THE POETICAL WORKS OF
WILLIAM BLAKE

I

William Blake.
1757 - 1827.

THE
POETICAL WORKS
OF
WILLIAM BLAKE

EDITED AND ANNOTATED BY

EDWIN J. ELLIS

IN TWO VOLUMES

VOL. I.

'Seeking the eternal, which is always present to the wise.'
'*Vala*,' *Night IX.*, *line* 170.

LONDON
CHATTO & WINDUS
1906

CONTENTS

CONTENTS

HOW BLAKE'S WORK HAS COME TO US

When Blake died in 1827 at seventy years of age, he left poetic work behind him in three different states. Some of it was still in manuscript ; some had been printed in ordinary type, and some had been printed with his own hands from copper and zinc plates on which he had first written in a kind of italic letter with a dark varnish ; then, having placed the plates in a bath of acid till all the parts not protected by this varnish were bitten away, he had rolled ordinary printing ink over the lines thus left in high relief, and so had been enabled to obtain copies by simply placing paper over the plates and passing them through a press. This process was his own.

His manuscripts are very inaccurate. The actual words are generally well written and properly spelled, but there are hundreds of lines in which wrong words have been left un-erased. Blake had an aversion to going over his work and removing errors. The mere idea often made him nervous and ill-tempered to such a degree that he became quite unfitted for the task. He was even afraid, when in this state, that he should injure his work in attempting to correct it, and his text is therefore almost as full of slips of the pen as of poetry. He wrote at a great pace, many lines at a time, and in a perfect fever of poetic excitement. His earliest work, the 'Poetical Sketches,' was published by his friends. He seems never to have read the proofs. His engraved work has fewest errors and misplaced or redundant words. He could not improvise with the varnish on metal as quickly as with the pen on paper. There is hardly any emendation necessary for these, such as his other work, whether earlier or later, so frequently requires. The paging of the books, however, is not always the same, and he seems to have sometimes forgotten his own intention in this matter.

We must always remember that whatever else Blake was, he was the only man of whom we have any knowledge at all who ever invented what may properly be called a myth. The allegories of the Elizabethan period and 'Pilgrim's Progress' belong to another order of symbolism. His myth is of value

xiii

for its beauty and its dramatic picturesqueness. It also has
a philosophy at its back which it will take us all many years
yet to estimate justly. But if the whole world had only one
volcano that was not extinct, or only one tree that was not a
fossil, that volcano and that tree would be of value to geologists
and botanists much as Blake is of value to mythologists. We
have living knowledge of him, and of no other man of his kind.

His myth has not come to us completely. Much was lost,
and a great deal which cannot be replaced was deliberately
destroyed by the friend to whom he left the manuscripts that
were in his hands when he died. The remainder consists of
poems and rhapsodies written at odd times during nearly half
a century without a connected system or a drawn-up and
arranged plan. That such a system can be found in them,
and such a plan drawn from them, is in itself a testimony to
the vigour and sanity of his mind which nothing can set
aside.

BLAKE'S PORTRAITS

We know now fairly well what manner of man we should
have seen had we lived when Blake was still going about
among us, a part of the daily life of our world. Not only
the big, square jaw, the short, eager-breathing nose, and
the immense rounded forehead, whose curves looked like the
full-shaped muscles of an athlete, are known to us now by the
portraits, but we can see him in the living expression that
spoke out the soul before the first word was uttered. We can
see the man of his race and of his time, the eighteenth century
Irishman of good descent—his father was born O'Neil before
his grandfather took the name of Blake with a wife to whom it
belonged,—and we can see the man of genius, for this face is
positively flaring with life, conscious of power and of its own
proud exuberance and generous giving out of mental wealth.
It is resentful to the unappreciative, grim to the incompetent,
kind to the simple, and savage to the pretentious.

We know also that if we had seen him while living, we
should have seen with his greatness something of his evident
deficiencies—his half-educated scrappiness, his lack of the
judicial spirit, and of any sympathetic mental patience. We
should have understood his hasty adoption of new words that
caught his fancy, and his vivacious incapacity to control his
own genius, or to do justice to other kinds of genius that were
repugnant to him.

*We should have seen in him the living spirit of rebellious-
ness, crowned with fidelity, so long as fidelity and partisanship were the same thing. We should have seen him incapable
of saving, incapable of serving, and incapable of fearing.*

*But when all was balanced, we should have seen a man to
love with some wonder, yet always to love; and to revere with
some regret, yet always to revere.*

*And the man we should have seen was the man that truly
was; for of hypocrisy, deception, or even of reasonable reserve
this face had no fragment, no suggestion, and no possibility.*

*And, last of all, we should have seen a face not easy to
record in one picture—the face of two portraits at least.*

*Fortunately we have these two portraits of Blake; and of
that on which the shadow of will, of pride, and of rebellion
lies most deeply, we have several.*

*In Quaritch's facsimile edition; in Gilchrist's 'Life'
(Macmillan); in Yeats's selections (Laurence and Bullen)
and in Perugini's (Methuen), we have altogether more than
half a dozen portraits from original and trustworthy sources.*

*Tatham's drawing in the Quaritch edition shows Blake
from the stern and fierce side of his character. The long-
lipped yet thin mouth, wide and sad, is held close with
determination. The corners go downwards, the whole line
of the lips forming a low-crowned arch, the line of stern and
permanent sorrow. The eyes glitter and burn with a fanatic
light. The brow-lines are seen not to have come by accident,
nor without their full equivalent of mental and personal
experience. The wide, open nostril and the wide, open ear
seem to have been carved by a sculptor's imperious and un-
flinching hand to show how well he knew that the spirit
that breathes and the spirit that hears needed a free passage
for inspiration and life—for the air of this world and the
messages of the other. At first this seems an exaggeration in
the portrait, but the photographs taken from the cast made
from Blake's head for Deville the phrenologist, show that it
is not so. In the Works (Quaritch) and in Perugini's Selections (Methuen) this cast is given, once in profile, once three-
quarter face, from photographs. It is even more stern and
uncompromising than Tatham's portrait, and the closed eyes
do not suggest either sleep or blindness.*

*To turn to Linnell's portrait, engraved for Gilchrist and
photographed from the original ivory for Yeats, is turning
from fierceness to sweetness, from anger to happiness, from
war to love.*

*The face is dimpled all over, right up into the temples, with
the kindliness and innocence of the smile, in which kindness is
the informing and moulding power. There is very little
amusement and absolutely no sarcasm or derision in it.*

There is a curious look as though the man were smiling and whistling at the same time, as people smile and whistle to little pet birds.

What has happened to the face to change it so much ; and, above all, what has become of the great, long, slit-like mouth ? The upper lip used to be slightly pressed forward, as though air were blown behind it, which bowed it above the thin, long, sad red line in a curve just the reverse of the Greek line of beauty. In lips of Cupid's bow form, a smile widens and flattens the red part, but in Blake's the opposite is what happens. A smile shortens the mouth. The line takes two new curves, one upward, just on each side of the central point, which now descends a hair's-breadth, and again one at each corner, where is now a slight rise. The Cupid's bow form has come in the act of smiling—the very action that obliterates it in a face of Greek beauty. The result of this shortening of a mouth while the other lines of the face show that it is smiling, is to give that whistling look, that appearance of addressing the smile along with little shrill sounds of endearment, to a bird.

To understand such a change in a face, it must be seen. Yet it is almost unknown outside Ireland. Even there it is not common in anything of the perfection which Blake's face possessed as an example of its paradoxical charms ; but it is well known, and is as distinctively Irish as were Blake's open nostril, large flashing eyes, and the square jaw, wide mouth, short nose, and round head.

In Tatham's portrait, the depression below the under lip and above the large chin is sudden and deeply carved. In Linnell's it is flatter, and as if water-worn. This also is a change belonging to the passage from a serious to a smiling look, and it occurs as part of the same movement, while the nostril grows more oval and less defiant.

The portrait given as frontispiece to this volume, made up as it is from all the others, has neither the advantages nor the disadvantages of such a picture as must have been drawn from life. It represents a man of extremes at neither one nor other of his extreme moments. If two of Blake's own favourite terms may be used for art-criticism, this may be said to be neither a Spectre portrait, like Tatham's, nor an Emanation portrait, like Linnell's. It shows the man—perhaps as he listens to what some visitor was saying—passing from one stage to the other ; and it is intended by the editor, who has made it for this purpose and has no other apology to offer for it, as a key by which the mystery of the transition may be unlocked.

PERSONAL IMPRESSION OF BLAKE

Blake's personality, as it impressed all those who came near him, has come down to us without the discussions that perturb our enjoyment of his work, and free from the miscomprehension that followed his poetry for so long, and alone caused the theory that he was a madman.   No one who knew him thought him mad except Mr. Crabbe Robinson, who tried to understand him without taking the trouble to understand Swedenborg first.   The greatest of his modern critics—D. G. Rossetti and Mr. Swinburne—always felt that he was sane, even if they could not prove it.

He was not only sane, but urbane.   His politeness to every one, whether above or below him in social standing, only failed three times, and then it gave place to indignation, not to raving: once when he obliged his wife to apologise to his brother, who handsomely and lovingly repudiated the apology; once when he suspected a circus proprietor of being cruel to a boy; and once when he bodily turned a soldier out of his garden before knowing that the gardener had asked him into it.

He felt much wrath at different times against more than one person, but there is no record that it broke the firmness of his personal bearing, during his years of manhood.

Of those who in later days felt the charm of Blake's personality, Gilchrist, his biographer, has done most to cause it to come down as a valuable and pleasant influence to our own day.   If there were nothing else than this personal impression to be got out of his book, it would be one of the best worth having and best worth remembering of biographies.   Its author held firmly that Blake knew what he meant himself, and that some one would come some day and explain him.   In fact, it was to a direct challenge (omitted since the first edition) to say what the poem 'To the Jews' meant in 'Jerusalem,' page 27, that the present editor owed so long ago as 1870 his own first impulse to investigate, and the first substantial results of investigation.

As an account of Blake's personality, no one could hope to improve on Gilchrist, but there is no space to quote a whole volume here.

Mr. Swinburne in the essay, in which he also calls for an interpreter, and avows his belief that there is sane matter for interpretation, has a few sentences, picturesque and stimulating, that are worth recalling now.   He describes Blake as—

'A man perfect in his way and beautifully unfit for walking in the way of any other man. . . . No one, artist or poet'

(*he continues*), '*of whatever school, who had any insight, or any love of things noble and lovable, ever passed by this man without taking away some pleasant or exalted memory of him. Those with whom he had nothing in common but a clear, kind nature, and sense of what was sympathetic in men and acceptable in things—those men whose work lay quite apart from his —speak of him still with as ready affection and as full remembrance of his sweet or great qualities as those nearest and likest him. There was a noble attraction in him which came home to all people with any fervour or candour of nature in themselves.*'

Mr. Swinburne *also adds much to this that, being criticism, has had its day, but the personal tribute remains as fresh and living as when it was written. Notwithstanding a note that is near, yet not too near to apology, in a writer who did not really understand why 'grave errors' are not—in the Prophetic Books, at any rate—the things that they seem to be, the closing lines of* Mr. Swinburne's *three hundred pages of essay are too fine and still too appropriate to be allowed to pass unrepeated—*

'*If it should now appear to any reader that too much has been made of slight things, and too little said of grave errors, this must be taken well into account: that praise enough has not yet been given, and blame can always be had for the asking; that when full honour has been done and full thanks rendered to those who have done great things, then and then only will it be no longer an untimely and unseemly labour to map out and mark down their shortcomings for the profit and pleasure of their inferiors and our own; that however pleasant for common palates and feeble fingers it may be to nibble or pick holes, it is not only more profitable, but should be more delightful, for all who desire or who strive after any excellence of mind or of achievement to do homage wherever it may be due; to let nothing great pass unsaluted or unenjoyed; but as often as we look backwards among past days and dead generations, with glad and ready reverence to answer the noble summons—"Let us now praise famous men and our fathers who were before us." Those who refuse them that are none of their sons; and among all those "famous men and our fathers," no names seem to demand so loudly as theirs who, while alive, had to dispense with the thanksgiving of men. To them, doubtless, it may be said, this is now more than ever indifferent; but to us it had better not be so. And especially in the works and in the life of Blake there is so strong and special a charm for those to whom the higher ways of work are not sealed ways, that none will fear to be too grudging of*

*blame or too liberal of praise. A more noble memory is
hardly left us, and it is not for his sake that we should
contend to do him honour.'*

BLAKE'S PHILOSOPHY

*Blake's philosophy was religion to him, as theirs was to the
Pagans; and it is the subject of all his poetry, as theirs was
to the myth-making teachers of the Pagans; and unless we
know something about it we cannot read a page of his writing,
however beautiful the melody or imagery of it may be, without
feeling that all our pleasure is spoilt. One of two opposite
thoughts will constantly assert itself and take away our
enjoyment, and, with our enjoyment, our intelligent apprecia-
tion. Either we shall know, with irritated humility, that we
are not understanding what was meant by the author; or we
shall fall back on the usual resource of the ignorant, and
conclude that the author did not understand what he meant
himself.*

*The latter theory was used freely whenever a difficulty
occurred by every reader and critic of Blake, very much to
the comfort of their own minds, but very little to the help of
the public, all the way from Blake's own time, through the
Gilchrist, Rossetti, and Swinburne period of criticism, and
only became obsolete after the appearance of the Quaritch
edition ten years ago. Dr. Garnel alone endeavoured to
revive it after that date to conceal his own invincible incapacity to understand Blake's manner of writing even after
it was explained to him.*

*In these volumes the present editor has taken up again the
system of comparing passage with passage in Blake himself,
which led to the obtaining of the clue that is developed in that
edition.*

*But a word of introduction, without references, giving the
summing up of the whole matter, may be of help to those who
have not the time to perform this task.*

*As is the case with each of us, Blake's philosophy was the
offspring of a union between his education and his personal
peculiarities. When speaking of his philosophy, of course we
mean his habitual conviction on the question of what is good
and what is bad, what is real and what is illusory, among the
mass of experiences and ideas that go to make up life.*

*His education was that of a child to whom the fundamental
ideas of Swedenborg are presented daily as entirely true and
not startlingly eccentric, and of a youth who acquired a*

mental dwelling-house of eighteenth century rationalistic materialism, and added it to their foundation.

Then he began to read the Bible for himself, continued to do so 'day and night' all his life, and picked up a little of the current critical knowledge as he read ; but very soon he struck out a new path of interpretation in harmony with Sweden-borgianism and Rationalism, and weaving in the Berkeleyan view of matter, and a good deal of Gnosticism into this, he formed his own theory of things, and having once formed this he held to it, worked for it, lived for it, and died exultingly in the enthusiasm of it.

His personal peculiarities, which, as he slowly and imperfectly learned, were not possessed by him in the average and normal degree in which people about him possessed the same, included a capacity of seeing through people and visions of people, while awake, as only hypnotically influenced nervous constitutions enable most persons to do, unless they are assisted by modern methods of producing fluorescence medicinally, and so illuminating the interior of their own or other physical bodies.

This clairvoyant capacity he believed to be not a physically developed, if abnormal and interesting nervous gift, as the people called 'psychics,' and others have so fully shown it to be, but a means of grace, a medium of brotherhood, a basis of religious and immortal hope—as it may be presumed this bodily gift is in actual fact on the way to really becoming. Such development would be a miracle less wonderful and more to be expected than childbirth. Blake was probably only a pioneer of an army whose methods are hardly yet understood by the inhabitants of the country which it is invading. He preached visions as others preach whatever they consider necessary to salvation, but he was always careful to add that there was no personal and egotistic permanence in it, but 'self-annihilation' and eternal brotherhood, which would develop into unity, and so become Humanity. This he called the fading away of the mortal in improved knowledge.

This ultimate Humanity was revealed, symbolically, in one man, he held, namely Christ, whose bodily person (the real chief of sinners) was Jesus. Christianity consisted in understanding this, and in being aroused to faith, love, and action by it. We cannot doubt that if Marcus Aurelius had read Blake, he would have believed every word.

Corporeally Blake was exceptionally strong. He spent his whole life in wasting his strength in nervous excitement, and undermining it by lack of fresh air and exercise, with over-much sedentary labour. If he left off work for a while, he could walk thirty miles without training, as a matter of course, and great physical power is revealed in his verse, his drawings, and his very handwriting.

Like some who are thus vigorous, he had also a super-abundance of physical passion. He takes account of this, and demands at first indulgence, then forgiveness for it. But he very soon gave up even in idea all egotistic demands other than the demand to do his spiritual duty. Still, he always to the end insisted on one liberty—that of being allowed to transform passion through the alchemy of the imagination and turn it all into inward light—into the helium (gold, he called it) of the mind. That all could, and should do the same, that Art was the process, and universal brotherhood and Christian love, with no more war and covet the result, he never doubted.

But repression of the body by morality, leading to hypocrisy and impurity; repression of the imagination by rationalism, or sense, leading to ambition and combat; and the loss or extinction of clairvoyance, of sympathy and of brotherhood, resulting from the egotism engendered by such repression, was to Blake the Antichrist and the enemy.

This enemy he knew, in his own day, as 'moral virtue,' and he could not denounce it too much. The only moral virtue he admitted was artistic industry, and this he showed in his own life. 'Self-annihilation,' by which he meant sense-annihilation, was to be its final and eternal result. We were to reach it by multiplication and development of senses, as Los rose into regeneration, or unity, after falling into generation, or division. The story of this, promised in the opening of 'Vala,' is related in all the 'Prophetic Books,' so called for that reason.

In the matter of that decency which is an avoidance of light laughter at passionate love, Blake was as far ahead of his age as in imaginative designing, philosophy, and poetry. But this is not surprising. Jests that degrade human passion are not common among those who have it greatly along with other greatness, but among boys who have not understood it or attained to it, men who are deficient in it, or who are goaded by the upside down modesty that is more shy of seeming to be better than their neighbours than of any other undecorum, and among those who have fallen into the vindictive ribaldry of senility.

Apart from what is personal, it is necessary to understand what is formal in Blake's philosophy if we are to follow his meaning.

The latter part of page 12, the former half of page 13 of 'Jerusalem,' being known practically by heart, and the explanatory scraps between pages 32 and 37 sought out and read with the opening paragraphs in pages 53, 59, 60, 64, 65,

66, 69, 71, *and all the last eight or ten pages of the same poem—a firm foundation may be obtained for understanding the rest. But in 'Jerusalem' almost all is explanation, the mass being poetic explanation. The poetry is apt to distract the attention of the mind from the task of seizing the skeleton of the idea until this is firmly grasped by the joints which are found in the more laboured and prosaic passages. The prose prefaces to the four chapters rather add to the difficulty until the language of the myth is understood by seeming too separate from it to belong to it, but all turns out to be one philosophic myth in the end.*

The story of the four Zoas, which, in the Quaritch edition, is traced in a chapter of references through the chief books, is briefly this:—

The origin of the world is a mental activity, condensing and contracting and identifying—condensing into tangibility and identifying into variety. This produces what we call existence. Blake did not call the process evolution, but he meant the same thing. Before, and while it is producing individuals, it appears in broader divisions. One resembles our intellect, that by trying to control us and stand above our emotions becomes an evil. Its effeminate side is a dream. Call it Urizen, call its feminine Ahania; consent to read the analysis of the thought in mythic form, and you are at one with the first quarter of life, or first life, or 'Zoa,' if you please. The South, Gold; the Sun, the Eyes; Fire, the Zenith, are among convenient symbols that further suggest its qualities.

The emotional part of life—older than the life of any one of us—is the enemy and rival of this power, and also seeks to tyrannise over us. Call it Luvah; call its material side Vala; call its fiery form Orc; give it for further symbols the East, Silver, Air; let it seek to rule by rising into the Sun; give it the Nostrils for organ; give it the Centre or Heart for region, and poetry will tell its philosophic story. Give it and all the others names of cities, and of elementary spirits; keep their places coherent; give them for symbols Height and Depth as ever contrary to Length and Breadth.

But there is, since the world was made by a word (logos), the 'Parent' or verbal power. We know it too well in dumb nature as Vegetation. Call it Tharmas; give it the region of sunset— West; give it Brass for metal, Water for element, the Tongue for organ; add any poetic adjunct you please so long as it is coherent, and it will tell its tale. Despair is its male form, Hope its female. Watch it try to tyrannise over us by its evil side—Uncertainty. Give it and take from it Outwards as a motion, and Accident or Chance as a power.

Finally, see in the night the dark labour of the mind and

the dark labour of mind we call matter. Give it the Ear
that receives the word as Organ, *and* Generation *as function. Give it* Earth *as element, the* Nadir *as place,* Iron
(magnetically attractive) as metal. Call it Urthona; *see in it
the revelation of* Time; *call him* Los—*reverse of Sol, and* Space;
*call her his female part; give to his revelation and his emotion
good powers friendly to man. See Orc himself as their sun,
and make Los no tyrant, but a prophet—the source of all our
knowledge of good. See him in the darkest hour before dawn,
write his philosophy as a sun-myth; follow the course of the
sun; keep the zodiac in your mind as a hint for plot; then
sum up all the religious history of the world and call it the
' Covering cherub' of the final and only religion, that which is
taught us by Imagination (the body of the Saviour in our
minds), and re-entering the bosom of God in a mass by brotherhood, since none of us can get there alone, defeat the tyranny
of the four Zoas, quarters, or moods, or powers of life; and
then whoever does this has himself lived through what Blake
writes, and can read it.*

BLAKE AND VISION

*Blake's own advice to an artist, ' Cultivate imagination to
the point of vision,' shows that he meant something by ' vision'
that was not the same as ' imagination,' but was its legitimate
offspring. All the senses are believed to be developments of the
sense of touch. Their uses could not have been foreseen by any
one who had only their undeveloped origin. The question
whether imagination or Vision can present us with truth or
not, is very much like the prehistoric question whether sight
or hearing could present us with truth or not, as it might
have been asked while these were still developing.*

*Blake hoped, and his hope was scientifically justifiable, that
all men would one day be as gifted as himself in visionary
faculty. Not only would it then be accepted, as ordinary
sight is now, and used as a means to bring truth to the mind,
but we should have a ready means of finding out when it was
likely to deceive us by comparing notes. We all know well
that illness, prejudice, and the mixture of the two that is
imitated by hypnotic suggestion, deceive us about objects of
sight.*

*Vision may also be made to bring an untrue report to the
mind. We have Blake's acknowledgment of this in his paper*

explaining his 'Vision of the Last Judgment' ('Works,' vol. ii. p. 393) :—

'The Greeks represent Chronos, or Time, as a very aged man. This is fable; but the real vision of Time is an eternal youth. I have, however, somewhat accommodated my figure of Time to the common opinion, as I myself am also infected with it, and I see Time aged,—alas! too much so.'

The use of the word infected *here helps to explain Blake's use of the word 'disease' elsewhere.*

He was only at his best in 'vision' in his most energetic moments. Under depression, the idleness of the mind, under doubt of the validity of imagination, forced even on him by the pressure of imaginative minds around him, and under influences that diverted and perverted when it did not destroy the best qualities of the visionary life, the visions were no longer those ideal 'gifts of the Holy Spirit' which he cultivated as a religious duty.

In 'Jerusalem,' the very first page contains this, in the appeal to 'perverted Man' not to turn away down the 'dark valleys' of unimaginative life—

'Thy nurses and thy mothers, thy sisters and thy daughters,
   Weep at thy soul's disease, and the Divine Vision is darkened.'

' The Divine Vision' was Divine in a double manner. It was of deific origin, and its result was to be brotherhood.

This also is a hope scientifically justified by the greater facilities for brotherly sympathy to be found among men who are united by delighting together in beautiful sights, as artists and Alpinists do, than when shut off as those are who are blind from birth, or who do not delight in beauty, except when it belongs to what they may personally possess, boast of, or enjoy—

'When souls mingle and join through all the fibres of Brotherhood,
Can there be any secret joy on earth greater than this?'

as Blake says near the close of the poem that opened with the appeal to throw off the 'soul's disease.'

The resemblance between our difficulty when using visionary sight as it is, and that which we should experience in employing ordinary sight as it would be if there were as few men in the world gifted with this as there are now gifted with visionary sight, is so close that one will almost explain the other.

Long before the value of this comparison is exhausted as a means of psychological explanation, in fact almost as soon as its utility is first perceived, it enables us to throw aside all the undue and foolish excitement that is apt to cling about the word 'vision' used in this emphatic and religiously poetic, or poetically religious, sense. We are enabled to put it into its right place in the general history of human development, and to deal with its best results with safety and with delight, while not allowing ourselves to be reduced to despair when the few owners of it show an occasional lack of sense of proportion. Proportion is, of course, one of the last results of brotherhood, and needs many generations of brothers to give it the authority of tradition.

THE PASSIONS

(Under this name a version of the following fragment, not identical with what here follows, appeared after the present collection was in type. It is probably among Blake's earliest pieces of writing, produced along with the 'Samson,' after first reading 'Milton,' though Mr. Rossetti has suggested that it might possibly be as late as 1785, though not later.)

—— THEN she bore pale Desire,
Father of Curiosity,—virgin young ;—
    And after, leaden Sloth,
From whom came Ignorance, who brought forth
    Wonder.
5 These are the sexless gods which come from fear ;
For gods like these nor male nor female are,
But single are pregnate, or if they list,
Together mingling bring forth mighty powers.
She knew them not ; yet they all war with Shame,
10   And strengthen her weak arm.

But Pride awoke, nor knew that Joy was born,
And taking poisonous seed from her own bowels
    In the monster Shame infused.
Forth came Ambition, crawling like a toad ;

15 Pride bears it in her bosom, and the gods
     All bow to it.   So great its power is
     That Pride, inspired by it, prophetic saw
     The kingdoms of the world and all their glory.

     Giants of mighty arm, before the Flood,
20   Cain's city built with murder.
     Then Babel mighty reared him to the skies—
        Babel with a thousand tongues.
     Confusion it was called, and given to Shame.

     This, Pride observing, inly grieved to see,
25 But knew not that the rest was given to Shame
        As well as this.
     Then Nineveh, and Babylon, and Tyre,
     And even Jerusalem, the Holy City,
        Was shown ;
30 Then Athens' learning, and the pride of Greece,
     And, further from the rising sun, was Rome,
        Seated on seven hills,
     The mistress of the world—emblem of Pride.
     She saw the Arts their generous treasures bring,
35 And Luxury his bounteous table spread.

     But now a cloud o'ercasts, and back to the East,
     To Constantine's great city empire fled
        Ere long to bleed and die,
     A sacrifice done by a priestly hand.
40 So, once, the Sun his chariot drew back
        To prolong a good King's life.
     The cloud o'erpassed, and Rome now shone again,
     Mitred and crowned with triple crown.   Then Pride
     Was better pleased : she saw the world fall down
45   In adoration.

     But now full to the setting Sun, a Sun
        Arose out of the Sea.
     It rose, and shed sweet influence o'er the earth.
     Pride fearèd for her City,—but not long,

50 For looking steadfastly, she saw that Pride
        Reigned here.

Now direful pains accost her, and still pregnant,
Till Envy came, and Hate, from progeny.
Envy hath a serpent's head of fearful bulk,
55 Hissing with a hundred tongues. Her poisonous
      breath
Breeds Satire—foul contagion—from which none
Are free. O'erwhelmed by ever-during thirst,
She swalloweth her own poison, which consumes
Her nether parts, from whence a river springs.
60 Most black and loathsome through the land it runs,
Rolling with furious noise; but at the last
It settles in a lake callèd Oblivion.

      'Tis at this river's fount
Where every mortal's cup, at birth, is mixed.
65 *My* cup is filled with Envy's rankest draught;
A miracle, no less, can set me right.
Desire still pines but for one cooling drop,
      And 'tis denied.
While others in Contentment's nest do sleep,
70 It is the cursèd thorn wounding my breast
      That makes me sing.
However sweet, Envy inspires my song.
Prickt by the fame of others, how I mount,
And my complaints are sweeter than their joys;
75 But, oh! could I at Envy shake my hands,
My notes should rise to meet the newborn day!

Hate, meagre hag! ever sets Envy on.
Unable to do aught herself alone,
She, worn away, a bloodless demon sits:
80 The Gods all bow and serve her at her will.
      So great her power is,
Like Hecate, she binds them to her law.
Far in a direful cave she sits unseen,
Closed from the eye of day,—to the hard rock

85 Transfixt by Fate,—she works her witcheries,
   And when she groans she shakes the solid ground.
   Now Envy she controls with numbing trance,
   And Melancholy sprang from her dark womb.

   There is a Melancholy, O how lovely 'tis !
90 When heaven is dwelling in the heavenly mind,
   For she from heaven came, and where she goes,
   Heaven still doth follow her.   She brings true joy
   Once fled, and Contemplation is her daughter.
           Sweet Contemplation !
95 'Tis she who brings Humility to Man.
   'Take her,' she says, ' and wear her in thy heart,
   Lord of thyself, then thou art Lord of all.'
   'Tis Contemplation teacheth how to know,
   Re-seating Knowledge on his throne, once lost,—
100 How lost, I 'll tell.   But stop the motley song !
   I 'll show how Conscience came at first from Heaven.
   But oh ! who listens to his voice on earth ?
   'Twas Conscience who brought Melancholy down,—
   Conscience who first was sent, a guard to Reason,—
105 Reason, once shining fairer than the light.
   For Knowledge drove sweet Innocence away ;
   And Reason would have gone.   Fate suffered not ;
   Then down came Conscience with his lonely band.

   And now the song goes on, telling how Pride
110 Against her Father warred and overcame.
   Down his white beard the silver torrents roll,
   And swelling sighs burst forth,—his children all
   In arms appear to tear him from his throne.
           Black was the deed,—most black.
115 Shame in a mist sat round his troubled head,
       And fillèd him with pale confusion.
   Fear as a torrent wild roared round his throne :
       The mighty pillars shake.

   Now all the gods in blackening ranks appear,
120 And like to a tempestuous thundercloud
       Pride leads them on.

Now they surround the god and bind him fast;—
Pride bound him, then usurped o'er all the gods.
She rode on high upon the swelling wind,
125 And scattered all who durst oppose her will.

But Shame opposing fierce
And hovering o'er her in the darkening storm,
She brought forth Rage.
And Shame bore Honour, and made league with Pride.
130 Meanwhile Strife, Mighty Prince, was born,—for Envy,
In direful pains him bore, then brought forth Care.
Care sitteth on the wrinkled brow of Kings;
Strife, shapeless, under thrones, like smould'ring fire
Sits, or in buzz of cities flies abroad.
135 Care brought forth Covet, eyeless and prone to th'
Earth,
And strife brought forth Revenge.

Hate, brooding in her dismal den, grew pregnant,
And bore both Scorn and Slander.
Scorn waits on Pride, but Slander flies around
140 The world to do the evil work of Hate,
Her drudge and elf.

But Policy doth also drudge for Hate
As well as Slander, and oft makes use of her,—
Policy, son of Shame.
145 Indeed, Hate controls all the gods at will.
Then Policy brought forth both Guile and Fraud.
These gods, last named, live in the smoke of cities
On dusky wing,
Breathing forth clamour and destruction.
150 Alas, in cities, where's the man whose face
Is not the mask to's heart?

Pride made a goddess fair, or image rather,
Till Knowledge gave it life; 'twas called Self-love.
The gods admiring, loaded her with gifts,
155 As once Pandora.   She 'mongst men was sent,
And worser ills attended her by far.

Conceit and Policy do dwell with her,
By whom she had Mistrust and cold Suspicion.
Then bore a daughter—Emulation,
160   Who married Honour ;
And all these follow her around the world.

Go see the city, friends joined hand in hand,
Go see the natural tie of flesh and blood,
Go see more strong the ties of marriage-love,
165 Thou scarce shall find but Self-love stands between.

Such appears to have been this early fragment as Blake thought he had written it. His perception of what he meant was always so much stronger than his perception of what he wrote, that all through life he constantly was liable to the misfortune of calling Dick (if one may say so) when he meant Harry, and then if Harry did not come, feeling aggrieved. Where it is obvious that Harry was meant, the substitution is here made. In other poems a little doubt may sometimes be felt, but the present work offers few such instances, and gives fairly evident indications of its own intention.

Even to the editor who prepared it for its first public appearance (in the August number of the Monthly Review, *1903), it was evident that Blake had not written the piece as he meant it to be read, for he had put it down as prose with no verse-division indicated at all. Those who study the version in the Review where this defect is supplied will see that mere versifying reveals many small errors while correcting one great one, and that the versifying itself is open to revision. While treating this to occasional mending, an attempt is made here to go further on the same path and take the necessary steps to enable the reader to enjoy Blake's poem without being harassed by the stuttering and stammering of the pen with which he marred it. Probably his own ear heard it much more as it is now printed than as he left it in MS., for he seldom aroused his senses to the necessary attentiveness for discovering what he had put on paper. When he had the experience of hearing himself sing his own songs, as in the case of some lyrics that he sang to his friends, he escaped the perpetual slips that annoy us in most of his pages. Strong power of enthusiasm, such as that which produced the central Nights* of 'Vala,' *would carry him a long way without error; and perhaps the repeated consideration necessary for engraving, as in 'Thel' or the 'Visions,' had an arousing effect, in early life, that was spoiled when his ear became trampled with argument, as in the ' Jerusalem' period.*

The following words being removed from the present version, namely—

In line	5, *sexless*	In line	105, *shining*
,,	7, *or*	,,	108, *gone*
,,	16, *is*	,,	110, *And now*
,,	24, *to see*	,,	117, *pale*
,,	29, *was shown*	,,	121, *And . . . to*
,,	34, *generous*	,,	125, *on high*
,,	64, *at birth*	,,	126, *her will*
,,	77, *ever*	,,	128, *o'er*
,,	78, *alone*	,,	131, *for Envy*
,,	79, *she . . . sits*	,,	133, *of Kings*
,,	81, *bow and*	,,	135, *sits*
,,	82, *binds*	,,	139, *both*
,,	86, *and*	,,	141, *evil*
,,	90, *dwelling*	,,	143, *also*
,,	95, *'Tis . . . who*	,,	147, *Then . . . both*
,,	99, *re-seating knowledge*	,,	152, *to 's*
,,	101, *at first*	,,	154, *gave it life*
,,	102, *on earth*	,,	159, *cold*
,,	104, *who first*		

and after their removal the re-instatement of the following—

Line 2, *a* (*before* virgin), *ever* (*before* young),
  ,, 27, *costly* (*before* Tyre),
  ,, 28, *was shown* (*after* Jerusalem),
  ,, 69, *downy* (*before* nest),
  ,, 79, *But* (*at beginning of line*),
  ,, 82, *fabled* (*before* Hecate), *doth bind* (*before* them),
  ,, 85, *and here* (*before* she),
  ,, 98, *knowledge truly* (*before* how),
  ,, 99, *And re-instates him on* (*at beginning of line*),
  ,, 108, *followed, but* (*before* Fate),
  ,, 132, *Envy* (*before* in, *and before* brought),
  ,, 134, *sitteth* (*before* under), *of Kings* (*end of line*),
  ,, 135, *the* (*before* buzz),
  ,, 152, *unto his* (*before* heart),
  ,, 154, *animated it* (*before* 'twas),
  ,, 160, *called* (*before* Emulation),

will, if the poem be now completely copied out as so many

prose pages, enable us to see what the MS. of Blake was when he left it.

Perhaps a tithe of this labour will convince any one that it had better be left undone, though the means to do it are here offered that no one may feel that the editor has disguised instead of emending his author.

VALUE AS INTERPRETATION

Blake's ideas and symbols were so persistent, like his designs, of which he writes that they are

> 'Re-engraved time after time,
> Ever in their youthful prime,'

that this early sketch helps to explain writings of a quarter of a century later.

It explains also his way of looking at the real relationship between various 'states of the human soul' when it is remembered that they were, to him, permanent things (like the gods), and were also like countries into which we enter, and through which we pass while travelling along our paths of life. We can see how naturally, when writing myth later on, he called them by fancy names, and treated their origins as paternity, their changes as personal events, and their results and detailed effects as children. His myths then are seen not to tell of mere unprofitable vagaries of fairy-tale monsters, made to employ an over-fluent poetic habit of writing, but to contain a psychology as the ancient myths did.

Blake saw after writing this poem that to continue to describe these gods (or moods and states) with personal adjectives, attributing to them also personal actions—like procreation—could not rightly be done while he called them by their prose names—shame, pride, etc. He must give them mythic names. He did so, and it is the giving of these names that made him become a myth-writer, for he at once perceived that each name grew to mean a great deal more than the idea from which it first sprang. To attempt to sort up the Zoas and the ungenerated sons of Los, or even those that went through the gates of Reuben, under words like Pride, Shame, Fear, etc., would be to make nonsense instead of suggestiveness of half what he wrote about them. Yet if we forget that the invention of his ideal personages was only the next stage in mental development after that which enabled him to see the vitality and vital narrative in the generation of the moods, we lose the use of this 'Poetical Sketch.'

But the notes here have no room for an interpretation of Blake, and only aim at giving useful hints as to what mood of our own minds to seek in, or what habit of his pen to study, or portion of his books to read when interpreting suggestions are desired.

'Reason once fairer than the light' is of course the germ of the idea to be called Urizen *presently, and the* Melancholy, *that* Conscience *(first set as his guard) brought down, is partly the parent idea of* Ahania, *who afterwards had visions that were full of wisdom, though* Urizen *cast her down and cast her out, when he became 'fouled in* Knowledge's *dark prison-house.'*

Conscience is not, in Blake's *language, the attribute which our newspapers teach us to attribute especially to Nonconformists. He has himself said in a prose paragraph that he means by it* Innate Science, *by which he seems to have meant transcendental intuition, or the faculty that* Swedenborg *called the 'celestial man.' This explains the last line of 'Vala.'*

The lake called Oblivion *afterwards revealed itself as the lake called* Udan Adan *in 'Jerusalem,' into which man should cast his selfish reasoning power that teaches him to be separate from his fellow man, and that Blake calls his 'spectre.'*

The passage about Knowledge *driving* Innocence *away helps to show Blake's idea of Knowledge, as meaning the source of argument, the 'knowledge of good and evil.' Argument is symbolised by the sexual warfare, and must be read with this later dictum—'Innocence dwells with wisdom, but not with ignorance.' 'Conscience,' or 'innate science,' is, of course, not 'ignorance.'*

In the passage where 'the song goes on telling how Pride *against her father warred,' we see into that part of Blake's mind where the foundation of the myth of* Urizen *and the* Net of Religion *was laid.* Shame *and* Pride *are both* Rahab *afterwards, and the binding fast done by the spirits (or gods) of the thunder-cloud is the enrooting round* Urizen *of the* Tree of Mystery. *There are (we shall learn) two clouds, that of blood and that of human souls. The blood-cloud (Rahab's red cord in the window) is now sending out its 'bands of influence' against* Urizen—*now the* Father of Pride. *Rahab is herself the* Tree, *and* Shame *is part of her* Mystery.

But so paradoxical are the generations of these human qualities that they act just as living people do who, when their families are of the nobility or gentry, and have self-admiring thoughts about their name and order, that make nine out of ten of them brave, delicate, kind, and true, and the tenth the blackest of black sheep. That is because 'Men they seem to one another.' See 'Vala,' Night VIII., line 119, and Blake's notes to Swedenborg, printed in 'The Real Blake,' published also by Mr. Grant Richards.

In this poem the qualities change their sexes at will. Shame 'opposing' and 'hovering o'er' fructifies, as a male, Pride, who is female, and who consequently had issue—she 'brought forth' Rage.' Shame becomes female, bears 'Honour,' and 'makes league with' Pride, the two fusing once more into what will later on be the state called Rahab. Such is the result of the amazing liberty of mind that we have in considering these symbols, after allowing to them the qualities described in the opening lines here—qualities that are natural in snails, perhaps, who are all Hermaphrodites, but inconceivable except in a mystic sense if applied to human beings. But if we keep the mystic sense close before us—that is to say, keep thinking of the actual facts of human states underlying the type, while not forgetting the appearance of the type—we shall not lose our way. Blake did not lose his, though there seem to be here and there contradictions at first sight; for example, it will be seen later that the 'spectre' is a guard in 'Jerusalem,' and that an emanation, 'Leutha,' is a guard in 'Milton.'

The Song of Experience called 'To Tirzah,' and the whole of the 'Prophetic Books,' especially 'Jerusalem,' are elaborations of the story of Shame and Pride, of which a portion is found in this early and fragmentary poem.

POETICAL SKETCHES, Etc.

POETICAL SKETCHES, ETC.

POETICAL SKETCHES

1753

TO SPRING

O THOU with dewy locks, who lookest down
Through the clear windows of the morning, turn
Thine angel eyes upon our western isle,
Which in full choir hails thy approach, O Spring!

The hills do tell each other, and the listening
Valleys hear; all our longing eyes are turned
Up to thy bright pavilions: issue forth,
And let thy holy feet visit our clime!

Come o'er the eastern hills, and let our winds
Kiss thy perfumèd garments; let us taste
Thy morn and evening breath; scatter thy pearls
Upon our lovesick land that mourns for thee.

Oh deck her forth with thy fair fingers; pour
Thy soft kisses on her bosom; and put
Thy golden crown upon her languished head,
Whose modest tresses were bound up for thee!

TO SUMMER

O THOU who passest through our valleys in
Thy strength, curb thy fierce steeds, allay the heat
That flames from their large nostrils! Thou, O
    Summer,

Oft pitchedst here thy golden tent, and oft
Beneath our oaks hast slept, while we beheld
With joy thy ruddy limbs and flourishing hair.

Beneath our thickest shades we oft have heard
Thy voice, when Noon upon his fervid car
Rode o'er the deep of heaven.   Beside our springs
Sit down, and in our mossy valleys, on
Some bank beside a river clear, throw thy
Silk draperies off, and rush into the stream !
Our valleys love the Summer in his pride.

Our bards are famed who strike the silver wire :
Our youth are bolder than the southern swains,
Our maidens fairer in the sprightly dance.
We lack not songs, nor instruments of joy,
Nor echoes sweet, nor waters clear as heaven,
Nor laurel wreaths against the sultry heat.

TO AUTUMN

O AUTUMN, laden with thy fruit, and stained
With the blood of the grape, pass not, but sit
Beneath my shady roof ; there thou mayst rest,
And tune thy jolly voice to my fresh pipe,
And all the daughters of the year shall dance !
Sing now the lusty song of fruits and flowers.

' The narrow bud opens her beauties to
The sun, and love runs in her thrilling veins ;
Blossoms hang round the brows of Morning, and
Flourish down the bright cheek of modest Eve,
Till clustering Summer breaks forth into singing,
And feathered clouds strew flowers round her head.

' The Spirits of the Air live on the smells
Of fruit ; and Joy, with pinions light, roves round
The gardens, or sits singing in the trees.'
Thus sang the jolly Autumn as he sat ;
Then rose, girded himself, and o'er bleak hills
Fled from our sight ; but left his golden load.

TO WINTER

O WINTER ! bar thine adamantine doors :
The north is thine ; there hast thou built thy dark
Deep-founded habitation. Shake not thy roofs,
Nor bend thy pillars with thine iron car.

He hears me not, but o'er the yawning deep
Rides heavy ; his storms are unchainèd, sheathed
In ribbèd steel ; I dare not lift mine eyes
For he hath reared his sceptre o'er the world.

Lo ! now the direful monster, whose skin clings
To his strong bones, strides o'er the groaning rocks :
He withers all in silence, and in his hand
Unclothes the earth, and freezes up frail life.

He takes his seat upon the cliffs,—the mariner
Cries out in vain.   Poor little wretch, that deal'st
With storms !—till heaven smiles, and drives the
      monster
Yelling beneath Mount Hecla to his caves.

TO THE EVENING STAR

THOU fair-haired Angel of the Evening,
Now, whilst the sun rests on the mountains, light
Thy [own] bright torch of love—thy radiant crown
Put on, and smile upon our evening bed !
Smile on our loves ; and, while thou drawest the
Blue curtains of the sky, scatter thy dew
On every flower that shuts its sweet eyes [now]
In timely sleep.   Let thy west wind sleep on
The lake ; speak silence with thy glimmering eyes,
And wash the dusk with silver.—Soon, full soon,
Dost thou withdraw ; then the wolf rages wide,
And then the lion glares through the dun forest.
The fleeces of our flocks are covered with
Thy sacred dew : protect them with thine influence !

TO MORNING

O ʜᴏʟʏ virgin, clad in purest white,
Unlock heaven's golden gates, and issue forth;
Awake the dawn that sleeps in heaven; let light
Rise from the chambers of the east, and bring
The honeyed dew that cometh on waking day.
O radiant Morning, now salute the Sun,
Roused like a huntsman to the chase, and with
Thy buskined feet appear upon our hills.

FAIR ELENOR

Tʜᴇ bell struck one, and shook the silent tower
The graves give up their dead : fair Elenor
Walked by the castle-gate, and lookèd in :
A hollow groan ran through the dreary vaults.

She shrieked aloud, and sunk upon the steps,
On the cold stone, her pale cheeks. Sickly smells
Of death issue as from a sepulchre,
And all is silent but the sighing vaults.

Chill Death withdraws his hand, and she revives :
Amazed she finds herself upon her feet,
And, like a ghost, through narrow passages
Walking, feeling the cold walls with her hands.

Fancy returns, and now she thinks of bones
And grinning skulls, and corruptible death
Wrapt in his shroud ; and now fancies she hears
Deep sighs, and sees pale, sickly ghosts gliding.

At length, no fancy, but reality
Distracts her. A rushing sound, and the feet
Of one that fled, approaches.—Ellen stood,
Like a dumb statue, froze to stone with fear.

The wretch approaches, crying: 'The deed is done!
Take this, and send it by whom thou wilt send;
It is my life—send it to Elenor:—
He's dead, and howling after me for blood!

'Take this,' he cried; and thrust into her arms
A wet napkin, wrapt about; then rushed
Past, howling.   She received into her arms
Pale death, and followed on the wings of fear.

They passed swift through the outer gate; the wretch,
Howling, leaped o'er the wall into the moat,
Stifling in mud.   Fair Ellen passed the bridge,
And heard a gloomy voice cry 'Is it done?'

As the deer wounded, Ellen flew over
The pathless plain; as the arrows that fly
By night, destruction flies, and strikes in darkness.
She fled from fear, till at her house arrived.

Her maids await her; on her bed she falls,
That bed of joy where erst her lord hath pressed.
'Ah woman's fear!' she cried, 'ah cursed duke!
Ah my dear lord! ah wretched Elenor!

'My lord was like a flower upon the brows
Of lusty May! Ah life as frail as flower!
O ghastly Death! withdraw thy cruel hand!
Seek'st thou that flower to deck thy horrid temples?

'My lord was like a star in highest heaven
Drawn down to earth by spells and wickedness;
My lord was like the opening eyes of Day,
When western winds creep softly o'er the flowers.

'But he is darkened; like the summer's noon
Clouded; fall'n like the stately tree, cut down;
The breath of heaven dwelt among his leaves.
O Elenor, weak woman, filled with woe!'

Thus having spoke, she raisèd up her head,
And saw the bloody napkin by her side,
Which in her arms she brought ; and now, tenfold
More terrified, saw it unfold itself.

Her eyes were fixed ; the bloody cloth unfolds,
Disclosing to her sight the murdered head
Of her dear lord, all ghastly pale, clotted
With gory blood ; it groaned, and thus it spake :

' O Elenor, behold thy husband's head,
Who, sleeping on the stones of yonder tower,
Was reft of life by the accursed duke :
A hired villain turned my sleep to death.

' O Elenor, beware the cursed duke ;
Oh give not him thy hand, now I am dead.
He seeks thy love ; who, coward, in the night,
Hired a villain to bereave my life.'

She sat with dead cold limbs, stiffened to stone ;
She took the gory head up in her arms ;
She kissed the pale lips ; she had no tears to shed ;
She hugged it to her breast, and groaned her last.

SONG

How sweet I roamed from field to field,
   And tasted all the summer's pride,
Till I the Prince of Love beheld
   Who in the sunny beams did glide.

He showed me lilies for my hair,
   And blushing roses for my brow ;
He led me through his gardens fair
   Where all his golden pleasures grow.

With sweet May-dews my wings were wet,
   And Phœbus fired my vocal rage ;
He caught me in his silken net,
   And shut me in his golden cage.

He loves to sit and hear me sing,
  Then, laughing, sports and plays with me;
Then stretches out my golden wing,
  And mocks my loss of liberty.

SONG

My silks and fine array,
  My smiles and languished air,
By love are driven away;
  And mournful lean Despair
Brings me yew to deck my grave:
Such end true lovers have.

His face is fair as heaven
  When springing buds unfold;
Oh why to him was't given,
  Whose heart is wintry cold?
His breast is love's all-worshipped tomb,
Where all love's pilgrims come.

Bring me an axe and spade,
  Bring me a winding-sheet;
When I my grave have made,
  Let winds and tempests beat:
Then down I'll lie, as cold as clay.
True love doth pass away!

SONG

Love and harmony combine,
And around our souls entwine,
While thy branches mix with mine,
And our roots together join.

Joys upon our branches sit,
Chirping loud and singing sweet;
Like gentle streams beneath our feet,
Innocence and virtue meet.

Thou the golden fruit dost bear,
I am clad in flowers fair ;
Thy sweet boughs perfume the air,
And the turtle buildeth there.

There she sits and feeds her young,
Sweet I hear her mournful song ;
And thy lovely leaves among
There is Love ; I hear his tongue.

There his charming nest doth lay,
There he sleeps the night away ;
There he sports along the day,
And doth among our branches play.

SONG

I LOVE the jocund dance,
  The softly breathing song,
Where innocent eyes do glance,
  And where lisps the maiden's tongue.

I love the laughing vale,
  I love the echoing hill,
Where mirth does never fail,
  And the jolly swain laughs his fill.

I love the pleasant cot,
  I love the innocent bower,
Where white and brown is our lot,
  Or fruit in the mid-day hour.

I love the oaken seat
  Beneath the oaken tree,
Where all the old villagers meet,
  And laugh our sports to see.

I love our neighbours all—
  But, Kitty, I better love thee ;
And love them I ever shall,
  But thou art all to me.

SONG

MEMORY, hither come,
  And tune your merry notes :
And, while upon the wind
  Your music floats,
I 'll pore upon the stream
Where sighing lovers dream,
And fish for fancies as they pass
Within the watery glass.

I 'll drink of the clear stream,
  And hear the linnet's song,
And there I 'll lie and dream
  The day along :
And, when night comes, I 'll go
To places fit for woe,
Walking along the darkened valley
With silent Melancholy.

MAD SONG

THE wild winds weep,
  And the night is a-cold ;
Come hither, Sleep,
  And my griefs enfold :
But lo ! the morning peeps
Over the eastern steeps,
And the rustling beds of dawn
The earth do scorn.

Lo ! to the vault
  Of pavèd heaven,
With sorrow fraught,
  My notes are driven :
They strike the ear of night,
  Make weep the eyes of day ;
They make mad the roaring winds,
  And with tempests play.

Like a fiend in a cloud,
    With howling woe
After night I do crowd
    And with night will go;
I turn my back to the east
From whence comforts have increased;
For light doth seize my brain
With frantic pain.

SONG

Fresh from the dewy hill, the merry year
Smiles on my head, and mounts his flaming car;
Round my young brows the laurel wreathes a shade,
And rising glories beam around my head.

My feet are winged, while o'er the dewy lawn
I meet my maiden risen like the morn.
Oh bless those holy feet, like angels' feet;
Oh bless those limbs, beaming with heavenly light!

Like as an angel glittering in the sky
In times of innocence and holy joy;
The joyful shepherd stops his grateful song
To hear the music of an angel's tongue.

So, when she speaks, the voice of Heaven I hear;
So, when we walk, nothing impure comes near;
Each field seems Eden, and each calm retreat,
Each village, seems the haunt of holy feet.

But that sweet village where my black-eyed maid
Closes her eyes in sleep beneath night's shade
Whene'er I enter, more than mortal fire
Burns in my soul, and does my song inspire.

SONG

When early Morn walks forth in sober grey,
Then to my black-eyed maid I haste away.

When Evening sits beneath her dusky bower,
And gently sighs away the silent hour,
The village bell alarms, away I go,
And the vale darkens at my pensive woe.

To that sweet village where my black-eyed maid
Doth drop a tear beneath the silent shade
I turn my eyes; and pensive as I go
Curse my black stars, and bless my pleasing woe.

Oft, when the Summer sleeps among the trees,
Whispering faint murmurs to the scanty breeze,
I walk the village round; if at her side
A youth doth walk in stolen joy and pride,
I curse my stars in bitter grief and woe,
That made my love so high, and me so low.

Oh should she e'er prove false, his limbs I'd tear
And throw all pity on the burning air!
I'd curse bright fortune for my mixèd lot,
And then I'd die in peace, and be forgot.

TO THE MUSES

WHETHER on Ida's shady brow,
    Or in the chambers of the East,
The chambers of the Sun, that now
    From ancient melody have ceased;

Whether in heaven ye wander fair,
    Or the green corners of the earth,
Or the blue regions of the air
    Where the melodious winds have birth;

Whether on crystal rocks ye rove,
    Beneath the bosom of the sea,
Wandering in many a coral grove;
    Fair Nine, forsaking Poetry;

How have you left the ancient love
 That bards of old enjoyed in you !
The languid strings do scarcely move,
 The sound is forced, the notes are few !

GWIN, KING OF NORWAY

COME, Kings, and listen to my song.—
 When Gwin, the son of Nore,
Over the nations of the North
 His cruel sceptre bore ;

The nobles of the land did feed
 Upon the hungry poor ;
They tear the poor man's lamb, and drive
 The needy from their door.

'The land is desolate ; our wives
 And children cry for bread ;
Arise, and pull the tyrant down !
 Let Gwin be humblèd !'

Gordred the giant roused himself
 From sleeping in his cave ;
He shook the hills, and in the clouds
 The troubled banners wave.

Beneath them rolled, like tempests black,
 The numerous sons of blood ;
Like lions' whelps, roaring abroad,
 Seeking their nightly food.

Down Bleron's hill they dreadful rush,
 Their cry ascends the clouds ;
The trampling horse and clanging arms
 Like rushing mighty floods !

Their wives and children, weeping loud,
 Follow in wild array,
Howling like ghosts, furious as wolves
 In the bleak, wintry day.

'Pull down the tyrant to the dust,
   Let Gwin be humblèd,'
They cry, 'and let ten thousand lives
   Pay for the tyrant's head!'

From tower to tower the watchmen cry
   'O Gwin, the son of Nore,
Arouse thyself! the nations, black
   Like clouds, come rolling o'er!'

Gwin reared his shield, his palace shakes
   His chiefs come rushing round;
Each like an awful thunder-cloud
   With voice of solemn sound:

Like rearèd stones around a grave
   They stand around the King;
Then suddenly each seized his spear,
   And clashing steel does ring.

The husbandman does leave his plough
   To wade through fields of gore;
The merchant binds his brows in steel,
   And leaves the trading shore;

The shepherd leaves his mellow pipe,
   And sounds the trumpet shrill;
The workman throws his hammer down
   To heave the bloody bill.

Like the tall ghost of Barraton
   Who sports in stormy sky,
Gwin leads his host as black as night
   When pestilence does fly,

With horses and with chariots—
   And all his spearmen bold
March to the sound of mournful song,
   Like clouds around him rolled,

Gwin lifts his hand—the nations halt ;
 ' Prepare for war ! ' he cries.
Gordred appears !—his frowning brow
 Troubles our northern skies.

The armies stand, like balances
 Held in the Almighty's hand ;—
' Gwin, thou hast filled thy measure up :
 Thou 'rt swept from out the land.'

And now the raging armies rushed
 Like warring mighty seas ;
The heavens are shook with roaring war,
 The dust ascends the skies !

Earth smokes with blood, and groans and
 shakes
 To drink her children's gore,
A sea of blood ; nor can the eye
 See to the trembling shore.

And on the verge of this wild sea
 Famine and death do cry ;
The cries of women and of babes
 Over the field do fly.

The King is seen raging afar,
 With all his men of might ;
Like blazing comets scattering death
 Through the red, feverous night.

Beneath his arm like sheep they die,
 And groan upon the plain ;
The battle faints, and bloody men
 Fight upon hills of slain.

Now death is sick, and riven men
 Labour and toil for life ;
Steed rolls on steed, and shield on shield,
 Sunk in this sea of strife !

The God of War is drunk with blood,
  The earth doth faint and fail ;
The stench of blood makes sick the heavens,
  Ghosts glut the throat of hell !

Oh what have kings to answer for
  Before that awful throne,
When thousand deaths for vengeance cry,
  And ghosts accusing groan !

Like blazing comets in the sky
  That shake the stars of light,
Which drop like fruit unto the earth
  Through the fierce burning night ;

Like these did Gwin and Gordred meet,
  And the first blow decides ;
Down from the brow unto the breast
  Gordred his head divides !

Gwin fell : the sons of Norway fled,
  All that remained alive ;
The rest did fill the vale of death,—
  For them the eagles strive.

The river Dorman rolled their blood
  Into the northern sea ;
Who mourned his sons, and overwhelmed
  The pleasant south country.

AN IMITATION OF SPENSER

Golden Apollo, that through heaven wide
  Scatter'st the rays of light, and truth's beams,
In lucent words my darkling verses dight,
  And wash my earthy mind in thy clear streams,
  That wisdom may descend in fairy dreams,
All while the jocund Hours in thy train
  Scatter their fancies at thy poet's feet ;
And, when thou yield'st to Night thy wide domain,
Let rays of truth enlight his sleeping brain.

For brutish Pan in vain might thee assay
  With tinkling sounds to dash thy nervous verse,
Sound without sense ; yet in his rude affray
  (For Ignorance is Folly's leasing nurse,
  And love of Folly needs none other's curse)
Midas the praise hath gained of lengthened ears,
  For which himself might deem him ne'er the worse
To sit in council with his modern peers,
  And judge of tinkling rhymes and elegances terse.

And thou, Mercurius, that with winged bow
  Dost mount aloft into the yielding sky,
And through heaven's halls thy airy flight dost throw,
  Entering with holy feet to where on high
  Jove weighs the counsel of futurity ;
Then, laden with eternal fate, dost go
  Down, like a falling star, from autumn sky,
  And o'er the surface of the silent deep dost fly :

If thou arrivest at the sandy shore
  Where nought but envious hissing adders dwell,
Thy golden rod, thrown on the dusty floor,
  Can charm to harmony with potent spell ;
  Such is sweet Eloquence, that does dispel
Envy and Hate, that thirst for human gore ;
  And cause in sweet society to dwell
  Vile savage minds that lurk in lonely cell.

O Mercury, assist my labouring sense
  That round the circle of the world would fly,
As the wing'd eagle scorns the towery fence
  Of Alpine hills round his high aëry,
  And searches through the corners of the sky,
Sports in the clouds to hear the thunder's sound,
  And see the winged lightnings as they fly ;
Then, bosomed in an amber cloud, around
  Plumes his wide wings, and seeks Sol's palace high.

And thou, O Warrior maid invincible,
  Armed with the terrors of Almighty Jove,
Pallas, Minerva, maiden terrible,
  Lov'st thou to walk the peaceful, solemn grove,

In solemn gloom of branches interwove?
Or bear'st thy ægis o'er the burning field
  Where like the sea the waves of battle move?
Or have thy soft, piteous eyes beheld
  The weary wanderer through the desert rove?
Or does the afflicted man thy heavenly bosom move?

BLIND-MAN'S BUFF

WHEN silver snow decks Susan's clothes,
And jewel hangs at th' shepherd's nose,
The blushing bank is all my care,
With hearth so red, and walls so fair.
' Heap the sea-coal, come, heap it higher;
The oaken log lay on the fire.'
The well-washed stools, a circling row,
With lad and lass, how fair the show!
The merry can of nut-brown ale,
The laughing jest, the love-sick tale,—
Till, tired of chat, the game begins,
The lasses prick the lads with pins.
Roger from Dolly twitched the stool;
She, falling, kissed the ground, poor fool!
She blushed so red, with sidelong glance
At hobnail Dick, who grieved the chance.
But now for Blind-man's Buff they call;
Of each incumbrance clear the hall.

Jenny her silken kerchief folds,
And blear-eyed Will the black lot holds.
Now laughing stops, with ' Silence, hush !
And Peggy Pout gives Sam a push.
The Blind-man's arms, extended wide,
Sam slips between :—' Oh woe betide
Thee, clumsy Will !'—But tittering Kate
Is penned up in the corner strait !
And now Will's eyes beheld the play;
He thought his face was t'other way.

'Now, Kitty, now! what chance hast thou?
Roger so near thee trips, I vow!'
She catches him—then Roger ties
His own head up—but not his eyes;
For through the slender cloth he sees,
And runs at Sam, who slips with ease
His clumsy hold; and dodging round,
Sukey is tumbled on the ground.—
'See what it is to play unfair!
Where cheating is, there's mischief there.'
But Roger still pursues the chase,—
'He sees! he sees!' cries softly Grace;
'O Roger, thou, unskilled in art,
Must, surer bound, go through thy part!'

Now Kitty, pert, repeats the rhymes,
And Roger turns him round three times,
Then pauses ere he starts.   But Dick
Was mischief-bent upon a trick:
Down on his hands and knees he lay
Directly in the Blind-man's way,
Then cries out 'Hem!'—Hodge heard, and ran
With hood-winked chance—sure of his man;
But down he came.—Alas, how frail
Our best of hopes, how soon they fail!
With crimson drops he stains the ground;
Confusion startles all around.
Poor piteous Dick supports his head,
And fain would cure the hurt he made.
But Kitty hasted with a key,
And down his back they straight convey
The cold relief: the blood is stayed,
And Hodge again holds up his head.

Such are the fortunes of the game;
And those who play should stop the same
By wholesome laws, such as—All those
Who on the blinded man impose
Stand in his stead; as, long agone,
When men were first a nation grown,

Lawless they lived, till wantonness
And liberty began to increase,
And one man lay in another's way ;
Then laws were made to keep fair play.

KING EDWARD THE THIRD

PERSONS

KING EDWARD.	SIR THOMAS DAGWORTH.
THE BLACK PRINCE.	SIR WALTER MANNY.
QUEEN PHILIPPA.	LORD AUDLEY.
DUKE OF CLARENCE.	LORD PERCY.
SIR JOHN CHANDOS.	BISHOP.

WILLIAM, *Dagworth's man.*
PETER BLUNT, *a common soldier.*

SCENE I.—*The Coast of France.*

KING EDWARD *and Nobles before it.* *The Army.*

KING

O THOU to whose fury the nations are
But as the dust ! maintain Thy servant's right.
Without Thine aid, the twisted mail, and spear,
And forgèd helm, and shield of beaten brass,
Are idle trophies of the vanquisher.
When confusion rages, when the field 's in flame,
When cries of blood tear horror out of heaven,
And yelling Death runs up and down the ranks,
Let Liberty, the chartered right of Englishmen,
Won by our fathers in many a glorious field,
Innerve my soldiers ; let Liberty
Blaze in each countenance, and fire the battle.
The enemy fight in chains, invisible, heavy ;
Their minds are fettered ; how can they be free?
While, like the mounting flame,
We spring to battle o'er the floods of death !
And these fair youths,—the flower of England,
Venturing their lives in my most righteous cause,—

Oh sheathe their hearts with triple steel, that they
May emulate their fathers' virtues ! Thou,
My son, be strong ; thou fightest for a crown
That death can never ravish from thy brow,
A crown of glory—From thy very dust
Shall beam a radiance, to fire the breasts
Of youth unborn ! Our names are written equal
In Fame's wide-trophied hall ; 'tis ours to gild
The letters, and to make them shine with gold
That never tarnishes : whether Third Edward,
The Prince of Wales, Montacute, Mortimer,
Or ev'n the least by birth gain brightest fame,
Is in His hand to whom all men are equal.
The world of men are like the numerous stars
That beam and twinkle in the depth of night,
Each clad in glory according to his sphere ;
But we, that wander from our native seats
And beam forth lustre on a darkling world,
Grow large as we advance ; and some perhaps
The most obscure at home, that scarce were seen
To twinkle in their sphere, may so advance
That the astonished world, with upturned eyes,
Regardless of the moon, and those once bright,
Stand only for to gaze upon their splendour.
    [*He here knights the Prince and other young Nobles.*
Now let us take a just revenge for those
Brave Lords who fell beneath the bloody axe
At Paris.   Noble Harcourt, thanks, for 'twas
By your advice we landed here in Brittany,
A country not yet sown with destruction,
And where the fiery whirlwind of swift war
Has not yet swept its desolating wing.—
Into three parties we divide by day,
And separate march, but join again at night :
Each knows his rank, and Heaven marshal all.
        [*Exeunt.*

SCENE II.—*English Court.*

LIONEL, DUKE OF CLARENCE, QUEEN PHILIPPA,
Lords, Bishop, etc.

CLARENCE

My Lords, I have by the advice of her
Whom I am doubly bound to obey, my parent
And my sovereign, called you together.
My task is great, my burden heavier than
My unfledged years ;
Yet with your kind assistance, Lords, I hope
England shall dwell in peace: that, while my father
Toils in his wars, and turns his eyes on this
His native shore, and sees commerce fly round
With his white wings, and sees his golden London
And her silver Thames, thronged with shining spires
And corded ships, her merchants buzzing round
Like summer bees, and all the golden cities
O'erflowing with their honey in his land,
Glory may not be dimmed with clouds of care.
Say, Lords, should not our thoughts be first to com-
    merce?
You, my Lord Bishop, commend agriculture?

BISHOP

Sweet Prince, I know the arts of peace are great
And no less glorious than those of war,
Perhaps more, in the philosophic mind.
When I sit at my home, a private man,
My thoughts are on my gardens and my fields,
How to employ the hand that lacketh bread.
If Industry is in my diocese,
Religion will flourish ; each man's heart
Is cultivated and will bring forth fruit :
This is my private duty and my pleasure.
But, as I sit in council with my prince,
My thoughts take in the general good of the whole,
And England is the land favoured by Commerce ;
For Commerce, though the child of Agriculture,

Fosters his parent, who else must sweat and toil,
And gain but scanty fare.   Then, my dear Lord,
Be England's trade our care; and we, as tradesmen
Looking to the gain of this our native land.

CLARENCE

O my good Lord, true wisdom drops like honey
From off your tongue, as from a worshipped oak !
Forgive, my Lords, my talkative youth, that speaks
Not merely from my narrow observation,
But what I have concluded from your lessons.
Now, by the Queen's advice, I ask your leave
To dine to-morrow with the Mayor of London.
If I get leave, I have another boon
To ask,—the favour of your company.
I fear Lord Percy will not give me leave.

PERCY

Dear Sir, a prince should always keep his state,
And grant his favours with a sparing hand,
Or they are never rightly valued.
These are my thoughts : yet it were best to go :
But keep a proper dignity, for now
You represent the sacred person of
Your father ; 'tis with princes as with the sun ;
If not sometimes o'erclouded, we grow weary
Of his officious glory.

CLARENCE

Then you will give me leave to shine sometimes,
My Lord ?

LORD (aside)

Thou hast a gallant spirit, which I fear
Will be imposed on by the closer sort.

CLARENCE

Well, I 'll endeavour to take
Lord Percy's advice ; I have been used so much
To dignity that I 'm sick on 't.

QUEEN PHILIPPA

Fie, fie, Lord Clarence! you proceed not to business,
But speak of your own pleasures.
I hope their lordships will excuse your giddiness.

CLARENCE

My Lords, the French have fitted out many
Small ships of war that, like to ravening wolves,
Infest our English seas, devouring all
Our burdened vessels, spoiling our naval flocks.
The merchants do complain, and beg our aid.

PERCY

The merchants are rich enough ;
Can they not help themselves?

BISHOP

They can, and may ; but how to gain their will
Requires both our countenance and help.

PERCY

When that they find they must, my Lord, they will:
Let them but suffer awhile, and you shall see
They will bestir themselves.

BISHOP

Lord Percy cannot mean that we should suffer
Disgrace like this. If so, we are not sovereigns
Of the sea,—our right, a right that Heaven gave
To England, when first at the birth of Nature
She in the deep was seated ; Ocean ceased
His mighty roar, and, fawning, played around
Her snowy feet, and owned his awful Queen.
Lord Percy, if the heart is sick, the head
Must be aggrieved ; if but one member suffer,
The heart doth fail. You say, my Lord, the merchants
Can, if they will, defend themselves against
These rovers : yet this is a noble scheme,
Worthy the brave Lord Percy, and as worthy
His generous aid to put it into practice.

PERCY

Lord Bishop, what was rash in me is wise
In you ; I dare not own the plan.   'Tis not
Mine.   Yet will I, if you please,
Quickly to the Lord Mayor, and work him onward
To this most glorious voyage ; on which cast
I 'll set my whole estate,
But we will bring these Gallic rovers under.

QUEEN PHILIPPA

Thanks, brave Lord Percy ; you have now the thanks
Of England's Queen, and will, ere long, of England.
                                                [Exeunt.

SCENE III.—*At Cressy.*

SIR THOMAS DAGWORTH *and* LORD AUDLEY *meeting.*

AUDLEY

Good-morrow, brave Sir Thomas ; the bright morn
Smiles on our army, and the gallant sun
Springs from the hills like a young hero leaping
Into the battle, shaking his golden locks
Exultingly : this is a promising day.

DAGWORTH

Why that, my good Lord Audley, I don't know.
Give me your hand, and now I 'll tell you what
I think you do not know.   Edward 's afraid
Of Philip.

AUDLEY

Ha, ha ! Sir Thomas ! you but joke ;
Did you e'er see him fear ?   At Blanchetaque,
When almost singly he drove down six thousand
French from the ford, did he fear then ?

DAGWORTH

                                    Yes, fear.
That made him fight so.

AUDLEY

By the same reason I might say 'tis fear
That makes you fight.

DAGWORTH

Mayhap you may.   Look upon Edward's face,
No one can say he fears; but, when he turns
His back, then I will say it to his face;
He is afraid : he makes us all afraid.
I cannot bear the enemy at my back.
Now here we are at Cressy; where to-morrow?
To-morrow we shall know.   I say, Lord Audley,
That Edward runs away from Philip.

AUDLEY

Perhaps you think the Prince too is afraid?

DAGWORTH

No ; God forbid !   I am sure he is not.
He is a young lion.   Oh, I have seen him fight
And give command, and lightning then has flashed
From his eyes across the field : I have seen him
Shake hands with Death, and strike a bargain for
The enemy ; he has danced in the field
Of battle, like the youth at morris-play.
I 'm sure he 's not afraid, nor Warwick, nor none,
None of us but me, and I am very much afraid.

AUDLEY

Are you afraid, too, Sir Thomas?   I believe that
As much as I believe the King 's afraid :
But what are you afraid of?

DAGWORTH

Of having my back laid open ; we must turn
Our backs to the fire, till we shall burn our skirts.

AUDLEY

And this, Sir Thomas, you call fear?   Your fear
Is of a different kind, then, from the King's ;

He fears to turn his face, and you your back.
I do not think, Sir Thomas, you know what fear is.

Enter Sir John Chandos

CHANDOS

Good morrow, Generals; I give you joy:
Welcome to the fields of Cressy.   Here we stop
And wait for Philip.

DAGWORTH

I hope so.

AUDLEY

There, there, Sir Thomas; do you call that fear?

DAGWORTH

I don't know; perhaps he takes it by fits.
Why, noble Chandos, and you, look you here—
One rotten sheep spoils always the whole flock;
And if the bell-wether is tainted, I wish
The Prince may not catch the distemper too.

CHANDOS

Distemper, ha! Sir Thomas! What distemper?
I have not heard.

DAGWORTH

Why, Chandos, you are a wise man,
I know you understand me; a distemper
The King caught here in France of running away.

AUDLEY

Sir Thomas, you say you have caught it too.

DAGWORTH

And so will the whole army; 'tis very catching,
For, when the coward runs, the brave man totters.
Perhaps the air of the country is the cause.

I feel it coming upon me, so I strive against it ;
You yet are whole ; but after a few more
Retreats, we all shall know how to retreat
Better than fight.—To be plain, I think retreating
Too often takes away a soldier's courage.

CHANDOS

Here comes the King himself : tell him your thoughts
Plainly, Sir Thomas.

DAGWORTH

I 've told him this before, but his disorder
Has made him deaf.

Enter KING EDWARD *and* BLACK PRINCE

KING

Good morrow, Generals ; when English courage fails,
Down goes our right to France ;
But we are conquerors everywhere, and nothing
Can stand before our soldiers ; each is worthy
Of a triumph.   Such an army—heroes all—
Ne'er shouted to the heavens, nor shook the field.
Edward, my son, thou art
Most happy, having such command : the man
Were more than base who were not fired to deeds
Above heroic, having such examples.

PRINCE

Sire, with respect and deference I look
Upon such noble souls, and wish myself
Worthy the high command that Heaven and you
Have given me.   When I 've seen the field a-glow,
And in each countenance the soul of war
Curbed by the manliest reason, I 've been winged
With certain victory ; and 'tis my boast,
And shall be still my glory, I was inspired
By these brave troops.

DAGWORTH

Your Grace had better make them
All Generals.

KING

Sir Thomas Dagworth, you must have your joke
And shall, while you can fight as you did at
The Ford.

DAGWORTH

I have a small petition to your Majesty.

KING

What can Sir Thomas Dagworth ask
That Edward can refuse?

DAGWORTH

I hope your Majesty cannot refuse so great
A trifle; I've gilt your cause with my best blood,
And would again, were I not now forbid
By him whom I am bound to obey: my hands
Are tied up, all my courage shrunk and withered,
My sinews slackened, and my voice scarce heard;
Therefore I beg I may return to England.

KING

I know not what you could have asked, Sir Thomas,
That I would not have sooner parted with
Than such a soldier as you, and such a friend:
Nay, I will know the most remote particulars
Of this your strange petition; that, if I can,
I still may keep you here.

DAGWORTH

Here on the fields of Cressy we are settled
Till Philip springs the timorous covey again.
The wolf is hunted down by causeless fear;
The lion flees, and fear usurps his heart,
Startled, astonished at the clamorous cock;
The eagle, that doth gaze upon the sun,

Fears the small fire that plays about the fen.
If, at this moment of their idle fear,
The dog doth seize the wolf, the forester the lion,
The negro in the crevice of the rock
Doth seize the soaring eagle ; undone by flight,
They tame submit : such the effect flight has
On noble souls.   Now hear its opposite :
The timorous stag starts from the thicket wild,
The fearful crane springs from the splashy fen,
The shining snake glides o'er the bending grass,
The stag turns head, and bays the crying hounds ;
The crane o'ertaken fighteth with the hawk ;
The snake doth turn, and bite the padding foot.
And if your Majesty's afraid of Philip,
You are more like a lion than a crane :
Therefore I beg I may return to England.

KING

Sir Thomas, now I understand your mirth,
Which often plays with wisdom for its pastime,
And brings good counsel from the breast of laughter.
I hope you'll stay and see us fight this battle,
And reap rich harvest in the fields of Cressy ;
Then go to England, tell them how we fight,
And set all hearts on fire to be with us.
Philip is plumed, and thinks we flee from him,
Else he would never dare to attack us.   Now,
Now the quarry's set ! and Death doth sport
In the bright sunshine of this fatal day.

DAGWORTH

Now my heart dances, and I am as light
As the young bridegroom going to be married.
Now must I to my soldiers, get them ready,
Furbish our armours bright, new-plume our helms ;
And we will sing like the young housewives busied
In the dairy.   Now my feet are wing'd, but not
For flight, an't please your grace.

KING

If all my soldiers are as pleased as you,
'Twill be a gallant thing to fight or die ;
Then I can never be afraid of Philip.

DAGWORTH

A raw-boned fellow t'other day passed by me ;
I told him to put off his hungry looks—
He said, 'I hunger for another battle.'
I saw a little Welshman, fiery-faced ;
I told him he looked like a candle half
Burned out ; he answered, he was '*pig* enough
To light another *pattle*.' Last night, beneath
The moon I walked abroad, when all had pitched
Their tents, and all were still ;
I heard a blooming youth singing a song
He had composed, and at each pause he wiped
His dropping eyes. The ditty was, ' If he
Returned victorious, he should wed a maiden
Fairer than snow, and rich as midsummer.'
Another wept, and wished health to his father.
I chid them both, but gave them noble hopes.
These are the minds that glory in the battle,
And leap and dance to hear the trumpet sound.

KING

Sir Thomas Dagworth, be thou near our person ;
Thy heart is richer than the vales of France :
I will not part with such a man as thou.
If Philip came armed in the ribs of death,
And shook his mortal dart against my head,
Thou'dst laugh his fury into nerveless shame !
Go now, for thou art suited to the work,
Throughout the camp ; inflame the timorous,
Blow up the sluggish into ardour, and
Confirm the strong with strength, the weak inspire,
And wing their brows with hope and expectation :
Then to our tent return, and meet to council.

[*Exit* DAGWORTH.

CHANDOS

That man's a hero in his closet, and more
A hero to the servants of his house
Than to the gaping world ; he carries windows
In that enlargèd breast of his, that all
May see what's done within.

PRINCE

He is a genuine Englishman, my Chandos,
And hath the spirit of Liberty within him.
Forgive my prejudice, Sir John ; I think
My Englishmen the bravest people on
The face of the earth.

CHANDOS

Courage, my Lord, proceeds from self-dependence.
Teach every man to think he's a free agent,
Give but a slave his liberty, he'll shake
Off sloth, and build himself a hut, and hedge
A spot of ground ; this he'll defend ; 'tis his
By right of Nature. Thus being set in action,
He will move on to plan conveniences,
Till glory fires him to enlarge his castle ;
While the poor slave drudges all day, in hope
To rest at night.

KING

O Liberty, how glorious art thou !
I see thee hovering o'er my army, with
Thy wide-stretched plumes; I see thee lead them on ;
I see thee blow thy golden trumpet while
Thy sons shout the strong shout of victory !
O noble Chandos, think thyself a gardener,
My son a vine, which I commit unto
Thy care. Prune all extravagant shoots, and guide
The ambitious tendrils in the path of wisdom ;
Water him with thy clear advice, and Heaven
Rain freshening dew upon his branches ! And,
O Edward, my dear son ! think lowly of

Thyself, as we may all each prefer other—
'Tis the best policy, and 'tis our duty.

[*Exit* KING EDWARD.

PRINCE

And may our duty, Chandos, be our pleasure.—
Now we are alone, Sir John, I will unburden
And breathe my hopes into the burning air,
Where thousand Deaths are posting up and down,
Commissioned to this fatal field of Cressy.
Methinks I see them arm my gallant soldiers,
And gird the sword upon each thigh, and fit
Each shining helm, and string each stubborn bow;
And dance to the neighing of our steeds.
Methinks the shout begins, the battle burns:
Methinks I see them perch on English crests,
And roar the wild flame of fierce war upon
The throngèd enemy! In truth, I am too full;
It is my sin to love the noise of war.
Chandos, thou seest my weakness; for strong Nature
Will bend or break us: my blood, like a springtide,
Does rise so high to overflow all bounds
Of moderation; while Reason, in her
Frail bark, can see no shore or bound for vast
Ambition. Come, take the helm, my Chandos,
That my full-blown sails overset me not
In the wild tempest. Condemn my venturous youth
That plays with danger, as the innocent child,
Unthinking, plays upon the viper's den:
I am a coward in my reason, Chandos.

CHANDOS

You are a man, my prince, and a brave man,
If I can judge of actions; but your heat
Is the effect of youth, and want of use:
Use makes the armèd field and noisy war
Pass over as a cloud does, unregarded,
Or but expected as a thing of course.
Age is contemplative; each rolling year
Brings forth her fruit to the mind's treasure-house:—

While vacant youth doth crave and seek about
Within itself, and findeth discontent,
Then, tired of thought, impatient takes the wing,
Seizes the fruits of time, attacks experience,
Roams round vast Nature's forest, where no bounds
Are set, the swiftest may have room, the strongest
Find prey ; till, tired at length, sated and tired
With the changing sameness, old variety,
We sit us down, and view our former joys
With distaste and dislike.

PRINCE

Then, if we must tug for experience,
Let us not fear to beat round Nature's wilds,
And rouse the strongest prey : then if we fall,
We fall with glory.   I know well the wolf
Is dangerous to fight, not good for food,
Nor is the hide a comely vestment ; so
We have our battle for our pains.   I know
That youth has need of age to point fit prey,
And oft the stander-by shall steal the fruit
Of the other's labour.   This is philosophy ;
These are the tricks of the world ; but the pure soul
Shall mount on native wings, disdaining little sport,
And cut a path into the heaven of glory,
Leaving a track of light for men to wonder at.
I 'm glad my father does not hear me talk ;
You can find friendly excuses for me, Chandos.
But do you not think, Sir John, that, if it please
The Almighty to stretch out my span of life,
I shall with pleasure view a glorious action
Which my youth mastered ?

CHANDOS

                    Age, my Lord, views motives
And views not acts ; when neither warbling voice
Nor trilling pipe is heard, nor pleasure sits
With trembling age, the voice of Conscience then,
Sweeter than music in a summer's eve,
Shall warble round the snowy head, and keep

Sweet symphony to feathered angels, sitting
As guardians round your chair ; then shall the pulse
Beat slow, and taste and touch, sight, sound and
    smell,
That sing and dance round Reason's fine-wrought
    throne,
Shall flee away, and leave him all forlorn ;
Yet not forlorn if Conscience is his friend.

                          [*Exeunt.*

SCENE IV.—*In* Sir Thomas Dagworth's *Tent.*

Dagworth, *and* William *his man.*

DAGWORTH

Bring hither my armour, William.
Ambition is the growth of every clime.

WILLIAM

Does it grow in England, sir ?

DAGWORTH

Ay, it grows most in lands most cultivated.

WILLIAM

Then it grows most in France ; the vines here
Are finer than any we have in England.

DAGWORTH

Ay, but the oaks are not.

WILLIAM

What is the tree you mentioned ?   I don't think
I ever saw it.

DAGWORTH

Ambition.

WILLIAM

Is it a little creeping root that grows in ditches ?

DAGWORTH

Thou dost not understand me, William.
It is a root that grows in every breast;
Ambition is the desire or passion that one man
Has to get before another, in any pursuit after glory;
But I don't think you have any of it.

WILLIAM

Yes, I have; I have a great ambition to know
everything, sir.

DAGWORTH

But, when our first ideas are wrong, what follows
must all be wrong, of course; 'tis best to know a
little, and to know that little aright.

WILLIAM

Then, sir, I should be glad to know if it was not
ambition that brought over our king to France to
fight for his right.

DAGWORTH

Though the knowledge of that will not profit thee
much, yet I will tell you that it *was* ambition.

WILLIAM

Then, if ambition is a sin, we are all guilty in
coming with him, and in fighting for him.

DAGWORTH

Now, William, thou dost thrust the question home;
but I must tell you that, guilt being an act of the
mind, none are guilty but those whose minds are
prompted by that same ambition.

WILLIAM

Now, I always thought that a man might be guilty
of doing wrong without knowing it was wrong.

DAGWORTH

Thou art a natural philosopher, and knowest truth
by instinct ; while reason runs aground, as we have
run our argument.   Only remember, William, all
have it in their power to know the motives of their
own actions, and 'tis a sin to act without some reason.

WILLIAM

And whoever acts without reason may do a great
deal of harm without knowing it.

DAGWORTH

Thou art an endless moralist.

WILLIAM

Now there's a story come into my head, that I will
tell your honour, if you'll give me leave.

DAGWORTH

No, William, save it till another time ; this is no
time for story-telling.   But here comes one who is as
entertaining as a good story.

Enter PETER BLUNT.

PETER

Yonder's a musician going to play before the King;
it's a new song about the French and English.   And
the Prince has made the minstrel a squire, and given
him I don't know what, and can't tell whether he
don't mention us all one by one ; and he is to write
another about all us that are to die, that we may be
remembered in Old England, for all our blood and
bones are in France ; and a great deal more that we
shall all hear by and by.   And I came to tell your
honour, because you love to hear war-songs.

DAGWORTH

And who is this minstrel, Peter, dost know ?

PETER

Oh ay, I forgot to tell that; he has got the same name as Sir John Chandos that the Prince is always with—the wise man that knows us all as well as your honour, only ain't so good-natured.

DAGWORTH

I thank you, Peter, for your information, but not for your compliment, which is not true. There's as much difference between him and me as between glittering sand and fruitful mould; or shining glass and a wrought diamond, set in rich gold, and fitted to the finger of an Emperor; such is that worthy Chandos.

PETER

I know your honour does not think anything of yourself, but everybody else does.

DAGWORTH

Go, Peter, get you gone; flattery is delicious, even from the lips of a babbler. [*Exit* PETER.

WILLIAM

I never flatter your honour.

DAGWORTH

I don't know that.

WILLIAM

Why you know, sir, when we were in England, at the tournament at Windsor, and the Earl of Warwick was tumbled over, you asked me if he did not look well when he fell; and I said no, he looked very foolish; and you were very angry with me for not flattering you.

DAGWORTH

You mean that I was angry with you for not flattering the Earl of Warwick. [*Exeunt.*

Scene V.—Sir Thomas Dagworth's *Tent*.

Sir Thomas Dagworth. *To him enters* Sir Walter Manny.

Sir Walter

Sir Thomas Dagworth, I 've been weeping now
Over the men that are to die to-day.

Dagworth

Why, brave Sir Walter, you or I may fall.

Sir Walter

I know this breathing flesh must lie and rot,
Covered with silence and forgetfulness.
Death wons in cities' smoke, and in still night,
When men sleep in their beds, walketh about.
How many in walled cities lie and groan,
Turning themselves about upon their beds,
Talking with Death, answering his hard demands !
How many walk in darkness, terrors round
The curtains of their beds, destruction still
Ready without the door !   How many sleep
In earth, covered over with stones and deathy dust,
Resting in quietness, whose spirits walk
Upon the clouds of heaven, to die no more !
Yet death is terrible, though borne on angels' wings.
How terrible then is the field of death,
Where he doth rend the vault of heaven, and shake
The gates of hell !
O Dagworth, France is sick ! the very sky,
Though sunshine light it, seems to me as pale
As the pale fainting man on his death-bed,
Whose face is shown by light of sickly taper.
It makes me sad and sick at very heart ;
Thousands must fall to-day.

Dagworth

Thousands of souls must leave this prison-house,
To be exalted to those heavenly fields

Where songs of triumph, palms of victory,
Where peace and joy and love and calm content,
Sit singing in the azure clouds, and strew
Flowers of heaven's growth over the banquet-table.
Bind ardent hope upon your feet like shoes,
Put on the robe of preparation !
The table is prepared in shining heaven,
The flowers of immortality are blown ;
Let those that fight fight in good steadfastness,
And those that fall shall rise in victory.

SIR WALTER

I 've often seen the burning field of war,
And often heard the dismal clang of arms ;
But never, till this fatal day of Cressy,
Has my soul fainted with these views of death.
I seem to be in one great charnel-house,
And seem to scent the rotten carcases ;
I seem to hear the dismal yells of Death,
While the black gore drops from his horrid jaws :
Yet I not fear the monster in his pride—
But oh ! the souls that are to die to-day !

DAGWORTH

Stop, brave Sir Walter ; let me drop a tear,
Then let the clarion of war begin ;
I 'll fight and weep, 'tis in my country's cause ;
I 'll weep and shout for glorious liberty.
Grim War shall laugh and shout, bedecked in tears,
And blood shall flow like streams across the meadows,
That murmur down their pebbly channels, and
Spend their sweet lives to do their country service :
Then England's green shall shoot, her fields shall smile,
Her ships shall sing across the foaming sea,
Her mariners shall use the flute and viol,
And rattling guns, and black and dreary war,
Shall be no more.

SIR WALTER

Well, let the trumpet sound, and the drum beat ;

Let war stain the blue heavens with bloody banners;
I 'll draw my sword, nor ever sheathe it up
Till England blow the trump of victory,
Or I lie stretched upon the field of death.   [*Exeunt.*

Scene VI.—*In the Camp.*

*Several of the Warriors met at the King's Tent with a
Minstrel, who sings the following Song:*

O sons of Trojan Brutus, clothed in war,
Whose voices are the thunder of the field,
Rolling dark clouds o'er France, muffling the sun
In sickly darkness like a dim eclipse,
Threatening as the red brow of storms, as fire
Burning up nations in your wrath and fury!

Your ancestors came from the fires of Troy
(Like lions roused by lightning from their dens,
Whose eyes do glare against the stormy fires),
Heated with war, filled with the blood of Greeks,
With helmets hewn, and shields covered with gore,
In navies black, broken with wind and tide:

Landing in firm array upon the rocks
Of Albion; they kissed the rocky shore;
'Be thou our mother and our nurse,' they said;
'Our children's mother, and thou shalt be our grave,
The sepulchre of ancient Troy, from whence
Cities shall rise, thrones, arms, and awful powers.'

Our fathers swarm from the ships.   Giant voices
Are heard from all the hills, the enormous sons
Of Ocean run from rocks and caves; wild men,
Naked and roaring like lions, hurling rocks,
And wielding knotty clubs, like oaks entangled
Thick as a forest, ready for the axe.

Our fathers move in firm array to battle;
The savage monsters rush like roaring fire;

Like as a forest roars with crackling flames,
When the red lightning, borne by furious storms,
Lights on some woody shore ; the parchèd heavens
Rain fire into the molten, raging sea.

The smoking trees are strewn upon the shore,
Spoiled of their verdure.   Oh how oft have they
Defied the storm that howlèd o'er their heads !
Our fathers, sweating, lean on spears, and view
The mighty dead : giant bodies streaming blood,
Dread visages frowning in silent death.

Then Brutus spoke, inspired ; our fathers sit
Attentive on the melancholy shore :
Hear ye the voice of Brutus—'The flowing waves
Of time come rolling o'er my breast,' he said ;
' And my heart labours with futurity.
Our sons shall rule the empire of the sea.

' Their mighty wings shall stretch from east to west.
Their nest is in the sea, but they shall roam
Like eagles for the prey ; nor shall the young
Crave to be heard ; for plenty shall bring forth,
Cities shall sing, and vales in rich array
Shall laugh, whose fruitful laps bend down with ful-
          ness.

' Our sons shall rise up from their thrones in joy,
Each buckling on his armour ; and the dawn
Shall be prevented by their swords gleaming.
Evening shall hear their song of victory ;
Their towers shall be built upon the rocks,
Their daughters sing, surrounded with their spears.

' Liberty shall stand on cliffs of Albion,
Casting her blue eyes over the green sea ;
Or towering upon the roaring waves,
Stretching her mighty spear o'er distant lands ;
While with her eagle wings she covereth
Fair Albion's shore, and all her families.'

PROLOGUE

INTENDED FOR A DRAMATIC PIECE OF KING EDWARD THE FOURTH

OH for a voice like thunder, and a tongue
To drown the throat of war ! When the senses
Are shaken, and the soul is driven to madness,
Who can stand ? When the souls of the oppressed
Fight in the troubled air that rages, who can stand ?
When the whirlwind of fury comes from the throne
Of God, when the frowns of His countenance
Drive the nations together, who can stand ?
When Sin claps his broad wings over the battle,
And sails rejoicing in the flood of death ;
When souls are torn to everlasting fire,
And fiends of hell rejoice upon the slain,
Oh who can stand ? Oh who hath causèd this ?
Oh who can answer at the throne of God ?
The Kings and Nobles of the land have done it !
Hear it not, Heaven, thy ministers have done it !

PROLOGUE TO KING JOHN

JUSTICE hath heaved a sword to plunge in Albion's
    breast ;
For Albion's sins are crimson-dyed,
And the red scourge follows her desolate sons.
Then Patriot rose ; full oft did Patriot rise,
When Tyranny hath stained fair Albion's breast
With her own children's gore.
Round his majestic feet deep thunders roll ;
Each heart does tremble, and each knee grows slack.
The stars of heaven tremble; the roaring voice of war,
The trumpet, calls to battle. Brother in brother's
    blood
Must bathe, rivers of death. O land most hapless !

O beauteous island, how forsaken !
Weep from thy silver fountains, weep from thy gentle
    rivers !
The angel of the island weeps ;
Thy widowed virgins weep beneath thy shades.
Thy aged fathers gird themselves for war ;
The sucking infant lives, to die in battle ;
The weeping mother feeds him for the slaughter.
The husbandman doth leave his bending harvest.
Blood cries afar !   The land doth sow itself !
The glittering youth of courts must gleam in arms ;
The aged senators their ancient swords assume ;
The trembling sinews of old age must work
The work of death against their progeny.
For Tyranny hath stretched his purple arm,
And 'Blood !' he cries : 'The chariots and the horses,
The noise of shout, and dreadful thunder of
The battle heard afar !'
Beware, O proud ! thou shalt be humbled ;
Thy cruel brow, thine iron heart is smitten,
Though lingering Fate is slow.   Oh yet may Albion
Smile again, and stretch her peaceful arms,
And raise her golden head exultingly !
Her citizens shall throng about her gates,
Her mariners shall sing upon the sea,
And myriads shall to her temples crowd !
Her sons shall joy as in the morning—
Her daughters sing as to the rising year !

A WAR SONG

TO ENGLISHMEN

PREPARE, prepare the iron helm of war,
  Bring forth the lots, cast in the spacious orb ;
  The Angel of Fate turns them with mighty hands,
  And casts them out upon the darkened earth !
             Prepare, prepare !

Prepare your hearts for Death's cold hand ! prepare
Your souls for flight, your bodies for the earth !
Prepare your arms for glorious victory !
Prepare your eyes to meet a holy God !
                   Prepare, prepare !

Whose fatal scroll is that ?   Methinks 'tis mine !
Why sinks my heart, why faltereth my tongue?
Had I three lives, I'd die in such a cause,
And rise, with ghosts, over the well-fought field.
                   Prepare, prepare !

The arrows of Almighty God are drawn !
Angels of Death stand in the louring heavens !
Thousands of souls must seek the realms of light,
And walk together on the clouds of heaven !
                   Prepare, prepare !

Soldiers, prepare !   Our cause is Heaven's cause ;
Soldiers, prepare !   Be worthy of our cause :
Prepare to meet our fathers in the sky :
Prepare, O troops that are to fall to-day !
                   Prepare, prepare !

Alfred shall smile, and make his heart rejoice :
The Norman William, and the learned Clerk,
And Lion-Heart, and black-browed Edward with
His loyal queen, shall rise, and welcome us !
                   Prepare, prepare !

THE COUCH OF DEATH

THE veiled evening walks solitary down the western
hills, and silence reposed in the valley. The birds of
day were heard in their nests, rustling in breaks and
thickets, and the owl and bat flew round the darkening trees. All is silent when Nature takes her repose.

In former times, on such an evening, when the cold
clay breathed with life, and our ancestors who now
sleep in their graves walked on the steadfast globe,

the remains of a family of the tribes of Earth, a
mother and a sister, were gathered to the sick-bed
of a youth. Sorrow linked them together, leaning
on one another's necks alternately, like lilies ; dropping tears in each other's bosom they stood by the
bed like reeds bending over a lake when the evening
drops trickle down.

His voice was low, as the whisperings of the woods
when the wind is asleep, and the visions of Heaven
unfold their visitation.

'Parting is hard, and death is terrible. I seem to
walk through a deep valley, far from the light of
day, alone and comfortless. The damps of death fall
thick upon me. Horrors stare me in the face. I
look behind : there is no returning. Death follows
after me. I walk in regions of death where no tree
is, without a lantern to direct my steps, without a
staff to support me.'

Thus he laments through the still evening, till the
curtains of darkness were drawn.

Like the sound of a broken pipe the aged woman
raised her voice :—'O my son ! my son ! I know but
little of the path thou goest ! But lo ! there is a
God that made the world. Stretch out thy hand to
Him.'

The youth replied, like a voice heard from a
sepulchre :—'My hand is feeble ; how should I
stretch it out ? My ways are sinful ; how should I
raise mine eyes ? My voice hath used deceit ; how
should I call on Him who is Truth ? My breath is
loathsome ; how should He not be offended ? If I
lay my face in the dust, the grave opens its mouth
for me. If I lift up my head, sin covers me as a
cloak. O my dear friends ! pray ye for me. Stretch
forth your hands that my helper may come. Through
the void space I walk between the sinful world and
eternity. Beneath me burns eternal fire. O for a
hand to pluck me forth !'

As the voice of an omen heard in the silent valley
when the few inhabitants cling trembling together,

as the voice of the Angel of Death, when the thin
beams of the moon give a faint light, such was this
young man's voice to his friends.

Like the bubbling waters of the brook in the dead
of night the aged woman raised her cry and said :—
'O voice that dwellest in my breast, can I not cry
and lift my eyes to Heaven? Thinking of this, my
spirit is turned within me into confusion. O my
child! my child! is thy breath infected? So is
mine. As the deer, wounded, by the brooks of
water, so the arrows of sin stick in my flesh, the
poison hath entered into my marrow.'

Like rolling waves upon a desert shore, sighs
succeed sighs. They covered their faces and wept.

The youth lay silent, his mother's arm under his
head. He was like a cloud tossed by the winds, till
the sun shine, and the drops of rain glisten, the
yellow harvest breathes, and the thankful eyes of
villagers are turned up in smiles ; the traveller that
hath taken shelter under an oak, eyes the distant
country with joy. Such smiles were seen upon the
face of the youth. A visionary hand wiped away his
tears, and a ray of light beamed around his head.
All was still. The moon hung not out her lamp, and
the stars faintly glimmered in the summer sky. The
breath of night slept among the leaves of the forest.
The bosom of the lofty hill drank in the silent dew,
while on his majestic brow the voice of angels is heard,
and stringed sounds ride on the wings of night.

The sorrowful pair lift up their heads. Hovering
angels are around them. Voices of comfort are heard
over the couch of death, and the youth breathes out
his soul with joy into eternity.

CONTEMPLATION

WHO is this that with unerring step dares to tempt
the wilds where only Nature's step hath trod? 'Tis
Contemplation, daughter of the grey Morning.

Majestical she steppeth, and with pure quill on every
flower, writeth Wisdom's name. Now, lowly bending, whispers in mine ear :—'O man! how great,
how little thou ! O man ! slave of each moment,
Lord of Eternity, seest thou where Mirth sits on the
painted cheek? Doth it not seem ashamed of such a
place and grow immoderate to brave it out? O what
an humble garb true joy puts on! Those who want
Happiness must stoop to find it. It is a flower that
grows in every vale. Vain, foolish man that roams
on lofty rocks, where 'cause his garments are swollen
with wind he fancies he is grown into a giant ! Lo,
then, Humility. Take it, and wear it in thine heart.
Lord of thyself, then thou art lord of all. Clamour
brawls along the streets and destruction hovers in the
city's smoke, but on these plains and in these silent
woods true joys descend. Here build thy nest; here
fix thy staff. Delights blossom around. Numberless beauties blow. The green grass springs in joy,
and the nimble air kisses the leaves. The brook
stretches its arms along the silent meadow ; its silver
inhabitants sport and play. The youthful sun joys
like a hunter roused to the chase. He rushes up the
sky and lays hold of the immortal coursers of the
day : the sky glitters with the jingling trappings.
Like a triumph, season follows season, while the airy
music fills the world with joyful sounds.'

I answered, 'Heavenly goddess ! I am wrapped
in mortality. My flesh is a prison ; my bones the
bars of death. Misery builds over our cottage roofs,
and Discontent runs like a brook. Even in childhood
sorrow slept with me in my cradle. He followed me
up and down in the house when I grew up. He was
my schoolfellow. Thus he was in my steps and in
my play till he became to me as a brother. I walked
through dreary places with him, and in churchyards,
and I oft found myself sitting by sorrow on a tomb-
stone.'

SAMSON

SAMSON, the strongest of the sons of men,
I sing ; how he was foiled by woman's art;
By a false wife brought to the gates of death.
O Truth, that shinest with propitious beams,
Turning our earthly night to heavenly day,
From presence of the Almighty Father, thou
Visitest our darkling world with blessed feet,
Bringing good news of Sin and Death destroyed.
O white-robed Angel, guide my timorous hand
To write as on a rock with iron pen
The words of truth, that all who pass may read.

Now Night, the noontide of the damnèd spirits,
O'er silent earth spreads her pavilion,
While in dark counsel sat Philistea's lords ;
And where strength failed, black thoughts in ambush
    lay.
Their helmed youth and aged warriors
In dust together lie, and Desolation
Spreads his wings o'er the land of Palestine :
From side to side she groans, her prowess lost,
And the land seeks to hide her bruisèd head
Under the mists of night, breeding dark plots.
For Dalila's fair arts were tried in vain ;
In vain she wept in many a treacherous tear.
Go on, fair traitress, do thy guileful work !
For know, ere once again the changing moon
Her circuit hath performed, thou shalt o'ercome
And conquer him, by force unconquerable,
And wrest his secrets from him.   Call thine arts,—
Alluring arts, and honest-seeming brow—
Love's holy kiss, and the transparent tear.
Put on fair linen, that with the lily vies,
Purple and silver, and neglect thine hair
To seem more lovely in thy loose attire.
Put on thy country's pride, false eyes of love,
Decked in mild sorrow, and sell thy lord for gold.

             ·   ·   ·   ·   ·

For now upon her sumptuous couch reclined
In gorgeous pride she still entreats, and still
She grasps his vigorous knees with her fair arms.
'Thou lovest me not! Thou art War, thou art not Love!
O foolish Dalila! O thou weak woman!
It is Death, clothèd in the flesh thou lovest,
And thou hast been encircled in his arms!
Alas, my Lord, what am I calling thee?
Thou art my God! To thee I pour my tears,
For sacrifice I, morn and evening, pour.
My days are covered with sorrow, shut up, darkened,
By night I am deceived.
Who says that thou wast born of mortal kind?
Destruction was thy father; a lioness
Suckled thee; thy young hands tore human limbs
And thy young throat was gorged with human flesh!
Come hither, Death. Art thou not Samson's slave?
'Tis Dalila that calls,—thy master's wife.
No, stay; and let thy master do the deed.
One blow of that strong arm would ease my pain;
Then should I lie at quiet, and have rest.
Pity forsook thee at thy birth! O Dagon
Furious, and all ye gods of Palestine,
Withdraw your hand! I am but a weak woman.
Alas, I am wedded to your enemy!
I will go mad and tear my crispèd hair!
I'll run about and pierce the ears o' the gods!
O Samson, hold me not: thou lovest me not!
Look not upon me with those deathful eyes;
Thou would'st my death, and death approaches fast.

Thus in false tears she wept and bathed his feet,
And thus she day by day oppressed his soul.
He seemed a mountain: on his brow the clouds:
She seemed a silver stream, his feet embracing.
Dark thoughts rolled to and fro within his mind
Like thunderclouds troubling the sultry sky.
His visage was troubled, and his soul distressed.
'Though I tell all my heart, what need I fear?
Though I should tell this secret of my birth,

The utmost may be warded off, as now.'
She saw him moved, and thus resumed her wiles:
'Samson, I am thine; do with me what thou wilt;
My friends are enemies; my life is death;
I am traitor to my nation and despised;
My joy is given into the hands of him
Who hates me, and his bosom's wife deceives.
Thrice hast thou mockèd me, and grieved my soul.
Didst thou not tell me with green withes to bind
Thy nervous arms, and even after that,
When I had found thy falsehood, with new ropes
To bind thee fast? I knew thou didst but mock.
Alas, when in thy sleep I bound thee thus,
To try thy truth I cried, "The Philistines
Be on thee, Samson!" By suspicion woke,
How didst thou rend away the feeble ties?
Thou fearest nought! What hast thou need to fear?
Thy bones are made of brass—thy sinews iron.
Ten thousand spears are like the summer grass;
An army of mighty men as flocks in the vales.
What canst thou fear? I drink my tears like water:
I live on sorrow. O worse than wolves and tigers,
What givest thou me, such trifles being denied?
But oh! at last thou mockest me, to shame
My over-fond inquiries, telling me
To weave thee to the beam by thy strong hair.
I did even that to try thy truth, but when
I cried, "The Philistines be on thee!" then
I did bewail that Samson loved me not.'

He heard her voice: he sat and inward grieved;
He saw and loved the beauteous suppliant,
Nor could conceal aught that might her appease.
Then, leaning on her bosom, thus he spoke:—
'O Dalila, doubt no more Samson's love,
For that fair breast was made the ivory palace
Of my inmost heart where it shall lie at rest,
For sorrow is the lot of all men born.
For care was I brought forth, labour is my lot,
Nor matchless might, wisdom, nor gifts enjoyed

Can from the heart of man his sorrow hide.
Twice was my birth foretold from heaven, and twice
A sacred vow enjoined me I should drink
No wine, nor eat of any unclean thing.
For holy unto Israel's God I am,
A Nazarite, even from my mother's womb :
Twice was it told, that it might not be broken.
"Grant me a son, kind Heaven," Manoa cried ;
But Heaven refused.   Childless he mourned, but
          thought
His God knew best.   Lonely, though not obscure,
In Israel he lived, till age came on :
His flocks increased, and plenty crowned his board ;
Beloved, revered.   But God had other joys
In store.   Was burdened Israel his grief?
The son of his old age should set her free.
The venerable sweetener of his life
Received the promise first from Heaven.   She saw
The maidens play, and blessed their innocent mirth ;
She blessed each new-joined pair ; but now from her
The long-desired deliverer shall spring.
Pensive, alone, she sat within the house,
When busy day was fading, and calm evening,
The time for quiet contemplation, rose
From the forsaken east, and drew heaven's veil—
Pensive she sat, and thought on Israel's grief,
And, silent, prayed to Israel's God ; when lo !
An angel from the fields of light come down
Entered the house.   His form was manhood's prime,
And from his brow terrors shot through the shade.
But mild he hailed her : "Hail, O highly favoured !"
Said he ; "thou shalt conceive and bear a son,
And Israel's strength shall be upon his shoulders.
He shall be called Israel's deliverer.
Now drink no wine, nor eat of unclean things,
For he shall be a Nazarite to God."
Then, as a neighbour when his tale is told,
Departs, his blessing leaving, so went he.
She wondered with exceeding joy, nor knew
He was an angel.   Manoa left his fields

To sit at home and take his evening's rest,
The sweetest time that unto mortal man
God doth allot.   He sat and heard with joy
And praisèd God, who Israel still doth keep.
The time rolled on, Israel groaned, oppressed :
The sword was bright, the ploughshare rusted still,
And hope grew feeble, ready to give place
To doubting.   Then Manoa prayed : "O Lord,
Upon the hills the wolf doth tear Thy sheep,
Oppression lays his rod upon our land :
Our country is ploughed with swords and reaped in
        blood.
Echoes of slaughter reach from hill to hill.
Instead of peaceful pipe, the shepherd bears
A sword.   The goad is turned into a spear.
O when shall our Deliverer come ?   Behold,
The Philistine riots upon our flocks ;
Our vintage gathered by an enemy's band :
Stretch forth Thy hand and save !"   Thus prayed
        Manoa.
The aged woman walked into the field,
And lo ! the angel came again, now clad
As a traveller, fresh risen on his journey.
She called her husband, who thus talked with him :
"O man of God," said he, "thou com'st from far !
Let us detain thee ; we prepare a kid
That thou mayst eat, and tell thy name and way,
That we may honour thee, thy words being true."
The angel said, "My name is Wonderful.
Inquire no more : it is a secret thing ;
But if thou wilt, make offering to the Lord."'

HOW THE 'POETIC SKETCHES' ARE
EDITED HERE

These 'Poetic Sketches' are here printed in the same order as in the little volume published by Blake's friends, with only his initials on the title-page, in the year 1783. The two prose fragments called 'The Couch of Death' and 'Contemplation' are reproduced in the places then chosen for them, just as they were there printed. They would not perhaps be considered at the present day to have any right to inclusion among poetic works, even as 'sketches.' 'Samson,' which follows them, is evidently a poem. Yet it was printed at the end of this volume as prose. A good many of the lines were imperfect. While sorting them up as verses, it has been necessary to do for Blake what he cannot be held blameless for not endeavouring to do for himself, and verbal emendations have been made. The original text is still obtainable through Mr. Quaritch's facsimile, and elsewhere. But those who desire to compare it with the present text, without putting down this volume, can do so by the following :—

For the last line but one of the first paragraph read,—

> 'To write as on a lofty rock with iron pens,'

which, however fine as a line, is evidently not in the metre of the poem.

In the second paragraph almost every line has an annoying and careless slip left in, and the total effect is so worrying that it may safely be said that no one but a student would willingly go through it in its unamended form. On the other hand, no one can read with any pleasure a poem of Blake's that has been touched up by some one else unless he knows just what it would have been if not so treated. The following is the unrestored reading of the second paragraph, only divided into lines, the words as in the original :—

> Now Night, noontide of damned spirits,
> Over the silent earth spreads her pavilion,

While in dark counsel sat Philistia's lords,
And where strength failed black thoughts in ambush lay.
Their helmed youth and aged warriors
In dust together lie, and desolation
Spreads his wings over the land of Palestine ;
From side to side the land groans, her prowess lost,
And seeks to hide her bruised head
Under the mists of night, breeding dark plots.
For Dalila's fair arts have long been tried in vain,
In vain she wept in many a treacherous tear.
'Go on, fair traitress, do thy guileful work ;
Ere once again the changing moon
Her circuit have performed, thou shalt o'ercome
And conquer him by force unconquerable,
And wrest his secret from him.   Call thine alluring arts
And honest-seeming brow,
The holy kiss of love, and the transparent tear ;
Put on fair linen that with the lily vies,
Purple and silver ; neglect thy hair.' . . .

*The continuation needs no amendment, and has none, till
the line*

O foolish Dalila ! O [thou] weak woman,

*in which, as will be noted, the editor has inserted the omitted
word 'thou.'   Nine or ten lines further comes,—*

                                          a lioness
Suckled thee, thy young hands tore human limbs,
And thy young throat was gorged with human flesh,

but the last line of this sentence exists in the original thus—

And gorged human flesh,

*which, of course, is neither sense nor verse, as hands cannot
gorge.   In the line,—*

Come hither, Death ! Art thou not Samson's slave,

*the original has 'servant' for the last word.   The rest of this
paragraph has no emendation.   But in the next are many
slips, hardly two lines together being free from them.   Here is
the uncorrected original,—*

Thus in false tears she bathed his feet,
And thus she day by day oppressed his soul,

He seemed a mountain, his brow among the clouds,—
She seemed a silver stream his feet embracing.
Dark thoughts rolled to and fro in his mind
Like thunderclouds troubling the sky.
His visage was troubled, his soul was distressed.
'Though I should tell her all my heart, what can I fear?
Though I should tell the secret of my birth,
The utmost may be warded off as well when told as now.'
She saw him moved and thus resumed her wiles—
'Samson, I'm thine: do with me what thou wilt,
My friends are enemies; my life is death;
I am a traitor to my nation and despised.
My joy is given into the hands of him
Who hates me, using deceit to the wife of his bosom.
Thrice hast thou mocked me and grieved my soul.
Didst thou not tell me with green withes to bind
Thy nervous arms, and after that,
When I had found thy falsehood, with new ropes
To bind thee fast? I knew thou didst but mock me.
Alas, when in thy sleep I bound thee with them
To try thy truth, I cried, "The Philistines
Be on thee, Samson!" Then did suspicion wake thee:
How didst thou rend away the feeble ties!
Thou fearest nought: what shouldst thou fear?
Thy bones are made of brass, thy sinews are iron;
Ten thousand spears are like the summer grass:
An army of mighty men are as flocks in the valleys—
What canst thou fear? I drink my tears like water;
I live upon water! Oh worse than wolves and tigers,
What canst thou give me when such a trifle is denied?
But oh! at last thou mockest me to shame
My overfond inquiry! Thou toldest me
To weave thee to the beam by thy strong hair;
I did even that to try thy truth, but when
I cried "The Philistines be upon thee," then
Didst thou leave me to bewail that Samson loved me not.

He sat and inward grieved.
He saw and loved the beauteous suppliant,
Nor could conceal aught that might appease her:
Then leaning on her bosom, thus he spoke:
'Hear, oh Dalila, doubt no more of Samson's love,
For that fair breast was made the ivory palace
Of my inmost heart, where it shall lie at rest,
For sorrow is the lot of all of woman born.
For care was I brought forth, and labour is my lot,
Nor matchless might, nor wisdom, nor every gift enjoyed
Can from the heart of man hide sorrow.

Twice was my birth foretold from heaven, and twice
A sacred vow enjoined me that I should drink
No wine, nor eat of any unclean thing,
For holy unto Israel's God I am,
A Nazarite even from my mother's womb.
Twice was it told, that it might not be broken.
'Grant me a son, kind Heaven!' Manoa cried,
But Heaven refused. Childless he mourned, but thought
His God knew best. In solitude, though not obscure,
In Israel he lived till venerable age came on ;
His flocks increased, and plenty crowned his board,
Beloved, revered of man. But God had other joys
In store. Is burdened Israel his grief ?
The son of his old age shall set it free.
The venerable sweetener of his life
Receives the promise first from Heaven. She saw
The maidens play and blessed their innocent mirth ;
She blessed each new-joined pair ; but from her
The long-desired deliverer shall spring.
Pensive, alone, she sat within the house,
When busy day was fading, and calm evening
Time for contemplation rose
From the forsaken east and drew the curtains of heaven.
Pensive she sat and thought on Israel's grief,
And silent prayed to Israel's God, when lo,
An angel from the fields of light
Entered the house ! His form was manhood in the prime,
And from his spacious brow shot terrors through the evening
    shade !
But mild he hailed her—'Hail, highly favoured !'
Said he, 'for lo, thou shalt conceive and bear a son,
And Israel's strength shall be upon his shoulders,
And he shall be called Israel's deliverer !
Now therefore drink no wine, and eat not any unclean thing,
For he shall be a Nazarite to God.'—
Then, as a neighbour when his evening tale is told
Departs, his blessing leaving, so seemed he to depart.
She wondered with exceeding joy, nor knew
He was an angel. Manoa left his fields
To sit in the house and take his evening's rest from labour,
The sweetest time that God has allotted to mortal man.
He sat and heard with joy,
And praised God who Israel still doth keep.
The time rolled on, and Israel groaned, oppressed,
The sword was bright, while the ploughshare rusted,
Till hope grew feeble and was ready to give place
To doubting ; then prayed Manoa—'O Lord,

Thy flock is scattered on the hills ! The wolf teareth them.
Oppression stretches his rod over our land,
Our country is ploughed with swords, and reaped in blood !
The echoes of slaughter reach from hill to hill !
Instead of peaceful pipe the shepherd bears
A sword ; the ox-goad is turned into a spear !
O when shall our Deliverer come ?
The Philistine riots upon our flocks,
Our vintage is gathered by bands of enemies !
Stretch forth Thy hand and save.'—Thus prayed Manoa.
The aged woman walked into the field,
And lo, again the angel came ! clad
As a traveller fresh risen on his journey.
She ran and called her husband, who came and talked with
    him.
'O Man of God,' said he, 'thou comest from far !
Let us detain thee while I make ready a kid,
That thou mayst sit and eat and tell us of thy name and
    warfare,
That when thy sayings come to pass, we may honour thee.'
The Angel answered, 'My name is Wonderful :
Inquire not after it, seeing it is a secret,
But if thou wilt, offer an offering unto the Lord.'

*So ends the last piece in the Poetical Sketches. It began as
a fine piece of Miltonic verse with a slip here and there. It
went on, still Miltonic, but with many slips. Finally, after
a long struggle between the style of the Biblical authorised
version of a Hebrew poem and that of true English blank verse,
the catchiness of the Biblical ended by so overmastering the ear
of the young poet, that only enough Miltonic intention was
left to injure, without transforming, the prose original. Yet
the English poem is there, and the incrustations that cling
round it, as shells might cling to and disguise a statue long
lost at sea, need but careful chipping away, no feature of the
hidden art being injured, and there is a beautiful work after
all.*

---

*Taking now the Songs in order as they are printed. In the
first line of the second verse of ' To Summer,' the word ' do ' is
inserted after ' hills.' A syllable of some kind is needed. This
emendation was made long ago by Mr. D. G. Rossetti.*

*In the first line of the second poem, ' To Autumn,' the word
' thy,' apparently dropped accidentally by Blake, is restored
after ' with.'*

The last two lines were printed in the original

Then rose, girded himself, and o'er the bleak
Hills fled from our sight, but left his golden load.

*We are left to guess whether the oversight was Blake's own
or the printer's.*
*In ' To Winter,' the last three lines in the original are left
in the following state—*

Cries in vain.   Poor little wretch that deal'st
With storms : till heaven smiles, and the monster
Is driven yelling to his caves beneath mount Hecla.

*In ' To the Evening Star,' two conjectural words are added
where the lines showed startling and unexpected gaps.   They
are* own, *the second word of the third line, and* now, *the last
of the seventh line.   D. G. Rossetti, in Gilchrist's* Life of
Blake, *has mended the lines by printing ' brilliant ' for
' bright,' and ' closes ' for ' shuts.'   But this is substitution,
and the operation, though indicated by the state in which
Blake left his verse, is more heroic than the gentle addition of
a needed syllable.*
*In ' To Morning,' the useful stop-gap word ' now ' is here
conjecturally supplied to the middle of the third line from
the end, where Blake unaccountably omits it.*
*The name in ' Fair Elenor ' is so spelled by Blake.   This
and the remaining poems of this group are exactly reproduced
from the 'Poetical Sketches' as printed in 1753, with the exception of the Edward III., in which there are a few verbal
emendations—none at all in the finest speeches.   The incorrect
text of the original edition is exactly reproduced without
emendation or comment in the selections from Blake published
in a cheap volume by Lawrence and Bullen, with Introduction by Mr. J. B. Yeats.*

SONGS OF
INNOCENCE AND OF EXPERIENCE

SHOWING THE TWO CONTRARY STATES
OF THE HUMAN SOUL

13

SONGS OF INNOCENCE
1789

THE AUTHOR AND PRINTER—W. BLAKE

INTRODUCTION

PIPING down the valleys wild,
   Piping songs of pleasant glee,
On a cloud I saw a child,
   And he laughing said to me:

'Pipe a song about a Lamb!'
   So I piped with merry cheer.
'Piper, pipe that song again';
   So I piped: he wept to hear.

'Drop thy pipe, thy happy pipe;
   Sing thy songs of happy cheer!'
So I sang the same again,
   While he wept with joy to hear.

'Piper, sit thee down and write
   In a book that all may read.'
So he vanished from my sight;
   And I plucked a hollow reed,

And I made a rural pen,
   And I stained the water clear,
And I wrote my happy songs
   Every child may joy to hear.

THE SHEPHERD

How sweet is the Shepherd's sweet lot !
From the morn to the evening he strays ;
He shall follow his sheep all the day,
And his tongue shall be fillèd with praise.

For he hears the lambs' innocent call,
And he hears the ewes' tender reply ;
He is watchful while they are in peace,
For they know when their Shepherd is nigh.

THE ECHOING GREEN

THE sun does arise,
And make happy the skies ;
The merry bells ring,
To welcome the spring ;
The skylark and thrush,
The birds of the bush,
Sing louder around
To the bells' cheerful sound ;
While our sports shall be seen
On the Echoing Green.

Old John, with white hair,
Does laugh away care,
Sitting under the oak,
Among the old folk.
They laugh at our play,
And soon they all say,
'Such, such were the joys
When we all—girls and boys—
In our youth-time were seen
On the Echoing Green.'

Till the little ones, weary,
No more can be merry :

The sun does descend,
And our sports have an end.
Round the laps of their mothers
Many sisters and brothers,
Like birds in their nest,
Are ready for rest,
And sport no more seen
On the darkening green.

THE LAMB

Little Lamb, who made thee,
Dost thou know who made thee,
Gave thee life, and bade thee feed
By the stream and o'er the mead ;
Gave thee clothing of delight,
Softest clothing, woolly, bright ;
Gave thee such a tender voice,
Making all the vales rejoice ?
     Little Lamb, who made thee ?
     Dost thou know who made thee ?

Little Lamb, I 'll tell thee ;
Little Lamb, I 'll tell thee :
He is called by thy name,
For He calls himself a Lamb.
He is meek, and He is mild,
He became a little child.
I a child, and thou a lamb,
We are callèd by His name.
     Little Lamb, God bless thee !
     Little Lamb, God bless thee !

THE LITTLE BLACK BOY

My mother bore me in the southern wild,
    And I am black, but oh, my soul is white !
White as an angel is the English child,
    But I am black, as if bereaved of light.

My mother taught me underneath a tree,
  And, sitting down before the heat of day,
She took me on her lap and kissèd me,
  And, pointing to the East, began to say :

' Look on the rising sun : there God does live,
  And gives His light, and gives His heat away,
And flowers and trees and beasts and men receive
  Comfort in morning, joy in the noonday.

' And we are put on earth a little space,
  That we may learn to bear the beams of love,
And these black bodies and this sunburnt face
  Are but a cloud, and like a shady grove.

' For, when our souls have learned the heat to bear
  The cloud will vanish, we shall hear His voice,
Saying, " Come out from the grove, My love and
    care,
  And round My golden tent like lambs rejoice." '

Thus did my mother say, and kissèd me,
  And thus I say to little English boy.
When I from black, and he from white cloud free,
  And round the tent of God like lambs we joy.

I 'll shade him from the heat till he can bear
  To lean in joy upon our Father's knee ;
And then I 'll stand and stroke his silver hair,
  And be like him, and he will then love me.

THE BLOSSOM

Merry, merry Sparrow !
Under leaves so green
A happy Blossom
Sees you, swift as arrow,
Seek your cradle narrow,
Near my Bosom.

Pretty, pretty Robin !
Under leaves so green
A happy Blossom
Hears you sobbing, sobbing,
Pretty, pretty Robin,
Near my Bosom.

THE CHIMNEY-SWEEPER

WHEN my mother died I was very young,
And my father sold me while yet my tongue
Could scarcely cry ' Weep ! weep ! weep ! weep !'
So your chimneys I sweep, and in soot I sleep.

There's little Tom Dacre, who cried when his head,
That curled like a lamb's back, was shaved ; so I
    said,
' Hush, Tom ! never mind it, for, when your head's
    bare,
You know that the soot cannot spoil your white hair.

And so he was quiet, and that very night,
As Tom was a-sleeping, he had such a sight !—
That thousands of sweepers, Dick, Joe, Ned, and
    Jack,
Were all of them locked up in coffins of black.

And by came an angel, who had a bright key,
And he opened the coffins, and set them all free ;
Then down a green plain, leaping, laughing, they
    run,
And wash in a river, and shine in the sun.

Then naked and white, all their bags left behind,
They rise upon clouds, and sport in the wind ;
And the angel told Tom, if he 'd be a good boy,
He 'd have God for his father, and never want joy.

And so Tom awoke, and we rose in the dark,
And got with our bags and our brushes to work.
Though the morning was cold, Tom was happy and
    warm :
So, if all do their duty, they need not fear harm.

THE LITTLE BOY LOST

' FATHER, father, where are you going?
    Oh do not walk so fast !
Speak, father, speak to your little boy,
    Or else I shall be lost.'

The night was dark, no father was there,
    The child was wet with dew ;
The mire was deep, and the child did weep,
    And away the vapour flew.

THE LITTLE BOY FOUND

THE little boy lost in the lonely fen,
    Led by the wandering light,
Began to cry, but God, ever nigh,
    Appeared like his father, in white.

He kissed the child, and by the hand led,
    And to his mother brought,
Who in sorrow pale, through the lonely dale,
    The little boy weeping sought.

LAUGHING SONG

WHEN the green woods laugh with the voice of joy,
And the dimpling stream runs laughing by ;
When the air does laugh with our merry wit,
And the green hill laughs with the noise of it ;

When the meadows laugh with lively green,
And the grasshopper laughs in the merry scene ;
When Mary and Susan and Emily
With their sweet round mouths sing ' Ha ha he ! '

When the painted birds laugh in the shade,
Where our table with cherries and nuts is spread :
Come live, and be merry, and join with me,
To sing the sweet chorus of ' Ha ha he ! '

A CRADLE SONG

Sweet dreams, form a shade
O'er my lovely infant's head !
Sweet dreams of pleasant streams
By happy, silent, moony beams !

Sweet Sleep, with soft down
Weave thy brows an infant crown !
Sweet Sleep, Angel mild,
Hover o'er my happy child !

Sweet smiles, in the night
Hover over my delight !
Sweet smiles, Mother's smiles,
All the livelong night beguiles.

Sweet moans, dovelike sighs,
Chase not slumber from thine eyes !
Sweet moans, sweeter smiles,
All the dovelike moans beguiles.

Sleep, sleep, happy child !
All creation slept and smiled.
Sleep, sleep, happy sleep,
While o'er thee doth mother weep.

Sweet babe, in thy face
Holy image I can trace ;
Sweet babe, once like thee
Thy Maker lay, and wept for me :

Wept for me, for thee, for all,
When He was an infant small.
Thou His image ever see,
Heavenly face that smiles on thee!

Smiles on thee, on me, on all,
Who became an infant small;
Infant smiles are His own smiles;
Heaven and earth to peace beguiles.

THE DIVINE IMAGE

To Mercy, Pity, Peace, and Love,
    All pray in their distress,
And to these virtues of delight
    Return their thankfulness.

For Mercy, Pity, Peace, and Love,
    Is God our Father dear;
And Mercy, Pity, Peace, and Love,
    Is man, His child and care.

For Mercy has a human heart,
    Pity, a human face;
And Love, the human form divine;
    And Peace, the human dress.

Then every man, of every clime,
    That prays in his distress,
Prays to the human form divine:
    Love, Mercy, Pity, Peace.

And all must love the human form,
    In heathen, Turk, or Jew.
Where Mercy, Love, and Pity dwell,
    There God is dwelling too.

HOLY THURSDAY

'Twas on a Holy Thursday, their innocent faces clean,
Came children walking two and two, in red, and blue,
    and green :
Grey-headed beadles walked before, with wands as
    white as snow,
Till into the high dome of Paul's they like Thames
    waters flow.

Oh what a multitude they seemed, these flowers of
    London town !
Seated in companies they sit, with radiance all their
    own.
The hum of multitudes was there, but multitudes of
    lambs,
Thousands of little boys and girls raising their in-
    nocent hands.

Now like a mighty wind they raise to heaven the voice
    of song,
Or like harmonious thunderings the seats of heaven
    among :
Beneath them sit the aged men, wise guardians of the
    poor.
Then cherish pity, lest you drive an angel from your
    door.

NIGHT

The sun descending in the west,
The evening star does shine ;
The birds are silent in their nest,
And I must seek for mine.
    The moon, like a flower
    In heaven's high bower,
    With silent delight,
Sits and smiles on the night.

Farewell, green fields and happy grove,
Where flocks have ta'en delight,
Where lambs have nibbled, silent move
The feet of angels bright;
    Unseen, they pour blessing,
    And joy without ceasing,
    On each bud and blossom,
    And each sleeping bosom.

They look in every thoughtless nest
Where birds are covered warm;
They visit caves of every beast,
To keep them all from harm:
    If they see any weeping
    That should have been sleeping,
    They pour sleep on their head,
    And sit down by their bed.

When wolves and tigers howl for prey,
They pitying stand and weep;
Seeking to drive their thirst away,
And keep them from the sheep.
    But, if they rush dreadful,
    The angels, most heedful,
    Receive each mild spirit,
    New worlds to inherit.

And there the lion's ruddy eyes
Shall flow with tears of gold:
And pitying the tender cries,
And walking round the fold:
    Saying: 'Wrath by His meekness,
    And, by His health, sickness,
    Are driven away
    From our immortal day.

'And now beside thee, bleating lamb,
I can lie down and sleep,
Or think on Him who bore thy name,
Graze after thee, and weep.

For, wash'd in life's river,
My bright mane for ever
Shall shine like the gold,
As I guard o'er the fold.'

SPRING

Sound the Flute !
Now 'tis mute !
Birds delight,
Day and Night,
Nightingale,
In the dale,
Lark in Sky,—
Merrily,
Merrily, Merrily to welcome in the Year.

Little Boy,
Full of joy ;
Little Girl,
Sweet and small ;
Cock does crow,
So do you ;
Merry voice,
Infant noise ;
Merrily, Merrily to welcome in the Year.

Little Lamb,
Here I am ;
Come and lick
My white neck ;
Let me pull
Your soft Wool ;
Let me kiss
Your soft face ;
Merrily, Merrily we welcome in the Year.

NURSE'S SONG

WHEN the voices of children are heard on the green,
　And laughing is heard on the hill,
My heart is at rest within my breast,
　And everything else is still.
'Then come home, my children, the sun is gone down,
　And the dews of night arise;
Come, come, leave off play, and let us away,
　Till the morning appears in the skies.'

'No, no, let us play, for it is yet day,
　And we cannot go to sleep;
Besides, in the sky the little birds fly,
　And the hills are all covered with sheep.'
'Well, well, go and play till the light fades away,
　And then go home to bed.'
The little ones leaped, and shouted, and laughed,
　And all the hills echoèd.

INFANT JOY

'I HAVE no name;
I am but two days old.'
What shall I call thee?
'I happy am,
Joy is my name.'
Sweet joy befall thee!

Pretty joy!
Sweet joy, but two days old.
Sweet joy I call thee:
Thou dost smile,
I sing the while;
Sweet joy befall thee!

A DREAM

ONCE a dream did weave a shade
O'er my angel-guarded bed,
That an emmet lost its way
Where on grass methought I lay.

Troubled, wildered, and forlorn,
Dark, benighted, travel-worn,
Over many a tangled spray,
All heart-broke, I heard her say :

'Oh my children ! do they cry,
Do they hear their father sigh ?
Now they look abroad to see,
Now return and weep for me.'

Pitying, I dropped a tear :
But I saw a glow-worm near,
Who replied, 'What wailing wight
Calls the watchman of the night ?

'I am set to light the ground,
While the beetle goes his round :
Follow now the beetle's hum ;
Little wanderer, hie thee home !'

ON ANOTHER'S SORROW

CAN I see another's woe,
And not be in sorrow too ?
Can I see another's grief,
And not seek for kind relief ?

Can I see a falling tear,
And not feel my sorrow's share ?
Can a father see his child
Weep, nor be with sorrow filled ?

Can a mother sit and hear
An infant groan, an infant fear?
No, no! never can it be!
Never, never can it be!

And can He who smiles on all
Hear the wren with sorrows small,
Hear the small bird's grief and care,
Hear the woes that infants bear—

And not sit beside the nest,
Pouring pity in their breast,
And not sit the cradle near,
Weeping tear on infant's tear?

And not sit both night and day,
Wiping all our tears away?
Oh no! never can it be!
Never, never can it be!

He doth give His joy to all:
He becomes an infant small,
He becomes a man of woe,
He doth feel the sorrow too.

Think not thou canst sigh a sigh,
And thy Maker is not by:
Think not thou canst weep a tear,
And thy Maker is not near.

Oh, He gives to us His joy,
That our grief He may destroy:
Till our grief is fled and gone
He doth sit by us and moan.

SONGS OF EXPERIENCE

1794

The Author and Printer—W. Blake

INTRODUCTION

Hear the voice of the Bard,
Who Present, Past, and Future sees ;
Whose ears have heard
The Holy Word
That walked among the ancient trees ;

Calling the lapsèd Soul,
And weeping in the evening dew ;
That might control
The starry pole,
And fallen, fallen light renew !

' O Earth, O Earth, return !
Arise from out the dewy grass !
Night is worn,
And the morn
Rises from the slumbrous mass.

' Turn away no more ;
Why wilt thou turn away ?
The starry floor,
The watery shore,
Are given thee till the break of day.'

EARTH'S ANSWER

EARTH raised up her head
From the darkness dread and drear,
Her light fled,
Stony, dread,
And her locks covered with grey despair.

' Prisoned on watery shore,
Starry Jealousy does keep my den
Cold and hoar ;
Weeping o'er,
I hear the father of the ancient men.

' Selfish father of men !
Cruel, jealous, selfish fear !
Can delight,
Chained in night,
The virgins of youth and morning bear ?

' Does spring hide its joy,
When buds and blossoms grow ?
Does the sower
Sow by night,
Or the ploughman in darkness plough ?

' Break this heavy chain,
That does freeze my bones around !
Selfish, vain,
Eternal bane,
That free Love with bondage bound. '

THE CLOD AND THE PEBBLE

' LOVE seeketh not itself to please,
  Nor for itself hath any care,
But for another gives its ease,
  And builds a Heaven in Hell's despair. '

So sang a little clod of clay,
   Trodden with the cattle's feet,
But a pebble of the brook
   Warbled out these metres meet :

' Love seeketh only Self to please,
   To bind another to Its delight,
Joys in another's loss of ease,
   And builds a Hell in Heaven's despite. '

HOLY THURSDAY

Is this a holy thing to see
   In a rich and fruitful land—
Babes reduced to misery,
   Fed with cold and usurous hand ?

Is that trembling cry a song ?
   Can it be a song of joy ?
And so many children poor ?
   It is a land of poverty !

And their sun does never shine,
   And their fields are bleak and bare,
And their ways are filled with thorns :
   It is eternal winter there.

For where'er the sun does shine,
   And where'er the rain does fall,
Babe can never hunger there,
   Nor poverty the mind appall.

THE LITTLE GIRL LOST

   In futurity
   I prophetic see
   That the earth from sleep
   (Grave the sentence deep)

Shall arise, and seek
For her Maker meek ;
And the desert wild
Become a garden mild.

In the southern clime,
Where the summer's prime
Never fades away,
Lovely Lyca lay.

Seven summers old
Lovely Lyca told.
She had wandered long,
Hearing wild birds' song.

' Sweet sleep, come to me
Underneath this tree ;
Do father, mother, weep?
Where can Lyca sleep ?

' Lost in desert wild
Is your little child.
How can Lyca sleep
If her mother weep?

' If her heart does ache,
Then let Lyca wake ;
If my mother sleep,
Lyca shall not weep.

' Frowning, frowning night,
O'er this desert bright
Let thy moon arise,
While I close my eyes.'

Sleeping Lyca lay
While the beasts of prey,
Come from caverns deep,
Viewed the maid asleep.

The kingly lion stood,
And the virgin viewed :
Then he gambolled round
O'er the hallowed ground.

Leopards, tigers, play
Round her as she lay ;
While the lion old
Bowed his mane of gold,

And her bosom lick
And upon her neck,
From his eyes of flame,
Ruby tears there came ;

While the lioness
Loosed her slender dress,
And naked they conveyed
To caves the sleeping maid.

THE LITTLE GIRL FOUND

ALL the night in woe
Lyca's parents go
Over valleys deep,
While the deserts weep.

Tired and woe-begone,
Hoarse with making moan,
Arm in arm, seven days
They traced the desert ways.

Seven nights they sleep
Among shadows deep,
And dream they see their child
Starved in desert wild.

Pale through pathless ways
The fancied image strays,
Famished, weeping, weak,
With hollow, piteous shriek.

Rising from unrest,
The trembling woman pressed
With feet of weary woe ;
She could no further go.

In his arms he bore
Her, armed with sorrow sore ;
Till before their way
A couching lion lay.

Turning back was vain :
Soon his heavy mane
Bore them to the ground,
Then he stalked around,

Smelling to his prey ;
But their fears allay
When he licks their hands,
And silent by them stands.

They look upon his eyes,
Filled with deep surprise ;
And wondering behold
A spirit armed in gold.

On his head a crown,
On his shoulders down
Flowed his golden hair—
Gone was all their care.

' Follow me,' he said ;
' Weep not for the maid ;
In my palace deep,
Lyca lies asleep.'

Then they followèd
Where the vision led,
And saw their sleeping child
Among tigers wild.

To this day they dwell
In a lonely dell,
Nor fear the wolvish howl
Nor the lion's growl.

THE CHIMNEY SWEEPER

A LITTLE black thing among the snow,
Crying 'weep! weep!' in notes of woe!
'Where are thy father and mother? Say!'—
'They are both gone up to the church to pray.

'Because I was happy upon the heath,
And smiled among the winter's snow,
They clothed me in the clothes of death,
And taught me to sing the notes of woe.

'And because I am happy and dance and sing,
They think they have done me no injury,
And are gone to praise God and his priest and king,
Who make up a heaven of our misery.'

NURSE'S SONG

WHEN the voices of children are heard on the green,
And whisperings are in the dale,
The days of my youth rise fresh in my mind,
My face turns green and pale.

Then come home, my children, the sun is gone down,
And the dews of night arise;
Your spring and your day are wasted in play,
And your winter and night in disguise.

THE SICK ROSE

O ROSE, thou art sick!
The invisible worm,
That flies in the night,
In the howling storm,

Has found out thy bed
    Of crimson joy,
And his dark, secret love
    Does thy life destroy.

THE FLY

LITTLE Fly,
    Thy summer's play
My thoughtless hand
    Has brushed away.

Am not I
    A fly like thee?
Or art not thou
    A man like me?

For I dance,
    And drink, and sing,
Till some blind hand
    Shall brush my wing.

If thought is life
    And strength and breath,
And the want
    Of thought is death;

Then am I
    A happy fly,
If I live,
    Or if I die.

THE ANGEL

I DREAMT a Dream! What can it mean?
And that I was a maiden Queen
Guarded by an Angel mild:
Witless woe was ne'er beguiled!

And I wept both night and day,
And he wiped my tears away;
And I wept both day and night,
And hid from him my heart's delight.

So he took his wings, and fled;
Then the morn blushed rosy red.
I dried my tears, and armed my fears
With ten thousand shields and spears.

Soon my Angel came again;
I was armed, he came in vain;
For the time of youth was fled,
And grey hairs were on my head.

THE TIGER

TIGER, Tiger, burning bright
In the forests of the night,
What immortal hand or eye
Could frame thy fearful symmetry?

In what distant deeps or skies
Burnt the fire of thine eyes?
On what wings dare he aspire?
What the hand dare seize the fire?

And what shoulder and what art
Could twist the sinews of thy heart?
And, when thy heart began to beat,
What dread hand and what dread feet?

What the hammer? what the chain?
In what furnace was thy brain?
What the anvil? what dread grasp
Dare its deadly terrors clasp?

When the stars threw down their spears,
And watered heaven with their tears,
Did he smile his work to see?
Did he who made the lamb make thee?

Tiger, Tiger, burning bright
In the forests of the night,
What immortal hand or eye
Dare frame thy fearful symmetry ?

MY PRETTY ROSE TREE

A FLOWER was offered to me,
    Such a flower as May never bore ;
But I said, 'I've a Pretty Rose tree,'
    And I passed the sweet flower o'er.

Then I went to my Pretty Rose tree,
    To tend her by day and by night ;
But my Rose turned away with jealousy,
    And her thorns were my only delight.

AH SUNFLOWER

AH Sunflower, weary of time,
    Who countest the steps of the sun ;
Seeking after that sweet golden clime
    Where the traveller's journey is done ;

Where the Youth pined away with desire,
    And the pale Virgin shrouded in snow,
Arise from their graves, and aspire
    Where my Sunflower wishes to go !

THE LILY

THE modest Rose puts forth a thorn,
The humble Sheep a threat'ning horn :
While the Lily white shall in love delight,
Nor a thorn nor a threat stain her beauty bright.

THE GARDEN OF LOVE

I WENT to the Garden of Love,
  And saw what I never had seen;
A Chapel was built in the midst,
  Where I used to play on the green.

And the gates of this Chapel were shut
  And 'Thou shalt not' writ over the door;
So I turned to the Garden of Love
  That so many sweet flowers bore.

And I saw it was filled with graves,
  And tombstones where flowers should be;
And priests in black gowns were walking their
    rounds,
  And binding with briars my joys and desires.

THE LITTLE VAGABOND

DEAR mother, dear mother, the Church is cold;
But the Alehouse is healthy, and pleasant, and warm.
Besides, I can tell where I am used well;
Such usage in heaven will never do well.

But, if at the Church they would give us some ale,
And a pleasant fire our souls to regale,
We'd sing and we'd pray all the livelong day,
Nor ever once wish from the Church to stray.

Then the Parson might preach, and drink, and sing,
And we'd be as happy as birds in the spring;
And modest Dame Lurch, who is always at church,
Would not have bandy children, nor fasting, nor
    birch.

And God, like a Father, rejoicing to see
His Children as pleasant and happy as He,
Would have no more quarrel with the Devil or the
    barrel,
But kiss him, and give him both drink and apparel.

LONDON

I WANDER through each chartered street,
  Near where the chartered Thames does flow,
A mark in every face I meet,
  Marks of weakness, marks of woe.

In every cry of every man,
  In every infant's cry of fear,
In every voice, in every ban,
  The mind-forged manacles I hear:

How the chimney-sweeper's cry
  Every blackening church appals,
And the hapless soldier's sigh
  Runs in blood down palace-walls.

But most, through midnight streets I hear
  How the youthful harlot's curse
Blasts the new-born infant's tear,
  And blights with plagues the marriage-hearse.

THE HUMAN ABSTRACT

PITY would be no more
If we did not make somebody poor,
And Mercy no more could be
If all were as happy as we.

And mutual fear brings Peace,
Till the selfish loves increase;
Then Cruelty knits a snare,
And spreads his baits with care.

He sits down with his holy fears,
And waters the ground with tears;
Then Humility takes its root
Underneath his foot.

Soon spreads the dismal shade
Of Mystery over his head,
And the Caterpillar and Fly
Feed on the Mystery.

And it bears the fruit of Deceit,
Ruddy and sweet to eat,
And the Raven his nest has made
In its thickest shade.

The Gods of the earth and sea
Sought through Nature to find this Tree,
But their search was all in vain:
There grows one in the Human Brain.

INFANT SORROW

My mother groaned, my father wept:
Into the dangerous world I leapt,
Helpless, naked, piping loud,
Like a fiend hid in a cloud.

Struggling in my father's hands,
Striving against my swaddling-bands,
Bound and weary, I thought best
To sulk upon my mother's breast.

CHRISTIAN FORBEARANCE

I was angry with my friend:
I told my wrath, my wrath did end.
I was angry with my foe:
I told it not, my wrath did grow.

And I watered it in fears
Night and morning with my tears,
And I sunnèd it with smiles
And with soft, deceitful wiles.

And it grew both day and night,
    Till it bore an apple bright,
And my foe beheld it shine,
    And he knew that it was mine,—

And into my garden stole
    When the night had veiled the pole;
In the morning, glad, I see
    My foe outstretched beneath the tree.

A LITTLE BOY LOST

Nought loves another as itself,
    Nor venerates another so,
Nor is it possible to thought
    A greater than itself to know.

And, father, how can I love you
    Or any of my brothers more?
I love you like the little bird
    That picks up crumbs around the door.

The Priest sat by and heard the child;
    In trembling zeal he seized his hair,
He led him by his little coat,
    And all admired the priestly care.

And standing on the altar high,
    Lo, what a fiend is here! said he:
One who sets reason up for judge
    Of our most holy mystery.

The weeping child could not be heard,
    The weeping parents wept in vain:
They stripped him to his little shirt,
    And bound him in an iron chain,

And burned him in a holy place
    Where many had been burned before;
The weeping parents wept in vain.
    Are such things done on Albion's shore?

A LITTLE GIRL LOST

CHILDREN of the future Age,
Reading this indignant page,
Know that in a former time
Love, sweet love, was thought a crime.

In the Age of Gold,
Free from winter's cold,
Youth and maiden bright,
To the holy light,
Naked in the sunny beams delight.

Once a youthful pair,
Filled with softest care,
Met in garden bright
Where the holy light
Had just removed the curtains of the night.

Then, in rising day,
On the grass they play ;
Parents were afar,
Strangers came not near,
And the maiden soon forgot her fear.

Tired with kisses sweet,
They agree to meet
When the silent sleep
Waves o'er heaven's deep,
And the weary, tired wanderers weep.

To her father white
Came the maiden bright ;
But his loving look,
Like the holy book,
All her tender limbs with terror shook.

Ona, pale and weak !
To thy father speak !
Oh the trembling fear !
Oh the dismal care !
That shakes the blossoms of my hoary hair.

TO TIRZAH

WHATE'ER is Born of Mortal Birth
Must be consumèd with the Earth,
To rise from Generation free :
Then what have I to do with thee?

The Sexes sprang from Shame and Pride,
Blowd in the morn, in evening died ;
But Mercy changed Death into Sleep ;
The Sexes rose to work and weep.

Thou, Mother of my Mortal part,
With cruelty didst mould my Heart,
And with false self-deceiving tears
Didst bind my Nostrils, Eyes, and Ears,

Didst close my Tongue in senseless clay,
And me to Mortal Life betray.
The Death of Jesus set me free :
Then what have I to do with thee?

THE SCHOOLBOY

I LOVE to rise in a summer morn,
    When the birds sing on every tree ;
The distant huntsman winds his horn,
    And the skylark sings with me :
    Oh what sweet company !

But to go to school in a summer morn,—
    Oh it drives all joy away !
Under a cruel eye outworn,
    The little ones spend the day
    In sighing and dismay.

Ah then at times I drooping sit,
    And spend many an anxious hour ;
Nor in my book can I take delight,
    Nor sit in learning's bower,
    Worn through with the dreary shower.

How can the bird that is born for joy
  Sit in a cage and sing?
How can a child, when fears annoy,
  But droop his tender wing,
  And forget his youthful spring?

Oh father and mother, if buds are nipped,
  And blossoms blown away;
And if the tender plants are stripped
  Of their joy in the springing day,
  By sorrow and care's dismay,—

How shall the summer arise in joy,
  Or the summer fruits appear?
Or how shall we gather what griefs destroy,
  Or bless the mellowing year,
  When the blasts of winter appear?

THE VOICE OF THE ANCIENT BARD

YOUTH of delight! come hither
And see the opening morn,
Image of Truth new-born.
Doubt is fled, and clouds of reason,
Dark disputes and artful teazing.
Folly is an endless maze;
Tangled roots perplex her ways;
How many have fallen there!
They stumble all night over bones of the dead;
And feel—they know not what but care;
And wish to lead others, when they should be led.

THE PRESENT ARRANGEMENT OF THE
'SONGS OF INNOCENCE AND EXPERIENCE'

*These poems were collected and engraved by Blake with
illustrations and decorative setting of his own. Figures and
fragments of landscape were drawn with the same varnish
used for writing the songs. The whole page was bitten with
acid at once, in the manner already described, and printed at
one printing. The ink used for this was of a dull brick-red,
or yellowish brown. Black lines were added by hand afterwards in places, and the whole was tinted in light washes
with water-colours. The pages were nowhere left colourless,
and the poems were seen through pale rainbows, or through
cloudy fumes of transparent flame-colours mixed with purple
or dark blue, where a gloom was needed in places to heighten
the delicacy of the sky-colours of dawn-like paleness elsewhere.
The collection was not always exactly the same, but nearly so.
The set here followed was chosen by Blake in his old age, and
coloured with unusual elaboration and care.*

*There is not the alteration of a single word in the text, the
ungrammatical plurals or singulars in the* smiles *and* beguiles
*of the first Cradle Song, the word 'bosom' where the two words
'breast did' should have been in the last stanza but one of
'The Little Girl Lost,' and one or two more slips, such as
'blowd' in the poem 'To Tirzah,' are reproduced exactly.*

*They are so few and so easy for the reader to alter im-
promptu as he goes along, that it was thought that the gain of
correction would not have justified the loss of the historical
value to be obtained from a complete view of the Songs just as
Blake engraved them. They were, at the time, his highest
achievement of accuracy, and have remained what they also
were from the beginning, his most popular work.*

*Some other verses exist, written originally for these songs,
including two stanzas preceding the 'Garden of Love' in
Gilchrist, but not so engraved by Blake; and two Songs of
Experience, 'A Divine Image' and 'A Cradle Song,' counterparts to the Songs of Innocence of the same name, were intended*

94

THE THISTLES AND THORNS

I laid me down upon a bank,
    Where Love lay sleeping:
I heard among the bushes dank,
    Weeping, weeping.

Then I went to the Heath and the Wild,
    To the Thistles and Thorns of the Waste,
And they told me how they were beguiled,
    Driven out and compelled to be chaste.

A DIVINE IMAGE

Cruelty has a human heart,
    And Jealousy a human face,
Terror the human form divine,
    And Secrecy the human dress.

The human dress is forgèd iron,
    The human form a fiery forge,
The human face a furnace sealed,
    The human heart its hungry gorge

A CRADLE SONG

Sleep, sleep, beauty bright,
Dreaming in the joys of night,
Sleep, sleep, in thy sleep,
Little sorrows sit and weep.

Sweet babe, in thy face
Soft desires I can trace,
Secret joys and secret smiles,
Little pretty infant wiles.

As thy softest limbs I feel,
Smiles as of the morning steal
O'er thy cheek and o'er thy breast
Where thy little heart doth rest.

Oh the cunning wiles that creep
In in thy little heart asleep,
When thy little heart shall wake,
Then the dreadful lightnings break.

From thy cheek and from thine eye,
O'er the youthful harvests nigh,
Infant wiles and infant smiles,
Heaven and earth of peace beguiles.

This last verse was not engraved at all. Here is the first instance of the symbol of the harvest. Blake wrote female twice and altered the word into infant in the last line but one.

There is a verse belonging to the 'Tiger' which was also omitted by Blake when engraving. It followed verse 3, and continues the sentence there left unfinished.

Could filch it from the furnace deep,
And in thy horrid ribs dare steep?
In what clay or in what mould
Were thy eyes of fury rolled?

There is a line in the middle of this stanza, 'In the well of sanguine woe,' which Blake inadvertently did not cross out. In the preface to Quaritch's facsimile of the Songs, the present editor mistakenly included it in the sentence.

There exist in manuscript, though crossed out, verses that amount to practically a complete second version of the song. They have been printed elsewhere. The present stanza seems merely to have been left out to give room for a drawing, after the first three verses were already on the plate. Perhaps Blake did not notice that he left his third verse by this omission in the state of a broken sentence. Perhaps he noticed and did not care. It is just possible that he thought that the reader would look on some such completing words as could twist the sinews of it? as implied in what was already said if nothing else were put to take their place and give another turn to the phrase.

The Song of Experience called 'London' was also retouched in manuscript. The word 'chartered' twice repeated is an afterthought. 'Dirty' was the first version. This song seems to have been deprived of its last verse, which is found in the MS. as a separate poem, with the title 'An Ancient Proverb.' These are the lines—

Remove away that blackening church,
Remove away that marriage hearse,
Remove away that man of blood,—
You'll quite remove the ancient curse.

This short song seems to have been written as a sequel to 'London' at the time when the word 'chartered' was foisted into its text. It was not engraved.

THAMES AND OHIO

Why should I care for the men of the Thames,
And the cheating waters of chartered streams, —
Or shriek at the little blasts of fear
That the hireling blows into mine ear?

Though born on the cheating banks of Thames,
Though his waters bathed my infant limbs,
The Ohio shall wash his stains from me:
I was born a slave, but I go to be free.

The following, only existing in pencil, written among the pages which contain many of the songs, seems to have escaped by accident, or by being written too late, from inclusion among them. It has no title. It might be called

THE CHAIN OF DECEIT

Love to faults is always blind,
Always is to joy inclined, —
Lawless, winged, unconfined,
And breaks the chains from every mind.

The souls of men are bought and sold
In milk-fed infancy for gold,
And youth to slaughter-houses led,
And beauty for a bit of bread.

Deceit to seeming love inclined,
Most cruel is when most refined, —
To everything but interest blind,
And forges fetters of the mind.

The first two stanzas only of this have been printed by Mr. Yeats, who calls it 'Freedom and Captivity.' It is almost illegible. The present editor reads the difficult and obscure words somewhat differently from Mr. Yeats and from Mr. Rossetti, though even now he has no absolute certainty that the words love inclined *in the first line of the last verse, and* cruel is when most *in the second, are really Blake's. They are the best conjecture he can make.*

Following the two verses engraved that make up the whole

*Song of Experience called 'Infant Sorrows,' are the following
in manuscript:—*

(Not engraved.)

3

And I grew day after day,
Till upon the ground I lay,
And I grew night after night,
Seeking only for delight.

4

And I saw before me shine
Clusters of the wandering vine,
And many a lovely flower and tree,
And beyond, a myrtle tree.

5

But a priest with holy look,
In his hands a holy book,
Pronounced curses on my head
And bound me in a myrtle shade.

6

I beheld the priests by night:
I beheld the priests by day:
They embraced my myrtle bright,
Underneath my vine they lay.

7

Like to holy men by day,
Underneath the vines they lay:
Like to serpents in the night,
They embraced my myrtle bright.

8

So I smote them, and their gore
Stained the roots my myrtle bore,
But the time of youth is fled,
And grey hairs are on my head.

*There are retouchings of this. A new verse 3 was schemed
later, and written at the end, for use as numbered.*

When I saw that rage was vain
And to sulk would nothing gain,
Turning many a trick and wile,
I began to soothe and smile,

To suit this new verse 3, some words in the standing verse 3, which would now have to be made verse 4, were altered,—grew in the first line to soothed ; *and the same word, where it recurs in the third line, to* smiled.

An attempt was made to get rid of the myrtle. *In the standing verse 4,* And beyond a myrtle tree *was altered to* Stretched their blossoms out to me ; *but the first form of the line shows the place of the poem in Blake's thoughts at the time. In verse 5,* But a priest *was changed into* My father then. *Verse 7 is overlooked, and the plural form of* serpents *and* men *left untouched, while in verse 8,* Them *and their is changed to* him *and* his.

Blake's own disapproval of these changes is seen in the fact that he abandoned the verses, and did not engrave them. But they help us to understand other poems. The two verses 'In a Myrtle Shade,' usually printed among 'Ideas of Good and Evil,' are all that is left of another portion or version of this poem, full of recomposed (one can hardly say corrected) lines.

Both are to be read with the last verse of 'Earth's Answer,' in which the 'Father' here spoken of is identified. It must never be forgotten that Blake was always a convinced Christian of the early type, once orthodox, but counted as heretical since the day when Gnosticism was decreed heresy by the Church.

The following rejected verses follow the two that make up the poem 'In a Myrtle Shade,' and connect it with 'Infant Sorrow' :—

Oft my myrtle sighed in vain
To behold my heavy chain ;
Oft my father saw us sigh,
And laughed at our simplicity.

So I smote him, and his gore
Stained the roots my murtle bore :
But the time of youth is fled
And grey hairs are on my head.

But, unable apparently to disentangle the two poems, they were abandoned by their author. An editor who should, on his own authority, substitute the words 'the priests' for 'my father' in the first of these two verses would enable it to be used in 'Infant Sorrow' as it stands, notwithstanding the unexpected allusion to the chain, which will be taken rightly as another form of the winding serpent and the swaddling-clothes, all companion symbols of one idea under several aspects.

Here are the two verses making the separate poem—

IN A MYRTLE SHADE

To a lovely Myrtle bound,
Blossoms showering all around,
Oh how weak and weary I
Underneath my Myrtle lie.

Why should I be bound to thee,
Oh my lovely Myrtle Tree?
Love, free love, will not be bound
To any tree that grows on ground.

In this final form it was probably intended, but never engraved, as a companion or counterpart to ' Infant Sorrow,' also reduced to two verses only when actually engraved.

The two following songs, not usually associated with the collection, are evidently early in date, and bear internal evidence of having been rejected when the ' Songs of Innocence' were first made up.

SONG BY A SHEPHERD

Welcome, little stranger, to this place,
Where joy doth sit on every bough,
Paleness flies from every face,
We reap not what we do not sow.

Innocence doth, like a rose,
Bloom on every maiden's cheek.
Honour twines around her brows,
The jewel health adorns her neck.

SONG BY AN OLD SHEPHERD

When silver snow decks Silvia's clothes,
And jewel hangs at shepherd's nose,
We can abide life's pelting storm,
That makes our limbs quake if our hearts be warm.

Whilst Virtue is our walking staff
And Truth a lantern to our path,
We can abide life's pelting storm,
Which makes our limbs quake if our hearts be warm.

Blow boist'rous wind, stern winter frown,
Innocence is a winter's gown.
So clad, we'll abide life's pelting storm,
That makes our limbs quake if our hearts be warm.

*This also can have been nothing but a 'Song of Innocence,
written, as it was, among others engraved in the same manuscript volume, but perhaps rejected as being composed too late
for the first section, and having no place in the second. It is
usually printed with the following conjectural title:—*

THE LAND OF DREAMS

Awake, awake, my little boy!
Thou wast thy mother's only joy.
Why dost thou weep in thy gentle sleep?
Awake,—thy father doth thee keep.

Oh what land is the land of dreams?
What are its mountains and what are its streams?
Oh Father, I saw my mother there,
Among the lilies, by waters fair.

Among the lambs clothèd in white,
She walks with her Thomas in sweet delight.
I wept for joy: like a dove I mourn:
Oh when shall I again return?

Dear child, I also by pleasant streams
Have wandered all night in the land of dreams,
And though calm and warm the waters wide,
I could not get to the other side.

Father, O Father, what do we here,
In this land of unbelief and fear?
The land of dreams is better far,
Beyond the light of the morning star.

*The last fragment which was designed for the 'Songs,' but
not included, is the following, bearing a title that leaves no
doubt at all:—*

MOTTO FOR SONGS OF INNOCENCE AND EXPERIENCE

The Good are attracted by men's perceptions,
And think not for themselves,
Till Experience teaches them to catch
And cage the fairies and elves.

Then the Knave begins to snarl,
   And the Hypocrite to howl,
And all his good friends show their private ends,
   And the eagle is known from the owl.

'The cage' will be recognised from an early 'Poetical Sketch,' and in 'The Island in the Moon' later on. The fairies—in the sense of minor spirits whose inspiration leads to love and marriage—will be met again.

Here we may leave the most popular of Blake's volumes with the reminder that the two sections of which it is made up were written five years apart, 1789 to 1794, and that between these dates Blake's Myth—the main invention of his life—began to grow up in his mind, and more than one of the 'Books' which here follow was composed. Traces of them are to be found more often than at first appears in the songs, and without familiarity with their stories a great deal will pass not fully understood or enjoyed.

IDEAS OF GOOD AND EVIL

IDEAS OF GOOD AND EVIL

An incomplete collection not made up into a volume by Blake. The date seems to range from 1794 till nearly 1800. No single piece can be stated with certainty to have been destined for it, and the contrasts were not sorted in pairs. The following were most probably to have been reserved for selection:—

DAYBREAK

To find the Western Path
Right through the gates of wrath
    I urge my way :
Sweet morning leads me on ;
With sweet, repentant moan
    I see the break of day.

The war of swords and spears
Melted by dewy tears
    Exhales on high ;
The sun is freed from fears
And with soft, grateful tears
    Ascends the sky.

MAMMON (Gilchrist's Title)
THE TWO THRONES (Mr. Yeats's Title)

I rose up at the dawn of day.
'Get thee away ! get thee away !
Pray'st thou for riches?   Away ! away !
This is the throne of Mammon grey.'

105

I said, ' This sure is very odd,
I took it to be the throne of God.
Everything else besides I have,
It's only riches I can crave.

' I have mental joys and mental health,
Mental friends and mental wealth.
I've a wife that I love and that loves me,
I've all but riches bodily.

' I am in God's presence night and day,
He never turns His face away.
The Accuser of Sins by my side does stand,
And he holds my money-bags in his hand.

' For my worldly things God makes him pay,
And he'd pay for more if to him I would pray.
And you may do the worst you can do ;
Be assured, Mr. Devil, I won't pray to you.

' Then if for riches I must not pray,
God knows it's little prayers I need say.
So, as a church is known by its steeple,
If I pray, it must be for other people.

' He says, if I don't worship him for a god,
I shall eat coarser food and go worse shod ;
But as I don't value such things as these,
You must do, Mr. Devil, just as God please.'

RICHES

SINCE all the riches of this world
    May be gifts from the devil and earthly kings,
I should suspect that I worshipped the devil
    If I thanked my God for worldly things.

The countless gold of a merry heart,
    The rubies and pearls of a loving eye,
The idle man never can bring to the mart,
    Nor the cunning hoard up in his treasury.

OPPORTUNITY

HE who bends to himself a joy
Does the winged life destroy;
But he who kisses the joy as it flies
Lives in eternity's sunrise.

If you trap the moment before it's ripe,
The tears of repentance you'll certainly wipe;
But, if once you let the ripe moment go,
You can never wipe off the tears of woe.

NIGHT AND DAY

SILENT, silent Night,
Quench the holy light
Of thy torches bright;

For, possessed of Day,
Thousand spirits stray
That sweet joys betray.

Why should joys be sweet
Usèd with deceit,
Nor with sorrows meet?

But an honest joy
Doth itself destroy
For a harlot coy.

THE WILL AND THE WAY

I ASKED a thief to steal me a peach:
    He turned up his eyes.
I asked a lithe lady to lie her down:
    Holy and meek, she cries.

As soon as I went,
    An Angel came.
He winked at the thief,
    And smiled at the dame ;

And, without one word spoke,
    Had a peach from the tree,
And 'twixt earnest and joke
    Enjoyed the lady.

BARREN BLOSSOM

I FEARED the fury of my wind
    Would blight all blossoms fair and true,
And my sun it shined and shined,
    And my wind it never blew.

But a blossom fair or true
    Was not found on any tree ;
For all blossoms grew and grew
    Fruitless, false, though fair to see.

CUPID

WHY was Cupid a boy,
    And why a boy was he?
He should have been a girl
    For all that I can see.

For he shoots with his bow
    And a girl shoots with her eye,
And they both are merry and glad,
    And laugh when we do cry.

Then to make Cupid a boy
    Was surely a woman's plan,
For a boy never learns so much
    Till he becomes a man.

And then he's so pierced with cares
And wounded with arrowy smarts,
That the whole business of his life
Is to pull out the heads of the darts.

LOVE'S SECRET

NEVER seek to tell thy love,
Love that never told can be;
For the gentle wind doth move
Silently, invisibly.

I told my love, I told my love,
I told her all my heart,
Trembling, cold, in ghastly fears.
Ah! she did depart!

Soon after she was gone from me,
A traveller came by,
Silently, invisibly:
He took her with a sigh.

THE BIRDS

HE

WHERE thou dwellest, in what grove,
Tell me, fair one, tell me, love;
Where thou thy charming nest doth build,
O thou pride of every field!

SHE

Yonder stands a lonely tree:
There I live and mourn for thee.
Morning drinks my silent tear,
And evening winds my sorrow bear,

HE

O thou summer's harmony,
I have lived and mourned for thee;
Each day I moan along the wood,
And night hath heard my sorrows loud.

SHE

Dost thou truly long for me?
And am I thus sweet to thee?
Sorrow now is at an end,
O my lover and my friend!

HE

Come! on wings of joy we'll fly
To where my bower is hung on high;
Come, and make thy calm retreat
Among green leaves and blossoms sweet.

YOUNG LOVE

ARE not the joys of morning sweeter
    Than the joys of night;
And are the joys of vigorous youth
    Ashamed of the light?

Let age and sickness silent rob
    The vineyard in the night,
But those who burn with vigorous youth
    Pluck fruits before the light.

SEED-SOWING

'THOU hast a lapful of seed,
And this is a fair country.
Why dost thou not cast thy seed,
And live in it merrily?'

'Shall I cast it on the sand,
And turn it into fruitful land?
For on no other ground can I sow my seed
Without tearing up some stinking weed.'

THE DEFILED SANCTUARY

I SAW a chapel all of gold
    That none did dare to enter in,
And many, weeping, stood without,
    Weeping, mourning, worshipping.

I saw a serpent rise between
    The carved pillars of the door,
And he forced and forced and forced,
    Till he the golden hinges tore,

And along the pavement sweet
    Set with pearls and rubies bright,
All his shining length he drew,
    Till upon the altar white

He vomited his poison out
    On the bread and on the wine ;
So I turned into a sty,
    And laid me down among the swine.

THE TWO VOICES

I HEARD an Angel singing
    When the day was springing :
' Mercy, pity, and peace,
    Are the world's release.'

So he sang all day
    Over the new-mown hay,
Till the sun went down,
    And haycocks looked brown,

I heard a Devil curse
Over the heath and the furze:
'Mercy could be no more
If there were nobody poor,
And pity no more could be
If all were happy as ye:
And mutual fear brings peace.
Misery's increase
Are mercy, pity, peace.'
At his curse the sun went down
And the heavens gave a frown.

THE WILD FLOWER'S SONG

As I wandered in the forest
    The green leaves among,
I heard a wild-flower
    Singing a song.

'I slept in the earth
    In the silent night;
I murmured my thoughts,
    And I felt delight.

'In the morning I went,
    As rosy as morn,
To seek for new joy,
    But I met with scorn.

THE GOLDEN NET

BENEATH a white-thorn's lovely may
Three virgins at the break of day.—
'Whither, young man, whither away,
Alas for woe! alas for woe!'
They cry, and tears for ever flow,

The first was clothed in flames of fire,
The second clothed in iron wire ;
The third was clothed in tears and sighs
Dazzling bright before my eyes.
They bore a net of golden twine
To hang upon the branches fine.
Pitying I wept to see the woe
That love and beauty undergo—
To be clothed in burning fires
And in ungratified desires,
And in tears clothed night and day ;
It melted all my soul away.
When they saw my tears, a smile
That might heaven itself beguile
Bore the golden net aloft,
As on downy pinions soft,
Over the morning of my day.
Underneath the net I stray,
Now entreating Flaming-fire,
Now entreating Iron-wire,
Now entreating Tears-and-sighs.—
Oh when will the morning rise ?

In the MS. ' Iron wire ' was at first written ' Sweet desire.'

SMILE AND FROWN

THERE is a smile of Love,
    And there is a smile of Deceit,
And there is a smile of smiles
    In which these two smiles meet.

And there is a frown of Hate,
    And there is a frown of Disdain,
And there is a frown of frowns
    Which you strive to forget in vain

For it sticks in the heart's deep core
    And it sticks in the deep backbone.
And no smile ever was smiled
    But only one smile alone.

(And betwixt the cradle and grave
    It only once smiled can be),
That when it once is smiled
    There's an end to all misery.

THE MARRIAGE RING

COME hither, my sparrows,
My little arrows,
If a tear or a smile
Will a man beguile,
If an amorous delay
Clouds a sunshiny day,
If the *tread* step of a foot
Smites the heart to its root,
'Tis the marriage ring
Makes each fairy a king.

So a fairy sang ;—
From the leaves I sprang.
He leaped from the spray
To flee away,
But in my hat caught
He soon shall be taught.
Let him laugh, let him cry
He's my butterfly ;
For I've pulled out the sting
Of the marriage ring.

THE FAIRY

A FAIRY leapt upon my knee
Singing and dancing merrily.
I said, ' Thou thing of patches, rings,
Pins, necklaces, and such like things,
Disgracer of the female form,
Thou pretty gilded poisonous worm !'

Weeping he fell upon my thigh—
And thus in tears did soft reply,
'Knowest thou not, Fairies' Lord,
How much by us contemned, abhorr'd,
Whatever hides the female form
That cannot bear the mortal storm?
Therefore in pity still we give
Our lives to make the female live,
And what would turn into disease
We turn to what will joy and please.'

THEOLOGICAL IRONICAL FRAGMENT

'I WILL tell you what Joseph of Arimathea
    Said to my Fairy: was it not queer?
Priestly—Bacon? What, are you here?
    Come before Joseph of Arimathea,
Listen patient, when Joseph is done
I'll make a fool laugh at a Fairy's fun.'

LONG JOHN BROWN AND LITTLE
MARY BELL

LITTLE Mary Bell had a fairy in a nut,
Long John Brown had the devil in his gut;
Long John Brown loved little Mary Bell,
And the fairy drew the devil into the nutshell.

Her fairy skipp'd out, her fairy skipp'd in,
He laughed at the devil, saying 'Love is a sin.'
The devil he raged and the devil he was wroth,
And the devil entered into the young man's broth.

He was soon in the gut of the loving young swain,
For John eat and drank to drive away love's pain,
But all he could do he grew thinner and thinner,
Though he eat and drank as much as ten men for his
    dinner.

Some said he had a wolf in his stomach day and
  night,
Some said he had the devil, and they guessed right,
The fairy skipped about in his glory, love and
  pride,
And he laughed at the devil till poor John Brown
  died.

Then the fairy skipp'd out of the old nutshell,
And woe and alack for pretty Mary Bell,
For the devil crept in when the fairy skipp'd out,
And there goes Miss Bell with her fusty old nut.

MARY

Sweet Mary, the first time she ever was there,
Came into the ballroom among the fair ;
The young men and maidens around her throng,
And these are the words upon every tongue :

' An angel is here from the heavenly climes,
Or again return the golden times ;
Her eyes outshine every brilliant ray,
She opens her lips—'tis the month of May.'

Mary moves in soft beauty and conscious delight,
To augment with sweet smiles all the joys of the
  night,
Nor once blushes to own to the rest of the fair
That sweet love and beauty are worthy our care.

In the morning the villagers rose with delight,
And repeated with pleasure the joys of the night,
And Mary arose among friends to be free,
But no friend from henceforward thou, Mary, shalt
  see.

Some said she was proud, some called her a whore,
And some when she passed by shut-to the door;
A damp cold came o'er her, her blushes all fled,
Her lilies and roses are blighted and shed.

'Oh why was I born with a different face?
Why was I not born like this envious race?
Why did Heaven adorn me with bountiful hand,
And then set me down in an envious land?

'To be weak as a lamb and smooth as a dove,
And not to raise envy, is called Christian love;
But, if you raise envy, your merit's to blame
For planting such spite in the weak and the tame.

'I will humble my beauty, I will not dress fine,
I will keep from the ball, and my eyes shall not
    shine;
And, if any girl's lover forsake her for me,
I'll refuse him my hand, and from envy be free.'

She went out in the morning attired plain and neat;
'Proud Mary's gone mad,' said the child in the
    street;
She went out in the morning in plain neat attire,
And came home in the evening bespattered with
    mire.

She trembled and wept, sitting on the bedside,
She forgot it was night, and she trembled and cried;
She forgot it was night, she forgot it was morn,
Her soft memory imprinted with faces of scorn;

With faces of scorn and with eyes of disdain,
Like foul fiends inhabiting Mary's mild brain;
She remembers no face like the human divine;
All faces have envy, sweet Mary, but thine.

And thine is a face of sweet love in despair,
And thine is a face of mild sorrow and care,
And thine is a face of wild terror and fear
That shall never be quiet till laid on its bier.

To understand what portion of Blake's own life and art is
impersonated under the name 'Mary,' who might be called
the 'Spirit of Spontaneity,' compare not only the later stories
of 'Thel' and 'Oothoon,' but the 'Wild Flower's Song' and
the few lines given below under the title 'A Cry,' and taken
from Blake's letter to Mr. Butts, August 1803.

WILLIAM BOND

I WONDER whether the girls are mad,
    And I wonder whether they mean to kill,
And I wonder if William Bond will die,
    For assuredly he is very ill.

He went to church on a May morning,
    Attended by fairies, one, two, and three ;
But the angels of Providence drove them away,
    And he returned home in misery.

He went not out to the field nor fold,
    He went not out to the village nor town,
But he came home in a black black cloud,
    And took to his bed, and there lay down.

And an angel of Providence at his feet,
    And an angel of Providence at his head,
And in the midst a black black cloud,
    And in the midst the sick man on his bed.

And on his right hand was Mary Green,
    And on his left hand was his sister Jane,
And their tears fell through the black black
    cloud
To drive away the sick man's pain.

'Oh William, if thou dost another love,
    Dost another love better than poor Mary,
Go and take that other to be thy wife,
    And Mary Green shall her servant be.'

'Yes, Mary, I do another love,
    Another I love far better than thee,
And another I will have for my wife:
    Then what have I to do with thee?

'For thou art melancholy pale,
    And on thy head is the cold moon's shine,
But she is ruddy and bright as day,
    And the sunbeams dazzle from her eyne.'

Mary trembled, and Mary chilled,
    And Mary fell down on the right-hand floor,
That William Bond and his sister Jane
    Scarce could recover Mary more.

When Mary woke and found her laid
    On the right hand of her William dear,
On the right hand of his loved bed,
    And saw her William Bond so near;

The fairies that fled from William Bond
    Danced around her shining head;
They danced over the pillow white,
    And the angels of Providence left the bed.

'I thought love lived in the hot sunshine,
    But oh he lives in the moony light!
I thought to find Love in the heat of day,
    But sweet Love is the comforter of night.

'Seek Love in the pity of others' woe,
    In the gentle relief of another's care.
In the darkness of night and the winter's snow,
    With the naked and outcast,—seek Love there.'

*Some truth may be found in the attempt to interpret this
poem in ' Gilchrist,'—the enlarged edition, vol. ii. p. 87.
' Day' and ' sunshine' mean also poetic life, and 'night' and
'moonshine' merely personal emotion.*

THE CRYSTAL CABINET

THE maiden caught me in the wild
 Where I was dancing merrily ;
She put me into her cabinet,
 And locked me up with a golden key.

This cabinet is formed of gold,
 And pearl and crystal shining bright,
And within it opens into a world
 And a little lovely moony night.

Another England there I saw,
 Another London with its Tower,
Another Thames and other hills,
 And another pleasant Surrey bower.

Another maiden like herself,
 Translucent, lovely, shining clear,
Threefold, each in the other closed,—
 Oh what a pleasant, trembling fear !

Oh what a smile ! A threefold smile
 Filled me that like a flame I burned ;
I bent to kiss the lovely maid,
 And found a threefold kiss returned.

I strove to seize the inmost form
 With ardour fierce and hands of flame,
But burst the crystal cabinet,
 And like a weeping babe became :

A weeping babe upon the wild,
  And weeping woman pale reclined,
And in the outward air again
  I filled with woes the passing wind.

The key to the explanation of this poem is in 'Jerusalem,'
page 70, line 25. There seem to be only two maidens mentioned,
yet they give a threefold smile. It is made up of the smile of
the first, then that of the second, then that of the two combined.

BROKEN LOVE

My Spectre before me night and day
Like a wild beast guards my way.
My Emanation far within
Weeps incessantly for my sin.

A fathomless and boundless deep ;
There we wander, there we weep ;
On the hungry, craving wind,
My spectre follows thee behind.

He scents thy footsteps in the snow,
Wheresoever thou dost go,
Through the wintry hail and rain.
When wilt thou return again ?

Dost thou not in pride and scorn
Fill with tempests all my morn,
And with jealousies and fears,
Fill my pleasant nights with tears?

Seven of thy sweet loves thy knife
Has bereaved of their life.
Their marble tombs I build with fears
And with cold and shadowy tears.

Seven more loves weep night and day
Round the tombs where my loves lay,
And seven more loves attend at night
Around my couch with torches bright.

And seven more loves in my bed
Crown with vine my mournful head,
Pitying and forgiving all
Thy transgressions, great and small.

When wilt thou return and view
My loves, and them to life renew?
When wilt thou return and live?
When wilt thou pity as I forgive?

Never, never I return.
Still for victory I burn.
Living, thee alone I'll have,
And when dead I'll be thy grave.

Through the Heaven and Earth and Hell
Thou shalt never, never quell,
I will fly and thou pursue,
Night and morn the flight renew.

Till I turn from female love
And root up the infernal grove,
I shall never worthy be
To step into Eternity.

And I to end thy cruel mocks
Annihilate thee on the rocks,
And another form create
To be subservient to my fate.

Let us agree to give up love
And root up the infernal grove,
Then shall we return and see
The worlds of happy Eternity.

And throughout all Eternity
I forgive you, you forgive me.
As our dear Redeemer said :—
This the wine and this the bread.

The order of the stanzas here used is not the same as that employed in 'Gilchrist,' and in the 'Aldine,' for which there is no authority.   It is Blake's finally chosen order as directed in the MS. book.   The poem has no title.   Mr. Yeats calls it 'Spectre and Emanation.'

The poem is extremely difficult to edit correctly, as Blake changed his mind while writing it, and again while numbering the stanzas.   No. 1 is always No. 1, and presents no difficulty.   There are three called No. 2.   The first, mistakenly used as such in the Quaritch edition as No. 2, is this—

> A deep winter, dark and cold,
> Within my heart thou didst unfold;
> A fathomless and boundless deep—
> There we wander, there we weep.

The second is the No. 2 finally chosen by Blake, and properly placed by Mr. Yeats in the Lawrence and Bullen edition.

The third is later—

> What transgressions I commit
> Are for thy transgressions fit,
> They thy harlots, thou their slave,
> And my bed becomes their grave.

This appears as the ninth in 'Gilchrist.'   In the MS. book it is followed, on the remote part of the page where it is written, by this,—not numbered at all,—given as the fourth in 'Gilchrist,' with two lines taken off and two others substituted from another stanza erased by Blake—to be presently quoted here.

> Poor, pale, pitiable form,
> That I follow in a storm,
> Iron tears and groans of lead
> Bind around my aching head.

This and the previous stanza seem to have been once intended by Blake to be used as part of a short poem of three, whose first was this, beside which a No. 1 can be faintly made out—

> O'er my sins thou dost sit and moan—
> Had thou no sin of thine own?
> O'er my sins thou dost sit and weep,
> And lull thine own sins fast asleep.

It is given as the seventh in 'Gilchrist. Returning to the main track of the poem, we find that the stanza No. 2 at first written, before any were numbered, and never numbered at all, still remains on the page of MS. exactly under the original No. 1, legible, though boldly crossed out. It is this—

thou

This weeping she shall ne'er give o'er,

thee

I sin against her more and more,

And never will from sin be free,

Till she forgives and comes to me.

The general erasure is thus seen to have been decided on after the first two lines had received a verbal alteration, and before the last was changed to fit them, so that it was no longer worth while to change it. The editor of 'Gilchrist' does so on his own responsibility, and gives the last couplet, thus amended, as the last of the fourth stanza of his arbitrary and un-Blakean arrangement.

Under it Blake's MS. shows what was at first his third stanza, all crossed out now. It bears both the number 6 and 5—first 6, then 5—put in afterwards, and both crossed out, and is as follows—

Thou hast parted from my side,

Once thou wast a virgin bride,

true love

Never shalt thou a lover find,

My Spectre follows thee behind.

The last line of this seems to have inspired the stanza numbered 2, and used as such in 'Gilchrist' and here.

Stanza 3 in the present text is so numbered by Blake, though he first numbered it 6, and crossed that out. It was the fourth actually written. It is third in 'Gilchrist' also.

There is another which Blake has numbered 3, and afterwards 9—the 3 not being crossed out—by inadvertence—which seems to have been intended for a moment to follow number 3, as a sort of answer to it, but a stanza at another part of the page, numbered first 6, then 4, both numbers crossed out, was chosen finally, and lines drawn from it to a place just above stanza 5, with the direction written between them that it was 'to come in' there. It is given as fourth in this text, and sixth in 'Gilchrist.'

The fifth in this text bears the number 5 in Blake's MS., and previously bore numbers 7 and 4, both crossed out. It unaccountably appears as tenth in 'Gilchrist.'

The sixth in this text bears that number in MS., and pre-

*viously had the number 8, twice written and twice crossed out.
It is eleventh in 'Gilchrist.'*

*The seventh in this text is marked 7 in MS., and also bore
the numbers 4 and 6, both crossed out. It is twelfth in
'Gilchrist.'*

*The No. 4 is given four times in the MS. One stanza,
written just after that beginning 'a deep winter dark and
cold,' bears it, and also the number 3, but was all struck out
with a bold line, and appears neither in this text nor in
'Gilchrist.' It has its own value for purposes of interpretation, as we learn from it that the warmth of the poet's passion,
and not coldness or infidelity, was accounted to him as 'sin'
—a most illuminating revelation.*

*Here at last is the crowded out stanza that was to have
served either as 3 or 4—*

> When my love did first begin,
> Thou didst call that love a sin,
> Secret trembling night and day,
> Driving all my loves away.

*To conclude. The eighth in this text is so marked in the
MS. The stanza had borne the numbers 10 and 7, both
crossed out. It is thirteenth in 'Gilchrist.' The ninth here
given bears that number in MS., as above stated, and also the
number 3, apparently—not crossed out. It is quietly omitted
in 'Gilchrist.' The tenth here bears no other number in MS.
It also is omitted on his own responsibility by the editor of
'Gilchrist,' who similarly concealed the existence of stanzas
11, 12, and 13, which bear no other numbers in the MS.,
having been written after the fluctuating resolutions of the
author became fixed.*

*Stanza 14—the last—also bears no other number, and ter-
minates the poem here as in 'Gilchrist,' whose fourteenth it
also is, which gives an air of spurious authenticity to a
version which nothing can justify. Its very title (followed
here because now so well known) loses most of its justification
with the omission of the verses 12 and 13.*

*A study of these variorum readings betrays the fact that the
bride is the 'Emanation' of the poet, and sometimes more,
as was Enitharmon, the 'vegetated mortal wife of Los; his
Emanation, yet his wife till the sleep of death is past.'—
'Jerusalem,' p. 14, l. 14. 'Sleep of death' means unimaginative experience.*

*A phrase from this poem in 'Jerusalem,' page 17, line 3,
places it in the myth, and places the myth in Blake's life.*

THE MENTAL TRAVELLER

I TRAVELLED through a land of men,
   A land of men and women, too,
And saw and heard such dreadful things
   As cold earth-wanderers never knew.

For there the babe is born in joy
   That was begotten in dire woe,
Just as we reap in joy the fruit
   That we in bitter tears did sow.

And if the babe is born a boy
   He's given to a woman old
Who nails him down upon a rock,
   Catches his shrieks in cups of gold.

She binds iron thorns about his head,
   She pierces both his hands and feet,
She cuts his heart out at his side
   To make it feel both cold and heat.

Her fingers number every nerve,
   Just as a miser counts his gold;
She lives upon his shrieks and cries,
   And she grows young as he grows old.

Till he becomes a bleeding youth,
   And she becomes a virgin bright;
Then he rends up his manacles
   And binds her down for his delight.

He plants himself in all her nerves,
   Just as a husbandman his mould,
And she becomes his dwelling place
   And garden fruitful seventyfold.

An aged shadow, soon he fades,
  Wandering round an earthly cot,
Full filled all with gems and gold
  Which he by industry has got.

And these are the gems of the human soul,
  The rubies and pearls of a lovesick eye,
The countless gold of the aching heart,
  The martyr's groan and the lover's sigh.

They are his meat, they are his drink,
  He feeds the beggar and the poor ;
To the wayfaring traveller
  For ever opens his door.

His grief is their eternal joy,
  They make the roofs and walls to ring,
Till from the fire upon the hearth
  A little female babe doth spring.

And she is all of solid fir,
  And gems and gold, that none his hand
Dares stretch to touch her baby form,
  Or wrap her in his swaddling band.

But she comes to the man she loves,
  If young or old, or rich or poor ;
They soon drive out the aged host,
  A beggar at another's door.

He wanders weeping far away,
  Until some other take him in ;
Oft blind and aged-bent, sore distressed,
  Until he can a maiden win.

And to allay his freezing age
  The poor man takes her in his arms ;
The cottage fades before his sight,
  The garden, and its lovely charms.

The guests are scattered through the land,
  For the eye altering, alters all ;
The senses roll themselves in fear,
  And the flat earth becomes a ball.

The stars, sun, moon, all shrink away,
  A desert vast without a bound :
And nothing left to eat or drink,
  And a dark desert all around.

The honey of her infant lips,
  The bread and wine of her sweet smile,
The wild game of her roving eye
  Do him to infancy beguile,

For as he eats and drinks he grows
  Younger and younger every day,
And on the desert wild they both
  Wander in terror and dismay.

Like the wild stag, she flees away,
  Her fear plants many a thicket wild ;
While he pursues her, night and day,
  By various arts of love beguiled.

By various arts of love and hate,
  Till the wild desert 's planted o'er
With labyrinth of wayward love,
  Where roam the lion, wolf, and boar.

Till he becomes a wayward babe,
  And she a weeping woman old ;
Then many a lover wanders here,
  The sun and stars are nearer rolled.

The trees bring forth sweet ecstasy
  To all who in the desert roam,
Till many a city there is built,
  And many a pleasant shepherd's home.

But when they find the frowning babe,
    Terror strikes through the region wild ;
They cry : ' The babe ! the babe is born ! '
    And flee away on every side.

For who dare touch the frowning form,
    His arm is withered to the root ;
Bears, lions, wolves, all howling fly,
    And every tree doth shed its fruit.

And none can touch that frowning form,
    Except it be a woman old ;
She nails him down upon a rock,
    And all is done as I have told.

The above text is not from original source. The editor has not seen the MS.—an admission accidentally and erroneously added to the chapter on 'Broken Love' in the Quaritch edition.

THE GREY MONK (Mr. Yeats's Title)

THE AGONY OF FAITH (Mr. Gilchrist's Title)

' I see, I see,' the Mother said,
' My children will die for lack of bread !
What more has the merciless Tyrant said ? '
The Monk sat him down on her stony bed.

His eye was dry, no tear could flow,
A hollow groan bespoke his woe,
He trembled and shuddered upon the bed :
(At length, with a feeble cry, he said) :

' When God commanded this hand to write
In the shadow hours of deep midnight,
He told me that all I wrote would prove
The bane of all that on earth I love.

' My brother starved between two walls,
My children's cry my soul appals,
I mock at the rack, the griding chain,
My bent body mocks at their torturing pain.

' My father drew his sword in the north,
With his thousands strong he is marched forth ;
My brother has armed himself in steel,
To revenge the wrongs thy children feel.'

But vain the sword and vain the bow,
They never can work war's overthrow ;
The hermit's prayer and the widow's tear
Alone can save the world from fear.

The hand of vengeance sought the bed
To which the purple tyrant fled ;
The iron hand crushed the tyrant's head,
And became a tyrant in his stead.

Until the tyrant himself relent,
The tyrant who first the black bow bent,
Slaughter shall heap the bloody plain,
Resistance and war is the tyrant's gain.

But the tear of love and forgiveness sweet,
And submission to death beneath his feet ;
The tear shall melt the sword of steel,
And every wound it has made shall heal.

For the tear is an intellectual thing,
And the sigh is the sword of an awful king,
And the bitter groan of a martyr's woe
Is an arrow from the Almighty's bow.

*This poem is found in the MS. book, where it forms part of
a longer piece, containing in all about twenty stanzas. Some
of them merely fragments, some were numbered by Blake, and
removed, leaving the remainder to form a separate poem. The
first four bore the numbers 1, 2, 3, 4, and are to be found now
where Blake transferred them, namely in the preface to the
third chapter of 'Jerusalem.' The fifth and sixth stanzas of
the piece there found were written sideways, as an afterthought, on the same page as the rest of the poem in the MS.,
and then the last stanza of the piece here given was numbered
7, and added to them, so it was used twice over, with the
trifling change of 'the tear' into 'a tear,' where engraved in
the 'Jerusalem,'*

NOTE ON SOURCES OF POEMS

'*A small autograph collection*' *of Blake's verses is referred to in vol. ii. of Gilchrist's* '*Life*,' *p.* 84, *as the source of some of the poems that are there printed. The present editor has made search for it, but can obtain no information. It was used by the editor of the Aldine edition, but since this it has practically been lost. Mr. Rossetti, Mr. Gilchrist, and Mr. Bell are alike unable to say what has become of it, and such clues as they have given conjecturally have not so far led to discovery—January* 1904. *The only important poem in this collection is the* '*Mental Traveller*,' *erroneously interpreted in* '*Gilchrist*' *and in the* '*Aldine*' *as representing* '*under a very ideal form the phenomena of gestation and birth.*' *To the reader who has been through* '*Vala*' *and* '*Jerusalem*' *it will need no interpretation.*

Also lost is an original copy of the '*Poetical Sketches*' *which Blake used as a note-book, since* '*a few short pieces*' *were found by Mr. Herne Shepherd—he does not say which— when this copy was lent to him—he does not say by whom.*

THE GATES OF PARADISE, AUGURIES
OF INNOCENCE, PROVERBS, VERSES
FROM LETTERS, MINIATURES,
GALLANTRIES, RESENT-
MENTS, ETC.

FURTHER IDEAS

(OF GOOD AND EVIL)

INTRODUCTION, KEYS, AND EPILOGUE TO

THE GATES OF PARADISE

'FOR CHILDREN'

(ENGRAVED 1793)

WITH AUGURIES OF INNOCENCE, VERSES FROM LETTERS, ETC.

'The Gates of Paradise' is the title of a set of small engravings, some of which have been reprinted in Gilchrist's 'Life.' A man drowning, one walking quickly near trees, a boy knocking down a Cupid like a butterfly with his hat, a caterpillar with a baby's face, some one wishing to mount to the moon, and other scattered fancies. There is no coherence in them. The verses here following were to serve as explanation. Sketches for the engravings occur in the centres of the pages of the manuscript book, and it must remain doubtful whether the title given since to the poems of various kinds written on the margins was not really designed by Blake for the engravings. The sixteenth line of the 'Keys of the Gates' gives colour to the suggestion. However this may be, Blake did not print the words 'Ideas of Good and Evil' at the head of these lines, nor did he cross them out, but left them, covering a whole page of his book, to the mercy of posterity, along with the mass of unsorted poetry that he wrote after them during a period of between ten and fifteen years.

INTRODUCTION TO THE GATES

MUTUAL forgiveness of each vice,
Such are the Gates of Paradise,

135

Against the Accuser's chief desire,
Who walked among the stones of fire,
Jehovah's fingers wrote the Law :
He wept ; then rose in zeal and awe,
And, in the midst of Sinai's heat,
Hid it beneath His Mercy-Seat.
O Christians ! Christians ! tell me why
You rear it on your altars high.

THE KEYS OF THE GATES

The caterpillar on the leaf
Reminds thee of thy mother's grief.
My Eternal Man set in repose,
The Female from his darkness rose ;
And she found me beneath a tree,
A mandrake, and in her veil hid me.
Serpent reasonings us entice
Of good and evil, virtue, vice.
Doubt self-jealous, watery folly,
Struggling through Earth's melancholy.
Naked in air, in shame and fear,
Blind in fire, with shield and spear,
Two horrid reasoning cloven fictions,
In doubt which is self-contradiction,
A dark hermaphrodite I stood,—
Rational truth, root of evil and good.
Round me, flew the flaming sword ;
Round her, snowy whirlwinds roared,
Freezing her veil, the mundane shell.
I rent the veil where the dead dwell :
When weary man enters his cave,
He meets his Saviour in the grave.
Some find a female garment there,
And some a male, woven with care,
Lest the sexual garments sweet
Should grow a devouring winding-sheet.
One dies ! alas ! the living and dead !
One is slain, and one is fled !

In vain-glory hatched and nursed,
By double spectres, self-accursed.
My son ! my son ! thou treatest me
But as I have instructed thee.
On the shadows of the moon,
Climbing through night's highest noon :
In Time's ocean falling, drowned :
In aged ignorance profound,
Holy and cold, I clipped the wings
Of all sublunary things :
And in depths of icy dungeons
Closed the father and the sons.
But, when once I did descry
The Immortal Man that cannot die,
Through evening shades I haste away
To close the labours of my day.
The door of Death I open found,
And the worm weaving in the ground :
Thou 'rt my mother, from the womb ;
Wife, sister, daughter, to the tomb :
Weaving to dreams the sexual strife,
And weeping over the web of life.

EPILOGUE

TO THE ACCUSER, WHO IS THE GOD OF THIS WORLD

TRULY, my Satan, thou art but a dunce,
    And dost not know the garment from the man ;
Every harlot was a virgin once,
    Nor canst thou ever change Kate into Nan.
Though thou art worshipped by the names divine
    Of Jesus and Jehovah, thou art still
The son of morn in weary night's decline,
    The lost traveller's dream under the hill.

AUGURIES OF INNOCENCE

(Not printed or engraved by Blake.   Date about 1793-4.)

To see a world in a grain of sand,
    And a heaven in a wild flower,
Hold infinity in the palm of your hand,
    And eternity in an hour.

The following were perhaps meant to be called ' Auguries of Innocence' also.   Mr. Herne Shepherd, who seems to have had access to Blake's manuscript of the piece, thinks so, as does Mr. Rossetti.   Mr. Shepherd's text is here followed blindly, as he is more generally strict than Mr. Rossetti.   Mr. Yeats's suggestion to call the couplets 'proverbs' is not adopted, as there is no Blakean authority for it, and it might add a difficulty of reference on account of the 'Proverbs of Hell,' Blake's own title for a section of the 'Marriage of Heaven and Hell.'

1   A ROBIN REDBREAST in a cage
           Puts all Heaven in a rage.

2   A dove-house filled with doves and pigeons
           Shudders Hell through all its regions.

3   A dog starved at his master's gate
           Predicts the ruin of the state.

4   A horse misused upon the road
           Calls to heaven for human blood.

5   Each outcry of the hunted hare
           A fibre from the brain doth tear.

6   A skylark wounded on the wing
           Doth make a cherub cease to sing.

7   The game-cock clipped and armed for fight
           Does the rising sun affright.

8   Every wolf's and lion's howl
           Raises from Hell a human soul.

9   The wild deer wandering here and there
           Keep the human soul from care.

10   The lamb misused breeds public strife,
           And yet forgives the butcher's knife.

11   The bat that flits at close of eve
     Has left the brain that won't believe.

12   The owl that calls upon the night
     Speaks the unbeliever's fright.

13   He who shall hurt the little wren
     Shall never be beloved by men.

14   He who the ox to wrath has moved
     Shall never be by woman loved.

15   The wanton boy that kills the fly
     Shall feel the spider's enmity.

16   He who torments the chafer's sprite
     Weaves a bower in endless night.

17   The caterpillar on the leaf
     Repeats to thee thy mother's grief.

18   Kill not the moth nor butterfly,
     For the last judgment draweth nigh.

19   He who shall train the horse to war
     Shall never pass the Polar Bar.

20   The beggar's dog and widow's cat,
     Feed them and thou shalt grow fat.

21   The gnat that sings his summer's song
     Poison gets from Slander's tongue.

22   The poison of the snake and newt
     Is the sweat of Envy's foot.

23   The poison of the honey-bee
     Is the artist's jealousy.

24   The prince's robes and beggar's rags
     Are toadstools on the miser's bags.

25   A truth that's told with bad intent
     Beats all the lies you can invent.

26   It is right it should be so;
     Man was made for joy and woe;

27   And, when this we rightly know,
     Through the world we safely go.

28   Joy and woe are woven fine,
      A clothing for the soul divine.

29   Under every grief and pine
      Runs a joy with silken twine.

30   The babe is more than swaddling-bands
      Throughout all these human lands.

31   Tools were made, and born were hands,
      Every farmer understands.

32   Every tear from every eye
      Becomes a babe in eternity ;

33   This is caught by females bright
      And returned to its own delight.

34   The bleat, the bark, bellow, and roar,
      Are waves that beat on heaven's shore.

35   The babe that weeps the rod beneath
      Writes revenge in realms of death.

36   The beggar's rags fluttering in air
      Do to rags the heavens tear.

37   The soldier armed with sword and gun
      Palsied strikes the summer's sun.

38   The poor man's farthing is worth more
      Than all the gold on Afric's shore.

39   One mite wrung from the labourer's hands
      Shall buy and sell the miser's lands,

40   Or, if protected from on high,
      Shall that whole nation sell and buy.

41   He who mocks the infant's faith
      Shall be mocked in age and death.

42   He who shall teach the child to doubt
      The rotting grave shall ne'er get out.

43   He who respects the infant's faith
      Triumphs over hell and death.

44   The child's toys and the old man's reasons
      Are the fruits of the two seasons.

45 The questioner who sits so sly
   Shall never know how to reply.

46 He who replies to words of doubt
   Doth put the light of knowledge out.

47 The strongest poison ever known
   Came from Cæsar's laurel-crown.

48 Nought can deform the human race
   Like to the armour's iron brace.

49 When gold and gems adorn the plough,
   To peaceful hearts shall Envy bow.

50 A riddle, or the cricket's cry,
   Is to doubt a fit reply.

51 The emmet's inch and eagle's mile
   Make lame philosophy to smile.

52 He who doubts from what he sees
   Will ne'er believe, do what you please.

53 If the sun and moon should doubt,
   They'd immediately go out.

54 To be in a passion good you may do,
   But no good if a passion is in you.

55 The whore and gambler, by the state
   Licensed, build that nation's fate.

56 The harlot's cry from street to street
   Shall weave old England's winding-sheet.

57 The winner's shout, the loser's curse,
   Shall dance before dead England's hearse.

58 Every night and every morn
   Some to misery are born;

59 Every morn and every night
   Some are born to sweet delight;

60 Some are born to sweet delight,
   Some are born to endless night.

61 We are led to believe a lie
   When we see *with*, not *through* the eye,

Which was born in a night to perish in a night
62   When the soul slept in beams of light.

God appears and God is light
63   To those poor souls who dwell in night;

But doth a human form display
64   To those who dwell in realms of day.

SCOFFERS

*These lines, the stanzas on Idolatry, and the Dedication
for the Picture of the Last Judgment belong to the mood and
almost to the date of the Felpham letters; they belong to no
sorted collection.*

Mock on, mock on, Voltaire, Rousseau,
   Mock on, mock on; 'tis all in vain;
You throw the sand against the wind,
   And the wind blows it back again.

And every sand becomes a gem,
   Reflected in the beams divine;
Blown back, they blind the mocking eye,
   But still in Israel's paths they shine.

The atoms of Democritus
   And Newton's particles of light,
Are sands upon the Red Sea shore
   Where Israel's tents do shine so bright.

IDOLATRY

IF it is true, what the Prophets write,
   That the Heathen Gods are all stocks and stones,
Shall we, for the sake of being polite,
   Feed them with the juice of our marrow bones?

And, if Bezaleel and Aholiab drew
What the finger of God pointed to their view,
Shall we suffer the Roman and Grecian rods
To compel us to worship them as Gods?

They stole them from
  The Temple of the Lord,
And worshipped them that they might make
  Inspired art abhorred.

The wood and stone were called the holy things,
And their sublime intent given to their kings ;
All the atonements of Jehovah spurned,
And criminals to sacrifices turned.

FOR A PICTURE OF THE LAST JUDGMENT

DEDICATION

THE caverns of the Grave I 've seen,
And these I showed to England's Queen ;
But now the caves of Hell I view,—
Whom shall I dare to show them to ?
What mighty soul in beauty's form
Shall dauntless view the infernal storm ?
Egremont's Countess can control
The flames of hell that round me roll.
If she refuse, I still go on,
Till the heavens and earth are gone ;
Still admired by noble minds,
Followed by Envy on the winds.
Re-engraved time after time,
Ever in their youthful prime,
My designs unchanged remain ;
Time may rage, but rage in vain ;
For above Time's troubled fountains,
On the great Atlantic mountains,
In my golden house on high,
There they shine eternally.

To my Dear Friend

MRS. ANNA FLAXMAN

ENCLOSED IN A LETTER FROM MRS. BLAKE TO HER, SEPTEMBER 1800

Some years divide these verses from those that close the 'Auguries,' but the last lines of these are a natural intro-duction to the letters of this period.

THIS song to the flower of Flaxman's joy ;
To the blossom of hope, for a sweet decoy;
Do all that you can, or all that you may,
To entice him to Felpham and far away.

Away to sweet Felpham, for heaven is there ;
The ladder of angels descends through the air ;
On the turret its spiral does softly descend,
Through the village then winds, at my cot it does end.

You stand in the village and look up to heaven ;
The precious stones glitter on flight seventy-seven ;
And my brother is there ; and my friend and thine
Descend and ascend with the bread and the wine.

The bread of sweet thought and the wine of delight
Feed the village of Felpham by day and by night ;
And at his own door the bless'd Hermit doth stand,
Dispensing unceasing to all the wide land.

TO MR. BUTTS

WRITTEN FROM FELPHAM, OCTOBER 2, 1800

To my friend Butts I write
My first vision of light,
On the yellow sands sitting.
The sun was emitting

His glorious beams
From heaven's high streams.
Over sea, over land,
My eyes did expand
Into regions of air,
Away from all care ;
Into regions of fire,
Remote from desire :
The light of the morning
Heaven's mountains adorning.
In particles bright,
The jewels of light
Distinct shone and clear.
Amazed and in fear
I each particle gazed,
Astonished, amazed ;
For each was a man
Human-formed. Swift I ran,
For they beckoned to me,
Remote by the sea,
Saying : ' Each grain of sand,
Every stone on the land,
Each rock and each hill,
Each fountain and rill,
Each herb and each tree,
Mountain, hill, earth, and sea,
Cloud, meteor, and star,
Are men seen afar.'

I stood in the streams
Of heaven's bright beams,
And saw Felpham sweet
Beneath my bright feet,
In soft female charms ;
And in her fair arms
My shadow I knew,
And my wife's shadow too,
And my sister and friend.
We like infants descend

In our shadows on earth,
Like a weak mortal birth.
My eyes more and more,
Like a sea without shore,
Continue expanding,
The heavens commanding,
Till the jewels of light,
Heavenly men beaming bright,
Appeared as one man,
Who complacent began
My limbs to infold
In his beams of bright gold ;
Like dross purged away
All my mire and my clay.
Soft consumed in delight,
In his bosom sun-bright
I remained.   Soft he smiled,
And I heard his voice mild,
Saying : 'This is my fold,
O thou ram horned with gold,
Who wakest from sleep
On the sides of the deep.
On the mountains around
The roarings resound
Of the lion and wolf,
The loud sea and deep gulph.
These are guards of my fold,
O thou ram horned with gold !'
And the voice faded mild,—
I remained as a child ;
All I ever had known
Before me bright shone :
I saw you and your wife
By the fountains of life.
Such the vision to me
Appeared on the sea.

TO MRS. BUTTS

(From the same letter.)

WIFE of the friend of those I most revere,
Receive this tribute from a harp sincere ;
Go on in virtuous seed-sowing on mould
Of human vegetation, and behold
Your harvest springing to eternal life,
Parent of youthful minds, and happy wife.

'LOS THE TERRIBLE'

(From a letter to Mr. Butts dated Felpham, Nov. 22, 1802.)

WITH happiness stretched across the hills
In a cloud that dewy sweetness distils,
With a blue sky spread over with wings,
And a mild sun that mounts and sings ;
With trees and fields full of fairy elves,
And little devils who fight for themselves,
(Remembering the verses that Hayley sung
When my heart knocked against the root of
    my tongue,)
With angels planted in hawthorn bowers,
And God Himself in the passing hours ;
With silver angels across my way,
And golden demons that none can stay ;
With my father hovering upon the wind,
And my brother Robert just behind,
And my brother John, the evil one,
In a black cloud making his moan ;
(Though dead, they appear upon my path,
Notwithstanding my terrible wrath ;
They beg, they entreat, they drop their tears,
Filled full of hopes, filled full of fears ;)
With a thousand angels upon the wind,
Pouring disconsolate from behind
To drive them off,—and before my way
A frowning Thistle implores my stay.

What to others a trifle appears
Fills me full of smiles or tears;
For double the vision my eyes do see,
And a double vision is always with me.
With my inward eye, 'tis an old man grey;
With my outward, a thistle across my way.

'If thou goest back,' the Thistle said,
'Thou art to endless woe betrayed;
For here does Theotormon lour,
And here is Enitharmon's bower,
And Los the terrible thus hath sworn,
Because thou backward dost return,
Poverty, envy, old age, and fear,
Shall bring thy wife upon a bier;
And Butts shall give what Fuseli gave,
A dark black rock and a gloomy cave.'
I struck the thistle with my foot,
And broke him up from his delving root.
'Must the duties of life each other cross?
Must every joy be dung and dross?
Must my dear Butts feel cold neglect
Because I give Hayley his due respect?
Must Flaxman look upon me as wild,
And all my friends be with doubts beguiled?
Must my wife live in my sister's bane,
Or my sister survive on my Love's pain?
The curses of Los, the terrible shade,
And his dismal terrors, make me afraid.'

So I spoke, and struck in my wrath
The old man weltering upon my path.
Then Los appeared in all his power:
In the sun he appeared, descending before
My face in fierce flames; in my double sight,
'Twas outward a sun,—inward, Los in his
        might.
'My hands are laboured day and night,
And ease comes never in my sight.

My wife has no indulgence given,
Except what comes to her from heaven.
We eat little, we drink less ;
This earth breeds not our happiness.
Another sun feeds our life's streams ;
We are not warmèd with thy beams.
Thou measurest not the time to me,
Nor yet the space that I do see :
My mind is not with thy light arrayed ;
Thy terrors shall not make me afraid.'

When I had my defiance given,
The sun stood trembling in heaven ;
The moon, that glowed remote below,
Became leprous and white as snow ;
And every soul of man on the earth
Felt affliction and sorrow and sickness and
    dearth.
Los flamed in my path, and the sun was hot
With the bows of my mind and the arrows of
    thought :
My bowstring fierce with ardour breathes,
My arrows glow in their golden sheaves.
My brother and father march before ;
The heavens drop with human gore.

Now I a fourfold vision see,
And a fourfold vision is given to me ;
'Tis fourfold in my supreme delight,
And threefold in soft Beulah's night,
And twofold always.   May God us keep
From single vision, and Newton's sleep !

MINIATURES

Under this sub-title are grouped for the first time the few very short pieces, chiefly quotations, that contain beauty without irony. They are of dates, not always ascertainable, ranging from 1795 to 1804.

I

AH, luckless babe, born under cruel star,
    And in dead parents' baleful ashes bred,
Full little reckest thou what sorrows are
    Left for the portion of thy livelihead !

II

THE Angel who presided at my birth
Said,—'Little Creature, formed for joy and mirth,
Go love, without the help of anything on earth.'

III

THE Sword sang on the barren heath,
    The Sickle in the fruitful field :
The Sword he sang a song of death,
    But could not make the Sickle yield.

IV

O LAPWING, that fliest around the heath,
Nor seest the net that is spread beneath ;
Why dost thou not fly among the corn-fields?
They cannot spread nets where a harvest yields.

V

I WALKED abroad on a snowy day,
I asked the soft Snow with me to play ;
She played and she melted in all her prime ;
And the Winter called it a dreadful crime.

VI

ABSTINENCE sows sand all over
  The ruddy limbs and flaming hair ;
But desire gratified
  Plants fruits of life and beauty there.

VII

THE look of love alarms,
  Because 'tis filled with fire,
But the look of soft deceit
  Shall win the lover's hire :
Soft deceit and idleness,
These are beauty's sweetest dress.

GALLANTRIES AND MOCKERIES

*Here are grouped the very short pieces that are amorous,
but yet are not without some intention of sarcasm or derision.
Four of the quatrains have titles in the MS. book, as printed
here.*

I

IF e'er I grow to man's estate,
O give to me a woman's fate !
May I govern all, both great and small,
Have the last word, and take the wall !

II

HER whole life is an epigram,
  Smart, smooth, and nobly penned,
Plaited quite neat to catch applause,
  With a strong noose at the end.

III

IF you play a game of chance,
  Know before you begin,
If you are benevolent
  You will never win.

THE QUESTION ANSWERED

IV

WHAT is it men in women do require?
The lineaments of gratified desire.
What is it women do in men require?
The lineaments of gratified desire.

V

An old maid early, e'er I knew
Ought but the love that on me grew,
And now I am covered o'er and o'er,
And wish that I had been a whore.

VI

O, I cannot, cannot find
The undaunted courage of a virgin mind;
For early I in love was crost,
Before my flower of love was lost.

MERLIN'S PROPHECY

VII

THE harvest shall flourish in wintry weather,
When two virginities meet together.
The king and priest must be tied in a tether,
Before two virgins can meet together.

VIII

When a man marries a wife,
He finds out whether
Her elbows and knees are only
Glued together.

ON THE VIRGINITY OF THE VIRGIN MARY AND
JOHANNA SOUTHCOTT

IX

WHATE'ER is done to her she cannot know ;
And if you ask her she will swear it so.
Whether 'tis good or evil, none's to blame ;
No one can take the pride and none the shame.

IMITATION OF POPE AND COMPLIMENT TO
THE LADIES

X

WONDROUS the gods, more wondrous are the men,
More wondrous, wondrous still the cock and hen.
More wondrous still the table, stool and chair,
But ah ! more wondrous still the charming fair.

XI

LET us approach the sighing dawns
    With many pleasing wiles.
If a woman does not fear your frowns,
    She will never reward your smiles.

XII

To Chloe's breast young Cupid slily stole,
But he crept in at Myra's pocket-hole.

XIII

GROWN old in love from seven till seven times seven,
I oft have wished for hell, for ease from heaven.

(*A Postscript labelled Stanza V, and originally intended
to close the poem called ' Cupid ' printed above on page
108.*)

XIV

'TWAS the Greek's love of war
    Turned Cupid into a boy,
And woman into a statue of stone,
    And away flew every joy.

THE ISLAND IN THE MOON

This was Blake's most sustained attempt at mere mockery, apart from resentment, a word here to be used further on to group the splenetic fragments of doggerel and epigram which he wrote later in life with some personal heat, and mainly to relieve his feelings. The 'Island in the Moon' was begun as a book—a real printable attempt at sarcasm. In a long rambling series of Platonic dialogues, interspersed with songs, evening-parties in literary drawing-rooms are represented and ridiculed. The work breaks off as it drifts into a higher poetic vein, some of the 'Songs of Innocence' being found in the last pages. This dates it, and had the verses of the earlier scenes been intended as poetry in earnest, they should have been placed in this collection next after the 'Poetical Sketches.'

The manuscript is in the library of Mr. Fairfax Murray, by whose kindness the first printed account of it appeared in Quaritch's edition of Blake's Works. He has permitted the present production of all the rhymed portions. The Platonic dialogue also, as far as it goes, deserves one day to be printed in its entirety.

MR. QUID'S FIRST SONG

LITTLE Phœbus came strutting in
With his fat belly and his round chin.
    What is it you would please to have?
      Ho! Ho!
    I won't let it go at only so so!
    Honour and Genius is all I ask,—
    And I ask the gods no more.
      Chorus, by the   } No more! No more!
      Three Philosophers. } No more! No more!

MR. QUID'S SECOND SONG

I

WHEN old corruption first begun,
Adorned in yellow vest,
He committed on flesh a whoredom—
O, what a wicked beast !

II

From there a callow babe did spring,
And old corruption smiled
To think his race should never end,
For now he had a child.

III

He called him Surgery, and fed
The babe with his own milk.
For flesh and he could ne'er agree :
She would not let him suck.

IV

And this he always kept on mind,
And formed a crooked knife,
And ran about with bloody hands,
To seek his mother's life.

V

And as he ran to seek his mother
He met with a dead woman.
He fell in love and married her :
A deed that is not common.

VI

She soon grew pregnant, and brought forth
Scurvy and spotted fever.
The father grinn'd and skipt about,
And said,—' I 'm made for ever !

VII

'For now I have procured these imps
  I'll try experiments.'
With that he tied poor scurvy down,
  And stopt up all its vents.

VIII

And when the child began to swell,
  He shouted out aloud,—
'I've found the dropsy out, and soon
  Shall do the world more good.'

IX

He took up fever by the neck,
  And cut out all its spots;
And thro' the holes which he had made
  He first discovered guts.

EPITAPH

(Quoted or composed by Mr. Steelyard.)

HEAR then the pride and knowledge of a sailor,
His sprit-sail, fore-sail, main-sail, and his mizen:
A poor frail man,—Got wot I know none frailer,
I know no greater sinner than John Tailor.

MISS GITTIPIN'S SONG

I

PHŒBE dressed like beauty's queen,
Jellicoe in faint pea-green,
Sitting all beneath a grot,
Where the little lambkins trot.

II

Maidens dancing ;—lovers sporting ;
All the country folks a-courting,
Susan, Johnny, Bob and Joe,
Lightly tripping on a row.

III

Happy people, who can be
In happiness compared to ye?
The pilgrim, with his crook and hat,
Sees your happiness complete.

'AN ANTHEM'

1st voice, Mr. Suction.

So the bat with leathern wing
    Winking and blinking,
    Winking and blinking,
    Winking and blinking,
Like Dr. Johnson.

2nd voice, Mr. Quid.

O ho, said Dr. Johnson
    To Scipio Africanus,
If you don't own me a philosopher,
I 'll kick your Roman * * * *

1st voice, Mr. Suction.

Ah ha, to Dr. Johnson,
    Said Scipio Africanus,
* * * * * * my Roman petticoat,
And kiss my Roman * * * *

(*The asterisks are not Blake's. They represent an indecorous
suggestion and a Latin word rhyming with 'Africanus.'*)

Grand Chorus.   Want matches?
                   Yes, yes, yes.
                   Want matches?
                   No!

MRS. NANNICATCHPOL'S SONG

I CRY my matches as far as Guildhall;
God bless the Duke and his aldermen all.

MR. STEELYARD'S SONG

As I walked forth one May morning
To see the fields so pleasant and gay,
Oh there did I spy a young Meadow-sweet,
Among the violets that smell so sweet,
          Smell so sweet,
          Smell so sweet,
Among the violets that smell so sweet.

MISS GITTIPIN'S SECOND SONG

A FROG he would a-wooing ride,
     Kitty alone,— Kitty alone;
This frog he would a-wooing ride,
     Kitty alone and I.

Sing, cock, I carry Kitty alone,
Kitty alone, Kitty alone,
Kitty alone and I.

THE JOVIAL MAN'S ITALIAN SONG

> FRA ra so bo ro,
> Fa ra bo ra,
> Fa ra za ba rara boro, etc.

MR. QUID'S THIRD SONG

I

HAIL, Matrimony, made of love,
To thy wide gates how great a drove
On purpose to be yoked do come,
Widows and maids and youths also,
That lightly trip on beauty's toe,
Or sit on beauty's b . . .

II

Hail, finger-footed lovely creatures,
The females of our human natures,
Formed to suckle all mankind.
'Tis you that come in time of need :
Without you we should never breed,
Or any comfort find.

III

For if a damsel's blind or lame,
Or Nature's hand has crooked her frame,
Or if she 's deaf, or is wall-eyed,
Some friend or lover she shall find
That panteth for a bride.

IV

The universal poultice this
To cure whatever is amiss,

In damsel or in widow gay,
It makes them smile, it makes them skip,
Like birds just curèd of the pip,
They chirp and hop away.

v

Then come, ye maidens, come, ye swains,
Come and be cured of all your pains
In Matrimony's golden cage.

MR. OBTUSE ANGLE'S SONG

I

To be or not to be
Of great capacity,
Like Sir Isaac Newton,
Or Locke, or Doctor South,
Or Sherlock upon Death,—
I'd rather be Sutton.

II

For he could build a house
For aged man or youth
With walls of brick or stone;
He furnished it within
With whatever he could win,
And all his own.

III

He drew out of the stocks
His money in a box,
And sent his servant
To Green the bricklayer,
And to the carpenter,
He was so fervent.

IV

The chimneys were three score,
The windows many more,
And for convenience
He sinks and gutters made,
And all the way he paved,
To hinder pestilence.

v

Was not this a good man,
Whose life was but a span,
Whose name was Sutton—
Like Locke, or Doctor South,
Or Sherlock upon Death,
Or Sir Isaac Newton?

MR. STEELYARD'S SONG

THIS city and this country has brought forth many
        Mayors
To sit in state and give forth Laws out of their old
        oak chairs,
With face as brown as any nut with drinking of
        strong ale—
Old English hospitality, O then it did not fail.

With scarlet gowns and broad gold lace, would make
        a yeoman sweat;
With stockings rolled above their knees, and shoes
        as black as jet;
With eating beef and drinking beer, O they were
        stout and hale—
Old English hospitality, O then it did not fail.

Thus sitting at the table wide the Mayor and the
        Aldermen
Were fit to give laws to the city: each eat as much
        as ten.

The hungry poor entered the hall to eat good beef
    and ale—
Good English hospitality, O then it did not fail.

MR. OBTUSE ANGLE'S SONG

*This song is here omitted, as it will be found under the
title 'Holy Thursday' among the 'Songs of Innocence.'*

MRS. NANNICANTRIP'S SONG

*This song also omitted, as it will be found under the title
'The Nurse's Song' among the 'Songs of Innocence.'*

MR. QUID'S SONG

*This will be found under the title 'The Little Boy Lost'
among the 'Songs of Innocence.'*

TILLY SALLY'S SONG

Oh I say, Joe,
    Throw up the ball,
I 've a good mind to go
And leave you all
    To bowl the ball in a t——d,
    And to clean it with my handkecher,
    Without saying a word !

That Bill 's a foolish fellow,—
[*A line here absolutely obliterated in the MS.*]
He has given me a black eye ;
He does not know how to handle a bat
Any more than a dog or cat.
He has knocked down the wicket
And broke the stumps,
And run without shoes to save his pumps.

MISS GITTIPIN'S SONG

I

LEAVE, O leave me to my sorrow,
Here I 'll sit and fade away
Till I 'm nothing but a spirit,
And I love this form of clay.

II

Then if chance along this forest
Any walk in pathless ways,
Through the gloom he 'll see my shadow,
Hear my voice upon the breeze.

MR. SCOPPREL'S SONG

THERE's Doctor Clash
And Signor Falasarole,—
Oh, they sweep in the cash
Into their purse bowl.

   Fa mi sol ! fa mi pol !
   Great A, little a,
   Bouncing B !
   Play away, play away :
   You 're out of the key.

Musicians should have
A pair of very good ears
And long fingers and thumbs,
And not like clumsy bears.

   Fa me sol, fa sol la sol,
   Gentlemen, gentlemen,
   Rap, rap, rap !
   Fiddle, fiddle, fiddle !
   Clap, clap, clap.
   Fa me sol ! fa me sol !

MR. SIPSOP'S SONG

A CROWNED king
On a white horse sitting,
With his trumpet sounding
And banners flying;
Through the clouds of smoke he makes his way.
And the shout of his thousands fills the heart
    with rejoicing and victory,
And the shout of his thousands fills the heart
    with rejoicing and victory.
Victory! Victory! 'Twas William the Prince of
    Orange.

[*The manuscript breaks off suddenly in the middle
    of a page.*]

RESENTMENTS

(*The dates of these are all from about* 1800 *to* 1808. *The titles when in parentheses are conjectural. The rest are Blake's.*)

(AFTER TOO MUCH 'KLOPSTOCK')

(*Unfinished; no title. Not decent in lines three and four. The rest of the gaps are where the manuscript is totally illegible or obliterated by Blake.*)

When Klopstock England defied,
Up rose William Blake in his pride
For old Nobodaddy. . . .

. . . . .

Then swore a great oath that would make
heaven quake,
And called aloud to English Blake.
Blake was away. His body was free
At Lambeth beneath the poplar tree.
From Lambeth then shouted he,
And . . . three times three.
The moon at that blushed fiery red;
The stars threw down their spears and fled.

. . . . .

Astonished felt the intrippled turn,
And all his bowells began to yearn,
His bowells turned round three times three,
And locked in his soul with a golden key,
That from his body it never could be
Till the last judgment. . . .
Then again old Nobodaddy swore
He never had seen such a thing before

Since Noah was shut in the ark,—
Since Eve first . . . her hell-found spark,
Since 'twas the fashion to go naked,
Since the old . . . was created,

.   .   .   .   .   .

TO NOBODADDY

WHY art thou silent and invisible,
    Father of Jealousy?
Why dost thou hide thyself in clouds
    From every passing eye?

Why darkness and obscurity
    In all thy words and laws,
That none can eat the fruit
    But from the wily serpent's jaws?

Or is it because Jealousy
    Gives Feminine applause?

LACEDEMONIAN INSTRUCTION

COME hither, boy: what see you there?
A fool caught in a religious snare.

AN ANSWER TO THE PARSON

WHY of the sheep do you not learn peace?
Because I don't want you to shear my fleece.

TO GOD

IF you have formed a circle to go into,
Go into it yourself, and see what you would do.

(A CRY)

(From a letter, August 1803.)

OH why was I born with a different face?
Why was I not born like this envious race?
If I look, each one starts: if I speak I offend;
Then I'm silent and passive and lose every friend.

Then my verse I dishonour, my pictures despise,
My person degrade, and my temper chastise;
And the pen is my terror, the pencil my shame;
All my talents I bury, and dead is my fame.

I am either too low, or too highly prized.
When elate I'm envied; when meek I'm despised.

(AN ALTERNATIVE)

GREAT things are done when men and mountains meet;
These are not done by jostling in the street.

MR. STOTHARD TO MR. CROMEK

FOR Fortune's favours you your riches bring,
But Fortune says she gave you no such thing.
Why should you be unfaithful to your friends,—
Sneaking and backbiting, and odds and ends?

MR. CROMEK TO MR. STOTHARD

FORTUNE favours the brave—old proverbs say—
But not with money—that is not her way:
Turn back, turn back, you travel all in vain;
Turn through the iron gate, down sneaking lane.

ON F—— AND I——

I FOUND them blind, I taught them how to see,
And now they know neither themselves nor me.
'Tis excellent to turn a thorn to a pin,
A fool to a bolt, a knave to a glass of gin.

TO F——. (FLAXMAN)

You call me mad, 'tis folly to do so,
To seek to turn a madman to a foe.
If you think as you speak, you are an ass,
If you do not, you are but as you was.

(HAYLEY AGAIN)

WHEN H——y finds out what you cannot do,
That is the very thing he'll set you to.
If you break not your back 'tis not his fault,
But pecks of poison are not pecks of salt.

ON HAYLEY

To forgive enemies H—— does pretend
Who never in his life forgave a friend,
And when he could not act upon my wife,
Hired a villain to bereave my life.

TO H——. (HAYLEY)

THY friendship oft has made my heart to ache:
Do be my enemy for friendship's sake.

ON H——, THE PICK THANK. (HAYLEY)

I WRITE the rascal thanks till he and I
With thanks and compliments are quite drawn dry.

(? STOTHARD)

SOME men created for destruction come
Into the world, to make the world their home.
For they are vile and base as e'er they can,
They'll still be called, The World's Honest Man.

ON S——.   (STOTHARD)

YOU say reserve and modesty he has,
Whose heart is iron, his head wood, and his face brass.
The fox, the owl, the beetle, and the bat,
By sweet reserve and modesty get fat.

(PROTESTS)

I

SOME people admire the work of a fool,
For it's sure to keep your judgment cool:
It does not reproach you with want of wit;
It is not like a lawyer serving a writ.

II

MY title as a genius thus is proved,
Not praised by Hayley or by Flaxman loved.

III

AND in melodious accents I
Will sit me down and cry I! I!

(CROMEK SPEAKS)

I ALWAYS take my judgments from a fool,
Because his judgments are so very cool.
Not prejudiced by feelings great or small:
Amiable state: he cannot feel at all.

(A HINT)

THE errors of a wise man make your rule
Rather than the perfections of a fool.

(ART SCHOOL WORK)

THE cripple every step smudges and labours
And says: 'Come, learn to walk of me, good
    Neighbours.'
Sir Joshua in astonishment cries out,
See what great labour! pain in modest doubt!
(His pains are more than others, there's no doubt,
He walks and stumbles as if he crep (*sic*)
And how high finished is every step!
Newton and Bacon! Being badly nursed,
He's all experiment from last to first.

(? TO HAYNES)

THE Sussex men are noted fools,
  And weak in their brain pan.
I wonder if H—— the painter
  Is not a Sussex man?

(? HAYNES)

MADMAN, I have been called. Fool, they call thee.
I wonder which they envy, thee or me?

TO H——. (? HAYNES)

YOU think Fuseli's not a great painter. I'm glad.
This is one of the best compliments he ever had.

(? HAYNES OR HAYLEY)

OF H——'s birth there was the happy lot;
His mother on his father him begot.

(REYNOLDS)

CAN there be anything more mean,
More malice in disguise ;
Than praise a man for doing what
That man does most despise?
Reynolds lectures exactly so
When he praises Michel Angelo.

(STOTHARD)

S——, in childhood, upon the nursery floor,
Was extreme old and most extremely poor.
He has grown old, and rich, and what he will.
He is extreme old, and extreme poor still.

TO NANCY F——. (FLAXMAN)

How can I help thy husband's copying me?
Should that make difference 'twixt thee and me?

TO CR——. (CROMEK)

A PETTY, sneaking knave I knew. . . .
Oh, Mr. Cromek, how d' you do?

CR——. (CROMEK)

CR—— loves artists as he loves his meat.
He loves the Art—but 'tis the art to cheat.

ON THE GREAT ENCOURAGEMENT GIVEN BY THE ENGLISH NOBILITY AND GENTRY

To Correggio, Rubens, Rembrandt, Reynolds,
Gainsborough, Catelaine, Ducrowe,
and Dilbury Doodle

I

As the ignorant Savage will sell his own wife
For a button, a buckle, a bead, or a knife,
So the wise savage Englishman gives his whole fortune
For a smear, or a squall, to destroy pictures or tune.

II

Give Pensions to the learned pig,
Or the hare playing on a Tabor;
Bunglers can never see perfection
But in the journeyman's labour.

III

And I call upon Colonel Warble
To give these rascals a dose of caudle.

(ARTIST MADMEN)

All pictures that's painted with sense and with thought
Are painted by madmen, as sure as a groat.
For the greater the fool is, the pencil more blest,
As when they are drunk they always paint best.
They never can Raphael it, Fuseli it, or Blake it,
If they can't see an outline, pray how can they make it?
When men will draw outlines begin you to jaw them;
Madmen see outlines, and therefore they draw them.

ENGLISH ENCOURAGERS OF ART

CROMEK'S OPINION PUT INTO RHYME

IF you mean to please everybody you will
Set to work both ignorance and skill.
For a great multitude are ignorant,
And skill to them seems raving and rant.
Like putting oil and water into a lamp,
'Twill make a great splutter with smoke and damp.
For there is no use, as it seems to me,
For lighting a lamp, when you don't wish to see.

(Later)

YOU say their pictures well painted be,
And yet they are blockheads, you all agree.
Thank heaven I never was sent to school
To be flogged into following the style of a fool.

(THE WASHERWOMAN'S SONG)

I WASHED them out, I washed them in:
And they told me it was a great sin.

(FROM A LOST BOOK)

DELICATE hands and heads will never appear
While Titian, etc.,—as in the *Book of Moonlight*, l. 5.

(The editor has inquired, without success, for any trace of this lost Book. It is not mentioned again by Blake, and this fragmentary allusion only remains to show us that—though it has been doubted—Blake really intended these sad epigrams for publication.)

TO I———D

YOU all your life observed the golden rule,
Till you're at last become the golden fool.
I sport with fortune, merry, blythe and gay,
Like to the lion sporting with his prey.
You have the hide and horns which you may wear ;
Mine is the flesh—the bones may be your share.

(HINTS FOR ARTISTS OR THEIR FRIENDS)

I

WHEN you look at a picture you always can see
If a man of sense has painted he.
Then, never flinch, but keep up a jaw
About freedom, and Jenny sink awa' !
As when it smells of the lamp, all can
Say all was owing to the skilful man.
For the smell of water is but small :
So e'en let ignorance do it all.

II

WHEN I see a Rembrandt or Correggio,
I think of crippled Harry or slobbering Joe,
And then I say to myself, are artists' rules
To be drawn from the works of two manifest fools ?
Then God defend us from the arts, I say,
Send battle, murder, sudden death, we pray.
Rather than be such a human fool
I 'd be a hog, a worm, a chair, a stool.

III

CALL that the public voice which is their error !
Like to a monkey peeping in a mirror,—
Admire all his colours, warm and brown,
And never once perceives his ugly form.

IV

ANGER and wrath my bosom rends,
I thought them the errors of friends ;
But all my limbs with warmth do glow,
I find them the errors of the foe.

V

AT a friend's errors anger show,
Mirth at the errors of a foe.

VI

I've given great provision to my foes,
And now I'll lead my false friends by the nose.

VII

These are Idiots' chiefest arts,
To blend and not define the parts.
To make out the parts is the wise man's aim,
But to loose them the fool makes his foolish aim.

VIII

The swallow sings in courts of kings,
That fools have their high finishings,
And this the Prince's golden rule,
The laborious stumble of a fool.

(FRIENDSHIPS)

I

The only man I ever knew
Who did not almost make me spue
Was Fuseli : (He was) both Turk and Jew.
And so, dear Christian (friends), how do you do?

II

Oh, this is being a friend just in the nick,
Not when he's well, but waiting till he's sick.
He calls you to his help,—but you're not moved,
Until by being sick his wants are proved.

III

You see him spend his soul in prophecy.
Do you believe it a confounded lie,
Till some bookseller, and the public tame,
Proves there is truth in his extravagant claim?

IV

Isn't it atrocious for a friend you love
To tell you anything that he can't prove?
And 'tis most wicked in a Christian Nation
For any one to pretend to inspiration.

V

False friends cry fie! on friendship: you shan't sever;
In spite we will be greater friends than ever.

(THE SUMMING-UP)

He's a blockhead who wants a proof of what he
    can't perceive,
And he's a fool who tries to make such a blockhead
    believe.

TO F——. (? Flaxman)

I

I mock thee not, though I by thee am mockèd,
Thou call'st me madman, but I call thee blockhead.

II

You don't believe: I won't attempt to make ye.
You are asleep; I won't attempt to wake ye.
Sleep on, sleep on, while in your pleasant dreams
Of Reason, you may drink of Life's clear streams,
Reason and Newton: they are quite two things,
For so the swallow, and the sparrow sings.

III

Reason says 'Miracle!' Newton says 'Doubt,
Ay, that's the way to make all nature out.
Doubt, doubt, and don't believe without experiment;
That is the very thing that Jesus meant
When He said, "Only believe, believe and try;
Try, try, and never mind the reason why."'

(SIR JOSHUA REYNOLDS)

I

SIR JOSHUA praises Rubens with a smile
By calling his the ornamental style,
And yet his praise of Flaxman was the smartest
When he called him the ornamental artist.

II

But, sure, such ornament we well may spare,
As crooked limbs or filthy heads of hair.

III

Sir Joshua praises Michael Angelo—
'Tis Christian charity when knaves praise so—
But 'twould be madness, all the world would say,
Should Michael Angelo praise Sir Joshua.
Christ used the Pharisees a rougher way.

IV

No real style of colouring now appears,
But advertising in the Newspapers.
Look here, you 'll see Sir Joshua's colouring ;
Look at his pictures : all has taken wing.

V

The villain at the gallows tree
When he is doomed to die,
To assuage his bitter misery
In virtue's praise does cry.

VI

So Reynolds, when he came to die,
To assuage his bitter woe,
Thus aloud did howl and cry :
'Michael Angelo ! Michael Angelo !'

VOL. I.   M

VII

When Joshua Reynolds died
All Nature was degraded.
  The King dropped a tear
  Into the Queen's ear,
And all his pictures faded.

FLORENTINE INGRATITUDE

Sir Joshua sent his own portrait to
The birthplace of Michael Angelo,
And in the hand of the simpering fool
He put a dirty paper scroll.
And on the paper—to be polite—
Did—'Sketches by Michael Angelo' write.
The Florentines said, ''Tis a Dutch-English-bore;
Michael Angelo's name writ on Rembrandt's door.'
The Florentines call it an English fetch;
Michael Angelo never did sketch.
Every line of his has meaning,
And needs neither suckling nor weaning.
Giotto's circle or Apelles' line
Were not the work of sketchers with wine,
Nor of the city clerk's running hand fashion,
Nor of Sir Isaac Newton's calculation,
(Nor of the city clerk's idle futilities
Which sprang of Sir Isaac Newton's great abilities.)
It will set his Dutch friends all in a roar
To write ' Michael Angelo' on Rembrandt's door.
But you must not bring in your hand a lie
If you mean the Florentines should buy.

(Postscript)

These verses were written by a very envious man
  Who, whatever likeness he may have to Michael
    Angelo,
Can never have any to Sir Jehoshuan.

TO THE ROYAL ACADEMY

A STRANGE erratum in all the editions
  Of Sir Joshua Reynolds' lectures,
Should be corrected by the young gentlemen,
  And the Royal Academy Directors.

Instead of *Michael Angelo*
  Read *Rembrandt*, for it is fit
To make mere common honesty
  Of all that he has writ.

(PATRONAGE)

To come in 'Barry: A Poem.

(This poem has not yet been found.)

I

I ASKED my dear friend Orator Prig,
'What's the first thing in oratory?' He said : 'A
    great Wig.'
'And what is the second?' Then dancing a jig
And bowing profoundly, he said : 'A great Wig.'
'And what is the third?' Then he snored like a pig,
And thrust out his cheeks, and replied : 'A great Wig.'

II

So, if to a painter the question you push,
'What's the first part of painting?' he'd say, 'A
    paint brush.'
'And what is the second?' with most modest blush
He'll smile like a cherub, and say, 'A paint brush.'
'And what is the third?' He will bow like a rush,
With a leer in his eye, and reply, 'A paint brush.'

III

Perhaps this is all that a painter can want,
But look yonder; that house is the house of Rembrandt.

IV

O dear mother Outline, of wisdom most sage,
'What's the first part of painting?' She said,
    'Patronage.'
'And what is the second—to please and engage?'
She frowned like a fury, and said, 'Patronage.'
'And what is the third?' She put off old age,
And smiled like a Syren, and said, 'Patronage.'

(A SARCASM)

THAT God is colouring, Newton does show,
And the devil is a black outline all of us know.

(THE TWO ARTS)

SOME look to see the sweet outlines
    And beauteous forms that love does wear.
Some look to find out patches, paint,
    Bracelets and stays and powdered hair.

TO VENETIAN ARTISTS

PERHAPS this little fable may make us merry.
A dog went over the water without a wherry.
A bone which he had stolen he had in his mouth,
He cared not whether the wind was north or south.
As he swam he saw the reflection of the bone.
This is quite perfection—generalising tone !
Snap ! snap !—and lost the substance and shadow too.
He had both these before.   Now how d' ye do ?
Those who have tasted colouring, love it more and more.

(PATRIOTIC ART)

'Now Art has lost its mental charms,
France shall subdue the world in arms.'

So spoke an Angel at my birth,
Then said—'Descend thou on the earth.
Renew the Arts on Britain's shore
And France shall fall down and adore.
With works of art her armies meet,
And war shall sink beneath thy feet.
But if thy nation arts refuse,
And if they scorn the immortal muse,
France shall the arts of Peace restore
And save thy works from Britain's shore.'

TO ENGLISH CONNOISSEURS

You must agree that Rubens was a fool,
And yet you make him master of your school,
And give more money for his slobberings
Than you will give for Raphael's finest things.

Raphael sublime, majestic, graceful, wise,—
His executive powers must I despise?
Rubens low, vulgar, stupid, ignorant,
His executive powers must I grant?

(ON THE CHRIST OF REUBENS)

I UNDERSTOOD Christ was a carpenter,
And not a brewer's servant, my good sir.

(THE STYE OF REUBENS)

SWELLED limbs with no outline that you can descry,
That stink in the nose of the passer-by,
But all the pulp washed, painted, finished with labour,
Of a hundred journeymen:—How do you do, good
    neighbour?

A PRETTY EPIGRAM FOR THE ENCOURAGE-MENT OF THOSE WHO HAVE GREAT SUMS IN THE VENETIAN AND FLEMISH OOZE

NATURE and Art in this together suit,
What is most grand is always most minute.
Rubens thinks tables, chairs, and stools are grand,
And Raphael thinks a head, a foot, a hand.

(THE SEQUEL)

RAPHAEL, sublime, majestic, graceful, wise—
His executive powers must I despise?
Rubens—low, vulgar, stupid, ignorant—
His powers of execution must I grant?
Go send your children to the slobbering school
To learn the laborious stumble of a fool.

(THE CONTRAST)

RUBENS was a statesman and a saint.
Deceptions? And so I'll learn to paint.

(A RESOLUTION)

HAVING given great offence by writing prose,
I'll write in verse as soft as Bartoloze.
Some blush at what others can see no crime in,
But nobody sees any harm in rhyming.
Dryden in rhyme cries 'Milton only planned.'
Every fool shook his bells throughout the land.
Tom Cook cut Hogarth down with his clean graving:
Thousands of connoisseurs with joy ran raving.
Thus Hayley, on his toilet seeing the soap,
Cries—'Homer is very much improved by Pope.'
Some say I've given provision to my foes,
And now I lead my false friends by the nose.
Flaxman and Stothard, smelling a sweet savour,
Cry—'Blakéfied drawing spoils painter and engraver,'
While I, looking up to my umbrella,
Resolved to be a very contrary fellow,

Cry, looking quite from circumference to centre,
'No one can finish so high as the original inventor.'
Then poor Schiavonetti died of the Cromek,
A thing that's tied about the Examiner's neck.
This is my sweet apology to my friends,
That I may put them in mind of their latter ends.

(SOME EPITAPHS)

I

Come, knock your heads against this stone,
For sorrow that poor John Thompson's gone.

II

I was buried near this dyke,
That my friends may weep as much as they like.

III

Here lies John Trot, the friend of all mankind,
He has not left one enemy behind.
Friends were quite hard to find, old authors say,
But now they stand in everybody's way.

(A POSTSCRIPT TO POPE'S COUPLET)

When France got free, Europe 'twixt fools and knaves
Were savage first to France, and after, slaves.

(A WARNING)

I am no Homeric hero, you all know,
I profess not generosity to a foe.
The generous to enemies promote their ends,
And becomes the enemy and betrayer of his friends.

ADVICE TO POPES WHO SUCCEEDED THE
AGE OF RAPHAEL

DEGRADE first the arts, would you nations degrade ;
Hire idiots to paint with cold light and hot shade ;
Give high price for the worst, leave the best in
    disgrace,
And with labour of idleness fill every place.

A WARNING

WHEN nations grow old,
    The arts grow cold,
And commerce settles on every tree ;

And the poor and the old
    Can live upon gold,
For all are born poor.   (Aged sixty-three.)

(ENEMIES AND IRONY)

I

COSWAY, Fraser, and Baldwin of Egypt's lake,
Fear to associate with Blake.
This life is a warfare against evils ;
They heal the sick, he casts out devils.
Hayley, Flaxman, and Stothard are also in doubt
Lest their virtue should be put to the rout.
One grins, another spits and in corners hides,
And all the virtuous have shaved their b——sides.

(HIS TITLE)

MY title as a Genius thus is proved,
Not praised by Hayley nor by Flaxman loved.

II

*Key to the characters in the following doggerel—
conjectured. Not Blake's own.*

DEATH (*in a disguise*),	Blake.
BOB SCREWMUCH (*the Man of Men*),	Robert Cromek.
FELPHAM BILLY,	William Hayley.
QUIBBLE,	Hayley's Lawyer.
BILLY'S DRAGOON,	Schofield.
JACK HEMP—called '*Yorkshire Jack*,'	John Flaxman.
CUR,	Stothard's Lawyer.
DADDY—'*Jack Hemp's Parson*,'	Dr. Malchin.

*The souls of Stothard and Blake : their works of
art on the ' Canterbury Pilgrims.'*

(*The beginning is lost. There is only this fragment.*)

STOTHARD (*loq.*) And his legs covered it like a long fork
Reached all the way from Chichester to York,
From York across Scotland to the sea,—
That was a Man of Men, as seems to me.
Not only in his mouth his own soul lay,
But my soul also would he bear away.
Like as a pedlar bears his weary pack,
He would bear my soul buckled to his back.
But once, alas ! committing a mistake,
He bore the wretched soul of William Blake,
That he might turn it into eggs and gold,
But neither back nor mouth those eggs could hold.
His under jaw dropped as those eggs he laid,
And all my eggs are addled and decayed.
O that I never had seen William Blake,
Or could from Death Assassinette (*sic*) awake !
We thought—alas, that such a thought could be !—
That Blake would etch for him and draw for me.
For 'twas a kind of bargain Screwmuch made,
That Blake's design should be by us displayed,

Because he makes designs so very cheap.
Then Screwmuch at Blake's soul took a long leap.
'Twas not a mouse, 'twas Death in a disguise.
And I, alas! live to weep out my eyes.
And Death sits laughing on their monuments
On which he's written—'Received the contents.'
But I have writ, so sorrowful my thought is,
His epitaph, for my tears are aquafortis.
'Come, Artists, knock your head against this stone,
For sorrow that our friend Bob Screwmuch's gone.'
And now the muses in me smile and laugh,
I'll also write mine own dear epitaph;
And I'll be buried near a dyke,
That my friends may weep as much as they like—
'Here lies Stothard, the Friend of all Mankind,
Who has not left one enemy behind.'

*The fragment ends here. It is satisfactory to be able to
gather, by the fact that the epitaphs were cut out of it and
written separately to be exhibited (without even the nick-
names here used) for their own wit, that Blake gave up the
idea of publishing this. A last fragment from the same note-
book:—*

III

THE *Examiner*, whose very name is Hunt,
Called 'Death' a madman; trembling for the
    affront,
Like trembling hare, he sits on his weekly paper
On which he used to dance and shout and caper.
And—Yorkshire Jack Hemp, and Quibble blushing
    saw—
Clapped Death into the corner of his jaw,
And Felpham Billy rode out every morn,
Horseback with Death, over the fields of corn,
Who, with iron hand, cuff'd in the afternoon
The ears of Billy's lawyer and dragoon.
And Cur, my lawyer, and Daddy, Jack Hemp's
    parson,
Both went to law with Death to keep our ears on.

For now to starve Death we had laid a plot
Against his price ; but death was in the pot.
He made him pay his price,—alack-a-day !
He knew both law and gospel better than they.

IV

Was I angry with Hayley who used me so ill,
Or can I be angry with Felpham's old mill?
Or angry with Flaxman, or Cromek, or Stothard,
Or poor Schiavonetti whom they to death bothered,
Or angry with Malchin, or Boydel, or Bowyer,
Because they did not say, 'O what a beau ye are !'?
At a friend's errors anger show,
Mirth at the errors of a foe.

(TWO LAST FRAGMENTS)

*(No date to be ascertained with any certainty. The key to
the personal allusions and the bad English is lost.)*

When you look at a picture you always can see
If a man of sense has painted he.
Then never flinch but keep up a jaw
About freedom and Jenny sink away ;
As when it smells of the lamp all can
Say it was owing to the skilful man,
For the smell of water is but small,
So e'en let ignorance do it all.

———

Great men and fools do often me inspire,
But the greater fool the greater liar.

After this period, personality, unsweetened by imagination or poetry or symbolism, vanishes from Blake's writing, and all the rest was in a higher vein. He experienced revulsion of feeling when, after these misunderstandings, Hayley came forward, finding he was in trouble, and stood by him, and risked and spent money and character and peace for him while he was under trial on a false accusation of treason. This taught him, through gratitude and compunction, to be rid for ever of resentment, as a dangerous and foolish mood, best avoided, whether justified apparently at the moment or not. The 'Epigrams,' however, must be well known and remembered constantly by any reader who wishes to enjoy and understand the inner meaning of the 'Everlasting Gospel,' and much of the 'Milton,' 'Jerusalem,' and 'Vala.' They are the flotsam and jetsam, the wreckage of once living troubles and excitements from whose death these poems arose, as in a new and better world.

Of the titles given here to these fugitive rhymes collected under the editorial sub-heading 'Resentments,' those in parentheses are proposed for use merely because titles are convenient for reference. Those not printed in parentheses are Blake's own, as they stand in his MS. book.

THE EVERLASTING GOSPEL

BLAKE'S POEMS   132

THE EVERLASTING GOSPEL

The probable date of most of this poem is 1810. *But it was
not all written at once. Part seems a little earlier.*

In Gilchrist's 'Life,' vol. ii. p. 96, *a poem is printed called*
The Woman taken in Adultery, *described as* Extracted from a
Fragmentary Poem entitled 'The Everlasting Gospel.'

*This extract begins with twelve lines, to be referred to here
in their place. They are not, properly, part of the poem at
all. There should be fourteen lines to this first section, if it is
to be understood as Blake meant it, but the third and fourth
are quietly removed without any mark made to show that they
had been dropped. This deceives the reader, because a few
asterisks and a blank space later on seem to indicate where the
first omission occurs in the straightforward and continuous
presentation of the poem.*

*The portion which follows appears to be a continuation, an
extract from some longer work. There are forty-two lines of
it. But once more the reader is deceived. In Blake's MS.
this portion has fifty-seven lines. The suppressed sixteen are
dropped out, some here, some there, and not a sign is made.*

*The Aldine Edition of Blake's Poems appeared next with a
much fuller and less misleading text. But even this is not
free from very serious garbling. Had any indication of its
alterations been given, or had it been entitled a selection or
arrangement from the original, no complaint could have been
made. But a footnote professed to give the poem in full.*

*There are omissions, divisions, and rejoinings in it that are
not marked, and that were neither necessary nor justifiable.*

*Both as a key to much of Blake's mystical and symbolic
method, and as a contribution to his biography, the poem is of
very great interest and value. Not the least use was made of
it in Gilchrist's 'Life' or in the Aldine Edition from either
point of view, and the reader was not permitted to see a text
that might have enabled him to do for himself what the editors
and biographers had not done for him.*

*This seems almost incredible, but neither Mr. Gilchrist nor
the brothers Rossetti ever knew what the poem was about. In*

191

*their treatment of it they were guided by mere fancy or per-
sonal taste, working without comprehension and in a patron-
ising spirit.*

*It is true that Blake never properly prepared the original
manuscript for the printer. He wrote it by fits and starts,
filling with it irregular blanks accidentally left in an already
somewhat crowded note-book. He only partly sorted the fragments in any coherent order. Marginal numbers written by
him against the lines here and there show that he made an
attempt to do so, but his directions are not complete; they do
not include all the sections of the poem, and therefore a
coherent and complete text, based on the authority of the
author himself, is not to be obtained. The intervention of an
editor is absolutely necessary if the poem is to be given to the
public.*

*But as in both the first two attempts to present it, whether for
Mr. Macmillan by Mr. D. G., or for Mr. Bell by Mr. W. M.
Rossetti, the reader had been treated with little frankness, and
the author with little scrupulosity, the present editor, acting
with Mr. Yeats, took an opposite course in the Quaritch
edition of Blake's works. In this, vol. ii. pp. 42-60, all that
could be found in Blake's MS., and all that could be conjectured about the order of the lines and their date, was given
so that the reader might at last edit the poem for himself, and
come to his own conclusion both as to its order of composition
and as to its meaning. In this way the feeling of distrust
with which any one would have turned to a fresh form of the
poem arranged by a new editor was avoided. This unsorted
revelation of all the material of the poem having once been
made did not need to be repeated, and on the next printing
of the 'Everlasting Gospel' a fresh attempt to get it into some
sort of order which would have been approved by Blake, even
if not originally intended by him, was certain to be made.*

*For this task the account of the MS., and the very full pre-
sentment of its matter in the Quaritch edition, was practically
sufficient. But though the original had been returned to its
owner in America, a MS. copy made by the present writer
remained, in which the arrangement of the lines was exactly
reproduced, whether written in sequence, in reverse order, or
sideways, whether with or without marginal numberings. The
value of this consisted partly in the way in which the insertion
of the fragments among other matter in the book offered hints
by which their order and dates could be inferred.*

*It happened that the next editor to whom the duty of dealing
with the question fell was Mr. Yeats. To him the present
editor passed his copy, as he records in a note, and he
arranged from it the form of the poem printed by Messrs.*

*Lawrence and Bullen. In his editorial observations Mr.
Yeats says of it:—*

'This poem is not given in full in the present book; for it
is not possible to do so without many repetitions, for Blake
never made a final text. The MS. book contains three
different versions of a large portion of the poem, and it is not
possible to keep entirely to any one of them without sacrificing
many fine passages. Blake left, however, pretty clear directions for a great part of the text-making, and these directions
were ignored by Mr. Rossetti.'

*Mr. Yeats also says of his own method of editing the poem
that it omits*

'. . . a few fragmentary lines here and there, of whose
place no indication is given,'

*adding that they are all to be found in the complete Quaritch
edition.*

*The present editor cannot now touch the work of his former
collaborator without here paying a tribute to the ability with
which his arrangement is made, and the conscientiousness
with which it is described in the notes. Mr. Yeats was
guided by considerations of readability and of space, and he
worked with a knowledge that he must needs produce a result
a little short of perfection, because no critical skill and no
poetic insight could make an ideally coherent and consecutive
poem out of the material Blake left. What Mr. Yeats did in
his arrangement was never done so well before, and it is hardly
to be supposed that it will be done any better by any one working after him under similar conditions.*

*In the present volumes the first consideration that guides
the editor is completeness. Here therefore now follow the
isolated fragments which were omitted, without disingenuous
concealment, by Mr. Yeats.*

*The first appears to have been intended as the opening of a
sustained paragraph like those that have a similar style of
commencement. It, however, went no further, and whatever
caused the interruption, Blake did not resume the subject, and
preferred to drop the lines.*

They are as follows:—

> ' Did Jesus preach doubt, or did he
> Give any lessons in philosophy,
> Charge visionaries with deceiving
> And call men wise for not believing?'

This was written in pencil, sideways, and in the same

pencil, at the top of that page which contains the long passage beginning 'Was Jesus chaste,' we read,

'This was spoken by my Spectre to Voltaire, Bacon,' etc.,

a note which probably only referred to the quatrain.

Later in the poem is another quatrain, squeezed in sideways, as Blake was reading over his first draft of the portion, 'Was Jesus humble,' etc. It is omitted from the fairer copy—

'He who loves his enemies hates his friends,
    This surely is not what Jesus intends ;
He must mean the mere love of civility,
    And so he must mean concerning humility.'

Another fragment, in a slightly different metre, is found on a page containing no part of the MS. of the rest of 'The Everlasting Gospel.' Though written in two long lines, it perhaps is more naturally to be printed as a quatrain with a reiteration imbedded in it—

'Nail his neck to the cross,
    Nail it with a nail :
Nail his neck to the cross,
    Ye all have power over his tail.'

There is another quatrain belonging to no part of the poem in particular. Its handwriting suggests that it was composed separately in an outburst of indignation one day when Blake had been turning over the leaves of his MS. :—

'What can be done with those desperate fools
    Who follow after the heathen schools ?
I was standing by when Jesus died.
    What they called Humility, I called pride.'

All these quatrains are essentially separate poems, though they help the main subject, and could all be woven into the text with a little straining. To do so would somewhat violate literary propriety, as nautical propriety would be violated if we collected the sprit-sails of a ship and sowed them on to the main-sail.

Another fragment is more puzzling—

'Seeing this false Christ, in fury and passion,
    I made my voice heard all over the nation,
What are those,' etc.

*So it breaks off.   It seems by its handwriting and its place
on the page to have been written immediately after the passage
that begins ' Was Jesus chaste,' and ends ' That never was
meant for man to eat.'   We have only the fragment, and it is
not improbable that it was the opening of a long passage, now
lost, that was written on a separate piece of paper, there being
no room for it on the page, already crowded with other notes,
sketches, and fragments of the poems.   Blake often wrote bits
belonging to long poems on separate scraps.   This one may
have been the opening of a portion lost through being written
in this manner.*

*The key to the meaning of the entire poem is perfectly
simple.   To comprehend it we need only remember that in
Blake's view of the Christian doctrine, the Second Person of
the Trinity was, before all things, the Logos, a word which
he translated Human Imagination, for without this, for us
at least, ' was not anything made that was made.'   Jesus of
Nazareth lived and died to offer to the world a moving
symbol, an allegorical figure not of marble, or of literary
descriptive phrases, not of art or poetry, but of the same stuff
as ourselves, if, indeed, it be not an error to look on ourselves
as made of any stuff other than that of dreams.*

*It was in connection with this portion of his Christianity
that Blake found the life of any imaginary or poetic personage,
even if invented entirely by himself, to have a sacredness such
as we all attribute to human life, and it logically followed that
to kill such a personage was a ' murder.'   He used the word
during his life, both in writing and conversation, in this non-
popular and purely technical sense, more than once.   He uses
' adultery' in a similarly symbolic manner.*

*He wrote ' The Everlasting Gospel' when raging against
Stothard, whose design illustrating Chaucer's Canterbury
Pilgrims was made under an arrangement with Cromek the
publisher, with the intention of rivalling that on which he was
engaged.   He looked on the publisher's action as wicked, and
on Stothard as unimaginative.   Stothard's view of imagination
in its ' logos' aspect—that is to say, his ' vision of Christ'—
was different in every way from Blake's own.   In the dedication of the poem to Stothard, the reference to the nose must be
read with the remembrance that Blake held body to be a part of
mind, made by mind, if perceived only by the five senses.*

*Probably Blake saw later on that it was out of keeping with
the higher intention of his poem to write of the nose in this
personal and hasty manner, and it is conceivable that he
dropped the whole of the dedication from his poem for the sake
of the second and third line, which Mr. Yeats omits with a
note, and the editor of ' Gilchrist' without one,*

*This dedication was not labelled with any such word as
'Proem,' 'Introduction,' or 'Preludium,' and we find no
place for it in the body of the work.   Here it is:—*

> 'The Vision of Christ that thou dost see
> Is my vision's greatest enemy.
> Thine has a long hooked nose like thine,
> Mine has a snub nose like mine.
> Thine is the Friend of All Mankind,
> Mine speaks in parables to the blind.
> Thine loves the same world that mine hates,
> Thy heaven-doors are my hell-gates.
> Socrates taught what Melitus
> Loathed as a nation's bitterest curse,
> And Caiaphas was, in his own mind,
> A benefactor to mankind.
> Both read the Bible day and night,
> But thou read'st black where I read white.'

*In actual drawings Blake so far modified his 'vision of
Christ' as to lengthen the nose at least to the conventional proportion.   Changing his will, he changed his vision.   He always
asserted that vision was, and should be, subject to will.   Will
alone, of all human attributes, must not be subjugated, though
it may be improved and varied by inspiration 'of the Holy Ghost,
or by the advice of a friend.'   In this doctrine of the power
of the will over vision, we find a refutation of the theory that
Blake was mad, though he never himself put it forward for
the purpose of vindicating his sanity.   Compare 'Jerusalem,'
p. 44, ll. 1-20, and p. 92, l. 12.*

*Blake seems to have begun to write the present poem merely
as a plea, with Biblical sanction, for a wrathful and violent
mood of mind under injuries.   He was probably roused to it
by being addressed (in some verses) by Hayley as 'gentle,
visionary Blake.'   It has therefore no claim to the title that
belongs to the second form of it only.*

*The poem was therefore as much an outcome of resentment
as most of the epigrams, or as the 'Screwmuch' lines.   But
Blake's mind was in the act of liberating itself from the merely
personal mood and rising to the imaginative.   Or, in his
way of understanding Biblical language, he was leaving the
Satanic and entering the Christian state.   To preach this and
its only way of attainment, namely, by considering sin from
so high a point of view that our minds can meet it with forgiveness, was actually and precisely the 'Everlasting Gospel.'
He therefore gave this title to the remaining fragments, and
dropped Part I. out of his scheme.   In the writing of this
first form of the poem, the appearance of the MS. suggests that*

*it was copied all at once into the MS. book after all the rest,
from some scraps outside, in which the words themselves and the
fact that they were outside, suggest that they must have formed
an earlier and now rejected poem.   Then the MS. book began
to be used to jot down a new composition on the same subject.*

*Readers wishing to follow Mr. Yeats's treatment of this can
do so by omitting the first twelve lines of it, and placing the
remainder between the line ' When the soul slept in beams of
light' and ' Was Jesus chaste, or did he' of the still fragmentary second part.   The only drawback to this arrangement
is that it disguises the changes of mood under which Blake
wrote by weaving a first mental impulse among the second
thoughts that arose out of it and one complete poem among the
fragments of another.   The advantage of presenting as many
'fine passages' as possible from the author's MS. in the
semblance of a single composition is rather dearly purchased.
We lose a real and personal comprehension of the author himself, which the present, or as it may be called the biographical,
method of printing enables us to retain.*

*Some differences may be seen between the text and that
arranged by Mr. Yeats in the order of the lines in the second
form of the poem that begins ' Was Jesus humble.'   They are
of secondary importance, and have been made unwillingly
after much revision.*

FIRST FORM : WITHOUT TITLE

I

Was Jesus gentle, or did He
Give any marks of gentility?
When twelve years old He ran away,
And left His parents in dismay.
When after three days' sorrow found,
Loud as Sinai's trumpet's sound,—
' No, earthly parents, I confess
My heavenly Father's business.
Ye understand not what I say,
And, angry, force me to obey.'
Obedience is a duty, then,
And favour gains with God and men.
John from the wilderness loud cried ;
Satan gloried in his pride.
'Come,' said Satan, 'come away ;
I 'll soon see if you obey.'

John for disobedience bled,
But you can turn the stones to bread.
God's high king and God's high priest
20 Shall plant their glories in your breast,
If Caiaphas you will obey.
If Herod you with bloody prey
Feed with the sacrifice, and be
Obedient; fall down, worship me.'
25 Thunders and lightnings broke around,
And Jesus' voice in the thunders sound.
'Thus I seize the spiritual prey.
Ye smiters with disease make way.
I come, your King and God, to seize.
30 Is God a smiter with disease?'
The God of this world raged in vain,
He bound old Satan in His chain,
And, bursting forth, His furious ire
Became a chariot of fire.
35 Throughout the land He took His course,
And traced diseases to their source.
He cursed the scribe and Pharisee,
Trampling down hypocrisy.
Where'er His chariot took its way,
40 The gates of Death let in the day,
Broke down from every chain a bar,
And Satan in his spiritual war
Dragged at His chariot-wheels.   Loud howl'd
The God of this world.   Louder rolled
45 The chariot-wheels, and louder still
His voice was heard from Zion's hill,
And in His hand the scourge shone bright.
He scourged the merchant Canaanite
From out the temple of his mind,
50 And in his body tight does bind
Satan and all his hellish crew;
And thus with wrath He did subdue
The serpent bulk of Nature's dross,
Till He had nailed it to the cross.
55 He took on sin in the virgin's womb,
And put it off on the cross and tomb,
To be worshipped by the Church of Rome.

Final Version; first use of Title

Lines 3 and 4 are written in later. Line 26 ended a paragraph, and line 47 was next, until Blake wrote in all that now comes between, covering a pencil sketch with them. The interpolation was to have ended at line 34. The next are re-numbered, and rearranged puzzlingly among themselves. Then the lines 41 to 44 were added, and the insertion was to have ended there; but lines 45 and 46 were crammed in along the margin at the last moment.

Was Jesus humble, or did He
Give any proofs of humility;
Boast of high things with a humble tone,
And give with charity a stone?
5 When but a child He ran away,
And left His parents in dismay.
When they had wandered three days long
This was the word upon His tongue:
'No, earthly parents, I confess
10 I am doing My Father's business.'
When the rich learned Pharisee
Came to consult Him secretly,
Upon his heart with iron pen
He wrote, 'Ye must be born again.'
15 He was too proud to take a bribe;
He spoke with authority, not like a scribe.
He says, with most consummate art,
'Follow me: I am meek and lowly of heart,'
As that is the only way to escape
20 The miser's net and the glutton's trap.
He who loves his enemies hates his friends.
This surely was not what Jesus intends,
But the sneaking pride of heroic schools,
And the scribes' and Pharisees' virtuous rules;
25 But he acts with honest triumphant pride,
And this is the cause that Jesus died.
He did not die with Christian ease,
Asking pardon of His enemies.
If He had, Caiaphas would forgive:
30 Sneaking submission can always live.

He had only to say that God was the Devil,
And the Devil was God, like a Christian civil.
Mild Christian regrets to the Devil confess
For affronting him thrice in the wilderness.
35 Like to Priestley, and Bacon, and Newton,
Poor spiritual knowledge is not worth a button.
But thus the Gospel St. Isaac confutes,
'God can only be known by His attributes.'
He had soon been bloody Cæsar's elf,
40 And at last he would have been Cæsar himself.
And as for the indwelling of the Holy Ghost,
Or Christ and His Father, it's all a boast,
Or pride and fallacy of the imagination,
That disdains to follow this world's fashion.
45 To teach doubt and experiment,
Certainly was not what Christ meant.

What was He doing all that time,
From ten years old to manly prime?
Was He then idle, or the less,
50 About His Father's business?
Or was His wisdom held in scorn,
Before His wrath began to burn,
In miracles throughout the land,
That quite unnerved the (?) seraph hand?
55 If He had been Antichrist—creeping Jesus—
He'd have done anything to please us:
Gone sneaking into synagogues,
And not used the elders and priests like dogs,
But humble as a lamb or ass,
60 Obeyed Himself to Caiaphas.
God wants not man to humble himself.
That is the trick of the ancient elf.
This is the race that Jesus ran:
Humble to God, haughty to man,
65 Cursing the rulers before the people,
Even to the temple's highest steeple.
And when He humbled Himself to God,
Then descended the cruel rod.
If thou humblest thyself thou humblest Me.
70 Thou also dwellest in eternity.

Thou art a man.   God is no more.
Thy own humanity learn to adore ;
For that is my spirit of life.
Awake, arise to spiritual strife,
75 And thy revenge abroad display,
In terrors at the last judgment day.
God's mercy and long suffering
Are but the sinner to justice to bring.
Thou on the cross for them shall pray,
80 And take revenge at the last day.
Jesus replied in thunders hurled,
' I never will pray for the world ;
Once I did so when I prayed in the garden.
I wished to take with Me a bodily pardon.
85 Can that which was of women born,
In the absence of the morn,
When the soul fell into sleep,
And archangels round it weep,
Shooting out against the light,
90 Fibres of a deadly night,
Reasoning upon its own dark fiction,
In doubt, which is self-contradiction?
Humility is only doubt,
And does the sun and moon blot out,
95 Roofing over with thorns and stems
The buried soul and all its gems.
This life's five windows of the soul
Distort the heavens from pole to pole,
And leads you to believe a lie,
100 When you see *with*, not *through* the eye,
Which was born in a night to perish in a night,
When the soul slept in beams of light.'

Was Jesus chaste, or did He
Give any lessons in chastity?
105 The Morning blushed fiery red.
Mary was found in adulterous bed.
Earth groaned beneath, and Heaven above
Trembled at discovery of love.

Jesus was sitting in Moses' chair.
110   They brought the trembling woman there.
Moses commands she be stoned to death.
What was the sound of Jesus' breath?
He laid His hand on Moses' law.
The ancient heavens in silent awe,
115   Writ with curses from pole to pole,
All away began to roll.
The Earth trembling and naked lay
In secret bed of mortal clay.
On Sinai fell the hand Divine,
120   Putting back the bloody shrine,
And she heard the breath of God
As she heard by Eden's flood.
' Good and evil are no more;
Sinai's trumpets cease to roar.
125   Cease, finger of God, to write;
The heavens are not clean in Thy sight.
Thou art good, and Thou alone;
Nor may the sinner cast one stone.
To be good only, is to be
130   As God or else a Pharisee.
Thou Angel of the Presence Divine,
That didst create this body of mine,
Wherefore hast thou writ these laws
And created Hell's dark jaws?
135   My presence I will take from thee,
A cold leper thou shalt be,
Though thou wast so pure and bright
That Heaven was not clean in thy sight;
Though thy oath turned Heaven pale,
140   Though thy covenant built Hell's jail;
Though thou dost all to chaos roll
With the serpent for its soul.
Still the breath Divine does move,
And the breath Divine is love.
145   Mary, fear not.   Let me see
The seven devils that torment thee.
Hide not from my sight thy sin,
That forgiveness thou mayst win.

Has no man condemned thee?'
150 'No man, Lord.'   'Then what is he
Who shall accuse thee?   Come ye forth,
Fallen fiends of Heavenly birth
That have forgot your ancient love
And driven away my trembling dove.
155 You shall bow before her feet;
You shall lick the dust for meat,
And though you cannot love, but hate,
You shall be beggars at love's gate.
What was thy love?   Let me see it.
160 Was it love, or dark deceit?'
'Love too long from me has fled.
'Twas dark deceit to earn my bread.
'Twas covet, or 'twas custom, or
Some trifle not worth caring for,
165 That they may call a shame and sin;
Love's temple that God dwelleth in,
And hide in secret hidden shrine
The naked human form divine
And render that a lawless thing
170 On which the soul expands her wing.
But this, O Lord, this was my sin,
When first I let the devils in,
In dark pretence to chastity,
Blaspheming love, blaspheming Thee.
175 Thence rose secret adulteries,
And thence did covet also rise.
My sin thou hast forgiven me.
Canst thou forgive my blasphemy?
Canst thou return to this dark hell,
180 And in my burning bosom dwell?
And canst thou die that I may live,
And canst thou pity and 'forgive'?
Then rolled the shadowy Man away
From the limbs of Jesus to make them his
            prey,
185 An ever-devouring appetite,
Glistering with festering venoms bright,

Saying,—'Crucify this cause of distress,
Who don't keep the secret of holiness!'
The mental powers by disease we bind,
190   But he heals the deaf, the dumb, the blind.
Whom God hath afflicted for secret ends,
He comforts and heals and calls them friends.'
But when Jesus was crucified,
Then was perfected His galling pride.
195   In three days he devoured his prey,
And still devours this body of clay.
For dust and clay is the serpent's meat
That never was meant for man to eat.

Was Jesus born of a virgin pure
200   With narrow soul and looks demure?
If He intended to take on sin
His mother should an harlot have been,
Just such a one as Magdalen
With seven devils in her pen.
205   Or were Jew virgins still more cursed,
And with more sucking devils nursed?
Or what was it that he took on
That he might bring salvation?
A body subject to be tempted,
210   From neither pain nor grief exempted,—
Or such a body as might not feel
The passions that with sinners deal?
Yes, but they say he never fell.
Ask Caiaphas, for he can tell.
215   He mocked the Sabbath, and he mocked
The Sabbath's God, and he unlocked
The evil spirits from their shrines,
And turned fishermen to divines,
O'erturned the tent of secret sins,
220   And all its golden cords and pins;
'Tis the bloody shrine of war,
Poured around from star to star,—
Halls of justice, hating vice,
Where the devil combs his lice.

225 He turned the devils into swine
That he might tempt the Jews to dine;
Since when a pig has got a look
That for a Jew may be mistook.
'Obey your parents.'   What says he?
230 'Woman, what have I to do with thee?
No earthly parents I confess,
I am doing my father's business.'
He scorned earth's parents, scorned earth's God,
And mocked the one and the other rod;
235 His seventy disciples sent
Against religion and government,
They by the sword of Justice fell,
And him their cruel murderer tell.
He left his father's trade to roam
240 A wandering vagrant without home,
And thus he others' labours stole
That he might live above control.
The publicans and harlots he
Selected for his company,
245 And from the adultress turned away
God's righteous law that lost its prey.

POSTSCRIPT

I AM sure this Jesus will not do
Either for Englishman or Jew.

*The editor offers this as a mere guess at Blake's own
arrangement, after constantly studying the MS., which is
written in a mass of scraps, the later portions often preceding
the earlier, yet betraying themselves as not intended to be taken
first.*

LA FAYETTE

This short poem stands alone in Blake's work. It belongs to no series or collection. It seems to have been intended for ' The French Revolution,' a Book referred to by Blake as written, but of which nothing is known now but its title, and the bare fact mentioned in ' Gilchrist' that it was printed and is lost.

1

FAYETTE beside King Lewis stood,
He saw him sign his hand,
And soon he saw the famine rage
About the fruitful land.

2

Fayette liked the Queen to smile
And wink her lovely eye,
And soon he saw the pestilence
From street to street to fly.

3

Fayette beheld the King and Queen
In tears of iron bound,
And mute Fayette wept tear for tear
And guarded them around.

4

' Let the brothels of Paris be opened
With many an alluring dance,
To awake the pestilence through the city,'
Said the beautiful Queen of France.

5

The King awoke on his couch of gold
As soon as he heard these tidings told :
' Arise and come, both fife and drum,
And the famine shall eat both crust and
        crumb,'

6

The Queen of France just touched this globe,
And the pestilence darted from her robe ;
But our own good Queen quite grows to the ground,
And a great many suckers grow all around.

7

Who will exchange his own fireside
For the steps of another's door ?
Who will exchange his wheaten loaf
For the links of a dungeon floor ?

Blake often altered his mind about what verses he considered best to select as a final text of this poem.   In the Quaritch edition an attempt is made to give all that he wrote, much as they came from his mind, the purpose being there mainly interpretative.   Here a single principle is followed.   Only such verses are printed as were never at any time crossed out by Blake in the manuscript.   These, as will be seen here, form, in 'La Fayette,' a coherent symbolic poem —six verses of parable, and one of suggestive, though equally figurative, interpretation.   It must be supposed to be the author's definitive and final text.   The personages of the story are figures representing moods of the human mind.   If it is reread in the light of the Prophetic Books, and the analogies between Luvah (who was once imprisoned by Vala in the furnaces of affliction) and Urizen, with Fayette and the King of France are noted, an idea of what Blake saw in it may be obtained.

The metals here are also used as in the Prophetic Books— iron (love), and gold (intellect).   So are the tears (nets), pestilence (the deadly sin of mental idleness leading to materialistic deception and the mixed mood called harlotry), the own fireside (the natural heart), and so forth.

In the 'Resentment' epigrams this symbolic use is not to be found, and wherever it is absent the writing stands outside Blake's real life's work.

BLAKE'S OWN IDEA OF GOOD AND EVIL

Underneath all the fluctuating moods caused by his hopes, fears, troubles, and quarrels, a thread of coherence may be seen to bind Blake's fury, if we keep his chief moral beliefs always in sight. Blake held that Good is Existence and Fellowship, Evil is Illusion and Egotism. He had beyond this a number of particular beliefs of which this is the foundation.

To begin with, he was philosophically convinced that our apparently real world exists for us merely by a 'contraction' of our mind from the mind of God, of which it is a part. This contraction causes an appearance, but does not produce a fact. Therefore God cannot exist in it and outside us.

The simplest practical illustration of what this means may be found if we consider that we should never know the shape of anything by looking at it if we did not see it in perspective. Yet if we forget for a moment that perspective is no fact, but a disguise caused by limitation of visuality, we make just such a mistake as a child does when, on looking down a tunnel, it thinks the further end no bigger than its hand.

The All-seeing Eye, of course, does not see in perspective. It sees the inside of a box, the outside, the top, and the bottom at once—a manner of beholding so very uncontracted that if we could see a box in the same manner, we should not even perceive that it was a box at all.

Mind being unknown to us except as human, from which we conjecture all other, above or below, one of Blake's names for the Complete or Divine Mind was Humanity. For the most contracted or personal form, so long as this does not lead to illusion—to the child's error about the perspective of a tunnel— he took the name Adam. For illusion, from which we are never quite free now, he took the name of the great deceiver— Satan.

Besides perception, always tempting us to error, by leading through narrow to mistaken personality, there is 'Imagination' always inviting us to truth. For this Blake took the name of the Saviour, or Humanity free from Adam's narrowness or Satan's falseness. That we shall enter into this, he considered was what Scripture means when it says we shall 'meet the Lord in the air.'

Meanwhile we must remember that there are aspects of each of these realities or names that are full of vivid feeling. These emanate from them as Eve from the side of Adam. If separated altogether, the 'Emanation' leaves the personality a most abominable thing—Blake found for it the name 'Spectre.' It is life without love, yet with the desire of power and possession constituting a side of love.

The Emanation of the Man was the feeling, which the Son Himself has compared to the desire of a hen to gather together her chickens under her wing. Blake called it after the town which has stood for the greatest and longest felt desire of reunion that a long scattered race has shown in the world's history. He named it 'Jerusalem.' In most of its aspects, especially in the form called friendship, we all have to do with it. As we rise and expand, it becomes indistinguishable from the Holy Ghost, the Comforter, also discernible in Desire.

The Emanation of Adam is the contracted side of the same feeling. It is found in the true Feminine, affectionate and fruitful, wherever this is. It is Eve, in relation to Adam, but in other relations it has other names. It is constantly tending to evil, as the Emotion or Emanation of Contraction must. The emotion of smallness felt when the further end of a tunnel is seen would be evil if it checked our hope of going down the tunnel and kept us fixed in despair.

The Feminine is thus closely related to the Satanic (the Deceptive). The philosophy of this is, of course, familiar to us through the story of the Garden of Eden. The mystic symbol Virgo-scorpio repeats it. In 'Vala,' Blake gives it in poetry.

Satan's own Emanation is the False, or Opaque Feminine, the feelings that deceitfully mix themselves with ideas, thereby falsifying them. This is usually called, by Blake, 'Rahab.' The fatal mixture is referred to wherever harlotry is mentioned. In impersonal, or non-figurative language, it is to be explained conveniently by the term 'Natural Religion,' itself a contradiction in terms, since when we say Nature we mean the deceptive perspective opacity of things, or Satan, and when we say religion—unless we use the term in a popular or nonmystic manner—we mean the imaginative perception of the error of opacity, and our release from it through Faith.

The philosophic system worked out through these sources of description, these definitions, goes on to assert a relation between morality, law, and life that must also be studied in all its consequences, however paradoxical it may seem at first, before even the simplest of Blake's poems can be understood as he intended.

Such being (very briefly and incompletely) the account of Blake's idea of mental Good and Evil, his idea of the Incarnation, of the Fall (the same thing in another aspect)—the Redemption and Judgment follow as a matter of course. Developments of his system between the date of the 'Marriage of Heaven and Hell,' 1790, and that of the 'Everlasting Gospel,' about twenty years later, are more numerous and elaborate than can be noted here. They are often highly paradoxical and subtle, but are always coherent.

In reading what he says in different places, we must watch continually to be sure when he uses his terms in popular sense, and when in mystical, that is to say, in accurate sense. When this caution is remembered, the apparent confusion of his upholding in one place what he denounces in another will generally turn into an interpretation, and cease to be a confusion. The meaning of the symbols of the Four Points, and of the Two Contraries, will put most of the rest of the seeming self-contradiction into clear order. Finally, all will be seen, when all is familiar, to be all significant and sane.

At the same time, we must expect to find him showing partisanship and taking sides, now all for energy and lawlessness, now for religious contemplation that is its own law,—always against restraint, since, at the best, the abnegation that bows under obedience checks the vitality that might go to spontaneous virtue. And yet, it must be also remembered—

'To be quite perfect is to be
A God—or else a Pharisee.'

THE BACKBONE OF THE SYMBOLISMS

The use of the word 'contraction' leads naturally to an understanding of the use of the word 'imagination,' which explains Blake's religious belief in it, and his employment of symbols. He invented these as an act of an essentially religious character. He told their stories as other men relate their heavenly hopes. He may have been, and was, biassed and injudicious. He himself tells how 'vision' may be 'infected.' It is certain that, notwithstanding this admission, he believed himself to be inspired. People without imagination are not deterred from believing their own eyes by knowing that we all see differently, and often, if not always, incorrectly.

Since all apparent Nature is the result of contraction on the faculties of unapparent Nature or Mind, we can elude the disadvantages of this contraction sometimes by considering things as symbols. Their suggestiveness expands, and with it their mentality or reality. If we go a step further, and actually invent things unknown to us by imagination from such as are so known, and take these as the instruments for realising to us what is beyond detailed perception, we are actually doing Divine work, that of Creation, since Mind is Real and Reality is One. That mathematicians do much the same thing when they deal with X, Y, and Z, Blake, fortunately for his readers, did not know. We cannot be too thankful for his hatred of Sir Isaac Newton, a man more like himself in shape of brow, expression of face, genius, and personal history, than any other of his age, and differing from him chiefly as the power of the sea and its methods differ from the power and methods of volcanic lava.

When Blake looked at the experiences of his own life, and when he read the Bible, he was always strongly moved to see *symbolic opportunity in both, and did so.   In his later years he saw the same to a harassing degree in the map of the United Kingdom, its countries, towns, rivers, and hills.*

Blake's own justification of this is to be found in the 'Marriage of Heaven and Hell,' p. 11, and in 'Jerusalem,' p. 40, line 58.

In his early life he especially looked for symbol in the form of contraction of the Divine Mind that we call Anatomy.   The nerves lend themselves to many discoveries of the more expanded action of Mind,--the blood to many others.   A tale about this is told in the poem of the 'Mental Traveller' from a point impersonal to Blake himself, and an aspect of it is hinted in the 'Argument' of the 'Marriage of Heaven and Hell' from nearer home.   'Broken Love' tells another story of the descendants, as it were, of the persons in the 'Mental Traveller.'

In what sense attributes of the mind are persons, and even seem so to one another, is studied in the notes to 'Vala' further on.

Contraction and Expansion are not the only realities of motion (as distinct from realities of form) over which we have control.   There are Division and Reunion—a symbol may be divided into myths, understood and restored to simplicity, but no longer to monotony.   There is also Upward Motion, towards Reality and Mind's Sight; and Downward, towards the brute reason or Mind's Darkness, out of which Delusion will be perpetually formed unless Mind's Sight go continually and boldly into it, as a hero to death for a cause, and win from the enemy the opposite of what the enemy came to give. In this is one real and mental equivalent for that which is figured in the Christian ceremony which has come down to us in the form of the Mass.   Each man can do it as far as Divine Power allows him.   But, said Blake, one man cannot confer on another the power to do it, though he may enable the other to obtain that power.   Not being a theologian, he did not understand the enabling limitation implied in the doctrine whose whole statement is the single word 'grace,' whose logical outcome is not usually proclaimed from pastoral lips.   He was as violently against priests as against mathematicians.   As a matter of fact, it may be noted that all the priests and mathematicians together did not take a step towards helping any of the poets to understand Blake or rescue him from those who robbed him of his influence, and wounded him with the slander of insanity during the long century that is now over since his symbolic and imaginative philosophy of science and religion was first offered to the world.   They looked on him and passed by on the other side.

BLAKE'S EARLIEST EXPLANATION(?)

The exact date of the following is not yet ascertained. The 'First Principle' would have great philosophic value if we could only tell the meaning of the word 'derived.' The Fourth has a distinctly Socratic flavour. These 'Principles' are printed here from illustrated leaves in the possession of the Linnell family, and seem to be a first form of the set of short paragraphs in similar strain, printed perhaps about 1790, of which there is a copy in the British Museum Print-Room. If we add to it the word 'unintelligently' after the word 'travelling,' we may add to the accuracy of the statement, but the word 'therefore' ceases to be serious.

There is no Natural Religion.

The voice of one crying in the wilderness.

The Argument.

As the true method of knowledge is experiment, the true faculty of knowing must be the faculty which experiences. This faculty I treat of.

Principle First.

That the Poetic Genius is the true Man, and that the body or outward form of Man is derived from the Poetic Genius. Likewise that the forms of all things are derived from their Genius, which by the Ancients was called an Angel, Spirit, and Demon.

Principle Second.

As all men are alike in outward form, so (and with the same infinite variety) are all alike in the Poetic Genius.

Principle Third.

No man can write or speak from his heart but he must intend truth. Thus all sects of Philosophy are from the Poetic Genius, adapted to the weakness of every individual.

Principle Fourth.

As none by travelling over known lands can find out the unknown, so, from already acquired knowledge, Man could not acquire more ; therefore an universal Poetic Genius exists.

Principle Fifth.

The Religions of all Nations are derived from each Nation's different reception of the Poetic Genius, which is everywhere called the Spirit of Prophecy.

Principle Sixth.

The Jewish and Christian Testaments are an original derivation from the Poetic Genius. This is necessary from the confined nature of bodily sensation.

Principle Seventh.

As all men are alike (though infinitely various), so all Religions, as all similars, have one source.

The True Man is the source, he being the Poetic Genius.

PRINTED MANIFESTO FROM THE BRITISH MUSEUM.

(No title.)

The Argument.

Man has no notion of moral fitness but from Education. Naturally he is only a natural organ subject to sense.

I

Man's perceptions are not bound by organs of perception ; he perceives more than sense (though ever so acute) can discover.

II

Reason, or the ratio of all we have already known, is not the same that it shall be when we shall know more.

III

From a perception of only three senses or three elements, none could deduce a fourth or fifth.

IV

None could have other than natural or organic thoughts if he had none but organic perceptions.

V

Man's desires are limited by his perceptions. None can desire what he has not perceived.

VI

The desires and perceptions of man, untaught by anything but organic sense, must be limited to objects of sense.

Therefore,

God becomes as we are, that we may be as he is.

I

Man cannot naturally perceive but through his natural or bodily organs.

II

Man by his reasoning power can only compare and judge of what he has already perceived.

These two last paragraphs are, like each of those preceding, from plates on which they were written in varnish for ink, and then the metal round the letters bitten away by acid, and the result rolled and printed like ordinary type or blocks. Each paragraph is on a little plate by itself. It is impossible to know now whether or not these last two were a first two, lost, and found again after substitutes were made. The little book has one more plate, a drawing, a picture of pastoral life, and so ends.

There is another issue of these little fragments in the possession of Mr. Muir, who has made a facsimile copy of it (Quaritch, 15 Piccadilly).   Its title is

ALL RELIGIONS ARE ONE.

Then follows Nos. I. and II., as in the British Museum example printed above.   No. III. is not in Mr. Muir's set. The rest are as follows:—

IV

The bounded is loathed by its possessor.   The same dull round, even of a universe, would soon become a mill with complicated wheels.

V

If the many become the same as the few, when possessed, 'More! More!' is the cry of a mistaken soul.   Less than all cannot satisfy Man.

VI

If any could desire what he is incapable of possessing, despair must be his eternal lot.

VII

The desire of Man being Infinite, the possession is Infinite, and himself Infinite.

Application.

He who sees the Infinite in all things, sees God. He who sees the Ratio only, sees himself only.

Therefore

God becomes as we are that we may be as He is.

ON HOMER'S POETRY

*The following, introduced here as part of the author's
explanation of himself, was printed by Gilchrist on two pages
and called 'Sybilline Leaves.' This is a fancy title. Blake
printed both the short essays from one plate, prepared like the
pages of all his work later in date than 1787. Its period may
be conjectured from the style to be later than 1802. Its handwriting is like plates of 'Jerusalem' that are later than this.
The matter probably belongs to this period, because he was
now learning Greek and reading Homer with Hayley at
Felpham, as a letter from Hayley to Johnson, dated February
3, 1802, relates. Traces of irritation, produced by Hayley's
tutorship, are found in the very first lines.*

*The title 'On Homer's Poetry' is written in a bold hand at
the head of his first five paragraphs, and 'On Virgil' similarly
at the head of the next four.*

Every poem must necessarily be a perfect Unity,
but why Homer's is peculiarly so I cannot tell. He
has told the story of Belerophon, and omitted the
Judgement of Paris, which is not only a part, but a
principal part of Homer's subject.

But when a work has Unity, it is as much in a part
as in the whole. The Torso is as much a Unity as
the Laocoon.

As Unity is the cloak of folly, so Goodness is the
cloak of knavery. Those who will have Unity ex-
clusively in Homer, come out with a Moral like a
sting in the tail. Aristotle says Characters are either
Good or Bad. Now Goodness or Badness has nothing
to do with Character. An Apple tree, a Pear tree, a
Horse, a Lion, are Characters, but a Good Apple
tree or a Bad is an Apple tree still. A Horse is not
more a Lion for being a Bad Horse; that is its
Character : its Goodness or Badness is another consideration.

It is the same with the Moral of a whole Poem as
with the Moral Goodness of its parts. Unity and
Morality are secondary considerations, and belong to
Philosophy and not to Poetry, to Exception and not

to Rule, to Accident and not to Substance. The
Ancients called it eating the tree of good and evil.

The Classics ! It is the Classics, and not Goths nor
Monks that Desolate Europe with Wars.

ON VIRGIL

Sacred Truth has pronounced that Greece and
Rome, as Babylon and Egypt, so far from being
parents of Arts and Sciences, as they pretend, were
destroyers of all Art.   Homer, Virgil, and Ovid confirm this opinion, and make us reverence the Word
of God, the only light of antiquity that remains
unperverted by War.   Virgil in the *Æneid*, Book vi.,
line 848, says—'Let others study Art. Rome has
somewhat better to do, namely, War and Dominion.'

Rome and Greece swept Art into their maw and
destroyed it.   A Warlike state can never produce Art.
It will Rob and Plunder and accumulate into one
place, and Translate and Copy, and Buy and Sell and
Criticise, but not Make.   Grecian is Mathematic
Form.

Mathematic Form is Eternal in the Reasoning
Memory ; Living Form is Eternal Existence.

Gothic is Living Form.

THE PROPHETIC BOOKS

With 'The Prophetic Books' a new kind of literature began in the modern world. In matter they were grafted on older ideas. They arose directly from what Blake had learned from Swedenborg and Bœhmen, and what he picked up of the Kabalists and other mystics from sources that we can only conjecture. The one thing in which these prophetic books stand alone is the telling what was new, and interpreting what was old, in the form of poetic myth, a form practically out of use since history began.

The word prophecy was adopted by Blake mainly after the manner of the use of it that describes the Vision of Ezekiel as Prophetic writing. He believed himself to have a perfect right to do this, being inspired in the same sense in which Ezekiel was inspired. Such a belief is not uncommon in persons suffering from religious mania. Those who know Blake's works best are least likely to attribute it, in his case, to this deplorable cause. It is due to his Swedenborgian education. Swedenborg says, 'To prophesy means to teach.'

It will be noticed that the title 'Prophecy' was at first given by Blake only to 'America' and 'Europe,' dated 1793, 1794. They dwell particularly on mental release from unimaginativeness following the uprising of bodily passions and employing hints from the terms of these for symbol. This suggests that they were written as part of the Bible of Hell—promised in the 'Marriage of Heaven and Hell.' The term 'prophetic' has been popularly remembered and extended.

So far as possible, the Prophetic Books here follow in the order in which they were written. But in the later books are pages written during the days of the earlier; and some of the earlier had thrust into them pages, or terms, belonging to a later period of Blake's mental progress than the rest of their composition.

All these books Blake engraved himself. In 'Jerusalem,' for which he claimed verbal accuracy, his misprints are followed, though not his punctuation.

The numberings by which pages are indicated when any of Blake's words are quoted in any note here are not to be understood as the numberings of the pages in these volumes, but in whichever of Blake's own books is under reference. 'Vala' is an exception, since the references are to lines that are numbered through each 'Night.' Blake has left no page numberings for this poem, and none are referred to in quotations from it, though they are given in descriptive notes on the state of the MS. All page numberings given by Blake are indicated in this text.

THE GHOST OF ABEL

A Revelation in the Vision of Jehovah, seen by WILLIAM BLAKE

TO LORD BYRON IN THE WILDERNESS

    WHAT dost thou here, Elijah?
Can a Poet doubt the Visions of Jehovah?
Nature has no Outline, but Imagination has.
Nature has no Tune, but Imagination has.
Nature has no Supernatural, and dissolves.
Imagination is Eternity.

SCENE—*A rocky Country.* EVE *fainted over the dead
body of* ABEL, *which lays near a Grave.* ADAM
kneels by her. JEHOVAH *stands above.*

JEHOVAH. Adam!
ADAM.   I will not hear thee more, thou Spiritual
 Voice.
 Is this Death?
JEHOVAH.   Adam!
ADAM.   It is in vain: I will not hear thee
 henceforth.
 Is this thy Promise, that the Woman's Seed
 Should bruise the Serpent's head? Is this the
 Serpent?
 Ah! Seven times, O Eve, thou hast fainted over the
 Dead. Ah! Ah!

      EVE *revives.*

 Is this the Promise of Jehovah? O, it is all a vain
 delusion,

This Death, and this Life, and this Jehovah!

JEHOVAH.   Woman, lift thine eyes.

A Voice is heard coming on.

VOICE. O Earth, cover not thou my Blood; cover not
thou my Blood.

Enter the Ghost *of* ABEL.

EVE. Thou Visionary Phantasm, thou art not the real
Abel.

ABEL. Among the Elohim a Human Victim I wander.
I am their House,
    Prince of the Air, and our dimensions compass
    Zenith and Nadir.
    Vain is thy Covenant, O Jehovah! I am the
    Accuser and Avenger
    Of Blood. O Earth, cover not thou the Blood of
    Abel.

JEHOVAH. What Vengeance dost thou require?

ABEL.   Life for Life! Life for Life!

JEHOVAH. He who shall take Cain's life must also Die,
O Abel,
    And who is He? Adam, wilt thou, or Eve, thou, do
    this?

ADAM. It is all a vain delusion of the all-creative
Imagination.
    Eve, come away, and let us not believe these vain
    delusions.
    Abel is dead, and Cain slew him. We shall also Die
    a Death,
    And then, what then? be as poor Abel, a Thought:
    or as
    This! O what shall I call thee, Form Divine,
    Father of Mercies,
    That appearest to my Spiritual Vision? Eve, seest
    thou also?

EVE. I see him plainly with my Mind's Eye. I see
also Abel living.
    Though terribly afflicted as we also are, yet Jehovah
    sees him

Alive and not Dead.   Were it not better to believe
Vision
With all our might and strength, tho' we are fallen
and lost?

ADAM. Eve, thou hast spoken truly : let us kneel
before His feet.

They kneel before JEHOVAH.

ABEL. Are these the Sacrifices of Eternity, O Jehovah ?
A Broken Spirit and a Contrite Heart, O, I cannot
forgive !
The Accuser hath entered into me as into his
House, and I loathe thy Tabernacles.
As thou hast said, so is it come to pass.   My
desire is unto Cain,
And He doth rule over Me : therefore my Soul in
Fumes of Blood
Cries for Vengeance : Sacrifice on Sacrifice, Blood
on Blood.

JEHOVAH. Lo ! I have given you a Lamb for an Atonement instead
Of the Transgressor, or no Flesh or Blood could
ever live.

ABEL. Compelled I cry, O Earth, cover not the Blood
of Abel.

ABEL *sinks down into the Grave, from which arises* SATAN,
armed in glittering scales, with a Crown and a Spear.

SATAN. I will have Human Blood, and not the blood of
Bulls or Goats,
And no Atonement.   O Jehovah, the Elohim live on
Sacrifice
Of Men : hence I am God of Men : Thou Human,
O Jehovah.
By the Rock and Oak of the Druid, creeping
Mistletoe, and Thorn,
Cain's City built with Human Blood, not Blood
of Bulls and Goats,

Thou shalt Thyself be Sacrificed to Me, thy God, on
Calvary.
JEHOVAH. Such is My Will, [*Thunders*] that thou
Thyself go to Eternal Death
In Self-Annihilation, even till Satan Self-subdued
Put off Satan
Into the Bottomless Abyss, whose torment arises for
ever and ever.

*On each side a Chorus of Angels entering, sing the
following.*

The Elohim of the Heathen Swore Vengeance for Sin,
Then Thou stoodst
Forth, O Elohim Jehovah, in the midst of the dark-
ness of the Oath, All Clothed
In Thy Covenant of the Forgiveness of Sins. Death,
O Holy ! Is this Brotherhood ?
The Elohim saw their Oath, Eternal Fire ; they rolled
apart, trembling over the
Mercy Seat, each in his station fixt in the firmament
by Peace, Brotherhood, and Love.

The Curtain falls.

1822. W. Blake's original stereotype was 1788.

---

*The stage directions here printed in italic type are Blake's,
and the account of the two dates was also engraved and printed
by him as here given.*

*These dates suggest that this book was his first. However,
it is neither probable nor credible that he engraved it in
1822, which is the date of the plate, as it has come to us,
without making any changes : for though Blake hated to
correct his work, he seldom took up again any piece of writing
that had lain aside for a while without inserting among its
sentences newer symbolic terms to bring it abreast of the part
of his system with which his mind was now occupied.*

*In the copy used for the photographic facsimile in the
Quaritch edition, the date was injured, and appears to read
1780. But other copies have been seen to bear 1788 distinctly.*

*What changes were made cannot be precisely known now.
The general tone implies that it was a very early composition.
The term 'Prince of the Air' is not likely to have been used*

in this way after the story of Luvah was invented. The reference to Lord Byron, who was born in 1788, probably belongs to the year before the plate was re-engraved, when it may have been written in a notebook. In 1820 Byron was in Italy conspiring against the Papal government with the friends of Countess Guiccioli. This may be the wilderness from which Blake would recall him to his duties as a poet. The Swiss passages in 'Childe Harold' may have provoked Blake's reproach, as in his later life he was much opposed to 'Nature' as different from 'Art,' Landscape as opposed to Design. In 'Jerusalem,' page 44, line 31 says of 'Los,' the mystic replacer of Apollo, the inspirer of poets beyond classic limits—'Naming him the Spirit of Prophecy—calling him Elijah.'

There is one design to this book. It represents Abel lying face downwards, dead on the ground, while a floating and pained figure called 'The Voice of Abel's Blood' floats away calling sadly for revenge.

THE

BOOK

OF

THEL

The author and printer, WILLM. BLAKE
1789

THE

BOOK

OF

THEL

The author and printer, W. Blake, 1789

THEL'S MOTTO

Does the Eagle know what is in the pit,
Or wilt thou go ask the Mole?
Can Wisdom be put in a silver rod,
Or Love in a golden bowl?

I

THE daughters of The Seraphim led round their
  sunny flocks,
All but the youngest: she in paleness sought the
  secret air,
To fade away like morning beauty from her mortal
  day :
Down by the river of Adona her soft voice is heard,
And thus her gentle lamentation falls like morning
  dew :—

O life of this our spring ! why fades the lotus of the
  water ?
Why fade these children of the spring, born but to
  smile and fall?
Ah ! Thel is like a wat'ry bow, and like a parting
  cloud ;
Like a reflection in a glass ; like shadows in the water;
Like dreams of infants, like a smile upon an infant's
  face ;
Like the dove's voice ; like transient day ; like music
  in the air
Ah ! gentle may I lay me down and gentle rest my
  head,

And gentle sleep the sleep of death, and gently hear
   the voice
Of him that walketh in the garden in the evening
   time.

The Lilly of the valley breathing in the humble grass
Answered the lovely maid and said : I am a wat'ry
   weed,
And I am very small, and love to dwell in lowly vales,
So weak, the gilded butterfly scarce perches on my
   head.
Yet I am visited from heaven, and he that smiles on all
Walks in the valley, and each morn over me spreads
   his hand
Saying, Rejoice, thou humble grass, thou new-born
   lilly-flower,
Thou gentle maid of silent valleys and of modest
   brooks;
For thou shalt be clothed in light, and fed with
   morning manna,
Till summer's heat melts thee beside the fountains
   and the springs
To flourish in eternal vales : then why should Thel
   complain ?

(2)

Why should the mistress of the vales of Har utter a
   sigh ?
She ceas'd, and smil'd in tears, then sat down in her
   silver shrine.

Thel answered : O thou little virgin of the peaceful
   valley,
Giving to those that cannot crave, the voiceless, the
   o'ertired ;
Thy breath doth nourish the innocent lamb, he
   smells thy milky garments,
He crops thy flowers while thou sittest smiling in his
   face,

Wiping his mild and meekin mouth from all con-
    tagious taints.
Thy wine doth purify the golden honey; thy perfume,
Which thou dost scatter on every little blade of grass
    that springs,
Revives the milked cow, and tames the fire-breathing
    steed.
But Thel is like a faint cloud kindled at the rising
    sun.
I vanish from my pearly throne, and who shall find
    my place?
Queen of the vales, the Lilly answered, ask the tender
    cloud,
And it shall tell thee why it glitters in the morning
    sky,
And why it scatters its bright beauty thro' the humid
    air.
Descend, O little cloud, and hover before the eyes of
    Thel.

The Cloud descended, and the Lilly bowed her modest
    head,
And went to mind her numerous charge among the
    verdant grass.

(3)

II

O little Cloud, the virgin said, I charge thee tell to me
Why thou complainest not when in one hour thou
    fade away;
Then we shall seek thee, but not find.   Ah, Thel is like
    to Thee.
I pass away, yet I complain, and no one hears my
    voice.
The cloud then shew'd his golden head and his bright
    form emerg'd,
Hovering and glittering on the air before the face of
    Thel.

O virgin, know'st thou not our steeds drink of the
    golden springs
Where Luvah doth renew his horses? look'st thou on
    my youth,
And fearest thou because I vanish and am seen no
    more?
Nothing remains.   O maid, I tell thee, when I pass
    away,
It is to tenfold life, to love, to peace, and raptures holy:
Unseen descending, weigh my light wings upon balmy
    flowers,
And court the fair-eyed dew, to take me to her
    shining tent.
The weeping virgin, trembling, kneels before the
    risen sun,
Till we arise link'd in a golden band and never part,
But walk united, bearing food to all our tender
    flowers.

Dost thou, O little Cloud? I fear that I am not like
    thee,
For I walk through the vales of Har, and smell the
    sweetest flowers;
But I feed not the little flowers. I hear the warbling
    birds,
But I feed not the warbling birds; they fly and seek
    their food:
But Thel delights in these no more, because I fade
    away,
And all shall say, without a use this shining woman
    liv'd,
Or did she only live to be at death the food of worms?

The Cloud reclin'd upon his airy throne, and
    answer'd thus :—

Then if thou art the food of worms, O virgin of the
    skies,
How great thy use, how great thy blessing; every-
    thing that lives
Lives not alone nor for itself: fear not, and I will call

The weak worm from its lowly bed, and thou shalt
    hear its voice.
Come forth, worm of the silent valley, to thy pensive
    queen.

The helpless worm arose, and sat upon the Lilly's leaf,
And the bright Cloud sail'd on, to find his partner in
    the vale.

(4)

III

Then Thel astonish'd view'd the Worm upon its dewy
    bed.

Art thou a Worm? Image of weakness, art thou
    but a Worm?
I see thee like an infant wrapped in the Lilly's leaf.
Ah weep not, little voice, thou canst not speak, but
    thou canst weep.
Is this a Worm? I see thee lay helpless and naked,
    weeping,
And none to answer, none to cherish thee with
    mother's smiles.

The Clod of Clay heard the Worm's voice and rais'd
    her pitying head;
She bow'd over the weeping infant, and her life exhal'd
In milky fondness, then on Thel she fix'd her humble
    eyes.

O beauty of the vales of Har, we live not for ourselves.
Thou seest me the meanest thing, and so I am indeed.
My bosom of itself is cold, and of itself is dark,

(5)

But he that loves the lowly, pours his oil upon my
    head
And kisses me, and binds his nuptial bands around
    my breast,

And says : Thou mother of my children, I have
    loved thee,
And I have given thee a crown that none can take
    away,
But how this is, sweet maid, I know not, and I cannot
    know.
I ponder, and I cannot ponder ; yet I live and love.

The daughter of beauty wip'd her pitying tears with
    her white veil,
And said, Alas ! I knew not this, and therefore did I
    weep ;
That God would love a Worm I knew, and punish the
    evil foot
That wilful bruis'd its helpless form ; but that He
    cherish'd it
With milk and oil I never knew, and therefore did I
    weep,
And I complain'd in the mild air, because I fade away,
And lay me down in thy cold bed, and leave my
    shining lot.

Queen of the vales, the matron Clay answered ; I
    heard thy sighs,
And all thy moans flew o'er my roof, but I have call'd
    them down :
Wilt thou, O Queen, enter my house ? 'tis given thee
    to enter
And to return : fear nothing, enter with thy virgin
    feet.

                                                (6)

IV.

The eternal gate's terrific porter lifted the northern
    bar :
Thel enter'd in and saw the secrets of the land
    unknown.
She saw the couches of the dead, and where the
    fibrous roots
Of every heart on earth infixes deep its restless twists :

A land of sorrows and of tears where never smile
    was seen.

She wander'd in the land of clouds thro' valleys dark,
    list'ning
Dolours and lamentations; waiting oft beside a dewy
    grave
She stood in silence, list'ning to the voices of the
    ground,
Till to her own grave plot she came, and there she
    sat down,
And heard this voice of sorrow breathed from the
    hollow pit.

Why cannot the Ear be closed to its own destruction?
Or the glist'ning Eye to the poison of a smile?
Why are Eyelids stor'd with arrows ready drawn,
Where a thousand fighting men in ambush lie!
Or an Eye of gifts and graces show'ring fruits and
    coined gold!

Why a Tongue impress'd with honey from every
    wind?
Why an Ear, a whirlpool fierce to draw creations in?
Why a Nostril wide inhaling, terror, trembling, and
    affright?
Why a tender curb upon the youthful, burning boy?
Why a little curtain of flesh on the bed of our desire?

The Virgin started from her seat, and with a shriek
Fled back unhinder'd till she came into the vales
    of Har.

THE END

THE MEANING OF THEL

  '*Thel*' *is not a name for a heroine of romance, but, as it is
essential to remember in order not to miss the whole of Blake's
meaning in the poem, for one of those* '*spirits*' *by whom all*

things are managed for us, 'no less than digestion or sleep.'
That phrase belongs to another Book.

In 'The Book of Thel,' on the first line, the word 'the' before
Seraphim is a conjectural correction. Blake left 'Mne,'
having begun to write Mnetha, and then changed his mind.
On the title-page, Thel as a shepherdess stands under a
bending tree, while the human forms of the love or the
generative substance of two flowers rush out as graceful
floating figures, the female half in flight, the male in joyous
pursuit. The motto has a page to itself without pictures.
Page 1 has some small figures at the head—a minute female
playing with a child in the air above a minute male who
reclines on one ear of corn. In the sky another lets fly
an eagle after a figure with sword and shield, the human
form of a hawk. On page 2 Thel, without her crook, under
the tree, stands bowing gracefully to the human form of the
lily, a small white feminine figure who bows humbly before
her. On page 4 she stands with her back to us, lifting both
arms almost level with her shoulders in mild surprise
at the sweet and childlike form of the baby-worm who smiles
up at her as it lies on its back in grass. The human form
of the cloud, a youth draped in a scarf only, floats gracefully away in the sky, looking back to take leave of her. On
page 5 the Matron Clay sits on the ground facing us, her
head completely bowed over arms folded on her knees. She
looks down at the lily and the worm, a pretty, naked, minute
girl and baby who lie and roll like kittens at her feet. Long
grasses bend over her. At the end the same design of children
riding on a big snake as in 'America' fills the page.

'Thel' is therefore a Western symbol, a dweller in the world
of Tharmas, as it was in the days of innocence.

To follow the ideas in the books, the arrangement of the four
Zoas with the four points of the compass, as given in the early
pages of 'Jerusalem,' and analysed in the notes, must be
familiarly known and clearly understood.

In 'Vala,' Night IX., line 507, etc., the Innocence of
Tharmas renews, yet her business in life, as she is a merely
evanescent influence of beauty, is to be (when she shall enter
her grave-plot—or mortal body—any mortal female) the food
or emotional excitement, or worms, or corporeal mortal men.

Tharmas is called 'the father of worms and clay' in 'Vala,'
Night IV., line 39, and Urthona the 'keeper of the Gates of
Heaven' in line 42 of the same Night.

The passage in 'Jerusalem,' lines 70 to 75 of page 82, and
the context also should be read with 'Thel.'

See also 'Vala,' Night III., lines 144 and 145; Night VIII.,
lines 525 and following; and Night IX., lines 725, etc.

THE MARRIAGE

OF

HEAVEN

AND

HELL

*(There are no other words on Blake's title-page to this book.
A design shows figures in the lower half of it, beneath the
surface of the earth, of feminine youthful forms, one from
flames on the left, one from smoke on the right, that reach to
each other and embrace. The date of the book was 1790.)*

(2)

THE ARGUMENT

RINTRAH roars and shakes his fires in the
    burden'd air ;
Hungry clouds swag on the deep.

Once meek, and in a perilous path,
The just man kept his course along
The vale of death.
Roses are planted where thorns grow,
And on the barren heath
Sing the honey bees.

Then the perilous path was planted,
And a river and a spring
On every cliff and tomb ;
And on the bleached bones,
Red clay brought forth ;

Till the villian left the paths of ease,
To walk in perilous paths, and drive
The just man into barren climes.

Now the sneaking serpent walks
In mild humility,
And the just man rages in the wilds
Where lions roam.

Rintrah roars and shakes his fires in the
    burden'd air ;
Hungry clouds swag on the deep.

(3)

As a new heaven is begun, and it is now thirty-three years since its advent, the Eternal Hell revives. And lo! Swedenborg is the Angel sitting at the tomb; his writings are the linen clothes folded up. Now is the dominion of Edom, and the return of Adam into Paradise. See Isaiah xxxiv. and xxxv. Chap.

Without Contraries is no progression. Attraction and Repulsion, Reason and Energy, Love and Hate, are necessary to Human existence.

From these contraries spring what the religious call Good and Evil. Good is the passive that obeys Reason. Evil is the active springing from Energy. Good is Heaven. Evil is Hell.

(4)

THE VOICE OF THE DEVIL

ALL Bibles or sacred codes have been the causes of the following Errors :—

1. That Man has two real existing principles, viz. a Body and a Soul.

2. That Energy, called Evil, is alone from the Body; and that Reason, called Good, is alone from the Soul.

3. That God will torment Man in Eternity for following his Energies.

But the following Contraries to these are True :—

1. Man has no Body distinct from his Soul, for that called Body is a portion of Soul discerned by the five Senses, the chief inlets of Soul in this age.

2. Energy is the only life and is from the Body, and Reason is the bound or outward circumference of Energy.

3. Energy is Eternal Delight.

(5)

Those who restrain desire, do so because theirs is

weak enough to be restrained ; and the restrainer or
reason usurps its place and governs the unwilling.

And being restrained it by degrees becomes passive
till it is only the shadow of desire.

The history of this is written in *Paradise Lost,* and
the Governor or Reason is called Messiah.

And the original Archangel or possessor of the
command of the heavenly host is called the Devil or
Satan, and his children are called Sin and Death.

But in the Book of Job, Milton's Messiah is called
Satan.

For this history has been adopted by both parties.

It indeed appeared to Reason as if Desire was cast
out, but the Devil's account is, that the Messiah fell,

(6)

and formed a heaven of what he stole from the
Abyss.

This is shown in the Gospel, where he prays to the
Father to send the comforter or Desire that Reason
may have Ideas to build on, the Jehovah of the Bible
being no other than he who dwells in flaming fire.
Know that after Christ's death, he became Jehovah.

But in Milton, the Father is Destiny ; the Son, a
Ratio of the five senses ; and the Holy-ghost, Vacuum !

NOTE.—The reason Milton wrote in fetters when
he wrote of Angels and God, and at liberty when of
Devils and Hell, is because he was a true Poet and of
the Devil's party without knowing it.

A MEMORABLE FANCY

As I was walking among the fires of hell, delighted
with the enjoyments of Genius, which to Angels look
like torment and insanity, I collected some of their
Proverbs ; thinking that as the sayings used in a
nation mark its character, so the Proverbs of Hell
show the nature of Infernal wisdom better than any
description of buildings or garments.

When I came home, on the abyss of the five senses,
where a flat-sided steep frowns over the present
world, I saw a mighty Devil folded in black clouds
hovering on the sides of the rock. With corroding

(7)

fires he wrote the following sentence now perceived
by the minds of men, and read by them on earth :—

How do you know but ev'ry Bird that cuts the airy
    way,
Is an immense world of delight, clos'd by your senses
    five ?

PROVERBS OF HELL

In seed time learn, in harvest teach, in winter
enjoy.

Drive your cart and your plow over the bones of
the dead.

The road of excess leads to the palace of wisdom.

Prudence is a rich, ugly old maid courted by
Incapacity.

He who desires but acts not, breeds pestilence.

The cut worm forgives the plow.

Dip him in the river who loves water.

A fool sees not the same tree that a wise man
sees.

He whose face gives no light, shall never become a
star.

Eternity is in love with the productions of time.

The busy bee has no time for sorrow.

The hours of folly are measur'd by the clock, but of
wisdom no clock can measure.

All wholesome food is caught without a net or a trap.

Bring out number, weight, and measure in a year
of death.

No bird soars too high, if he soars with his own
wings.

A dead body revenges not injuries.

The most sublime act is to set another before you.

If the fool would persist in his folly he would become wise.

Folly is the cloak of knavery.

Shame is Pride's cloak.

(8)

Prisons are built with stones of Law, Brothels with bricks of Religion.

The pride of the peacock is the glory of God.

The lust of the goat is the bounty of God.

The wrath of the lion is the wisdom of God.

The nakedness of woman is the work of God.

Excess of sorrow laughs.   Excess of joy weeps.

The roaring of lions, the howling of wolves, the raging of the stormy sea, and the destructive sword, are portions of eternity too great for the eye of man.

The fox condemns the trap, not himself.

Joys impregnate.   Sorrows bring forth.

Let man wear the fell of the lion, woman the fleece of the sheep.

The bird a nest, the spider a web, man friendship.

The selfish, smiling fool, and the sullen, frowning fool, shall be both thought wise, that they may be a rod.

What is now proved was once only imagined.

The rat, the mouse, the fox, the rabbit watch the roots; the lion, the tiger, the horse, the elephant watch the fruits.

The cistern contains, the fountain overflows.

One thought fills immensity.

Always be ready to speak your mind, and a base man will avoid you.

Everything possible to be believed is an image of truth.

The eagle never lost so much time as when he submitted to learn of the crow.

(9)

The fox provides for himself, but God provides for the lion.

Think in the morning, Act in the noon, Eat in the evening, Sleep in the Night.

He who has suffered you to impose on him knows you.

As the plow follows words, so God rewards prayers.

The tigers of wrath are wiser than the horses of instruction.

Expect poison from the standing water.

You never know what is enough unless you know what is more than enough.

Listen to the fool's reproach; it is a kingly title!

The eyes of fire, the nostrils of air, the mouth of water, the beard of earth.

The weak in courage is strong in cunning.

The apple tree never asks the beech how he shall grow; nor the lion, the horse, how he shall take his prey.

The thankful receiver hears a plentiful harvest.

If others had not been foolish, we should be so.

The soul of sweet delight can never be defiled.

When thou seest an Eagle, thou seest a portion of Genius; lift up thy head!

As the caterpillar chooses the fairest leaves to lay her eggs on, so the priest lays his curse on the fairest joys.

To create a little flower is the labour of ages.

Damn braces: Bless relaxes.

The best wine is the oldest, the best water the newest.

Prayers plow not! Praises reap not!

Joys laugh not! Sorrows weep not!

(10)

The head Sublime, the heart Pathos, the genitals Beauty, the hands and feet Proportion.

As the air to a bird or the sea to a fish, so is contempt to the contemptible.

The crow wished everything was black, the owl that everything was white.

Exuberance is Beauty.

If the lion was advised by the fox, he would be cunning.

Improve[me]nt makes strait roads, but the crooked roads without Improvement are roads of Genius.

Sooner murder an infant in its cradle than nurse unacted desires.

Where man is not, nature is barren.

Truth can never be told so as to be understood, and not be believed.

Enough ! or Too much.

(11)

The ancient Poets animated all sensible objects with Gods or Geniuses, calling them by the names and adorning them with the properties of woods, rivers, mountains, lakes, cities, nations, and whatever their enlarged and numerous senses could perceive.

And particularly they studied the genius of each city and country, placing it under its mental deity.

Till a system was formed, which some took advantage of and enslaved the vulgar by attempting to realise or abstract the mental deities from their objects ; thus began Priesthood.

Choosing forms of worship from poetic tales.

And at length they pronounced that the Gods had ordered such things.

Thus men forgot that All deities reside in the human breast.

(12)

A MEMORABLE FANCY

THE Prophets Isaiah and Ezekiel dined with me, and I asked them how they dared so roundly to assert that God spake to them; and whether they did not think at the time that they would be misunderstood, and so be the cause of imposition.

Isaiah answered: I saw no God, nor heard any, in a finite organical perception; but my senses discovered the infinite in everything, and as I was then persuaded, and remain confirmed, that the voice of honest indignation is the voice of God, I cared not for consequences but wrote.

Then I asked: Does a firm persuasion that a thing is so, make it so?

He replied: All poets believe that it does, and in ages of imagination this firm persuasion removed mountains; but many are not capable of a firm persuasion of anything.

Then Ezekiel said: The philosophy of the east taught the first principles of human perception. Some nations held one principle for the origin, and some another; we of Israel taught that the Poetic Genius (as you now call it) was the first principle and all the others merely derivative, which was the cause of our despising the Priests and Philosophers of other countries, and prophesying that all Gods would at

(13)

last be proved to originate in ours and to be the tributaries of the Poetic Genius. It was this that our great poet King David desired so fervently and invokes so pathetically, saying by this he conquers enemies and governs kingdoms; and we so loved our God, that we cursed in his name all the deities of surrounding nations, and asserted that they had rebelled. From these opinions the vulgar came to think that all nations would at last be subject to the Jews.

This, said he, like all firm persuasions, is come to pass, for all nations believe the Jews' code and worship the Jews' god, and what greater subjection can be?

I heard this with some wonder, and must confess my own conviction. After dinner I asked Isaiah to

favour the world with his last works ; he said none of
equal value was lost.   Ezekiel said the same of his.

I also asked Isaiah what made him go naked and
barefoot three years ? He answered, the same that
made our friend Diogenes the Grecian.

I then asked Ezekiel why he eat dung, and lay so
long on his right and left side ? He answered, The
desire of raising other men into a perception of the
infinite. This the North American tribes practise, and
is he honest who resists his genius or conscience only
for the sake of present ease or gratification ?

(14)

The ancient tradition that the world will be consumed in fire at the end of six thousand years is true,
as I have heard from Hell.

For the cherub with his flaming sword is hereby
commanded to leave his guard at tree of life, and
when he does, the whole creation will be consumed
and appear infinite and holy, whereas it now appears
finite and corrupt.

This will come to pass by an improvement of
sensual enjoyment.

But first the notion that man has a body distinct
from his soul is to be expunged ; this I shall do by
printing in the infernal method, by corrosives, which
in Hell are salutary and medicinal, melting apparent
surfaces away, and displaying the infinite which was
hid.

If the doors of perception were cleansed everything
would appear to man as it is, infinite.

For man has closed himself up till he sees all things
thro' narrow chinks of his cavern.

(15)

A MEMORABLE FANCY

I was in a Printing-house in Hell, and saw the

method in which knowledge is transmitted from generation to generation.

In the first chamber was a Dragon-Man, clearing away the rubbish from a cave's mouth; within, a number of Dragons were hollowing the cave.

In the second chamber was a Viper folding round the rock and the cave, and others adorning it with gold, silver, and precious stones.

In the third chamber was an Eagle with wings and feathers of air. He caused the inside of the cave to be infinite. Around were numbers of Eagle-like men who built palaces in the immense cliffs.

In the fourth chamber were Lions of flaming fire raging around and melting the metals into living fluids.

In the fifth chamber were Unnamed forms, which cast the metals into the expanse.

There they were received by Men who occupied the sixth chamber, and took the forms of books and were arranged in libraries.

(16)

The Giants who formed this world into its sensual existence and now seem to live in it in chains are in truth the causes of its life and the sources of all activity, but the chains are the cunning of weak and tame minds which have power to resist energy. According to the proverb, the weak in courage is strong in cunning.

Thus one portion of being is the Prolific, the other the Devouring. To the devourer it seems as if the producer was in his chains; but it is not so, he only takes portions of existence and fancies that the whole.

But the Prolific would cease to be Prolific unless the Devourer as a sea received the excess of his delights.

Some will say, Is not God alone the Prolific? I answer, God only Acts and Is, in existing beings or Men.

These two classes of men are always upon earth, and they should be enemies. Whoever tries to reconcile them seeks to destroy existence.

(17)

Religion is an endeavour to reconcile the two.

NOTE.—Jesus Christ did not wish to unite, but to separate them, as in the Parable of sheep and goats. And He says, I came not to send Peace, but a Sword.

Messiah or Satan or Tempter was formerly thought to be one of the Antediluvians who are our Energies.

A MEMORABLE FANCY

AN Angel came to me and said, O pitiable, foolish young man! O horrible! O dreadful state! Consider the hot, burning dungeon thou art preparing for thyself to all eternity, to which thou art going in such career.

I said: Perhaps you will be willing to show me my eternal lot, and we will contemplate together upon it, and see whether your lot or mine is most desirable?

So he took me thro' a stable and thro' a church and down into the church vault, at the end of which was a mill. Thro' the mill we went, and came to a cave. Down the winding cavern we groped our tedious way, till a void boundless as a nether sky appeared beneath us, and we held by the roots of trees, and hung over this immensity. But I said, If you please, we will commit ourselves to this void, and see whether providence is here also. If you will not, I will. But he answered, Do not presume, O young man, but as we here remain, behold thy lot which will soon appear when the darkness passes away.

So I remained with him, sitting in the twisted root

(18)

of an oak. He was suspended in a fungus, which hung with the head downward into the deep.

By degrees we beheld the infinite Abyss, fiery as the smoke of a burning city. Beneath us, at an immense distance, was the sun, black but shining; round it were fiery tracks on which revolved vast spiders, crawling after their prey, which flew, or rather swum, in the infinite deep, in the most terrific shapes of animals sprung from corruption. And the air was full of them, and seemed composed of them. These are Devils, and are called Powers of the air. I now asked my companion which was my eternal lot? He said, Between the black and white spiders.

But now, from behind the black and white spiders, a cloud and fire burst and rolled thro' the deep, blackening all beneath, so that the nether deep grew black as a sea, and rolled with a terrible noise. Beneath us was nothing now to be seen but a black tempest, till looking east between the clouds and the waves we saw a cataract of blood mixed with fire, and not many stones' throw from us appeared and sunk again the scaly fold of a monstrous serpent. At last, to the east, distant about three degrees, appeared a fiery crest above the waves. Slowly it reared like a ridge of golden rocks, till we discovered two globes of crimson fire, from which the sea fled away in clouds of smoke; and now we saw it was the head of Leviathan. His forehead was divided into streaks of green and purple like those on a tiger's forehead. Soon we saw his mouth and red gulls hang just above the raging foam, tinging the black deep with beams of blood, advancing toward us with all the fury of a spiritual existence.

(19)

My friend the Angel climbed up from his station into the mill; I remained alone, and then this appearance was no more; but I found myself sitting on a pleasant bank beside a river, by moonlight, hearing a harper, who sung to the harp, and his theme was, The man who never alters his opinion is like standing water, and breeds reptiles of the mind.

But I arose and sought for the mill, and there I found my Angel, who, surprised, asked me how I escaped?

I answered: All that we saw was owing to your metaphysics; for when you ran away, I found myself on a bank by moonlight hearing a harper. But now we have seen my eternal lot, shall I show you yours? He laughed at my proposal, but I by force suddenly caught him in my arms, and flew westerly thro' the night, till we were elevated above the earth's shadow; then I flung myself with him directly into the body of the sun. Here I clothed myself in white, and taking in my hand Swedenborg's volumes, sunk from the glorious clime, and passed all the planets till we came to Saturn. Here I stay'd to rest, and then leaped into the void between Saturn and the fixed stars.

Here, said I, is your lot, in this space, if space it may be called. Soon we saw the stable and the church, and I took him to the altar and opened the Bible, and lo! it was a deep pit, into which I descended, driving the Angel before me. Soon we saw seven houses of brick. One we entered. In it

(20)

were a number of monkeys, baboons, and all of that species chained by the middle, grinning and snatching at one another, but withheld by the shortness of their chains. However, I saw that they sometimes grew numerous, and then the weak were caught by the strong, and with a grinning aspect, first coupled with and then devoured by plucking off first one limb and then another, till the body was left a helpless trunk. This, after grinning and kissing it with seeming fondness, they devoured too; and here and there I saw one savourily picking the flesh off of his own tail. As the stench terribly annoyed us both, we went into the mill, and I in my hand brought the skeleton of a body, which in the mill was Aristotle's Analytics.

So the Angel said, Thy phantasy has imposed upon me, and thou oughtest to be ashamed.

I answered, We impose on one another, and it is but lost time to converse with you whose works are only Analytics.

(21)

I have always found that Angels have the vanity to speak of themselves as the only wise. This they do with a confident insolence sprouting from systematic reasoning.

This Swedenborg boasts that what he writes is new, tho' it is only the Contents or Index of already published books.

A man carried a monkey about for a show, and because he was a little wiser than the monkey, grew vain, and conceived himself as much wiser than seven men. It is so with Swedenborg. He shows the folly of churches, and exposes hypocrites, till he imagines that all are religious, and himself the single one on earth that ever broke a net.

(22)

Now hear a plain fact. Swedenborg has not written one new truth. Now hear another : He has written all the old falsehoods.

And now hear the reason. He conversed with Angels who are all religious, and conversed not with Devils who all hate religion, for he was incapable thro' his conceited notions.

Thus Swedenborg's writings are a recapitulation of all superficial opinions, and an analysis of the more sublime, but no further.

Have now another plain fact. Any man of mechanical talents may, from the writings of Paracelsus or Jacob Behmen, produce ten thousand volumes of equal value with Swedenborg's, and from those of Dante or Shakespear an infinite number.

But when he has done this, let him not say that he knows better than his master, for he only holds a candle in sunshine.

A MEMORABLE FANCY

ONCE I saw a Devil in a flame of fire, who arose before an Angel that sat on a cloud, and the Devil uttered these words :—

The worship of God is, Honouring his gifts in other men, each according to his genius, and loving the

(23)

greatest men best.   Those who envy or calumniate great men hate God, for there is no other God.

The Angel hearing this became almost blue, but mastering himself he grew yellow, and at last white, pink, and smiling, and then replied :—

Thou Idolater, is not God One? and is not he visible in Jesus Christ? and has not Jesus Christ given his sanction to the law of ten commandments, and are not all other men fools, sinners, and nothings?

The Devil answered: Bray a fool in a morter with wheat, yet shall not his folly be beaten out of him. If Jesus Christ is the greatest man, you ought to love him in the greatest degree.   Now hear how he has given his sanction to the law of ten commandments. Did he not mock at the sabbath, and so mock the sabbath's God? murder those who were murdered because of him? turn away the law from the woman taken in adultery? steal the labor of others to support him? bear false witness when he omitted making a defence before Pilate? covet when he pray'd for his disciples, and when he bid them shake off the dust of their feet against such as refused to lodge them?   I tell you, no virtue can exist without breaking these ten commandments. Jesus was all virtue, and acted from impulse, not from rules.

(24)

When he had so spoken, I beheld the Angel, who stretched out his arms, embracing the flame of fire, and he was consumed, and arose as Elijah.

Note.—This Angel, who is now become a Devil, is my particular friend. We often read the Bible together in its infernal or diabolical sense, which the world shall have if they behave well.

I have also The Bible of Hell, which the world shall have whether they will or no.

One Law for the Lion and Ox is Oppression.

ABOUT 'THE MARRIAGE OF HEAVEN AND HELL'

It is still a question not quite certainly to be answered whether the 'Marriage of Heaven and Hell' came before or after 'Tiriel.' Its date, as indicated in the first lines, is 1790. The 'New Heaven,' whose advent had taken place thirty-three years before, is undoubtedly that which the author's own mind had brought into the world. He was born in 1757, and was therefore thirty-three in 1790. This Book is therefore placed before 'Tiriel,' because there is reason—presently to be given—for believing that at least the later pages were written in 1791, or early in 1792.

'The Argument,' as the first page is called in the 'Marriage,' is evidently later than the rest. In the original the style of printing is more upright, more mature, and is smaller than the rest of the Book, which, like the 'Songs of Innocence and Experience'—and all the prophetic works except 'Vala' and 'Tiriel,' that came down to us in the original manuscript—is written or printed by hand in an ink of varnish upon the backs of zinc or copper plates, which, being put for long in an acid bath, were so corroded and bitten away that the letters, protected by the varnish, now stood up in such bold relief that

they could be printed from like a page of compact or metal-cast type. The drawings in all cases, scattered through the pages, were done in the same way.

An exception must also be made of the Books called 'Los' and 'Ahania,' which were actually engraved on metal with a point, probably because they could be got into smaller space, and plates were scarcer in 1795 than in 1790.

Rintrah is second of the 'ungenerated' sons of Los—their list is given in 'Jerusalem.' Being 'ungenerated,' they 'fled not' through the 'gates' (of birth), but remained with imagination as forces. Rintrah, Palamabron, Theotormon, and Bromion are the four. See 'Jerusalem,' page 72, line 11, and again, page 74, line 2. Two of them are invoked, page 93, line 2; Rintrah, on lines 7, 10, and 13. This refers to the long myth in 'Milton.'

It will be seen that in these names the whole of Blake's 'prophetic' narratives are perceptibly united as a single intellectual scheme. The last passages of 'Jerusalem' belong to after 1810. Its title-page is of 1804, like that of 'Milton.' The scheme therefore was a single and coherent symbolic language to Blake for between fifteen and twenty years at the very least.

Rintrah's symbolic form is a lion. He is a name for intellectual fury—enthusiasm or (as Blake liked to call it) wrath. He belongs to that half of the two 'contraries of Humanity' of which Pity is the other. The two create the motive of all art. When they have done so, criticism gives them other names —the Sublime and the Pathos—that are not used by Blake till the close of 'Jerusalem,' page 90, lines 1 to 13, where, in the darkest hour before dawn, he speaks of them. They are essentially also Male and Female principles. 'Life' in art is not to be had if they separate and each assumes it. Then they are 'separate from Man'—from Mind—and Man—or Mind falls to grovelling outside art (himself) in mere matter-of-fact and temporary accidents of his blood.

To avoid this was Blake's especial mission in life, to preach 'brotherhood' through a true and united state of the imagination in each that each might delight in all.

He begins the work now under a furiously bold symbol, the marriage of Heaven (ideal) and Hell (passion).

Cloud is, as we shall see in 'Jerusalem,' blood. In page 21, lines 28, 31, Hand—an intellectual wrath, gone astray into abstract philosophy—punishes the poor 'animal spirits,' as metaphysics used to call what Blake called 'daughters' of Albion, for teaching the passion of the heart (called Luvah in the myth) to 'rise into my clouded heavens.' This is the 'Marriage' in a single phrase. The fruition of that marriage should be the Incarnation itself, as related in the last line of page 5 and first of page 6, here in the 'Marriage' in scriptural language, again in 'Jerusalem,' page 33, lines 48, 52, where it appears in mythical language. We have already had it in 'The Mental Traveller' in poetic language, where 'The Divine Appearance' is 'born a boy' and given to the old woman mentioned also in 'Jerusalem,' page 44, line 25, who, in page 85, lines 1 to 9, after the complicated changes of the life of symbols, turns out to be 'divine analogy' to live six thousand years, and to be related to Reuben the 'mental traveller,' or wanderer, who entered in after seeds of beauty had been planted here. In 'Jerusalem,' page 80, from line 66 to page 81, line 14, more of his travels through states are seen. Pilgrims pass, countries remain, men pass on, states remain.—'Jerusalem,' page 73, lines 42 and 43, as also page 49, line 74. We are the state in which we are. An example of this is seen in Luvah 'named' Satan, when in that state, page 49; again, line 68,—though it is 'eternal death,' whose contrary is good, though called 'little deaths'—the acts of kindness—as in 'Jerusalem,' page 96, line 27.

Jesus only enters eternal death and puts on Satan that He may put him off. This is the Incarnation; but as we each of us have to do bits of crucifixion, so we have to do bits of this. Reuben does it in Hyle and others, and becomes a 'winding worm' ('Jerusalem,' page 82, lines 47 and 49), when he is the mental traveller Merlin, page 56, line 28, who has been exploring Creation, Redemption, and Judgment, page 36, line 40, where the word Judgment in its Loins meaning is explained, and incidentally we have a light on the poem called 'Broken Love.'

In Gilchrist's 'Life' we have the solution. There is at first a vague gossiping story about how Blake thought of taking a concubine, quite in Old Testament style, after his marriage, and how his wife cried, and how, at the sight of her tears, he gave up his project.

It may be true, but even if it is mere invention, the gossips had good cause for error. They were not likely to guess the meaning of a poem like that called 'Broken Love,' and though they did justice to Blake's heart, they did not do so to his Head and Loins; nor has any writer seen the connection of that poem, and all the others—notably 'Jerusalem,' page 38, line 44, and page 30, lines 33 and following; and 'Milton,' page 32, lines 2 and following; 'Jerusalem,' pages 55, 60, and 62, and again page 40, line 41, where we find an expression already explained by the 'winding' worm that crushes the minute particulars with reason, and by Merlin (*first of the three—Merlin, Bladud, Arthur) being the Head, Heart, Loins of that worm seen under femininity as Christ, born of woman to 'put on' Satanic holiness. All this may be read with the following passage from Gilchrist's 'Life,' 2nd edition, p. 410 :—*

'*One complaint only she*' (Mrs. Blake) '*was ever known to make during her husband's life, and that gently. "Mr. Blake was so little with her, though in the body they were never separated ; for he was incessantly away from her in Paradise," which would not seem to have been "far off."* ' *This is quoted (or rather is misprinted) from a note to page 81 of Mr. Swinburne's essay, where the quotation-marks for Mrs. Blake's complaint are given only to the words 'Mr. Blake' and 'in Paradise.' The authority for this story is Blake's friend Mr. Kirkup.*

This brings us straight to 'Broken Love.' We are comforted to find the jealousy of Mrs. Blake was of immaterial personages after all—a kind not at all uncommon among artists' wives. It was not his old age, but her new education that eventually cured her of it. But it would be exacting to demand of gossips that they should understand a point such as this. One thing, however, may appeal to them. Blake, though an Irishman, was scrupulous about getting into debt, and though poor all his life, was never in what is gracefully called 'embarrassed circumstances.' If he had this rare (though less rare than used to be supposed) Irish quality of conscientiousness in money matters, he probably had the much more usual trait of fidelity in marriage.

In the ballad of 'William Bond' there is a threat, but the only effect 'the girls' there had on him was to make him ill. Even if William Bond was William Blake, illness is not adultery, though what has been known to pass for adultery in gossip may sometimes have been illness—hers, if not his.

In further explanation of the words 'In Paradise,' as connected with 'jealousy,' there remain the concluding lines of 'Broken Love'—

> '*Let us agree to give up love*
> *And root up the infernal grove*';

and the passage in 'Jerusalem,' page 77, at the beginning of the prose paragraph—'We are told to abstain from fleshly desires that we may lose no time from the work of the Lord.'

The general idea of 'The Marriage of Heaven and Hell' was to rebuke Swedenborg for having used his faculty of vision to no better purpose than that of reducing all the visions of scriptural writers to perpetual references in the incarnation and to the human form of God, and to the praise of 'good-ness.' He is derided for not having made prophetic books of his own. Blake now proceeds to 'out-do' him, and continues the same system ever afterwards.

'JEHOVAH,' 'HEAVEN,' AND 'HELL'

'Jehovah' is itself, of course, no more a sacred name than the French exclamation Par bleu! is a binding oath. The original name is well known to be irrecoverably lost, because during too long a period the commandment that forbids taking this name in vain was understood as forbidding its pronun-ciation in conversation or its record in history. The speaking of it once a year by the High Priest in the Holy of Holies having ceased,—we do not know why,—it was lost altogether. 'Jehovah' therefore is simply a guess-work substitute, and we may well ask ourselves how much of substitute and of guess-work on the subject of its meaning the Owner of the lost name allowed to arise among men, or how much of such conjecture represents truth.

Blake offers his own reading:—'After Christ's death, He (who dwells in flaming fire) became Jehovah.'—'Marriage of Heaven and Hell,' page 6. This He is the impersonation of fatherhood, and therefore in a more elementary state (before the death of Christ) was the great Desirer, the Spirit of Desire in all men—called (says Blake) Satan by Milton in 'Paradise Lost.'

Blake's own use of the word Satan, first indicated in the close of 'The Ghost of Abel,' is elaborated in 'Jerusalem.'

The Creator, as distinguished from the Father—or, in the 'Book of Genesis,' Elohim, as distinguished from Jehovah, is kept apart as a separate idea all through Blake's work. In the close of the book of 'The Ghost of Abel,' he writes the two names in a way that suggests an idea closely resembling that of Hengstenberg in the passage, 'Hitherto that Being who, in one aspect, was Jehovah, in another had always been Elohim. The great crisis now drew nigh in which Jehovah Elohim would be changed into Jehovah.' The obscurantism of all keepers of sacred tradition is not yet quite cast off even in our own day, for the authorised version of the Bible still fails to denote the particular places where the particular names come in either by printing them as they stood or by using uniform equivalents with an initial code vocabulary.

In Blake's last book, 'Milton,' the word Jehovah only occurs seven times—Page 6, line 27; page 7, line 22; page 10, lines 20, 24, and 25; page 11, lines 24, 26. The first mention connects the name with fatherhood through the symbols plough, rain, etc., and even the Satanic Molech; the second through blood (the cloud)—the seat of moral law and punishment; the third and fourth with thought (thunder) —not absent in any fatherhood; the fifth with stars—an aspect of heavenly eyes, in which the arguments of philosophy (sons of Albion) will be seen in 'Jerusalem'; then finally, in the sixth and seventh, as author of that strange fruit of mind, a mortal appearance called a body,—the work of all the soul's diseases,—which the Lamb (the Imagination) puts on and puts off.

In 'Jerusalem' the lines of verse on page 3 first refer to Him, but not by name. They explain the symbolic use of Thunder, Fire, and the Ear, as well as hint at the meaning of the expression 'Marriage of Heaven and Hell' (of purity and desire), with earth, the nerves, or unintellectualised experience, even if it be experience of inspiration, as in the first lines of 'Vala.' In page 22, line 3 of 'Jerusalem,' He is seen as Nimrod, Hunter of Men; but the explanation is for 'Vala,' and indirectly only is His. He is only mentioned passingly on page 30, line 32, yet in the mystic sense. In page 46, line 14, He is owner of the Plough.

In page 49, line 53, He is first connected with the place of the Moon, the symbol for feminine secrecy and maternal movement; also with Albion's tomb, for which see above, page 48, lines 36, 41; and page 59, line 6; page 72, line 49; page 73, line 16— (the first reference given in the Russell and Maclagan sketch index). The starry characters of Og and Anak are the literal meanings, the Letter' of Scripture, page 78, line 2. Imagination's Mind sleeps in the literal meaning, having become common-sense. Yet Jerusalem laments being excluded from the letter—in page 91, line 37, where the Rational Power (Spectre) reads; in page 94, line 2, where the Tomb is admittedly immortal in its way, as in line 12; 13—Erin, a form and love that once attained to prophecy, sits in it; and 19, where divine breath—spirit—awakes mind from the letter.

Compare for 'Erin'—who is a Westward symbol, as Thel is, and has her aged as well as her youthful form:—

JERUSALEM.

The Tomb differs but little from the Couch—page 32, line 13 ; page 42, line 66 ; page 44, line 35 ; page 48, line 6—where it is explained, and page 53, line 21.

To continue Jehovah from after the reference to page 49, see that on page 55, line 32, a very brief mention of the myth of the Seven Eyes that is told at length in 'Vala,' where the name Jehovah occurs in Night VIII. The references of page 61, on the lines 1, 2, 17, 21, 25, 48, belong to an interpolated section of myth, a story, a Book in itself, a page written later than the part of 'Jerusalem' where it occurs, and full of explanation. On page 63, lines 1, 10, 16, 27, 30, the earlier, and, as it were, more corporeal Jehovah is seen with his symbols.

Blake here was feeling thoroughly in accord with Biblical interpretation, remembering perhaps that the Ophites, who were Egyptians, gave the name 'Iaῶ to the Moon, and that in Coptic the moon is called Ioh, that Macrobius connected 'Iaω, which also denotes the Sun, or Dionysus, with the root of Jehovah. Mr. Mathew may have told him this. Page 68, line 39 ; page 81, line 13 ; page 98, lines 23, 40, 45, are the remaining references to Jehovah in 'Jerusalem.'

The name 'Scofield' referred to in these passages stands for Adam, or red (earth), similar to Edom, a title of Esau, from the red porridge of lentils for which he sold his birthright. Edom is mentioned in 'The Marriage of Heaven and Hell' and in 'Jerusalem.' 'Scofield' is a symbol for the part of Mind that produces the restricted state in which we have only the corporeal five senses and no imagination. Blake took 'Scofield' from an assistant gardener, so named, whom he once, at Felpham, bodily ejected from his own paradise or garden.

In Swedenborg's 'Angelic wisdom concerning the Divine Love,' which Blake read and annotated shortly before writing 'The Marriage of Heaven and Hell,' in avowed continuation and correction of all Swedenborgianism, we read in par. 283 that heaven is one Man distinguished into regions and provinces according to the members, viscera, and organs of a man,—all the provinces distinct from one another, and that 'the angels who constitute heaven are the recipients of love and wisdom from the Lord, and RECIPIENTS ARE IMAGES.'

The last three words contain what may be called the First Law of Mysticism, and explain why Imagination is the Logos.

The word Heaven was elaborately used in 'Jerusalem' in connection with the '27 Heavens' and the 'Mundane Shell' ; but the reference, page 43, line 16, is the most appropriate here. The references are the following :—

Heaven, and Heavens.

Page 3, verse			Page 68, lines 19		
,,	13,	*lines* 32, 51	,,	71, ,,	17, 57
,,	21,	,, 31	,,	75, ,,	20, 23, 27
,,	27,	,, *prose*	,,	77, ,,	*prose, and verses*
,,	33,	,, 50			3, 7, 34
,,	34,	,, 14	,,	79, ,,	71, 80
,,	41,	,, 2, 20	,,	80, ,,	15
,,	43,	,, 16, 18	,,	81, ,,	*picture*, 15
,,	49,	,, 13, 27, 61, 62, 64	,,	82, ,,	79
,,	5,	,, 26, 55	,,	91, ,,	32, 49
,,	60,	,, 1	,,	95, ,,	7, 21
,,	63,	,, 17, 19	,,	96, ,,	1, 40, 43
,,	65,	,, 5	,,	98, ,,	2, 8, 10, 27
,,	66,	,, 5, 40, 81			

Hell.

Page 8, lines 8, 38			Page 49, lines 61, 62		
,,	12,	,, 15	,,	75, ,,	21
,,	17,	,, 47, 54	,,	77, ,,	*prose, and verse*
,,	24,	,, 34			34
,,	41,	,, 2	,,	78, ,,	8
,,	43,	,, 16, 32			

As will be found noted in reference to the use of the words in other Books, Heaven, or Heavens, are spoken of in 'Vala,' Night VII., line 103, and notably in Night IX., lines 180, 296, 789, 790, 797, 820.

THE CLOSING OF THE WESTERN GATE.

With this symbol begins a period within a period—an epoch in the production of the Prophetic Books themselves.

In the first page—the Argument—of 'The Marriage of Heaven and Hell,' we have practically the entrance of what becomes the main subject of all the Books, and, at any rate, the explanation of the symbolic language and mythic form in which they are written. This is the censorship of modesty that closes the Western Gate, or Gate of the Tongue.

This censorship is aided by another—that of stupidity, that hates imagination and refuses to see Christ in Adam.

People will not have the Body spoken of freely, however much they may, in the abstract, admit that it is the Temple of God, 'not made with hands.'

This refusal is not Blake's fault. It results in a closing of frankness, the Gate of the Tongue—great parent of that wonderful race the 'all-powerful human words.' So they have to come forth in symbolic garment if at all.

It has led, in England generally, to the superiority of our novels—taken in the mass—over the French, and it produced Blake's poetry. But he always thought the closed gate a sad thing, if not wicked, and looked forward to its reopening.

This explanation of the 'closing of the Western Gate,' as the prohibition of such general excess in frankness as might endanger public decency, is not anywhere given in express terms by Blake, and is only offered here as one aspect of that terrible event. It is an aspect that followed almost as a matter of course from the very nature of our opaque bodies—themselves altogether Satanic ; for Satan, as must ever be remembered, is the limit of opaqueness, as will often be repeated in these notes, for which repetition the reader is asked to forgive the editor, who is more afraid of being obscure than of being dull.

This opaqueness of our bodies—once more to repeat—is itself the fault of our minds, for a state of mind makes all states of body, not merely the amorous state, the apoplectic, or the hysterical, and just as in a clairvoyant or hypnotic trance mind can see through bodies and brick walls, and escape the control of opacity, so, Blake held, would all men's normal minds end by conquering their normal and mortal bodies, and ('Vala,' Night VIII., line 544) these would 'disappear in improved knowledge.'

Meanwhile, since none of us can effect this for the race by living all alone, our business is to try to effect it all together by exalted sympathy, not only with 'trifles not worth caring for,' as the pleasures of the passions are called in the 'Everlasting Gospel,' written at least fourteen years after 'The Marriage of Heaven and Hell,' but—what would be of no less effect—with sympathy even for

'Loves and tears of brothers, sisters, sons, fathers, and friends,
Which, if Man ceases to behold, he ceases to exist,' etc.—
                    Jerusalem, page 38, line 12.

The closing of Albion's western gate caused all his sympathies to diminish, and all his opacities to increase, as will be read at full length in 'Jerusalem.'

In Blake's earlier Books, now to follow, will be found the voice of a visionary uttering (for the spirits Orc and Oothoon) the cry of passion, just as for the shy spirit of virgin beauty (Thel) he uttered the cry of humility and despondency.

DESIGNS TO 'THE MARRIAGE OF HEAVEN AND HELL'

*Whatever else Blake was thinking of in 1790, when he com-
posed 'The Marriage of Heaven and Hell,' his own career
was very much in his mind. The 'Argument' of this book
may be looked on as a companion composition to Tennyson's
little poem about his own writings, beginning*

> *'Once in a golden hour
> I cast to earth a seed.'*

*The days of the 'Poetical Sketches' were over. Seven years
had passed. Blake was no longer an unconsidered novice.
He was beginning to be considered rather as a dangerous
eccentric. Rintrah is his own spirit of energy. He is the
Just Man because he admitted the existence of his bodily
passions, and claimed his right to be imaginative at the same
time. He had ceased to be meek. Poets were ceasing to copy
Pope and Dryden only. The movement of the modern sweet
singers had begun. Then came the imitator—the villain.
Poetry became respectable sentiment once more, just as it was
ceasing to be respectable epigram. It was no longer a claim to
the liberty of a prophet. The man who had what modern
critics call an evangel, grew angry. The hungry clouds on
the deep are his passions. Blood is the cloud in the symbolic
system. So ends the 'Argument.' A supplementary interpretation is given along with that of all the Books in vol. ii. of the
Quaritch edition.*

*Blake in the book itself of the Marriage makes a manifesto.
He casts off allegiance to Swedenborg, and begins his main
gospel: 'Claim to be happy. Dare to be imaginative. Refuse
to be bound. Be good,—for that is the way to be free.'*

The book is full of designs.

*The title-page shows fire—a virgin, kissing cloud (her friend)
under the earth, while trees above are barren. These figures
are the passion kissing the mortality or opacity of the blood.*

*The Argument's page shows a fruit-gatherer, passion,
reaching down from a tree to one who stands below, the virgin
flesh.*

*Page 3 has above the text a female figure, who has eaten the
fruit now, lying back with outspread arms in a bath of flames,
and offering herself to them. Below the text she is seen putting
forth a child, while a boy and girl of four or five run away
alarmed. Compare the 'Mental Traveller.'*

*Page 4 shows, below the text, a young female, a mere girl,
carrying the babe, now three or four years old, with giant
strides across the sea out of the sunrise. A youth, chained by
one foot, dashes to meet her out of flames that follow him from*

his side of the picture as though the ocean opposite the sun were on fire.

The upper part of page 5 shows a man and a horse, separate, falling headlong from the sky into where the tops of flames are seen burning from somewhere below. A sword and a trumpet and a fire-ball fall with them.

On page 10, after the last of the proverbs, a diabolic angel is seen unrolling the list of them in a long strip across his knees, while two women make notes. They and their books are iron and brass—love and hate—on and by which moods such proverbs are written.

At the top of page 11 some flames are seen, as a sun-god, goddess, and babe. These figures are possibly Thel, the Lily, and the Golden Cloud, conceived in another aspect. They are 'sensible objects animated,' as by the ancient poets. A bearded head, and arms outstretched on a cloud below, fill half the foot of the page. A baby floats alone on the darkness of the other half. They are Jehovah and the Infant Son, as conceived usually in the 'human breast.' Above these, very small, is a caricature of a giant frightening four people into kneeling down to him. He has a sword.

On page 14 a female head, with arms extended in hovering attitude, bends towards us out of a world of flames, over a youth lying on his back on the ground. He is in profile. The two figures, if fully seen, would form a cross, as one lies floating across, though at half a yard above the other. It has several symbolic meanings. That of the emanation hovering over the Spectre suggests most of the rest.

Page 15 has an eagle flying up with its talons in a serpent. It almost seems as though Shelley had seen this before writing his opening to the 'Revolt of Islam,' though it is not probable. If he had known of Blake he would have said so. The eagle here is Luvah; the serpent probably Urizen; see page 20, below.

On page 16 the giants who formed this world sit sadly in a close-huddled group on the ground, like Job and his friends, but not as Blake afterwards drew that subject. They are the four Zoas and Albion, or the five senses, in all probability.

At the foot of page 20 the serpent is rolling and writhing its way through a foaming sea in great wheel-shaped coils. Urizen in the world of Tharmas. See 'Vala,' Night VIII., line 436.

At the head of page 21, a naked youth sits on a flattened human skin, or corpse, of a man, his 'dead-self,' and looks up into the sky.

On a separate plate Blake printed a picture of Nebuchadnezzar as crawling to grass on page 24.

'A Song of Liberty' has only some small drawings of prancing horses.

A SONG OF LIBERTY

(*The page numbers 25, 26, 27 continue those of 'The Marriage of Heaven and Hell' with which this Song was bound up.*)

A SONG OF LIBERTY

(25)

1. THE Eternal Female groan'd ! It was heard over all the Earth.

2. Albion's coast is sick, silent. The American meadows faint.

3. Shadows of Prophecy shiver along by the lakes and the rivers, and mutter across the ocean. France, rend down thy dungeon.

4. Golden Spain, burst the barriers of old Rome.

5. Cast thy keys, O Rome, into the deep down falling, even to eternity down falling.

6. And weep.

7. In her trembling hands she took the new born terror howling.

8. On those infinite mountains of light now barr'd out by the atlantic sea, the new born fire stood before the starry king.

9. Flag'd with grey brow'd snows and thunderous visages, the jealous wings wav'd over the deep.

10. The speary hand burn'd aloft, unbuckled was the shield ; forth went the hand of jealousy among the flaming hair, and hurl'd the new born wonder

(26)

thro' the starry night.

11. The fire, the fire, is falling !

12. Look up ! look up ! O citizen of London, enlarge thy countenance. O Jew, leave counting gold ! return to thy oil and wine. O African ! black African ! (Go, winged thought, widen his forehead.)

13. The fiery limbs, the flaming hair, shot like the sinking sun into the western sea.

267

14. Wak'd from his eternal sleep, the hoary element
roaring, fled away.

15. Down rush'd, beating his wings in vain, the
jealous king ; his grey brow'd councellors, thunderous
warriors, carl'd veterans, among helms, and shields,
and chariots, horses, elephants, banners, castles,
slings, and rocks.

16. Falling, rushing, ruining ! buried in the ruins,
on Urthona's dens.

17. All night beneath the ruins ; then their sullen
flames faded, emerge round the gloomy king.

18. With thunder and fire, leading his starry

(27)

hosts thro' the waste wilderness, he promulgates his
ten commands, glancing his beamy eyelids over the
deep in dark dismay.

19. Where the son of fire in his eastern cloud,
while the morning plumes her golden breast.

20. Spurning the clouds written with curses ; stamps
the stony law to dust ; loosing the eternal horses from
the dens of night, crying, Empire is no more !
And now the lion and wolf shall cease.

Chorus

Let the Priests of the Raven of dawn, no longer in
deadly black, with hoarse note curse the sons of joy.
Nor his accepted brethren, whom, tyrant, he calls
free. Lay the bound or build the roof. Nor pale
religions letchery call that virginity that wishes but
acts not.

For everything that lives is Holy.

MEANING OF 'A SONG OF LIBERTY

'A Song of Liberty,' though issued from Blake's own
press under the same cover as the 'Marriage,' is really a
separate book.

It is so entirely symbolic, as well as so early in date, and *so short, that while its earliness makes the coherence of its symbolism with that of the later books a guarantee that Blake always knew his own mind—though it took so long for any one else to do so—its shortness makes it serviceable if paraphrased as a sort of exercise in which some portion of Blake's peculiar language may conveniently be learned.*

And here the editor ventures to appeal to the readers, begging them first to take pains to learn all *the language—not merely the little bits that he can teach in these italic notes, and, having learned it, to read it to himself as he would read a foreign tongue which had become as familiar to him as his native language, so that he ceases to translate it into other words as he goes along, but allows his mind to vivify it straight into its meaning, passing through its images to its purposes. Then, and then only, will he understand Blake's position among the poets.*

1. *The Eternal Female, the corporeal instincts, groaned. It was felt through all flesh—the earth (Adam, Red Earth). She will not be happy until with Ahania, and 'all the lovely sex,' all the pathos, the instincts. She obeys the sublime, the male.—'Vala,' Night IX., line 215.*

2. *The world of generation—the North of the North, Albion's coast in Europe—is sick with restraint. The American, or western meadows, or the tissues from which instincts arise, faint under it.*

3. *The spirits that awake the flesh to action in each person timidly sent desires down the nerves. France, Passion of the Blood—Luvah and Orc in one (compare 'Jerusalem,' page 49, line 46 ; page 55, line 29 ; page 60, line 15 ; and 'Vala,' Night VIII., lines 59 and 60)—be no longer restrained! (as Urizen said in 'Vala,' Night IX., line 186, when Tharmas is America).*

4. *Intellect that learns from generation and regenerates the Man, cast off thy restraining half.*

5. *Cast thy restraint off on South of North—Rome in Europe ; religion in war—Rahab—or Urizen in the Net.*

6. *And lay thy heart open with a sword of tears (compare notes to 'Jerusalem' : the* sword).

7. *The 'woman old' of the Mental Traveller—who is both morality and Divine analogy—took the new-born spirit that discerns imaginative meaning through its desires (howling is symbol for desiring) in her hands, trembling.*

8. *It stood before Urizen (the Starry King) on those truly moral heights of unalloyed pure passion that were of the soul once, and that the body drowns now.*

9. *He was seen in vision waving over the lower passions,—wings—on which gloomy desiring and matter-of-fact elderly selfish faces appeared as though painted—in fact, as a flag's*

*device is embroidered on a flag; and the wings were jealousy
—they command the air, as jealousy commands the natural
heart.* (*Luvah, demon of the Heart, is Prince of the Air.*)

10. *Armed mental control seized the new-born meaning (of
the Bible and of the world, as about to be taught by Blake) and
hurled him jealously down into the body's lower impulses.*

11. *Into which it fell as fire falls.*

12. '*Come unto me all ye that labour and are heavy laden,
and I will give you rest.*'

13. *Imagination fell into flesh.*

14. *Whose matter-of-fact habits shrank from him.*

15. *Every argument that Reason could bring rushed down,
seeing Jealousy's mistake, to catch Imagination and destroy
him.*

16. *The fire that had risen in the East, stood in the South,
and been flung through the West (the direction is that of the
sun), entered the earth (the auricular nerves of human life, to
which inspiration whispers: compare 'Vala,' Night I., lines
14, 15): brought forth an eternal brood of ideas.*

17. *The desire to live will not be repressed. If imagination
be refused the mind, he will burn in the loins, and from thence
re-arise, for this is the real story of the Incarnation. Compare 'Vala,' last line of Night V.*

18, 19, 20. *The stony law that is stamped to dust is not
merely—whether or not it be partly—the moral law. The eternal
horses loosened from their dens of night suggest the idea, for
Swedenborg taught that in Scripture the horse is symbol of
the intellect, and the dens of night are evidently that literal
scripture now upheld by Rome, once otherwise treated by her
when all was given a spiritual meaning, even the 'daily
bread' in the Lord's prayer.*

*The last words describe the universal peace fellowship
without greed and law that Blake believed would come of
itself if all men's hands were filled with the priceless gold of
poetic imagination. Most certainly he was right, but in
believing that all could be so filled if they chose, he perhaps
did more than justice to his fellow-creatures.*

*The chorus is frankly physical. The Raven here dis-
appears from the scheme of symbolism to reappear picturesquely
in 'Vala,' Night IX., line 60.*

*In the last three Nights of 'Vala,' the problem of the value
and meaning, the danger and deception of mind that belong
to the simple passions of the flesh are argued out in poetry, and
are counterparts to the Night V., 66 to 182; Night VII., 5 to
99, 136 to 182, 171 to 126, and 439 to 699. In Night VIII.,
line 60 to end; in Night IX., 34, 69, 183, 186, 354, are the
indicative references.*

TIRIEL

TIRIEL.

TIRIEL

I

And aged Tiriel stood before the gates of his beautiful palace,
With Myratana, once the Queen of all the western plains;
But now his eyes were darkened, and his wife fading in death.
They stood before their once delightful palace; and thus the voice
Of aged Tiriel arose, that his sons might hear in their gates.

'Accursed race of Tiriel! behold your father;
Come forth and look on her that bore you. Come, you accursed sons.
In my weak arms I here have borne your dying mother;
Come forth, sons of the curse, come forth! see the death of Myratana.'

His sons ran from their gates, and saw their aged parents stand;
And thus the eldest son of Tiriel raised his mighty voice :—

'Old man! unworthy to be called the father of Tiriel's race!
For every one of those thy wrinkles, each of those grey hairs,
Are cruel as death, and as obdurate as the devouring pit!
Why should thy sons care for thy curses, thou accursed man?

Were we not slaves till we rebelled? Who cares for
 Tiriel's curse?
His blessing was a cruel curse; his curse may be a
 blessing.'

He ceased. The aged man raised up his right hand
 to the heavens;
His left supported Myratana, shrinking in pangs of
 death.
The orbs of his large eyes he opened, and thus his
 voice went forth :—

'Serpents, not sons, wreathing around the bones of
 Tiriel !
Ye worms of death, feasting upon your aged parent's
 flesh,
Listen, and hear your mother's groans. No more
 accursed sons
She bears; she groans not at the birth of Heuxos or
 Yuva.
These are the groans of death, ye serpents ! these are
 the groans of death !
Nourished with milk, ye serpents, nourished with
 mother's tears and cares !
Look at my eyes, blind as the orbless skull among the
 stones ;
Look at my bald head. Hark, listen, ye serpents,
 listen ! . . .
What, Myratana ! What, my wife ! O soul ! O
 spirit ! O fire !
What, Myratana, art thou dead? Look here, ye
 serpents, look !
The serpents sprung from her own bowels have
 drained her dry as this.
Curse on your ruthless heads, for I will bury her
 even here !'

So saying, he began to dig a grave with his aged
 hands ;

But Heuxos called a son of Zazel to dig their mother
a grave.

'Old cruelty, desist, and let us dig a grave for thee.'
Thou hast refused our charity, thou hast refused our
food,
Thou hast refused our clothes, our beds, our houses
for thy dwelling,
Choosing to wander like a son of Zazel in the rocks.
Why dost thou curse? Is not the curse now come
upon thine head?
Was it not thou enslaved the sons of Zazel? and they
have cursed,
And now thou feel'st it! Dig a grave, and let us
bury our mother.'

'There, take the body, cursed sons! and may the
heavens rain wrath,
As thick as northern fogs, around your gates, to
choke you up!
That you may lie as now your mother lies—like dogs,
cast out,
The stink of your dead carcases annoying man and
beast,
Till your white bones are bleached with age for a
memorial.
No! your remembrance shall perish; for, when your
carcases
Lie stinking on the earth, the buriers shall arise from
the East,
And not a bone of all the sons of Tiriel remain.
Bury your mother, but you cannot bury the curse of
Tiriel.'

He ceased, and darkling o'er the mountains sought
his pathless way.

II

He wandered day and night. To him both day and
night were dark:
The sun he felt, but the bright moon was now a useless globe.

O'er mountains and through vales of woe the blind
    and aged man
Wandered, till he that leadeth all led him to the
    vales of Har.

And Har and Heva, like two children, sat beneath
    the oak.
Mnetha, now aged, waited on them, and brought
    them food and clothing.
But they were as the shadow of Har, and as the years
    forgotten :
Playing with flowers and running after birds they
    spent the day,
And in the night like infants slept, delighted with
    infant dreams.
Soon as the blind wanderer entered the pleasant
    gardens of Har,
They ran weeping, like frighted infants, for refuge in
    Mnetha's arms.
The blind man felt his way, and cried : ' Peace to
    these open doors !
Let no one fear, for poor blind Tiriel hurts none but
    himself.
Tell me, O friends, where am I now, and in what
    pleasant place ? '

' This is the valley of Har,' said Mnetha, ' and this
    the tent of Har.
Who art thou, poor blind man, that takest the name
    of Tiriel on thee ?
Tiriel is King of all the West.   Who art thou ?   I am
    Mnetha ;
And this is Har and Heva, trembling like infants by
    my side.'

' I know Tiriel is King of the West, and there he
    lives in joy.
No matter who I am, O Mnetha !   If thou hast any
    food,
Give it me, for I cannot stay,—my journey is far
    from hence.'

Then Har said : ‘O my mother Mnetha, venture not
    so near him,
For he is the king of rotten wood, and of the bones
    of death ;
He wanders without eyes, and passes through thick
    walls and doors.
Thou shalt not smite my mother Mnetha, O thou
    eyeless man !’

‘A wanderer, I beg for food. You see I cannot weep.
I cast away my staff, the kind companion of my travel,
And I kneel down that you may see I am a harmless
    man.’

He kneeled down. And Mnetha said : ‘Come, Har
    and Heva, rise :
He is an innocent old man, and hungry with his
    travel.’

Then Har arose, and laid his hand upon old Tiriel’s
    head.

‘God bless thy poor bald pate, God bless thy hollow
    winking eyes,
God bless thy shrivelled beard, God bless thy many-
    wrinkled forehead !
Thou hast no teeth, old man ! and thus I kiss thy
    sleek bald head.
Heva, come kiss his bald head, for he will not hurt
    us, Heva.’

Then Heva came, and took old Tiriel in her mother’s
    arms.

‘Bless thy poor eyes, old man, and bless the old
    father of Tiriel !
Thou art my Tiriel’s old father ; I know thee through
    thy wrinkles,
Because thou smellest like the fig-tree, thou smellest
    like ripe figs.
How didst thou lose thy eyes, old Tiriel? Bless thy
    wrinkled face !’

Mnetha said : ' Come in, aged wanderer ; tell us of
thy name.
Why shouldst thou conceal thyself from those of
thine own flesh ? '

' I am not of this region,' said Tiriel dissemblingly.
' I am an aged wanderer, once father of a race
Far in the North ; but they were wicked, and were
all destroyed,
And I their father sent an outcast. I have told
you all :
Ask me no more, I pray, for grief hath sealed my
precious sight.'

' O Lord !' said Mnetha, ' how I tremble ! Are there
then more people,
More human creatures on this earth, beside the sons
of Har ?'

' No more,' said Tiriel, ' but I, remain on all this
globe ;
And I remain an outcast. Hast thou anything to
drink ?'

Then Mnetha gave him milk and fruits, and they sat
down together.

III

They sat and ate, and Har and Heva smiled on Tiriel.

' Thou art a very old old man, but I am older than thou.
How came thine hair to leave thy forehead, how came
thy face so brown ?
My hair is very long, my beard doth cover all my
breast.
God bless thy piteous face ! To count the wrinkles in
thy face
Would puzzle Mnetha. Bless thy face, for thou art
Tiriel !'

' Tiriel I never saw but once. I sat with him and ate ;

He was as cheerful as a prince, and gave me enter-
    tainment.
But long I stayed not at his palace, for I am forced
    to wander.'

'What! wilt thou leave us too?' said Heva. 'Thou
    shalt not leave us too,
For we have many sports to show thee, and many
    songs to sing;
And after dinner we will walk into the cage of Har,
And thou shalt help us to catch birds, and gather
    them ripe cherries;
Then let thy name be Tiriel, and never leave us more.'
'If thou dost go,' said Har, 'I wish thine eyes may
    see thy folly.
My sons have left me.—Did thine leave thee? Oh,
    'twas very cruel!'

'No, venerable man,' said Tiriel, 'ask me not such
    things,
For thou dost make my heart to bleed. My sons
    were not like thine,
But worse. Oh never ask me more, or I must flee
    away.'

'Thou shalt not go,' said Heva, 'till thou hast seen
    our singing-birds,
And heard Har sing in the great cage, and slept upon
    our fleeces.
Go not, for thou art so like Tiriel that I love thine
    head,
Though it is wrinkled like the earth parched with the
    summer heat.'

Then Tiriel rose up from the seat, and said: 'God
    bless these tents!
My journey is o'er rocks and mountains, not in
    pleasant vales;
I must not sleep nor rest, because of madness and
    dismay.'

And Mnetha said : 'Thou must not go to wander
    dark alone,
But dwell with us, and let us be to thee instead of eyes,
And I will bring thee food, old man, till death shall
    call thee hence.'

Then Tiriel frowned, and answered : 'Did I not
    command you, saying,
Madness and deep dismay possess the heart of the
    blind man,
The wanderer who seeks the woods, leaning upon his
    staff ? '

Then Mnetha, trembling at his frowns led him to
    the tent-door,
And gave to him his staff, and blessed him. He went
    on his way.

But Har and Heva stood and watched him till he
    entered the wood ;
And then they went and wept to Mnetha, but they
    soon forgot their tears.

IV

Over the weary hills the blind man took his lonely
    way ;
To him the day and night alike was dark and desolate.
But far he had not gone when Ijim from his woods
    came down,
Met him at entrance of the forest, in a dark and
    lonely way.

'Who art thou, eyeless wretch, that thus obstructest
    the lion's path ?
Ijim shall rend thy feeble joints, thou tempter of dark
    Ijim !
Thou hast the form of Tiriel, but I know thee well
    enough !
Stand from my path, foul fiend ! Is this the last of
    thy deceits—

To be a hypocrite, and stand in shape of a blind
    beggar?'

The blind man heard his brother's voice, and kneeled
    down on his knee.

' O brother Ijim, if it is thy voice that speaks to me,—
Smite not thy brother Tiriel, though weary of his life.
My sons have smitten me already ; and, if thou
    smitest me,
The curse that rolls over their heads will rest itself
    on thine.
'Tis now seven years since in my palace I beheld thy
    face.'

' Come, thou dark fiend, I dare thy cunning ! know
    that Ijim scorns
To smite thee in the form of helpless age and eyeless
    policy ;
Rise up, for I discern thee, and I dare thy eloquent
    tongue.
Come, I will lead thee on thy way, and use thee as a
    scoff.'

' O brother Ijim, thou beholdest wretched Tiriel :
Kiss me, my brother, and then leave me to wander
    desolate !'

' No, artful fiend, but I will lead thee ; dost thou
    want to go ?
Reply not, lest I bind thee with the green flags of the
    brook ;
Ay, now thou art discovered. I will use thee like a
    slave.'

When Tiriel heard the words of Ijim, he sought not
    to reply :
He knew 'twas vain, for Ijim's words were as the
    voice of Fate.

And they went on together, over hills, through woody
  dales,
Blind to the pleasures of the sight, and deaf to
  warbling birds.
All day they walked, and all the night beneath the
  pleasant moon,
Westwardly journeying, till Tiriel grew weary with
  his travel.

'O Ijim, I am faint and weary, for my knees forbid
To bear me further. Urge me not, lest I should die
  with travel.
A little rest I crave, a little water from a brook,
Or I shall soon discover that I am a mortal man,
And thou wilt lose thy once-loved Tiriel.   Alas! how
  faint I am !'

'Impudent fiend !' said Ijim, 'hold thy glib and
  eloquent tongue ;—
Tiriel is a king, and thou the tempter of dark Ijim.
Drink of this running brook, and I will bear thee on
  my shoulders.'

He drank ; and Ijim raised him up, and bore him on
  his shoulders.
All day he bore him ; and, when evening drew her
  solemn curtain,
Entered the gates of Tiriel's palace, and stood and
  called aloud.

'Heuxos, come forth !   I here have brought the fiend
  that troubles Ijim.
Look ! know'st thou aught of this grey beard, or of
  these blinded eyes ?'

Heuxos and Lotho ran forth at the sound of Ijim's
  voice,
And saw their aged father borne upon his mighty
  shoulders.
Their eloquent tongues were dumb, and sweat stood
  on their trembling limbs ;

They knew 'twas vain to strive with Ijim. They
　　bowed and silent stood.

'What, Heuxos! call thy father, for I mean to sport
　　to-night.
This is the hypocrite that sometimes roars a dreadful
　　lion;
Then I have rent his limbs, and left him rotting in
　　the forest
For birds to eat.　But I have scarce departed from
　　the place
But like a tiger he would come, and so I rent him too.
Then like a river he would seek to drown me in his
　　waves,
But soon I buffeted the torrent; anon like to a cloud
Fraught with the swords of lightning, but I braved
　　the vengeance too.
Then he would creep like a bright serpent, till around
　　my neck
While I was sleeping he would twine : I squeezed his
　　poisonous soul.
Then like a toad or like a newt would whisper in my
　　ears;
Or like a rock stood in my way, or like a poisonous
　　shrub.
At last I caught him in the form of Tiriel blind and
　　old,
And so I'll keep him.　Fetch your father, fetch forth
　　Myratana.'

They stood confounded, and thus Tiriel raised his
　　silver voice.

'Serpents, not sons, why do you stand? Fetch hither
　　Tiriel,
Fetch hither Myratana, and delight yourselves with
　　scoffs;
For poor blind Tiriel is returned, and this much-
　　injured head

Is ready for your bitter taunts.   Come forth, sons of
the curse !'

Meantime the other sons of Tiriel ran around their
father,
Confounded at the terrible strength of Ijim.   They
knew 'twas vain,
Both spear and shield were useless, and the coat of
iron mail,
When Ijim stretched his mighty arm ; the arrow from
his limbs
Rebounded, and the piercing sword broke on his
naked flesh.

'Then it is true, Heuxos, that thou hast turned thy
aged parent
To be the sport of wintry winds,' said Ijim : 'is this
true ?
It is a lie, and I am like the tree torn by the wind,
Thou eyeless fiend and you dissemblers !   Is this
Tiriel's house ?
It is as false as Matha, and as dark as vacant Orcus.
Escape, ye fiends, for Ijim will not lift his hand
against ye.'

So saying, Ijim gloomy turned his back, and silent
sought
The secret forests, and all night wandered in desolate
ways.

v

And aged Tiriel stood and said : 'Where does the
thunder sleep ?
Where doth he hide his terrible head ? and his swift
and fiery daughters,
Where do they shroud their fiery wings, and the
terrors of their hair ?
Earth, thus I stamp thy bosom ! rouse the earthquake
from his den,
To raise his dark and burning visage through the
cleaving ground,

To thrust these towers with his shoulders! Let his
    fiery dogs
Rise from the centre, belching flames and roaring
    dark smoke!
Where art thou, Pestilence, that bathest in fogs and
    standing lakes?
Raise up thy sluggish limbs, and let the loathsomest
    of poisons
Drop from thy garments as thou walkest, wrapped in
    yellow clouds!
Here take thy seat in this wide court; let it be strewn
    with dead;
And sit and smile upon these cursed sons of Tiriel!
Thunder, and fire, and pestilence, hear you not
    Tiriel's curse?'

He ceased. The heavy clouds confused rolled round
    the lofty towers,
Discharging their enormous voices at the father's
    curse.
The earth trembled, fires belched from the yawning
    clefts,
And, when the shaking ceased, a fog possessed the
    accursed clime.

The cry was great in Tiriel's place. His five daughters
    ran,
And caught him by the garments, weeping with cries
    of bitter woe.

'Ay, now you feel the curse, you cry! but may all
    ears be deaf
As Tiriel's, and all eyes as blind as Tiriel's, to your
    woes!
May never stars shine on your roofs, may never sun
    nor moon
Visit you, but eternal fogs hover around your
    walls!—
Hela, my youngest daughter, thou shalt lead me from
    this place;

And let the curse fall on the rest, and wrap them up
together !'

He ceased, and Hela led her father from the noisome
place.
In haste they fled, while all the sons and daughters
of Tiriel,
Chained in thick darkness, uttered cries of mourning
all the night.
And in the morning, lo ! an hundred men in ghastly
death,
The four daughters, stretched on the marble pavement, silent, all
Fallen by the pestilence,—the rest moped round in
guilty fears ;
And all the children in their beds were cut off in one
night.
Thirty of Tiriel's sons remained, to wither in the
palace—
Desolate, loathed, dumb, astonished — waiting for
black death.

VI

And Hela led her father through the silence of the
night,
Astonished, silent, till the morning beams began to
spring.

'Now, Hela, I can go with pleasure, and dwell with
Har and Heva,
Now that the curse shall clean devour all those guilty
sons.
This is the right and ready way ; I know it by the
sound
That our feet make. Remember, Hela, I have saved
thee from death ;
Then be obedient to thy father, for the curse is taken
off thee.

I dwelt with Myratana five years in the desolate
    rock ;
And all that time we waited for the fire to fall from
    heaven,
Or for the torrents of the sea to overwhelm you
    all.
But now my wife is dead, and all the time of grace is
    past.
You see the parent's curse. Now lead me where I
    have commanded.'

'O leagued with evil spirits, thou accursed man of
    sin,—
True, I was born thy slave. Who asked thee to save
    me from death ?
'Twas for thyself, thou cruel man, because thou
    wantest eyes.'

'True, Hela, this is the desert of all those cruel
    ones.
Is Tiriel cruel ? Look ! his daughter—and his youngest
    daughter—
Laughs at affection, glories in rebellion, scoffs at
    love.
I have not ate these two days ; lead me to Har and
    Heva's tent,
Or I will wrap thee up in such a terrible father's
    curse
That thou shalt feel worms in thy marrow creeping
    through thy bones ;
Yet thou shalt lead me. Lead me, I command, to
    Har and Heva.'

'O cruel ! O destroyer ! O consumer ! O avenger !
To Har and Heva I will lead thee ; then would that
    they would curse,—
Then would they curse as thou hast cursed ! But
    they are not like thee !

Oh they are holy and forgiving, filled with loving
  mercy,
Forgetting the offences of their most rebellious
  children,
Or else thou wouldest not have lived to curse thy
  helpless children.'

'Look on my eyes, Hela, and see (for thou hast eyes
  to see)
The tears swell from my stony fountains; wherefore
  do I weep?
Wherefore from my blind orbs art thou not seized
  with poisonous stings?
Laugh, serpent, youngest venomous reptile of the
  flesh of Tiriel!
Laugh, for thy father Tiriel shall give thee cause to
  laugh,
Unless thou lead me to the tent of Har, child of the
  curse!'

'Silence thy evil tongue, thou murderer of thy helpless children.
I lead thee to the tent of Har: not that I mind thy
  curse,
But that I feel they will curse thee, and hang upon
  thy bones
Fell shaking agonies, and in each wrinkle of that
  face
Plant worms of death to feast upon the tongue of
  terrible curses!'

'Hela, my daughter, listen! Thou art the daughter
  of Tiriel.
Thy father calls. Thy father lifts his hand unto the
  heavens,
For thou hast laughed at my tears, and cursed thy
  aged father:
Let snakes rise from thy bedded locks, and laugh
  among thy curls!'

He ceased. Her dark hair upright stood, while
    snakes infolded round
Her madding brows : her shrieks appalled the soul of
    Tiriel.

'What have I done, Hela, my daughter ? Fear'st
    thou now the curse,
Or wherefore dost thou cry ? Ah, wretch, to curse
    thy aged father !
Lead me to Har and Heva, and the curse of Tiriel
Shall fail. If thou refuse, howl in the desolate
    mountains.'

VII

She, howling, led him over mountains and through
    frighted vales,
Till to the caves of Zazel they approached at eventide.

Forth from their caves old Zazel and his sons ran,
    when they saw
Their tyrant prince blind, and his daughter howling
    and leading him.

They laughed and mocked ; some threw dirt and
    stones as they passed by ;
But, when Tiriel turned around and raised his awful
    voice,
Some fled away ; but Zazel stood still, and thus
    began :—

'Bald tyrant, wrinkled cunning, listen to Zazel's
    chains ;
'Twas thou that chained thy brother Zazel ! Where
    are now thine eyes ?
Shout, beautiful daughter of Tiriel ; thou singest a
    sweet song !
Where are you going ? Come and eat some roots,
    and drink some water.
Thy crown is bald, old man ; the sun will dry thy
    brains away,
And thou wilt be as foolish as thy foolish brother
    Zazel.'

The blind man heard, and smote his breast, and
        trembling passed on.
They threw dirt after them, till to the covert of a
        wood
The howling maiden led her father, where wild beasts
        resort,
Hoping to end her woes ; but from her cries the
        tigers fled.
All night they wandered through the wood ; and,
        when the sun arose,
They entered on the mountains of Har.   At noon the
        happy tents
Were frighted by the dismal cries of Hela on the
        mountains.

But Har and Heva slept fearless as babes on loving
        breasts.
Mnetha awoke ; she ran and stood at the tent-door,
        and saw
The aged wanderer led towards the tents.   She took
        her bow,
And chose her arrows, then advanced to meet the
        terrible pair.

VIII

And Mnetha hasted, and met them at the gate of the
        lower garden.
' Stand still, or from my bow receive a sharp and
        winged death !'

Then Tiriel stood, saying : ' What soft voice threatens
        such bitter things?
Lead me to Har and Heva ; I am Tiriel, King of the
        West.'

And Mnetha led them to the tent of Har ; and Har
        and Heva
Ran to the door.   When Tiriel felt the ankles of aged
        Har,
He said : ' O weak mistaken father of a lawless race,

Thy laws, O Har, and Tiriel's wisdom, end together
    in a curse.
Why is one law given to the lion and the patient ox,
And why men bound beneath the heavens in a reptile
    form,
A worm of sixty winters creeping on the dusty
    ground ?
The child springs from the womb; the father ready
    stands to form
The infant head, while the mother idle plays with her
    dog on her couch.
The young bosom is cold for lack of mother's nourish-
    ment, and milk
Is cut off from the weeping mouth with difficulty and
    pain.
The little lids are lifted, and the little nostrils
    opened ;
The father forms a whip to rouse the sluggish senses
    to act,
And scourges off all youthful fancies from the new-
    born man.
Then walks the weak infant in sorrow, compelled to
    number footsteps
Upon the sand. And, when the drone has reached
    his crawling length,
Black berries appear that poison all round him. Such
    was Tiriel,—
Compelled to pray repugnant and to humble the
    immortal spirit,
Till I am subtle as a serpent in a paradise,
Consuming all—both flowers and fruits, insects and
    warbling birds.
And now my paradise is fallen, and a drear sandy
    plain
Returns my thirsty hissings in a curse on thee, O
    Har,
Mistaken father of a lawless race !—My voice is past.'

He ceased, outstretched at Har and Heva's feet in
    awful death.

MANUSCRIPT AND MEANING OF 'TIRIEL'

This bears no date on the MS. Mr. Swinburne, who certainly had the original in his hands, gives it as his opinion that it was Blake's first book. In the 'First Book of Urizen' the name occurs as 'Thiriel.' He is first-born son of Urizen (in the South), and was 'astonished as a man from a cloud born' at his own birth. The name is probably modified from Ithuriel. That a whole book is lost referring to his youthful life is not improbable, unless this was contained in the possible 'Second Book of Urizen,' of which we know nothing, except that Blake seems to have intended to write it.

In any case, the words 'I am Tiriel, King of the West,' begin a portion which, as Mr. Rossetti's eye first observed, marks the handwriting of a later period, as though Blake had returned to the book after laying it aside, and had then finished it. Mr. Yeats has noticed a change of style towards the close of the poem. The book now begins with a conjunction. The true commencement has not come down to us. Perhaps only a line was struck out, while the conjunction was left. Blake made several incomplete corrections like this to the MS. of 'Vala.'

He probably omitted to copy out fairly the first sentences. The MS. as we have it is neatly written on a very bad soft paper bearing as watermark the letters G. R. (Georgius Rex) only. Blake used just such paper for the 'Island in the Moon.' On the limp grey cover into which it was stitched he wrote 'MS. of Mr. Blake,' showing that he intended it to go out of his hands.

In our own time the MS. had an adventure. It seems to have been unstitched to set up type from its separate leaves when the Aldine edition was published by Mr. Bell. For many years no one knew what had become of it. There were stories related of how it had gone to America, but these were not authoritative. In 1903 the present head of the firm of Bell and Son found it in a box, where it seems to have been placed by his father after returning from the printer at the time of the Aldine edition. He relates this himself, and it is well known that it was sold at Messrs. Sotheby's, and bought by Mr. Quaritch, who resold it soon after, but here the story ends, for Mr. Quaritch very properly never tells to whom he has sold anything that has once been disposed of.

While at Messrs. Sotheby's, before the sale, the MS. was open to inspection. There the present editor saw it, and was able to read the partly obliterated lines—obliterated by Blake himself—that were quoted incorrectly in a note to page 200 of

Mr. Swinburne's essay (John Camden Hotten, 2nd edition, 1868).

It is not permitted to copy at Messrs. Sotheby's, but the three extra lines were written down from memory by the present editor immediately on leaving the house, after careful reading, and are substantially accurate. But before we reach these, we find a few fragments.

The earliest, of no great importance, are dotted about in the fourth section of the poem, where Ijim appears. He at once calls out—

> 'Children, bring forth your father.'

A little later some words are struck out that seem to be

> 'We are the slaves of fortune, and this cruel man
> Desires our death. . . . We bow to the decree of fate.
> They kneeled down.'

And finally—

> 'Ijim set Tiriel on the ground, musing deeply
> If these things were so.'

But it is in a few meditative sentences which Blake cut out in order to keep the interest more to his myth towards the end that the lines occur that Mr. Swinburne first saw to be of poetic value.

Different kinds of men are described—the Lion and Ox, etc.—these words being imperfectly legible in broken lines, and then the list goes on—

'Some nostrils wide breathing out blood, some close shut
In silent deceit, poisons inhaling from the morning rose,
With danger hid beneath their lips and poison in their
    tongue,—
Or eye'd with little sparks of Hell, or with infernal brands
Flying flames of discontent and plagues of dark despair,—
Or those whose mouths are shut, whose teeth are gates of
    eternal death.
Can wisdom be hid in a silver rod, or love in a golden bowl?'

At the end this also is struck out of the summing up—

'Such was Tiriel. . . .
Hypocrisy, the folly of the wise man, the wisdom of the
    cunning.'

The obliteration of this line shows the changing state of Blake's mind, and the beginning of his adoption of at least a modicum of reticence, which his ideally frank nature felt to be a form of wisdom tinged with hypocrisy.

There is yet another crossed out fragment in 'Tiriel' that belongs to the time when Tom Paine was one of Blake's youthful associates—

'Is the King's son warmed without wool, or does he cry with
    a voice
Of Thunder, or look upon the sun and laugh, or streatch
His little hands to the depths of the ocean to draw up
The deadly cunning of the flatterer and spread it to the
    morning?'

It will be felt at once that these passages belong nowhere in the mythic poem, and are only of interest because they are so early that we can see symbolism in them half-born from the mother-earth of poetry, like the 'Tawny lion' in Milton's description of creation in 'Paradise Lost,' still only a head and shoulders visible, rising from the ground, and 'pawing to get free.'

There are also traces of a name or two composed for members of Tiriel's family, and never used again in Blake, so that his own rejection of them seems to have been decisive.

In Thel's Motto, at the head of the 'Book of Thel,' one of the lines here quoted will be found cut in half and dressed with two more above it into a quatrain. This also tends to date 'Tiriel' as at 1790 or 1791, as does the surprise at his birth mentioned at the close of the 'Book of Urizen.'

He is here mentioned as born of a cloud, and in the line where his name occurs in 'Vala' he is identified with a mountain, whose bald and snow-capped peak is suggested in the personal description of him here. In fact the word was struck out, and his name substituted in 'Vala,' Night I., line 357, and in an earlier line, 37 of the same Night, Jerusalem is described as hidden in him in darkness and silence.

He is looked on as hypocrisy, raising its mass to heaven. He becomes a mountain (in human form) from being a cloud by the hardening process belonging to restraint. Also, as restraint alone has no fruitful power in the mind, his story is told as that of an old man. In one line of the MS. we can make out the words 'desire is lost' obliterated. Eyes—which will be seen to be the symbol of desire—have left him: he is blind. The eyes, or desire, that he once had leads him now, in the person of his daughter Hela, whom he reviles. The whole allegoric basis of the story is analysed in the Quaritch edition.

In 'Vala,' Night VII., line 470, or thereabouts, to about

line 490, *there is a story that reveals part of the meaning of Tiriel as eldest son of Urizen, showing the relations to all points of the compass of human moods in this early symbol.*

All the evidence, therefore, that we can collect goes to show that 'Tiriel' was written about 1791—late in that year—when Blake was frequenting the shop of Johnson the publisher, for it was in 1791 that Johnson produced the first part of Blake's lost and never completed poem the 'French Revolution.' 'Tiriel' was copied out for Johnson at this time, and submitted to him. Instead of being printed it was lost. In 1797, when Blake was writing the list of the generations of Los in 'Vala,' Night VIII., line 350 and following, he no longer had it before him. He never utilised any passages from it except the words from the deleted lines in 'Thel's Motto'— probably written after Thel, and added while engraving— and the expression about the Lion and Ox, which is in the last line of 'The Marriage of Heaven and Hell,' and is later than all the rest, whose earlier copies show the last half page blank, without the design below which the words occur. They are used again near the end of page 4 of the 'Visions of the Daughters of Albion,' 1793.

VISIONS

OF

THE DAUGHTERS OF

ALBION

The Eye sees more than the Heart knows.

Printed by Willm. Blake

1793

The Argument

I LOVED Theotormon,
And I was not ashamed.
I trembled in my virgin fears,
And I hid in Leutha's vale!

I plucked Leutha's flower,
And I rose up from the vale;
But the terrible thunders tore
My virgin mantle in twain.

VISIONS

ENSLAV'D, the Daughters of Albion weep; a trembling
    lamentation
Upon their mountains: in their valleys, sighs toward
    America.

For the soft soul of America, Oothoon wander'd in
    woe
Along the vales of Leutha, seeking flowers to comfort
    her;
And thus she spoke to the bright Marygold of
    Leutha's vale:——

Art thou a flower? art thou a nymph? I see thee now
    a flower,
Now a nymph! I dare not pluck thee from thy dewy
    bed!

The Golden nymph replied: pluck thou my flower,
    Oothoon the mild.
Another flower shall spring, because the soul of sweet
    delight
Can never pass away. She ceas'd, and clos'd her
    golden shrine.

Then Oothoon pluck'd the flower, saying: I pluck
    thee from thy bed,
Sweet flower, and put thee here to glow between my
    breasts,
And thus I turn my face to where my whole soul
    seeks.

Over the waves she went in wing'd exulting swift
    delight,
And over Theotormon's reign took her impetuous
    course.

Bromion rent her with his thunders; on his stormy
    bed
Lay the faint maid, and soon her woes appall'd his
    thunders hoarse.

Bromion spoke: behold this harlot here on Bromion's
    bed,
And let the jealous dolphins sport around the lovely
    maid,
The soft American plains are mine, and mine thy
    north and south.
Stampt with my signet are the swarthy children of the
    sun.
They are obedient, they resist not, they obey the
    scourge:
Their daughters worship terrors and obey the violent.

(2)

Now thou must marry Bromion's harlot, and protect
    the child
Of Bromion's rage, that Oothoon shall put forth in
    nine moons' time.

Then storms rent Theotormon's limbs: he rolled his
    waves around;
And folded his black jealous waters round the
    adulterate pair.
Bound back to back in Bromion's caves, terror and
    meekness dwell.

At entrance Theotormon sits, wearing the threshold
    hard
With secret tears; beneath him sound like waves on
    a desert shore

The voice of slaves beneath the sun, and children
    bought with money,
That shiver in religious caves beneath the burning
    fires
Of lust, that belch incessant from the summits of the
    earth.

Oothoon weeps not; she cannot weep; her tears are
    locked up;
But she can howl incessant, writhing her soft snowy
    limbs,
And calling Theotormon's Eagles to prey upon her
    flesh.

I call with holy voice! kings of the sounding air,
Rend away this defiled bosom that I may reflect
The image of Theotormon on my pure transparent
    breast.

The Eagles at her call descend and rend their bleed-
    ing prey.
Theotormon severely smiles; her soul reflects the
    smile,
As the clear spring mudded with feet of beasts
    grows pure and smiles.

The Daughters of Albion hear her woes, and echo
    back her sighs.

Why does my Theotormon sit weeping upon the
    threshold,
And Oothoon hovers by his side, perswading him in
    vain?
I cry arise, O Theotormon, for the village dog
Barks at the breaking day: the nightingale has done
    lamenting;
The lark does rustle in the ripe corn, and the Eagle
    returns
From nightly prey, and lifts his golden beak to the
    pure east,

Shaking the dust from his immortal pinions to awake
The sun that sleeps too long.   Arise, my Theotormon,
        I am pure,
Because the night is gone that clos'd me in its deadly
        black.
They told me that the night and day were all that I
        could see :
They told me that I had five senses to inclose me up ;
And they inclos'd my infinite brain into a narrow
        circle,
And sunk my heart into the Abyss, a red, round
        globe, hot burning,
Till all from life I was obliterated and erased.
Instead of morn arises a bright shadow, like an eye,
In the eastern cloud : instead of night a sickly charnel
        house,
That Theotormon hears me not ! to him the night and
        morn
Are both alike ; a night of sighs, a morning of fresh
        tears :

(3)

And none but Bromion can hear my lamentations.

With what sense is it that the chicken shuns the
        ravenous hawk ?
With what sense does the tame pigeon measure out
        the expanse ?
With what sense does the bee form cells ?   Have not
        the mouse and frog
Eyes and ears and sense of touch ? yet are their
        habitations
And their pursuits as different as their forms and as
        their joys.
Ask the wild ass why he refuses burdens, and the
        meek camel
Why he loves man.   Is it because of eye, ear, mouth,
        or skin,
Or breathing nostrils ? No, for these the wolf and
        tyger have.

Ask the blind worm the secrets of the grave, and why
    her spices
Love to curl round the bones of death; and ask the
    rav'nous snake
Where she gets poison; and the wing'd eagle why he
    loves the sun;
And then tell me the thoughts of man, that have been
    hid of old.

Silent I hover all the night, and all day could be
    silent,
If Theotormon once would turn his loved eyes upon
    me.
How can I be defil'd when I reflect thy image pure?
Sweetest the fruit that the worm feeds on, and the
    soul prey'd on by woe;
The new wash'd lamb ting'd with the village smoke,
    and the bright swan
By the red earth of our immortal river; I bathe my
    wings,
And I am white and pure to hover round Theotor-
    mon's breast.

Then Theotormon broke his silence, and he answered:—

Tell me what is the night or day to one overflow'd
    with woe?
Tell me what is a thought? and of what substance is
    it made?
Tell me what is a joy? and in what gardens do joys
    grow?
And in what rivers swim the sorrows, and upon what
    mountains

(4)

Wave shadows of discontent? and in what houses
    dwell the wretched,
Drunken with woe, forgotten, and shut up from cold
    despair?

Tell me where dwell the thoughts, forgotten till thou
    call them forth?
Tell me where dwell the joys of old, and where the
    ancient loves?
And when will they renew again, and the night of
    oblivion past,
That I might traverse times and spaces far remote,
    and bring
Comforts into a present sorrow and a night of pain?
Where goest thou, O thought? to what remote land is
    thy flight?
If thou returnest to the present moment of affliction,
Wilt thou bring comforts on thy wing, and dews and
    honey and balm,
Or poison from the desert wilds, from the eyes of the
    envier?

Then Bromion said, and shook the cavern with his
    lamentation :—

Thou knowest that the ancient trees seen by thine
    eyes have fruit ;
But knowest thou that trees and fruits flourish upon
    the earth
To gratify senses unknown? trees, beasts, and birds
    unknown ;
Unknown, not unperciev'd, spread in the infinite
    microscope,
In places yet unvisited by the voyager, and in worlds
Over another kind of seas, and in atmospheres un-
    known.
Ah ! are there other wars, beside the wars of sword
    and fire?
And are there other sorrows beside the sorrows of
    poverty?
And are there other joys beside the joys of riches and
    ease?
And is there not one law for both the lion and the ox?
And is there not eternal fire, and eternal chains,

To bind the phantoms of existence from eternal life?

Then Oothoon waited silent all the day and all the
  night,

(5)

But when the morn arose, her lamentation renew'd;
The Daughters of Albion hear her woes, and echo
  back her sighs.

O Urizen! Creator of men! mistaken Demon of
  heaven;
Thy joys are tears, thy labour vain, to form men to
  thine image.
How can one joy absorb another? are not different joys
Holy, eternal, infinite? and each joy is a Love.
Does not the great mouth laugh at a gift? and the
  narrow eyelids mock
At the labour that is above payment? and wilt thou
  take the ape
For thy councellor, or the dog for a schoolmaster to
  thy children?
Does he who contemns poverty, and he who turns
  with abhorrence
From usury, feel the same passion, or are they moved
  alike?
How can the giver of gifts experience the delights of
  the merchant?
How the industrious citizen the pains of the husbandman?
How different far the fat fed hireling with hollow
  drum,
Who buys whole corn fields into wastes, and sings
  upon the heath!
How different their eye and ear! how different the
  world to them!
With what sense does the parson claim the labour of
  the farmer?
What are his nets and gins and traps, and how does
  he surround him

With cold floods of abstraction, and with forests of
   solitude,
To build him castles and high spires, where kings and
   priests may dwell,
Till she who burns with youth, and knows no fixed
   lot, is bound
In spells of law to one she loaths? and must she drag
   the chain
Of life in weary lust? must chilling, murderous
   thoughts obscure
The clear heaven of her eternal spring? to bear the
   wintry rage
Of a harsh terror, driv'n to madness, bound to hold
   a rod
Over her shrinking shoulders all the day, and all the
   night
To turn the wheel of false desire, and longings that
   wake her womb
To the abhorred birth of cherubs in the human form,
That live a pestilence and die a meteor, and are no
   more,
Till the child dwell with one he hates, and do the
   deed he loaths,
And the impure scourge force his seed into its unripe
   birth,
Ere yet his eyelids can behold the arrows of the day?

Does the whale worship at thy footsteps as the hungry
   dog?
Or does he scent the mountain prey because his
   nostrils wide
Draw in the ocean? does his eye discern the flying
   cloud
As the raven's eye? or does he measure the expanse
   like the vulture?
Does the still spider view the cliffs where eagles hide
   their young?
Or does the fly rejoice because the harvest is brought
   in?

Does not the eagle scorn the earth, and despise the
treasures beneath?
But the mole knoweth what is there, and the worm
shall tell it thee.
Does not the worm erect a pillar in the mouldering
church yard,

(6)

And a palace of eternity in the jaws of the hungry
grave?
Over his porch these words are written: Take thy
bliss, O Man!
And sweet shall be thy taste, and sweet thy infant
joys renew!

Infancy, fearless, lustful, happy! nestling for delight
In laps of pleasure; Innocence, honest, open, seeking
The vigorous joys of morning light, open to virgin
bliss.
Who taught thee modesty, subtil modesty? child of
night and sleep,
When thou awakest wilt thou dissemble all thy secret
joys,
Or wert thou not awake when all this mystery was
disclos'd?
Then com'st thou forth a modest virgin knowing to
dissemble,
With nets found under thy night pillow, to catch
virgin joy,
And brand it with the name of whore, and sell it in
the night
In silence, ev'n without a whisper, and in seeming
sleep.
Religious dreams and holy vespers light thy smoky
fires:
Once were thy fires lighted by the eyes of honest
morn.
And does my Theotormon seek this hypocrite modesty,
This knowing, artful, secret, fearful, cautious, trembling hypocrite?

Then is Oothoon a whore indeed ! and all the virgin
    joys
Of life are harlots ; and Theotormon is a sick man's
    dream,
And Oothoon is the crafty slave of selfish holiness.

But Oothoon is not so, a virgin fill'd with virgin
    fancies,
Open to joy and to delight where ever beauty appears.
If in the morning sun I find it, there my eyes are
    fix'd

(7)

In happy copulation ; if in evening mild, wearied
    with work,
Sit on a bank and draw the pleasures of this free
    born joy.

The moment of desire ! the moment of desire ! The
    virgin
That pines for man shall awaken her womb to
    enormous joys
In the secret shadows of her chamber ; the youth shut
    up from
The lustful joy shall forget to generate and create
    an amorous image
In the shadows of his curtains and in the folds of his
    silent pillow.
Are not these the places of religion, the rewards of
    continence,
The self enjoyings of self denial ? Why dost thou
    seek religion ?
Is it because acts are not lovely, that thou seekest
    solitude,
Where the horrible darkness is impressed with reflec-
    tions of desire ?

Father of Jealousy, be thou accursed from the earth !
Why hast thou taught my Theotormon this accursed
    thing ?

Till beauty fades from off my shoulders, darken'd and
  cast out,
A solitary shadow wailing on the margin of non-entity.

I cry: Love! Love! Love! happy happy Love! free
  as the mountain wind!
Can that be Love, that drinks another as a sponge
  drinks water?
That clouds with jealousy his nights, with weepings
  all the day;
To spin a web of age around him, grey and hoary,
  dark!
Till his eyes sicken at the fruit that hangs before his
  sight.
Such is self-love that envies all! a creeping skeleton
With lamplike eyes watching around the frozen
  marriage bed.

But silken nets and traps of adamant will Oothoon
  spread,
And catch for thee girls of mild silver, or of furious
  gold.
I'll lie beside thee on a bank and view their wanton
  play
In lovely copulation, bliss on bliss, with Theotormon.
Red as the rosy morning, lustful as the first born beam,
Oothoon shall view his dear delight, nor e'er with
  jealous cloud
Come in the heaven of generous love, nor selfish
  blightings bring.

Does the sun walk in glorious raiment, on the secret
  floor,

(8)

Where the cold miser spreads his gold? or does the
  bright cloud drop
On his same threshold? does his eye behold the beam
  that brings
Expansion to the eye of pity? or will he bind himself

Beside the ox to thy hard furrow ? does not that mild
    beam blot
The bat, the owl, the glowing tyger, and the king of
    night ?
The sea fowl takes the wintry blast for a cov'ring to
    her limbs ;
And the wild snake the pestilence to adorn him with
    gems and gold,
And trees and birds, and beasts and men, behold
    their eternal joy.
Arise, you little glancing wings, and sing your infant
    joy !
Arise, and drink your bliss, for every thing that lives
    is holy !

Thus every morning wails Oothoon, but Theotormon
    sits
Upon the margin'd ocean conversing with shadows
    dire.

The Daughters of Albion hear her woes, and echo
    back her sighs.

THE END

MEANING OF THE 'VISIONS OF THE DAUGHTERS OF ALBION'

It is practically certain that no reader who has not gone through 'Jerusalem' can possibly guess what this book, the 'Visions,' is about. Those who have will recall many passages the moment the words 'daughters of Albion' are seen on the title. The following in particular will come to mind :—

'In every bosom they controll our Vegetative powers,' 'Jerusalem,' page 5, line 39.

' Then all the Daughters of Albion became one before Los, even Vala,' page 64, line 6.

'And the twelve Daughters of Albion united in Rahab and Tirzah,' page 67, line 2.

'Vala, Mother of the Body of Death,' page 62, line 13.

'Vala was their Mother—Vala, Albion's wife,' page 65, line 71.

'No one can consummate female bliss in Los' world without Becoming a generated Mortal, a Vegetating Death,' page 69, line 31, and page 86, line 42.

' Her name is Vala in Eternity: in Time her name is Rahab,' page 63, line 7.

' Vala, Luvah's Daughter,' page 69, line 7.

Here again, as everywhere, the passages have no meaning unless we remember that Vala, like Rahab (her temporal name, used practically as though she were in the region of Time quite another person), is a state ('Jerusalem,' page 52) eternal, though influencing the temporary, and that it is these states (of mind) that both produce our bodies and own their blame or praise.

The Daughters of Albion, these mythical personages, described in 'Jerusalem' as also controlling in each of us the vegetative powers, inhabit the nutritive and procreative organs. It must never be lost sight of that 'body' is only a name for the visible and outer portion of mind.

Nothing that belongs to the region of the loins can be a secret to the Daughters of Albion. Their visions are the visions of the Eye of the Loins, not of the Eye of the Head, or the Eye of the Heart.

In 'Jerusalem' (p. 41, l. 15, and following) is a description of the dwelling-place of Oothoon. In a sense she does inhabit a region of space, but the material portion of her house and its mental dimensions are put in playfully emphatic contrast. She possesses a grain of sand in Lambeth—near the 'Parent' river—that Satan cannot find. That is to say, no accusation, for Satan is the accuser, can be brought successfully against that very small portion of material flame which attaches to her. This grain of sand opens miraculously within and reveals itself to be a palace. Here both 'Jerusalem' and 'Vala'—both poetic and natural love—may repose and be hidden from the terrible action of the mortal created-body, for which they have, maternally, a share of the responsibility, but which is identical with Satan, with Urizen in the North, and with the literal interpretation of the Scriptures, in its matter-of-fact and censorious aspect, and with Reason.

Oothoon is not always even confined to that palace. In 'Jerusalem' (p. 83, l. 27, and following) she is said to hide

herself in Oxford—used always as the name typical of a
'place of thought,' with Antamon, the 'Prince of the Pearly
Dew,' as he is called in 'Europe,' the artistic spirit to
whose hands we owe beauty in form ('Milton,' p. 27). Here
she conceals herself in 'chaste appearances,' lest Hand, the
chief of the Satanic personalities of fallen Man, those that
are moral and reasoning through fear of accusation of sin
or of stupidity, destroy his affection. In the poem of the
'Visions' Oothoon is not hiding at all, but revealing herself
in emphatically unchaste appearances, and it is difficult at
first to see her through the glamour of her own symbols.
The comment of most readers of these pages will be the reproach which Enitharmon in 'Europe' addresses to her: 'Why
wilt thou give up woman's secrecy, my melancholy child?'

'Woman's,' or nature's 'secrecy,' is a term for Theotormon,
and for the jealousy with which Jehovah himself hides from
us. Yet Oothoon is essentially a being of beauty. She equals
Thel; in a physical sense, perhaps, she surpasses Thel. She
is certainly more beautiful than Hela, for Hela's hair is filled
with serpents, and she is the Gorgon beauty whom thought has
turned to pain and poison, for thought changed the 'Infinite'
itself into a serpent ('Europe,' l. 120). And this serpent,
wherever found, in pictures or in poems, is 'The vast form of
nature' ('Jerusalem,' p. 29, l. 80).

Oothoon's beauty being spiritual is able to protect the poor
natural beauty of Leutha. She is her 'charming guard' when
she lives in the tent of Palamabron, the genius of the pen
('Milton,' p. 11, l. 44).

This idea that beauty was a protection was probably at the
root of Blake's decision to utter his philosophy in poetry. As
the scent of tropical flowers given out at evening makes an
atmosphere less penetrable to the chill of night than scentless
air, this helps to protect truth, its utterance, and its initiated
from the violences of Reason. 'When I tell a truth,' Blake
says, 'it is not to convince those who do not know it, but to
protect those who do.' Who these were is indicated in another
saying of his, not altogether consistent with it, but giving it
light none the less. 'I have innocence to defend, and ignorance to instruct' ('Jerusalem,' p. 42, l. 26). Those who know
truth are thus seen to be the Innocent. A picture on the
eleventh page of 'America,' reproduced long ago in 'Gilchrist,'
shows three of them as little naked children playing at horses
with the Great Serpent, whom they bridle with a thread, and
ride by moonlight.

Oothoon's importance is shown by the division of the region
of her influence into its own three regions of Head, Heart,
Loins. This is indicated by her three lovers. When she

hides in places of thought with the formative spirit ('Milton,' p. 27, l. 13), she is the Eye of the Loins in the Region of the Head. It is her last position when she is left in Oxford with Antamon. The present poem relates her grief because Theotormon, who is the sadness of the jealous heart, rejects her for having yielded to Bromion, who represents the violence of fleshly fury. He refuses to believe that if she leaves the state called Bromion, she would become pure again as a river, and reflect his image only. He 'attributes sin and righteousness to individuals, and not to states,' which deprives him of the very means by which he could have forgiven her, as the book 'Jerusalem' will presently teach.

Oothoon is of the region of the blood, of the cloud of the loins. She belongs to that 'Hell' or 'Abyss' from which, in 'The Marriage of Heaven and Hell,' we are told that Messiah stole something of that with which he formed Heaven. This is part of the symbolic suggestion contained also in the phrases about 'the divine members' being 'ideas,' and Christ and His apostles 'artists,' and Theotormon giving the gospel to Jesus, considered as the Man of Sorrows ('Africa,' line 24).

Antamon, like Oothoon, is a cloud—a blood symbol. He is related to Tiriel, the 'man from a cloud born,' but his functions are not separated from his origin. Tiriel passed from the province of the life-giving air to that of hard earth, seen as mountains or rock, and became a destroyer. Antamon is the 'golden cloud' who speaks in the book of 'Thel.' He is not named there. Of those who converse in the book of 'Thel,' only Thel herself is given by name. The rest are under common nouns, the names of their symbols. Oothoon is able to live with him finally because she also is a cloud. There is a picture of her as one, raining over a field of corn, in 'Milton,' page 44. But clouds are not only the kind nourishers with rain. Lightning has access to them, and they have no defence. Blood cannot resist the inroad of passion. Oothoon could not resist Bromion. After Bromion had rent her, she wept all her tears quickly away and had no more, but as a cumulus cloud in the high air showed snowy limbs within which the eagles could find pure water with the qualities of the river. But from such a cloud new lightning might yet fall, in the fulness of time (mythically Bromion's child), thus forming the link that binds Oothoon evermore to all violence and fury of fire, whether in the heights or the deeps, therefore she is chained to a flame given forth by the earth, when seen in the 'Visions,' floating over Theotormon and pleading with him.

Bromion also implies the violence of the Human Reason

destroying imagination. Those come under his power who pluck the flower of desire in the region of natural and not of imaginative beauty—the marigold of Leutha's vale. Leutha is the feminine personality of simple desire, and owns the 'dogs,' lusts, of the Isle of Dogs on the Thames ('Jerusalem,' p. 31, l. 16). For Leutha, see also 'Europe,' line 205, and 'Africa,' line 28, and 'Milton,' page 9, lines 23 and following.

'The Argument' of the poem shows us Oothoon as the 'Mary' of the ballads and the 'William Bond' mingled.

'I plucked Leutha's flower,' Oothoon says.

Oothoon's fault was that of Eve and Psyche, and Pandora. She passed, through curiosity, under the dominion of intellectual powers that are those of coercive reasoning, not of beautiful persuasion. 'The terrible thunders,' thoughts of passion ('Jerusalem,' p. 3, l. 24), 'tore my virgin mantle,' her realm of free, pure, unthinking joy, 'in twain.' It began to be double, and so to enter into the condition leading to war, for the single cannot fight in space.

The poem needs endless explanation. It will be noticed that the device of putting thoughts into a series of one-line questions is developed here from the rejected lines in 'Tiriel,' and helps us to date that poem as earlier than 1793. In this note the present editor quotes (with trifling changes) the opening pages of his much longer analysis in the Quaritch edition, as he ventures to do more than once in the succeeding notes.

DESIGNS TO THE 'VISIONS OF THE DAUGHTERS OF ALBION'

A virgin, Oothoon, is on the Frontispiece, seen as a tiny figure leaping wildly to earth from the part of the sky dominated by Urizen. Figures sit or fly about full of youth and passion.

'The Argument.' This page shows a graceful girl kneeling in the blaze of a sunrise, and crossing her hands on her breast. She sits on her heels in kneeling, and is not at prayer or meditation. Her object is to get down near the level of a straggling flower whose scent, as a similar virgin but a quarter the size—a miniature—floats out and kisses her on the

lips while flying past. Both nude. She is Oothoon. We have come on her as the 'wild flower' itself in the 'Wild-flower's Song' in the 'Ideas of Good and Evil.' She is, in fact, Vala, and all the females together.

Page 1. The upper part: archers in the air shooting the 'arrows of the day' down to the poem. Lower part: the virgin, no longer such now, flung exhausted on a rock. The owner of terrible thunders, a strong man, lies in a position of abandonment and relief, not far off, but looking the other way. Both nude.

Page 2. Inserted in middle a strong black male figure, writhing alone on the ground, rolling as he lies. Nude. Bromion perhaps in the gloom of Theotormon, a 'shadow dire,' if not Theotormon dressed in his own gloom.

Page 3. Oothoon on a cloud, flung back while kneeling, and letting an eagle tear her heart out as she lies with face lifted so far as to show him only the under side of the chin, and arms flung beyond and above the head.

Page 4. Oothoon hovering in a flame over the head of Theotormon, who sits by the sea with his hands on his raised knees and his forehead bowed on his hands. She is attached by a chain and ankle-ring to the sea, from which the flame itself rises. Both young; he, robed; she, nude.

Page 5. A small sketch. Oothoon, partly draped, rolling sadly on the ground, and hiding her face.

Page 6. Oothoon, nude, walking off hiding her face, striding over one leg of Theotormon, now nude, who, half raised from where he lay, flourishes a three-lashed scourge over his head at her. Each lash has a terrible set of prickly points at the end. In classic days the scourge would have been called a scorpion. The absence of any trace of voluptuous cruelty in the attitudes and expressions, and the fact that the scourge is being flourished rhetorically, not used practically, and that Oothoon hides her face and does not wince, suggests that Theotormon is scourging her with jealous accusations of sin.

Page 7. Three daughters of Albion hearing her woes as they sit in a heap by the sea; all robed. They represent also the fourfold sorrow of Theotormon.

Page 8. The same three. This time they see the woes and sighs as a figure on its breast on a cloud, with arms flung out and flames rising from between its body and the cloud, and curling round its arms: the daughters robed: the sighs, nude.

Last picture, an entire page. Bromion's cave. We see from within it the sea and the sun outside, beyond three figures in the entrance. A man with his hair on end, and his hands tied behind him, sits on his heels with his knees at his chin, as usual, and seems in great agitation. At his back a young and graceful woman kneels, with her hands tied behind her, and also tied to his hands. He is chained by the ankle as well. Another man sits a little way off them, rolling himself in distress, and folding his arms round his face to shut out the sight of the others. Bromion, Oothoon, and Theotormon, all nude.

AMERICA:

A

PROPHECY

LAMBETH :

Printed by WILLIAM BLAKE in the year 1793.

PRELUDIUM

THE shadowy daughter of Urthona stood before red
  Orc,
When fourteen suns had faintly journey'd o'er his
  dark abode.
His food she brought in iron baskets, his drink in
  cups of iron.
Crown'd with a helmet and dark hair the nameless
  female stood ;
5 A-quiver with its burning stores, a bow like that of
  night.
When pestilence is shot from heaven, no other arms
  she had ;
Invulnerable tho' naked, save where clouds roll round
  her loins ;
Their awful folds in the dark air ; silent she stood as
  night ;
For never from her iron tongue could voice or sound
  arise ;
10 But dumb till that dread day when Orc assay'd his
  fierce embrace.

Dark virgin, said the hairy youth, thy father stern
  abhorr'd,
Rivets my tenfold chains while still on high my spirit
  soars.
Sometimes an eagle screaming in the sky, sometimes
  a lion
Stalking upon the mountains, and sometimes a whale
  I lash
15 The raging fathomless abyss, anon a serpent folding
Around the pillars of Urthona, and round thy dark
  limbs,

On the Canadian wilds I fold, feeble my spirit folds,
For chain'd beneath I rend these caverns; when thou
bringest food
I howl my joy, and my red eyes seek to behold thy
face.
20 In vain ! these clouds roll to and fro, and hide thee
from my sight.

(2)

Silent as despairing love, and strong as jealousy,
The hairy shoulders rend the links, free are the wrists
of fire ;
Round the terrific loins he siez'd the panting, struggling womb ;
It joy'd : she put aside her clouds and smiled her
first-born smile,
5 As when a black cloud shews its lightnings to the
silent deep.

Soon as she saw the terrible boy then burst the virgin
cry.

I know thee, I have found thee, and I will not let
thee go :
Thou art the image of God who dwells in darkness
of Africa,
And thou art fall'n to give me life in regions of dark
death.
10 On my American plains I feel the struggling afflictions
Endur'd by roots that writhe their arms into the
nether deep.
I see a serpent in Canada who courts me to his love ;
In Mexico an Eagle, and a Lion in Peru ;
I see a Whale in the South-sea, drinking my soul
away.
15 O what limb-rending pains I feel, thy fire and my frost
Mingle in howling pains, in furrows by thy lightnings
rent ;
17 This is eternal death, and this the torment long
foretold.

A PROPHECY

THE Guardian Prince of Albion burns in his nightly
      tent,
Sullen fires across the Atlantic glow to America's
      shore,
Piercing the souls of warlike men who rise in silent
      night.
Washington, Franklin, Paine, and Warren, Gates,
      Hancock, and Green,
5 Meet on the coast glowing with blood from Albion's
      fiery Prince.

Washington spoke: Friends of America, look over
      the Atlantic sea;
A bended bow is lifted in heaven, and a heavy iron
      chain
Descends link by link from Albion's cliffs across the
      sea to bind
Brothers and sons of America, till our faces pale and
      yellow;
10 Heads deprest, voices weak, eyes downcast, hands
      work-bruis'd,
Feet bleeding on the sultry sands, and the furrows
      of the whip
Descend to generations that in future times forget.

The strong voice ceas'd, for a terrible blast swept over
      the heaving sea;
The eastern cloud rent; on his cliffs stood Albion's
      wrathful Prince,

15 A dragon form clashing his scales at midnight he arose,
   And flam'd red meteors round the land of Albion
      beneath ;
17 His voice, his locks, his awful shoulders, and his
      glowing eyes,

(4)

Appear to the Americans upon the cloudy night.

Solemn heave the Atlantic waves between the gloomy
      nations,
Swelling, belching from its deeps red clouds and
      raging fires.
Albion is sick. America faints ! enrag'd the Zenith
      grew,
5 As human blood shooting its veins all round the
      orbed heaven.
Red rose the clouds from the Atlantic in vast wheels
      of blood,
And in the red clouds rose a Wonder o'er the Atlantic
      sea ;
Intense ! naked ! a Human fire, fierce glowing, as the
      wedge
Of iron heated in the furnace ; his terrible limbs were
      fire
10 With myriads of cloudy terrors, banners dark and
      towers
Surrounded ; heat but not light went thro' the murky
      atmosphere.

12 The King of England looking westward trembles at
      the vision.

(5)

Albion's Angel stood beside the Stone of night, and
      saw
The terror like a comet, or more like the planet red
That once inclos'd the terrible wandering comets in
      its sphere.
Then Mars thou wast our center, and the planets
      three flew round

5 Thy crimson disk ; so e'er the Sun was rent from thy
    red sphere,
  The Spectre glow'd his horrid length staining the
    temple long
7 With beams of blood, and thus a voice came forth,
    and shook the temple :

(6)

The morning comes, the night decays, the watchmen
    leave their stations ;
The grave is burst, the spices shed, the linen wrapped
    up ;
The bones of death, the cov'ring clay, the sinews
    shrunk and dry'd,
Reviving shake, inspiring move, breathing ! awaken-
    ing !
5 Spring like redeemed captives, when their bonds and
    bars are burst.
Let the slave grinding at the mill run out into the
    field,
Let him look up into the heavens and laugh in the
    bright air ;
Let the inchained soul shut up in darkness and in
    sighing,
Whose face has never seen a smile in thirty weary
    years,
10 Rise and look out ; his chains are loose, his dungeon
    doors are open,
And let his wife and children return from the
    opressor's scourge ;
They look behind at every step and believe it is a
    dream,
Singing, The Sun has left his blackness, and has
    found a fresher morning,
And the fair Moon rejoices in the clear and cloudless
    night ;
15 For Empire is no more, and now the Lion and Wolf
    shall cease,

(7)

In thunders ends the voice. Then Albion's Angel
 wrathful burnt
Beside the Stone of Night; and like the Eternal
 Lion's howl
In famine and war, reply'd, Art thou not Orc, who
 serpent form'd
Stands at the gate of Enitharmon to devour her
 children?
5 Blasphemous Demon, Antichrist, hater of Dignities,
Lover of wild rebellion, and transgresser of God's
 Law,
7 Why dost thou come to Angels' eyes in this terrific
 form?

(8)

The terror answer'd : I am Orc, wreath'd round the
 accursed tree ;
The times are ended ; shadows pass, the morning 'gins
 to break ;
The fiery joy, that Urizen perverted to ten commands,
What night he led the starry hosts thro' the wide
 wilderness ;
5 That stony law I stamp to dust ; and scatter religion
 abroad
To the four winds as a torn book, and none shall
 gather the leaves ;
But they shall rot on desart sands, and consume in
 bottomless deeps ;
To make the desarts blossom, and the deeps shrink to
 their fountains,
And to renew the fiery joy, and burst the stony roof,
10 That pale religious letchery, seeking Virginity,
May find it in a harlot, and in coarse-clad honesty
The undefil'd tho' ravish'd in her cradle night and
 morn ;
For every thing that lives is holy, life delights in life ;
Because the soul of sweet delight can never be defil'd.
15 Fires inwrap the earthly globe, yet man is not
 consum'd ;

Amidst the lustful fires he walks; his feet become
like brass,

17 His knees and thighs like silver, and his breast and
head like gold.

(9)

Sound ! sound! my loud war-trumpets, and alarm my
Thirteen Angels.

Loud howls the eternal Wolf ! the eternal Lion lashes
his tail !

America is dark'ned ; and my punishing Demons
terrified

Crouch howling before their caverns deep like skins
dry'd in the wind.

5 They cannot smite the wheat, nor quench the fatness
of the earth.

They cannot smite with sorrows, nor subdue the plow
and spade.

They cannot wall the city, nor moat round the castle
of princes.

They cannot bring the stubbed oak to overgrow the
hills,

For terrible men stand on the shores, and in their
robes I see

10 Children take shelter from the lightnings, there stands
Washington,

And Paine, and Warren, with their foreheads rear'd
toward the east.

But clouds obscure my aged sight. A vision from afar !

Sound ! sound ! my loud war-trumpets, and alarm my
thirteen Angels :

Ah, vision from afar ! Ah, rebel form that rent the
ancient

15 Heavens ! Eternal Viper self-renew'd, rolling in
clouds,

I see thee in thick clouds and darkness on America's
shore,

Writhing in pangs of abhorred birth ; red flames the
crest rebellious

And eyes of death ; the harlot womb oft opened in
vain
Heaves in enormous circles; now the times are return'd
upon thee,
20 Devourer of thy parent ; now thy unutterable torment
renews.
Sound ! sound ! my loud war-trumpets, and alarm my
thirteen Angels.
Ah, terrible birth ! a young one bursting ! where is
the weeping mouth,
And where the mother's milk ? instead those ever-
hissing jaws
And parched lips drop with fresh gore ; now roll thou
in the clouds ;
25 Thy mother lays her length outstretch'd upon the
shore beneath.
Sound ! sound ! my loud war-trumpets, and alarm my
thirteen Angels ;
27 Loud howls the eternal Wolf, the eternal Lion lashes
his tail !

(10)

Thus wept the Angel voice, and as he wept the terrible
blasts
Of trumpets blew a loud alarm across the Atlantic
deep.
No trumpets answer ; no reply of clarions or of fifes.
Silent the Colonies remain and refuse the loud alarm.

5 On those vast shady hills between America and
Albion's shore,
Now barr'd out by the Atlantic sea, call'd Atlantean
hills,
Because from their bright summits you may pass to
the Golden world,
An ancient palace, archetype of mighty Emperies,
Rears its immortal pinnacles, built in the forest of
God
10 By Ariston the king of beauty for his stolen bride.

Here on their magic seats the thirteen Angels sat
    perturb'd,
12 For clouds from the Atlantic hover o'er the solemn
    roof.

(11)

Fiery the Angels rose, and as they rose deep thunder
    roll'd
Around their shores : indignant burning with the fires
    of Orc,
And Boston's Angel cried aloud as they flew thro' the
    dark night.

He cried : Why trembles honesty, and like a murderer,
5 Why seeks he refuge from the frowns of his immortal
    station ?
Must the generous tremble and leave his joy to the
    idle, to the pestilence
That mock him ? who commanded this ? what God ?
    what Angel ?
To keep the gen'rous from experience till the
    ungenerous
Are unrestrain'd performers of the energies of nature,
10 Till pity is become a trade, and generosity a science
That men get rich by, and the sandy desert is giv'n
    to the strong.
What God is he, writes laws of peace, and clothes him
    in a tempest ?
What pitying Angel lusts for tears, and fans himself
    with sighs ?
What crawling villain preaches abstinence and wraps
    himself
15 In fat of lambs ? no more I follow, no more obedience
    pay.

(12)

So cried he, rending off his robe and throwing down
    his scepter
In sight of Albion's Guardian, and all the thirteen
    Angels

Rent off their robes to the hungry wind, and threw
　　their golden scepters
Down on the land of America ; indignant they de-
　　scended
5 Headlong from out their heav'nly heights, descending
　　swift as fires
Over the land ; naked and flaming are their lineaments
　　seen
In the deep gloom ; by Washington and Paine and
　　Warren they stood,
And the flame folded roaring fierce within the pitchy
　　night,
Before the Demon red, who burnt towards America,
10 In black smoke thunders and loud winds rejoicing in
　　its terror,
Breaking in smoky wreaths from the wild deep, and
　　gath'ring thick
12 In flames as of a furnace on the land from North to
　　South.

(13)

What time the thirteen Governors that England sent
　　convene
In Bernard's house ; the flames cover'd the land, they
　　rouze, then
Shaking their mental chains, they rush in fury to the
　　sea
To quench their anguish : at the feet of Washington
　　down fall'n
5 They grovel on the sand and writhing lie, while all
The British soldiers thro' the thirteen states sent up
　　a howl
Of anguish, threw their swords and muskets to the
　　earth, and ran
From their encampments and dark castles seeking
　　where to hide
From the grim flames, and from the visions of Orc,
　　in sight
10 Of Albion's Angel ; who, enrag'd, his secret clouds
　　open'd

From north to south, and burnt outstretch'd on wings
    of wrath cov'ring
The eastern sky, spreading his awful wings across the
    heavens ;
Beneath him roll'd his num'rous hosts, all Albion's
    Angels camp'd
Darken'd the Atlantic mountains, and their trumpets
    shook the valleys,
15 Arm'd with diseases of the earth to cast upon the
    Abyss,
16 Their numbers forty millions, must'ring in the eastern
    sky.

(14)

In the flames stood and view'd the armies drawn out
    in the sky,
Washington, Franklin, Paine, and Warren, Allen,
    Gates, and Lee ;
All heard the voice of Albion's Angel give the
    thunderous command ;
His plagues, obedient to his voice, flew forth out of
    their clouds,
5 Falling upon America, as a storm to cut them off,
As a blight cuts the tender corn when it begins to
    appear.
Dark is the heaven above, and cold and hard the earth
    beneath ;
And as a plague wind fill'd with insects cuts off man
    and beast,
And as a sea o'erwhelms a land in the day of an earth-
    quake :
10 Fury ! rage ! madness ! in a wind swept through
    America,
And the red flames of Orc, that folded roaring, fierce,
    around
The angry shores, and the fierce rushing of th'
    inhabitants together ;
The citizens of New York close their books and lock
    their chests ;

The mariners of Boston drop their anchors and
    unlade ;
15 The scribe of Pensylvania casts his pen upon the
    earth ;
The builder of Virginia throws his hammer down in
    fear ;
Then had America been lost, o'erwhelm'd by the
    Atlantic,
And Earth had lost another portion of the infinite.
But all rush together in the night in wrath and
    raging fire.
20 The red fires rag'd ! the plagues recoil'd ! then roll'd
    they back with fury

(15)

On Albion's Angels : then the Pestilence began in
    streaks of red
Across the limbs of Albion's Guardian, the spotted
    plague smote Bristol's,
And the Leprosy London's Spirit, sickening all their
    bands :
The millions sent up a howl of anguish and threw off
    their hammer'd mail,
5 And cast their swords and spears to earth, and stood
    a naked multitude.
Albion's Guardian writhed in torment on the eastern
    sky,
Pale, quiv'ring toward the brain his glimmering eyes,
    teeth chattering,
Howling and shuddering, his legs quivering ; convuls'd
    each muscle and sinew,
Sick'ning lay London's Guardian, and the ancient
    miter'd York,
10 Their heads on snowy hills, their ensigns sick'ning in
    the sky.

The plagues creep on the burning winds driven by
    flames of Orc.
And by the fierce Americans rushing together in the
    night,

Driven o'er the Guardians of Ireland, and Scotland
    and Wales.
They spotted with plagues forsook the frontiers and
    their banners sear
15 With fires of hell, deform their ancient heavens with
    shame and woe.
Hid in his caves the Bard of Albion felt the enormous
    plagues,
And a cowl of flesh grew o'er his head and scales on
    his back and ribs ;
And rough with black scales all his Angels fright their
    ancient heavens.
The doors of marriage are open, and the Priests in
    rustling scales
20 Rush into reptile coverts, hiding from the fires of Orc,
That play around the golden roofs in wreaths of fierce
    desire,
Leaving the females naked and glowing with the lusts
    of youth.

For the female spirits of the dead, pining in bonds of
    religion,
Run from their fetters reddening, and in long drawn
    arches sitting ;
25 They feel the nerves of youth renew, and desires of
    ancient times,
26 Over their pale limbs as a vine when the tender grape
    appears.

(16)

Over the hills, the vales, the cities rage the red flames
    fierce ;
The Heavens melted from north to south ; and Urizen,
    who sat
Above all heavens in thunders wrap'd, emerg'd his
    leprous head
From out his holy shrine, his tears in deluge piteous
5 Falling into the deep sublime ; flag'd with grey-brow'd
    snows

And thunderous visages, his jealous wings wav'd over
　　the deep;
Weeping in dismal howling woe, he dark descended,
　　howling
Around the smitten bands, clothed in tears and
　　trembling, shudd'ring, cold.
His stored snows he poured forth, and his icy
　　magazines
10 He open'd on the deep, and on the Atlantic sea white
　　shiv'ring.
Leprous his limbs, all over white, and hoary was his
　　visage,
Weeping in dismal howlings before the stern Ameri-
　　cans,
Hiding the Demon red with clouds and cold mists
　　from the earth,
Till Angels and weak men twelve years should govern
　　o'er the strong;
15 And then their end should come, when France reciev'd
　　the Demon's light.

Stiff shudderings shook the heav'nly thrones! France,
　　Spain, and Italy
In terror view'd the bands of Albion, and the ancient
　　Guardians,
Fainting upon the elements, smitten with their own
　　plagues;
They slow advance to shut the five gates of their law-
　　built heaven,
20 Filled with blasting fancies and with mildews of
　　despair,
With fierce disease and lust, unable to stem the fires
　　of Orc;
But the five gates were consum'd, and their bolts and
　　hinges melted;
23 And the fierce flames burnt round the heavens, and
　　round the abodes of men.

FINIS

MEANING OF 'AMERICA'

'America' reappears in Blake's symbolic poetry, though the allusion was not published, in the earlier pages of 'Vala,' quite certainly not written later than 1797, the date of its title-page. In Night I., line 120, we hear how

' A frowning continent appeared, where Enion in the desert,
  Terrified at her own creation, viewing her woven shadow,
  Sat in a dread intoxication of Repentance and contrition.'

Enion is wife of Tharmas, ruler of uncertainty in mind, of vegetation and bodily instinct in nature. We never lose sight of him for long in the Prophetic Books.

Close to these lines we have the first account of the 'birth' of Los and Enitharmon, who will be fully spoken of later on, and then—after the creation of Beulah, also to be familiar to us later—it is seen that Tharmas must not be a personal ruler and prolific father any more, and the gate of the tongue (the Western Gate) is closed. Tharmas is the tongue, in a certain point of view. Compare 'Jerusalem,' page 14, line 4.

The object of this action seems to have been regarded by Blake as good, but afterwards we have its evil results continually before us.

We are definitely told how

' Albion closed the Western Gate and shut America out
  By the Atlantic for a curse, and for a hidden horror,
  And for an altar of victims offered to sin and repentance,'

after Albion had turned his back on the spirits of pity and love.

The preceding passages from line 50 are almost to be found in 'Jerusalem,' page 29, etc., where Blake first printed them. They had lain beside him not less than seven years in the 'Vala' manuscript. The previous 'hiding in shadow' of Los and Enitharmon, Night III., line 47, and their coming away from the scene that followed in 'Jerusalem,' page 30, lines 1 and 2, and from all the Tharmas story, show how sternly Blake contracted what he had to say in the engraved poem, from the more expanded account in the 'Vala' MS.

We know now that sin and repentance were shut out with 'America,' but only after reading all Blake do we get to see that sin meant, to him, in spite of his wild preaching of 'free love,' almost anything that leads us to be absorbed in nature, however beautiful, so that we attend to and believe in her, and forget imagination. This follows logically, of course, from the creed that Nature is essentially opaque or Satanic, and eternal death only its 'limit'; while Imagination, or the Saviour or eternal life, is essentially translucent, there being no limit to translucence ('Jerusalem,' page 42, line 35).

When we get to the account of the 'closing' in 'Jerusalem' corresponding to that already quoted from 'Vala,' it is in the end of page 30 and beginning of page 31 in this form—

'Albion covered
His Western heaven with rocky clouds of death and despair,'

to which even sin and repentance would seem preferable, though these two things join in Morality, personated poetically afterwards by Rahab, who, we are also told, is sin, in the useful explanatory passage, Night IX., lines 150 to 160.

Since Heavens are vessels of nourishing or generative power, as seen in 'Jerusalem,' page 21, line 31 ; page 43, lines 16, 17 ; page 49, lines 61, 62, which vessels are seen as the Eye, Marriage, or Beulah, and the Ear (generation), page 66, line 40, and in 'Vala,' Night IX., lines 786 to 797 and 820—the preface to the book of 'America' comes with no surprise now.

In 'Vala,' Night VII., lines 611 and following, we have the first form of this Preludium. Traces of the same portion of the myth will be found in extra, page 17, after 'Milton.'

As we read it in this book of 'America,' if we require to keep a running commentary of translation in mind, in order not to get ourselves lost among the symbols, the words to be chiefly noted are :—

To Orc (passion) the shadowy daughter (properly his sister, since his father's spectre or egotistic personality and Reasoning power was Urthona, but really his material counterpart) brings food in iron baskets, which symbolise incidents of excitement and attraction. Iron is magnetic. She is nameless, as we shall learn in the Preludium to 'Europe,' because not generated really—a mere portion of himself that seems external: the helmet is a sign of war—the war of passion: the bow is that of male and female love ('Jerusalem,' page 95, lines 14, 15, and page 97, line 12): the pestilence is the disease of languor and shame. She is invulnerable because naked—not clothed with even the 'little curtain of flesh' told of in 'Thel,' though clouds (blood: his blood really) roll round her loins. She is youth's ideal arising from his material needs; finally, in various forms obviously suggestive of meaning—eagle, serpent, etc. She becomes a real power in him and over him, though in torment. For torment, see 'Jerusalem,' prose passage, page 77. See for full explanation, 'Vala,' Night VII., lines 610 to 671.

The book that follows has puzzled people by its title. Why is it called 'A Prophecy'? Yet there is much less history in it than in such books of the Bible as Joshua, Ruth, Samuel, Kings, Chronicles, and Esther, which were called 'Prophets' as much as Isaiah. Our term 'Historical Books' has arbitrarily overlaid their title. Blake took them all for symbolic history, and saw no reason for treating the history of his own day otherwise than symbolically. In fact, he practically invented it as he went along merely for the purpose of his myth. The idea now current in respectable circles that we are to imitate the persons mentioned in Biblical narrative, though even this not too recklessly, while we are not to imitate Biblical authors at all, would have astounded him by its cool assumption of authority as much as we may fairly imagine that it would have astonished Moses himself, who was the first to check such prohibitions when applied to poor Eldad and Medad, who were prophesying in the camp,—Numbers, chap. xi. verse 26. This belongs to Blake's 'Bible of Hell,' promised in 'The Marriage of Heaven and Hell.' We are all so accustomed to our fleshly bodies and their limitations, that we are apt to forget that Blake believed clairvoyance to be no miracle, but the proper state of man, while corporeal solidity was the result of an intellectual error. Our opacity certainly increases with our common sense. The most frequent examples of telepathy, second sight, and so forth are not to be found where are most decorum and education, among the school-taught people of London.

It would seem that Albion's Angel here is an aspect of Urizen. 'Albion' becomes a personage in 'Vala,' and presumably his name was inserted into the MS. of that poem when such lines were used for it as those from page 6 here, that are in Night IX., ll. 667 and 823, and others that are rounded up with the close of the 'Song of Liberty,' evidently dated 1790, and issued with 'The Marriage of Heaven and Hell.' It will be noticed how the 'fiery limbs' that sunk into the Western Sea in that Song send up from it a 'human wonder' now, as told in page 4. That the 'falling fire' of the 'Song of Liberty' was Orc is made clear in page 8 here, where the words about stamping the Stony Law are the same; and close to them the 'everything that lives is holy' repeats the 'Visions of the Daughters of Albion.'

That restraint, the holding in of wild impulses in firm grip of 'heavens' was also holy, follows once more, and has no incoherence in its place.

After intricate symbolism, analysed with more or less success by the present editor in the Quaritch edition, and easily to be analysed over again, as well or better, by any one who knows 'Jerusalem' and 'Vala' reasonably well, we come, in the last page, on the doctrinal essence of the whole matter:—

It is bodily passion that burns the hard gates of the five senses, and ends by setting free the spiritual in man.

That this is not more often seen as a fact we must attribute to education as at present practised, being the enemy of sympathy and telepathy.

DESIGNS TO 'AMERICA'

Frontispiece.—A colossal winged giant sitting at night, and chained as he sits, in the opening where a massive wall has been broken through. His forehead is bowed forward on his knees. We do not see the face.

A woman, intended to be of natural size, but of a third of his height, sits on part of the broken wall, as on a chair. She seems waiting. A child is on her lap, another stands against her: all nude.

The large figure seems to be Urizen, as Albion's Angel, chained to the wall that became the Mundane Shell, or the Finite wall of the Flesh. Enion sits outside, with Los and Enitharmon as children. The wall has been breached, but the chained figure fills the gap. This is in the possible meaning also. As usual, there is no precise passage illustrated.

Title-page.—Mixed with the lettering, a robed male and dressed female figure sit at a little distance, sadly, back to back, and pay no heed to each other. Minute figures try in vain to invite them to happy thoughts. They are reading laws of Urizen.

Below, night and rain on a battle-field. A woman dressed, but without hat, and barefooted, crawls over a pavement of dead bodies, and kisses one of them, putting her arms round his neck. She is Pity as a female, repentant, trying to revive with kisses the lover she has slain through jealousy when she was Rahab. Compare 'Broken Love.'

Preludium.—A very strong and handsome boy of sixteen lies on a rock under a tree, sprawling. He is chained down by the wrists. A man and woman stand by, but are turning to leave him. The woman hides her face, the man throws up his hands and utters violent reproach. All nude: Los, Enitharmon, and Orc.

Below the roots of the tree, a doubled-up, nude, youthful figure, Orc, with a worm near him, sits deep in the soil, equally alive there, but in captivity.

Page 2. The doubled-up, youthful, nude figure, Orc, is rising through the soil and forcing his way out. We see his figure through the earth as before. His head is already above.

Page 3. A man and woman fly from flames. The man leads a child of seven. All nude: Los, Enitharmon, and Orc again.

Page 4. A dragon pursues through the air, casting lightning, a draped and bearded figure with a sceptre and book, who dives headlong out of space to avoid him—Tharmas and Urizen. Below, on the earth, people crouch in fear (nude), and trees are blown flat. Clouds roll, heavy and low.

It is difficult to see whether the falling figure is a man with a long beard, robed, or a woman with long hair. In either case, the subject of the design may be called war chasing away law, or religion.

Page 5. Among the best drawings and most difficult to interpret. It is reproduced in 'Gilchrist,' vol. i. Its text identifies the page, and occupies the central of three equal parts into which the page is divided. The upper part shows a strong man in the centre striding over clouds, and carrying another in a doubled-up heap on his back, while a figure on the left flies along with a balance (much weighed down, unequally, though empty), and another on the right carries a flaming sword. The general interpretation is easy. The figures at each side show the central one how, if the balance but be made to go decisively one way or the other, or all judgment be discarded and the sword adopted, Energy need no longer bear Restraint on his shoulders. In more Blakean terms, they are Albion as Ijim, bearing Tiriel on his shoulders between the East and West, between the Angel of the Flaming Sword, 'leaving his guard at the tree of life' (compare 'Marriage of Heaven and Hell'), who is Tharmas; and Luvah, who 'rent the scales from the faint heart of man' ('Vala,' Night II., line 141). These two Zoas in this aspect seem to be one another—the result of Albion's captivity to his own ancient spirit of restraint. Albion is, of course, 'Man,' the male principal, as distinguished from Humanity, which has no sex. Tharmas in this group points down to the lake of fire, from which a serpent rises coiling in the lower part of the page, below the text. There are two figures here, one falling and holding its head; one already fallen, head down, into the coils. Altogether the group may be best described as a pictorial equivalent for some words which we shall presently come to in the book called 'Jerusalem,' written ten years later.

> 'Each man is in his Spectre's Power
> Until the arrival of that hour
> When his Humanity awake,
> And cast his Spectre into the Lake.'

Page 6. *A youth nude, sitting on a rock and a skull, and looking up, in the upper part of the picture. Below, a lizzard catching a fly. The ' awakening' of man's ' Humanity,' and the consequent regeneration of Man.*

Page 7. *A little nude boy and girl of eight years old or less, asleep, one on the back of a big sleeping ram, one at his side. The time of innocence. They may be Tharmas and Enion among the flocks of Vala. The meaning is the same. Compare ' Vala,' Night IX., line* 507, *etc.*

Page 8. *The upper part, a figure representing Jehovah. The lower part, the dark waters on whose face this Spirit brooded at the beginning.*

Page 9. *A baby lying naked and alone in a whirling atmosphere of vague influences that circle round in dim light. Compare ' Jerusalem,' p.* 81, *line* 11, *etc.*—

' I have stripped off Joseph's beautiful integument for my beloved,
The cruel one of Albion, to clothe him in gems of my zone.
I have named him Jehovah, Lord of Hosts. Humanity is become
A weeping Infant in ruined, lovely Jerusalem's folding cloud.'

Page 10. *Orc, or Los, in his flames. A nude youth, with a rapt, ecstatic, and frowning face, climbing through fire.*

Page 11. *Above, a youth riding through the sky on a huge flying swan; below, three children riding a monster snake. This page is reproduced in Gilchrist's ' Life.' The power of innocence that controls the earth in childhood, controls the air in manhood. The swan occurs twice more in Blake's work. Compare picture ' Jerusalem,' p.* 11, *and the mention of it as a type of purity, ' Vala,' Night V., line* 194.

Page 12. *An old man, robed, walking on crutches into a tomb. This design is composed into one picture with that on page* 6, *and is well known as one of Blake's pictures to Blair's ' Grave.'*

Page 13. *A virgin torn by eagles, in the upper part of the page ; a drowned man eaten by fish at the bottom of the sea, in the lower. The pangs of virginity and those of jealousy—of Oothoon and of Theotormon.*

Page 14. *A stern prophetess, draped only in a veil that falls back and leaves her nude, sits under a leafless tree, sternly lecturing a youth who lies on the ground before, his body raised a little, his elbows on a heavy book in two volumes, his hands raised and clasped as in prayer. From between the knees of the woman a big snake is uncoiling itself, lifting its head and thrusting out its tongue at the youth, who is dressed in a*

*tight-fitting costume.   The woman is Rahab.   She is teaching
'Natural Religion' to innocence from beneath its own barren
growth—the tree of Mystery.*

*Page 15.   Happy and lawless innocence.   Women nude,
children, and large vine-branches with leaves and tendrils,
playing in a world of flames where they are not burned.*

*Page 16.   A colossal female figure kneeling under a barren
tree, and worshipping with raised hands and lowered head
and outspread hair.   She is so large that men, women, and
children grouped about her and walking over her look no
bigger than mice.   This is Rahab, of course—or an old Vala,
as Rahab—her 'locks spread on the pavement.'   At the foot
of the page, a snake among thorns, Nature itself.*

THE

BOOK

OF

URIZEN

LAMBETH

Printed by Wm. Blake

1794

PRELUDIUM

TO THE

FIRST BOOK OF URIZEN

OF the primeval Priest's assum'd power,
When Eternals spurn'd back his religion,
And gave him a place in the north,
Obscure, shadowy, void, solitary.

Eternals, I hear your call gladly.
Dictate swift winged words, and fear not
To unfold your dark visions of torment.

BLAKE'S POEMS

(3)

CHAP. I

1. Lo, a shadow of horror is risen
   In Eternity ! Unknown, unprolific,
   Self-clos'd, all-repelling. What Demon
   Hath form'd this abominable void,
   This soul-shudd'ring vacuum?   Some said
   It is Urizen. But unknown, abstracted,
   Brooding secret, the dark power hid.

2. Times on times he divided, and measur'd
   Space by space in his ninefold darkness,
   Unseen, unknown ; changes appear'd
   Like desolate mountains rifted furious
   By the black winds of perturbation.

3. For he strove in battles dire,
   In unseen conflictions with shapes
   Bred from his forsaken wilderness ;
   Of beast, bird, fish, serpent, and element,
   Combustion, blast, vapour, and cloud.

4. Dark, revolving in silent activity,
   Unseen in tormenting passions ;
   An activity unknown and horrible ;
   A self-contemplating shadow,
   In enormous labours occupied.

5. But Eternals beheld his vast forests ;
   Age on ages he lay, clos'd, unknown,
   Brooding, shut in the deep ; all avoid
   The petrific, abominable chaos.

6. His cold horrors silent, dark Urizen
   Prepar'd ; his ten thousands of thunders
   Rang'd in gloom'd array stretch out across
   The dread world ; and the rolling of wheels,
   As of swelling seas, sound in his clouds
   In his hills of stor'd snows, in his mountains
   Of hail and ice ; voices of terror
   Are heard, like thunders of autumn,
   When the cloud blazes over the harvests.

CHAP. II

1. Earth was not, nor globes of attraction ;
   The will of the Immortal expanded
   Or contracted his all flexible senses ;
   Death was not, but eternal life sprung.

2. The sound of a trumpet : the heavens
   Awoke, and vast clouds of blood roll'd
   Round the dim rocks of Urizen, so nam'd
   That solitary one in Immensity.

3. Shrill the trumpet, and myriads of Eternity

(4)

   In living creations appear'd
   In the flames of eternal fury.

(3.) Sund'ring, dark'ning, thund'ring,
   Rent away with a terrible crash,
   Eternity roll'd wide apart,
   Wide asunder rolling ;
   Mountainous all around
   Departing, departing, departing,

Leaving ruinous fragments of life
Hanging, frowning cliffs and all between
An ocean of voidness unfathomable.

4. The roaring fires ran o'er the heav'ns
In whirlwinds and cataracts of blood,
And o'er the dark desarts of Urizen
Fires pour thro' the void on all sides
On Urizen's self-begotten armies.

5. But no light from the fires; all was darkness
In the flames of Eternal fury.

6. In fierce anguish and quenchless flames
To the desarts and rocks he ran, raging
To hide, but he could not; combining,
He dug mountains and hills in vast strength,
He piled them in incessant labour,
In howlings and pangs and fierce madness,
Long periods in burning fires labouring,
Till hoary, and age-broke, and aged,
In despair and the shadows of death.

7. And a roof vast, petrific around,
On all sides he fram'd, like a womb,
Where thousands of rivers in veins
Of blood pour down the mountains to cool
The eternal fires beating without,
From Eternals; and like a black globe,
View'd by sons of Eternity, standing
On the shore of the infinite ocean
Like a human heart struggling and beating,
The vast world of Urizen appear'd.

8. And Los round the dark globe of Urizen
Kept watch for Eternals to confine,
The obscure separation alone;
For Eternity stood wide apart

(5)

As the stars are apart from the earth.

9. Los wept, howling around the dark Demon
And cursing his lot, for in anguish
Urizen was rent from his side,
And a fathomless void for his feet,
And intense fires for his dwelling.

10. But Urizen, laid in a stony sleep,
Unorganiz'd, rent from Eternity.

11. The Eternals said : What is this, Death ?
Urizen is a clod of clay.

(6)

12. Los howl'd in a dismal stupor,
Groaning ! gnashing ! groaning !
Till the wrenching apart was healed.

13. But the wrenching of Urizen heal'd not.
Cold, featureless, flesh or clay,
Rifted with direful changes,
He lay in a dreamless night

14. Till Los rouz'd his (his) fires affrighted
At the formless, unmeasurable death.

(7)

CHAP. III

(*Erroneously numbered IV. in Blake's engraved book.*)

1. Los, smitten with astonishment,
Frighten'd at the hurtling bones

2. And at the surging, sulphureous,
Perturbed, Immortal, mad, raging

3. In whirlwinds, and pitch, and nitre
Round the furious limbs of Los.

4. And Los formed nets and gins,
And threw the nets round about.

5. He watch'd in shudd'ring fear
   The dark changes, and bound every change
   With rivets of iron and brass.

6. And these were the changes of Urizen.

(9)

CHAP. IV

1. Ages on ages roll'd over him ;
   In stony sleep ages roll'd over him,
   Like a dark waste stretching, chang'able ;
   By earthquakes riv'n, belching sullen fires ;
   On ages roll'd ages in ghastly
   Sick torment ; around him in whirlwinds
   Of darkness the eternal Prophet howl'd,
   Beating still on his rivets of iron,
   Pouring sodor of iron ; dividing
   The horrible night into watches.

2. And Urizen (so his eternal name)
   His prolific delight obscur'd more and more ;
   In dark secresy hiding in surging,
   Sulphureous fluid his phantasies.
   The Eternal Prophet heard the dark bellows,
   And turn'd restless the tongs ; and the hammer
   Incessant beat, forging chains new and new ;
   Numb'ring with links, hours, days, and years.

3. The eternal mind bounded began to roll
   Eddies of wrath, ceaseless, round and round.
   And the sulphureous foam, surgeing thick,
   Settled, a lake, bright and shining clear,
   White as the snow on the mountains cold.

4. Forgetfulness, dumbness, necessity,
   In chains of the mind locked up,
   Like fetters of ice shrinking together,
   Disorganiz'd, rent from Eternity.

Los beat on his fetters of iron,
And heated his furnaces, and pour'd
Iron sodor and sodor of brass.

5. Restless turn'd the immortal, inchain'd,
Heaving dolorous ! anguish'd, unbearable,
Till a roof, shaggy, wild, inclos'd
In an orb his fountain of thought.

6. In a horrible, dreamful slumber,
Like the linked infernal chain,
A vast Spine writh'd in torment
Upon the winds, shooting pain'd
Ribs, like a bending cavern,
And bones of solidness froze
Over all his nerves of joy ;
And a first Age passed over,
And a state of dismal woe.

(10)

7. From the caverns of his jointed Spine
Down sunk with fright a red
Round globe, hot, burning deep,
Deep down into the Abyss;
Panting, Conglobing, Trembling,
Shooting out ten thousand branches
Around his solid bones ;
And a second Age passed over,
And a state of dismal woe.

8. In harrowing fear rolling round,
His nervous brain shot branches
Round the branches of his heart,
On high, into two little orbs,
And fixed in two little caves,
Hiding carefully from the wind,
His Eyes beheld the deep ;
And a third Age passed over,
And a state of dismal woe.

9. The pangs of hope began,
   In heavy pain striving, struggling;
   Two Ears in close volutions;
   From beneath his orbs of vision
   Shot spiring out, and petrified
   As they grew.   And a fourth Age passed,
   And a state of dismal woe.

10. In ghastly torment sick,
    Hanging upon the wind,

    (12)

    Two Nostrils bent down to the deep;
    And a fifth Age passed over,
    And a state of dismal woe.

11. In ghastly torment sick,
    Within his ribs bloated round,
    A craving, Hungry Cavern.
    Thence arose his channel'd Throat,
    And, like a red flame, a Tongue
    Of thirst and of hunger appear'd;
    And a sixth Age passed over,
    And a state of dismal woe.

12. Enraged and stifled with torment,
    He threw his right Arm to the north,
    His left Arm to the south,
    Shooting out in anguish deep,
    And his Feet stamp'd the nether Abyss
    In trembling and howling and dismay;
    And a second Age passed over,
    And a state of dismal woe.

CHAP. V

1. In terrors Los shrunk from his task,
   His great hammer fell from his hand,
   His fires beheld, and sickening
   Hid their strong limbs in smoke;

For with noises, ruinous, loud,
With hurtlings and clashings and groans,
The Immortal endur'd his chains,
Tho' bound in a deadly sleep.

2. All the myriads of Eternity,
All the wisdom and joy of life,
Roll like a sea around him,
Except what his little orbs
Of sight by degrees unfold.

3. And now his eternal life
Like a dream was obliterated.

4. Shudd'ring, the Eternal Prophet smote
With a stroke from his north to south region.
The bellows and hammer are silent now,
A nerveless silence, his prophetic voice
Siez'd, a cold solitude and dark void,
The Eternal Prophet and Urizen clos'd.

5. Ages on ages roll'd over them,
Cut off from life and light, frozen
Into horrible forms of deformity.
Los suffer'd his fires to decay,
Then he look'd back with anxious desire,
But the space, undivided by existence,
Struck horror into his soul.

6. Los wept, obscur'd with mourning ;
His bosom earthquak'd with sighs ;
He saw Urizen, deadly black
In his chains bound, and Pity began

7. In anguish dividing and dividing,
For pity divides the soul
In pangs, eternity on eternity.
Life in cataracts pour'd down his cliffs :
The void shrunk the lymph into Nerves,
Wand'ring wide on the bosom of night,
And left a round globe of blood
Trembling upon the void.

(14)

Thus the Eternal Prophet was divided
Before the death image of Urizen,
For in changeable clouds and darkness,
In a winterly night beneath,
The Abyss of Los stretch'd immense,
And now seen, now obscur'd in the eyes
Of Eternals, the visions remote
Of the dark separation appear'd.
As glasses discover Worlds
In the endless Abyss of space,
So the expanding eyes of Immortals
Beheld the dark visions of Los,
And the globe of life blood trembling.

(16)

8. The globe of life blood trembled,
   Branching out into roots,
   Fibrous, writhing upon the winds;
   Fibres of blood, milk, and tears,
   In pangs, eternity on eternity.
   At length in tears and cries imbodied,
   A female form trembling and pale
   Waves before his deathy face.

9. All Eternity shudder'd at sight
   Of the first female now separate,
   Pale as a cloud of snow,
   Waving before the face of Los.

10. Wonder, awe, fear, astonishment,
    Petrify the eternal myriads
    At the first female form now separate.

(17)

They call'd her Pity, and fled.

11. Spread a Tent with strong curtains around them,
    Let cords and stakes bind in the Void
    That Eternals may no more behold them.

12. They began to weave curtains of darkness,
They erected large pillars round the Void ;
With golden hooks fasten'd in the pillars.
With infinite labour the Eternals
A woof wove, and called it Science.

CHAP. VI

1. But Los saw the Female, and pitied ;
He embrac'd her ; she wept, she refus'd ;
In perverse and cruel delight
She fled from his arms, yet he follow'd.

2. Eternity shudder'd when they saw
Man begetting his likeness
On his own divided image.

3. A time passed over ; the Eternals
Began to erect the tent,
When Enitharmon, sick,
Felt a Worm within her womb.

4. Yet helpless it lay like a Worm
In the trembling womb
To be moulded into existence.

5. All day the worm lay on her bosom,
All night within her womb
The worm lay till it grew to a serpent,
With dolorous hissings and poisons
Round Enitharmon's loins folding.

6. Coil'd within Enitharmon's womb
The serpent grew, casting its scales ;
With sharp pangs the hissings began
To change to a grating cry.
Many sorrows and dismal throes,
Many forms of fish, bird, and beast,
Brought forth an Infant form
Where was a worm before.

7. The Eternals, their tent finished,
    Alarm'd with these gloomy visions,
    When Enitharmon, groaning,
    Produc'd a man Child to the light.

8. A shriek ran thro' Eternity,
    And a paralytic stroke,
    At the birth of the Human shadow.

9. Delving earth in his resistless way,
    Howling, the Child with fierce flames
    Issu'd from Enitharmon.

10. The Eternals closed the tent,
    They beat down the stakes with cords,

                                    (18)

    Stretch'd for a work of eternity :
    No more Los beheld Eternity.

11. In his hands he siez'd the infant,
    He bathed him in springs of sorrow,
    He gave him to Enitharmon.

                 CHAP. VII

1. They nam'd the child Orc ; he grew,
    Fed with milk of Enitharmon.

2. Los awoke her ; O sorrow and pain.
    A tight'ning girdle grew
    Around his bosom.   In sobbings
    He burst the girdle in twain ;
    But still another girdle
    Oppress'd his bosom.   In sobbings
    Again he burst it.   Again
    Another girdle succeeds.
    The girdle was form'd by day,
    By night was burst in twain.

3. These falling down on the rock
   Into an iron chain,
   In each other link by link lock'd.

4. They took Orc to the top of a mountain.
   O how Enitharmon wept!
   They chain'd his young limbs to the rock
   With the Chain of Jealousy,
   Beneath Urizen's deathful shadow.

5. The dead heard the voice of the child,
   And began to awake from sleep;
   All things heard the voice of the child,
   And began to awake to life.

6. And Urizen, craving with hunger,
   Stung with the odours of Nature,
   Explor'd his dens around.

7. He form'd a line and a plummet
   To divide the Abyss beneath.
   He form'd a dividing rule.

8. He formed scales to weigh,
   He formed massy weights;
   He formed a brazen quadrant,
   He formed golden compasses,
   And began to explore the Abyss;
   And he planted a garden of fruits.

9. But Los encircled Enitharmon
   With fires of Prophecy,
   From the sight of Urizen and Orc.

10. And she bore an enormous race.

CHAP. VIII

1. Urizen explor'd his dens,
   Mountain, moor, and wilderness,
   With a globe of fire lighting his journey,
   A fearful journey, annoy'd
   By cruel enormities; forms

(21)

Of life on his forsaken mountains.

2. And his world teem'd vast enormities,
   Fright'ning, faithless, fawning,
   Portions of life, similitudes
   Of a foot, or a hand, or a head,
   Or a heart, or an eye, they swam mischievous,
   Dread terrors, delighting in blood.

3. Most Urizen sicken'd to see
   His eternal creations appear,
   Sons and daughters of sorrow on mountains,
   Weeping, wailing.   First Thiriel appear'd,
   Astonish'd at his own existence,
   Like a man from a cloud born, and Utha
   From the waters emerging laments.
   Grodna rent the deep earth, howling,
   Amaz'd ; his heavens immense cracks
   Like the ground parch'd with heat ; then Fuzon
   Flam'd out, first begotten, last born,
   All his eternal sons, in like manner
   His daughters, from green herbs and cattle,
   From monsters and worms of the pit.

4. He in darkness clos'd view'd all his race,
   And his soul sicken'd ! he curs'd
   Both sons and daughters, for he saw
   That no flesh nor spirit could keep
   His iron laws one moment.

5. For he saw that life liv'd upon death.

(23)

The Ox in the slaughter house moans ;
The Dog at the wintry door ;
And he wept, and he called it Pity,
And his tears flowed down on the winds.

6. Cold he wander'd on high, over their cities,
In weeping and pain and woe :
And wherever he wander'd in sorrows
Upon the aged heavens,
A cold shadow follow'd behind him
Like a spider's web, moist, cold, and dim,
Drawing out from his sorrowing soul,
The dungeon-like heaven dividing,
Where ever the footsteps of Urizen
Walked over the cities in sorrow.

7. Till a Web dark and cold throughout all
The tormented element stretch'd
From the sorrows of Urizen's soul,
And the Web is a Female in embrio.
None could break the Web, no wings of fire,

8. So twisted the cords, and so knotted
The meshes ; twisted like to the human brain.

9. And all call'd it the Net of Religion.

CHAP. IX

1. Then the Inhabitants of those Cities
Felt their Nerves change into Marrow,
And hardening Bones began
In swift diseases and torments,
In throbbings and shootings and grindings,
Thro' all the coasts, till weaken'd
The senses inward rush'd, shrinking
Beneath the dark net of infection ;

2. Till the shrunken eyes, clouded over,
Discern'd not the woven hypocrisy,
But the streaky slime in their heavens,
Brought together by narrowing perceptions,
Appear'd transparent air ; for their eyes

Grew small like the eyes of a man,
And in reptile forms shrinking together
Of seven feet stature they remain'd.

3. Six days they shrank up from existence,
And on the seventh day they rested,
And they bless'd the seventh day, in sick hope,
And forgot their eternal life.

4. And their thirty cities divided
In form of a human heart.
No more could they rise at will
In the infinite void, but bound down
To earth by their narrowing perceptions,

(26)

They lived a period of years,
Then left a noisom body
To the jaws of devouring darkness.

5. And their children wept, and built
Tombs in the desolate places,
And form'd laws of prudence, and call'd them
The eternal laws of God.

6. And the thirty cities remain'd
Surrounded by salt floods, now call'd
Africa : its name was then Egypt.

7. The remaining sons of Urizen
Beheld their brethren shrink together
Beneath the Net of Urizen.
Persuasion was in vain,
For the ears of the inhabitants
Were wither'd and deafen'd and cold ;
And their eyes could not discern
Their brethren of other cities.

8. So Fuzon call'd all together
The remaining children of Urizen,
And they left the pendulous earth.
They called it Egypt, and left it.

9. And the salt ocean rolled englob'd.

THE END OF THE FIRST BOOK OF URIZEN

MEANING OF THE BOOK OF 'URIZEN'

Of all the moods of mind that Blake was least fitted by character to treat with any kind of justice, none was so certain to be ill-used by him as the mood of intellectual certainty. He saw it under two forms, living in his day, as it lives in ours. There is the dogmatic priest who himself is no prophet, and the believer in elementary mathematic education, who has not gone far enough into his subject to feel the frailness of the frontier that divides it from mysticism. He rolled the two into one as the schoolmaster of our souls ('Vala,' Night IX., line 130), called it Urizen, saw that its proper place was at the very centre of light, and that its evil tendency was to go to the mere darkness of repetition, restraint, unimaginative morality, and all that is the contrary of its ideal. It was likely to enter this condition, as each of the dominant moods that rule our life is liable to become an influence the reverse of its ideal and natural tendency, because it would be sure to grow proud, and that is the effect of pride.

In 'Vala' he wrote a sun-myth that fitted the psychology, much as in 'Alice through the Looking-Glass' we read in our own day a game of chess made the plot of a nursery tale. This he did in 1797, but already in 1794 he has taken a principal scene from the myth and given it an introduction and denouement, to make a separate bit of symbolic teaching (a separate Prophetic Book) from its matter. He even seems to have intended to do so in two volumes.

As this Book opens the time is night—not merely night after sunset, but the primal night, the absolute lack of imaginative art, love, beauty, or brotherhood in the soul of any one and every one. He assumes power as Primal Priest. He is mere restraint, without even such alleviations as the 'Visions of the

Daughters of Albion' so boldly describe. His 'divisions' are barren of all result. He is properly, when arisen, ploughman and sower, as 'Vala' (never published by Blake) tells us. But now his sowing lacks a field, for ' earth was not, nor globes of attraction,' and the division of himself into original and creative, into self and procreative, avails nothing. The intellectual result is dark fire and formless blood, or cloud. (Never to leave our remembrance for a moment is the formula 'the cloud is blood.'—'Vala,' Night IX., line 277.)

Urizen, as the spirit of ineffectually yet religiously restrained passion, unsupported by brotherhood, art, or hope, is described quite frankly in 'Vala,' Night IX., 149 to 157. This state, with its infectious 'stupor' (aimless, repressed desire), had to be rent away from the Spirit of Prophecy (Los), though it was a part of intellect in its way, and so the end of the third chapter of the 'Book of Urizen' sees him so rent and left formless. Los decides to form him because only form can be ultimately dealt with for good, and he gives him a body by watching and fixing his changes. It is a 'body of doctrine,' if you desire the phrase, and consists of a set of consciousnesses—that symbolised by spine, the ego of thought itself—a mere freezing of thought over that joy which is the spring, or nerves, of life, a condensation of communicative blood into a globe; Heart, the ego of feeling; Eyes, the origin of localised and aimed desire, according to the rule that we cannot desire that which we have not perceived; Ears, that should (and ultimately do, at close of the tale in ' Vala') receive inspired command and generate living words, thoughts, and moods. Tongue, the organ with which most good or evil could be done, and therewith the work of generating Urizen (in the North, the dark interior of matter where generation has its world) was completed.

Then by the law 'what we look on we become,' Los was so far generated also that he became this personality, as we shall hear elsewhere, with this difference, he was alive, and so the red drop of pathetic tendency in his heart separated and became revealed as the female, and is called Enitharmon.

In later books that intellectual thing called a tear is much heard of. Los now saw Enitharmon and pitied (she became Pity in consequence), but in the unpublished book ' Vala' (unpublished by Blake), Night IV., line 96, we see that she was animated by the tears of Los, as Vala herself was animated by the tears of Jerusalem, as told in the book 'Jerusalem' on the last line of page 11.

The story of the 'binding' of Urizen is given with variations that bring out even more clearly the purpose of the symbolism in Night IV. of 'Vala,' from line 170 to line 246. It is seen as part of a larger narrative. The paraphrase here offered attains only to truth along a narrow line of appropriateness. Urizen, and the part of Mind (afterwards called Albion) that was 'generated' in him afterwards, is seen to have put on a 'body of death'—in fact, to have died (Night IV., line 252). Many lines, notably the unforgettable 211th—

'Forgetfulness, dumbness, necessity, in chains of the mind locked up,'

will be recognised as verbally the same in the two accounts. An extra page belonging to some copies only of the book 'Milton' gives, in brief, a third version.

By reaction Los, after binding Urizen, has no choice but to give birth to Orc, his living opposite, whom he will, as told in 'Vala,' Night V., here and elsewhere, try also to bind to a rock, for lawless passion is as much likely to be the enemy of the Spirit of Prophecy as passionless law.

Urizen goes to the caves of Orc (the 'caverns of the grave,' or 'places of human seed,' where Thel herself just peeped in, and fled with virgin terror) in 'Vala,' Night VII., line 5, and from then to the time of regeneration the argument and contest of their natures comes and goes through the poem.

At the end of this book Urizen succeeds in getting sons at last. He had wept. Tiriel is one of them, but we look in vain for Ijim, who does not appear again in Blake's work except as one of three—Har, Ochim, Ijim—which appear among a list of the children of Los and Enitharmon, 'Vala,' Night VIII., line 351 and following. It seems that Blake simply forgot those of the names that interested him least. It must be remembered that he never imprinted on his memory by completely engraving either the book of 'Tiriel' or 'Vala.' Utha is the name of the Western son,

Tiriel, Fuzon, Utha, Grodna

being the four, in the usual order—

S.	E.	W.	N.
Fire	*Air*	*Water*	*Earth*
Urizen	*Luvah*	*Tharmas*	*Urthona,*

for Urizen's 'eternal' place is in the South, though here we are hearing about him in the North, where the sun goes at night.

So Tiriel, when he called himself 'King of the West,' was unusually hypocritical.

The name 'Tiriel,' as Mr. Perugini (a brother-editor, though not a collaborator) has just reminded me, is given in Francis Barrett's book on 'The Magus,' 1801, as meaning 'The intelligence of Mercury.'

In the end we learn that Urizen's fire-son, Fuzon, calls

all the influences, so multitudinous that there are cities-full,
and takes away those who will come, thirty only, that were, his
very heart remaining. It will be seen at any rate that the
'myriads' of Urizen 'built a temple in the image of the
human heart,' of which he laid the first stone.—'Vala,' Night
VII., line 510. We also find Africa referred to as 'heart-
shaped Africa' in another place. Those who left the pendulous earth called it 'Egypt,' which Swedenborg says denotes
'Science' when referred to in the Bible. Science is sometimes
used in a good sense, sometimes in a bad one. It opposes
'religion' when religion is bad, but also opposes 'imagination' when imagination is good. Restricted non-visionary
senses that shut out prophecy take root in Egypt—as told in
the whole page 49 of 'Jerusalem'—where Egypt is named in
line 4.

This book is printed with one editorial variation from
Blake. The chapters are now correctly numbered. In the
original, Blake had numbered Chap. III. as IV., as well as
Chap. IV. Thus there seemed two fourth chapters and no
third. The numberings of verses and chapters have usually a
symbolic suitability to their contents, and had there been any
such indication that there should be no Chap. III. to this book,
the error would have been left. But there is none at all, and
the unusual numbering was really an oversight of Blake's and
has therefore not been followed here.

DESIGNS TO 'URIZEN'

On the title-page of the 'Book of Urizen,' which seems to
have been intended for the first and second Book of the name,
is seen Urizen writing his books under the Tree of Mystery.
An exceedingly old and bearded man, with long hair and
closed eyes, sits in a heap on an open volume that is covered
with blood and blood-vessels. His knees are nearly up to his
ears, and higher than his hands, which stick out right and
left symmetrically, each with a pen in it, and write on a huge
volume that lies open behind him. They are apparently just
able to sign this without reaching too far to the rear. Over
his head rise the tables of the law, like the back of a throne,
and over them a mass of rock, from which their shape is
chiselled. A leafless tree rises over all. This is Urizen, old.
Page 2. The words 'Preludium to' at the top, then a vague

*atmospheric space in which a graceful female figure, draped,
but bare of arm and shoulder, floats away across from left to
right, the back toward us. She reaches out a long arm to
receive a baby that comes swimming through the space towards
her from the left, pursuing her, and laying its arm in the
upward palm of her hand as it comes within reach. Urizen,
innocent, with Vala. Below, the title and seven lines of
'preludium' are framed like a picture in a frame of flames.*

*Page 3.   At the top a nude male figure, Orc, or Los, not yet
inspired, but seeking, strides all across from right to left,
turning his face and shoulders from us and flinging an arm
forward and another backward as he goes. He does not
touch ground, but strides floatingly through a whirl of flames
which have no boundary.*

*Page 4.   The old man (Urizen, claiming to be Jehovah),
opening his book wide as his arms extend before him, and
reading in it. Its pages are covered with Hebrew characters.
Light flashes and irradiates from behind his head.*

*Page 5.   A youth (Luvah, as Christ) with spread arms
falls clear down head-first, bound round by a serpent, and
not struggling. On each side others, also in serpent coils,
fall, holding their heads (the thieves). They fall through fire
into the body of the flame that rises to meet them.*

*Page 6.   A youth (Los, in torments of Orc), with hair on
end, protecting his left ear with his right hand and his right
ear with his left, crawls kneeling towards us and stooping,
escaping from a mass of flame. His face is thrust forward,
with starting eyes and wide open mouth.*

*Page 7.   A skeleton (Urizen, as 'the Bones of Horeb') sitting
on the ground, profile, holding his head that is bowed between
his knees, so that his elbow touches the ground by his instep.
A halo of light clings around him. Beyond is darkness.*

*Page 8.   The old man (Urizen, as Reason in the dark caves
of the senses, unilluminated by imagination) is seen, quite
blind, naked, draped only in his own long beard, crawling on
his hands and knees towards us, and raising himself now
to the height of his straightened arms as he begins to escape
from under a mass of dark rock that has no visible limit.*

*Page 9.   A nude youth (Los) is going boldly away from us
into the same dark rock. He has hardly room to keep his feet.
His head is already hidden. He strides crawlingly, but with
determination. He goes to war with those rocks.*

*Page 10.   A chained and howling anatomy sitting in
flames. A nude youth beside him, picking up a hammer, and
sitting in the same flames. Urizen, with Los 'binding' his
'changes.'*

Page 11.   The same old man is floating with upward arms

and face, spread beard and paddling feet, in a vague darkness of water, through which we see him as if we were in it also. He is Urizen passing the world of Tharmas.

Page 12. A moonlike feminine figure, Ahania, dividing two pale clouds at night as a moon might seem to do.

Page 13. A male, beardless figure upside down, in and on dark clouds, standing on his hands, with bent elbows, and feet swaying in the cloudy air. Perhaps Los going ' North' after Urizen. Another version of his entering the rocks.

Page 14. Four figures, two young, two old, lean over the globed world from the sky, and one moves the waters from half the surface. They are Urizen, Luvah, Tharmas, and Urthona. An eagle is seen behind them. Tharmas is moving the waters. The other youth is Luvah.

Page 14ʌ. The youth, Los, who before crawled from the flames, is now descending through them on purpose. He has leaped in with his knees drawn up and his hands clasped behind his head.

Page 15. Perhaps Los howling over the drop of blood, perhaps Enitharmon leaning over the ' pendulous' world of blood that solidifies from her hair and her dress of blood-vessels. The figure stoops toward us so low that we only see the back of the head. The hands are over the ears.

Page 16. The youth, Los, coming happy and bold from the flames, walking in triumph, and carrying his hammer.

Page 17. Enitharmon appearing from the fire before Los. She hovers in the air and turns shyly from him, holding her head as if in thoughts of grief. He does the same, at the same time kneeling and bowing forward. Both nude and young.

Page 18. Birth of Orc. A baby, nude, diving joyously into a mass of flames.

Page 19. Enitharmon, mature but young, stands beside Los with drooped head. He (now bearded) stands at his forge touching her with his body from shoulder to hip; his hand reaching away from her leans on the handle of his hammer, resting on the anvil. His expression is anxious and frowning (jealousy). Hers is sad and perplexed (contrition). There is an iron belt round his waist, from the middle of which a chain droops to the ground, where it trails and is lost sight of. Between the two figures, and touching the mother with the whole front of his figure, the father with the side, stands Orc, a youth now of fourteen. His arms wound round her as high on the body as they will reach are raised above his head, as he looks upwards from a little below the height of her breasts. All the figures are nude, but a sort of cloak behind Enitharmon trails from one hand. A full page, graceful and impressive.

Page 20.   *Urizen sitting weeping on the ground, his wrists chained to his ankles, his knees as high as his chin, his beard and hair flowing to the earth. A full page. Tragic and masterful. 'Forgetfulness, dumbness, necessity, in chains of the mind locked up.'*—'*Vala,' Night IV., line* 211.

Page 21.   *Urizen exploring his dens—a bearded, patriarchal figure, but in the full vigour of life. He wears a robe with tight sleeves, and carries a radiating globe. A lion meets him, but does not threaten. Dreary hills and twilight behind.*

Page 22.   *Chiefly sky, out of which, from a cloud, comes an excited figure with hands out and long hair—Thiriel. Another, fully seen, floats nude with a look of horror, and wears a nimbus—Fuzon. Below is dark sea to the left, out of which a head is rising—Utha; and an athlete struggles out of the earth on a cliff to the right—Grodna. 'Thiriel,' we know by an earlier poem, was afterwards 'Tiriel.' He loses the 'h' from his name along with his youth, as Abram and Sarai in the Bible become Abraham and Sarah when they adopt 'the promise' or youth, or the divine element—becoming symbols which are most elaborately explained by Swedenborg in the 'Arcana Cœlestia.'*

Page 23.   *An involved group of female figures writhing on the ground. They are worms from the body downwards, and enwound all about with worm growth. One has a bat's wings. They are the emanations of the other four in their earth-aspects—the female and the worm in one. An aspect of conscious but uninspired mortality.*

Page 24.   *A large dog lying on the ground howling, with lifted head, outside a massive closed door. A youth like a young priest, in a robe, stands with his back to it, and looks up despairingly with clasped hands. This, 'the dog at the wintry door.' The youth is perhaps Orc, tamed and outcast. The dog is desire. The wintry door is morality, restraint of desire. Full page.*

Page 25.   *The back of an old man, Urizen again, is seen, in a long robe, floating away into clouds and darkness, and holding up hands of consternation as he sees where he is going. The 'white web' trails after him as he goes. It will become his net.*

Page 26.   *An old man, Urizen, is seated on a low stone throne with his arms supported on rocks at each side of him. A huge net of rope as thick as a cable fastens him in his place. He cannot rise. His eyes are open, and glance sideways in annoyance. He frowns. He is 'caught in his own net.'*

EUROPE:

A

PROPHECY

LAMBETH

Printed by Willm. Blake

1794

(In the copy of 'Europe' possessed by the brothers Linnell, the following preface is to be read. It is not in the British Museum copy. Blake seems to have disused it as out of keeping with the tone of the rest of the Book.)

FIVE windows light the caverned Man: through one he
  breathes the air ;
Through one hears music of the spheres; through one the
  eternal Vine
Flourishes that he may receive the grapes ; through one can
  look
And see small portions of the eternal world that ever groweth;
Through one himself pass out, what time he please, but he
  will not,
For stolen joys are sweet and bread eaten in secret pleasant.

So sang a Fairy, mocking, as he sat on a streaked tulip,
Thinking none saw him. When he ceased I started from the
  trees
And caught him in my hat, as boys knock down a butterfly.

How know you this, said I, small sir, where did you learn
  this song ?
Seeing himself in my possession thus he answered me,—
My Master, I am yours, command me, for I must obey.

Then tell me, what is the material world, and is it dead?
He, laughing, answered, I will write a book on leaves of
  flowers,
If you will feed me on love-thoughts, and give me now and
  then
A cup of sparkling poetic fancies, and when I am tipsy
I will sing you to this soft lute, and show you all alive
This world, where every particle of dust breathes forth its joy.

I took him home in my warm bosom. As we went along
Wild flowers I gathered, and he show'd me each eternal
  flower.
He laughed aloud to see them whimper because they were
  plucked,
Then hovered round me like a cloud of incense. When I came
Into my parlour and sat down and took my pen to write,
My Fairy sat upon the table and dictated Europe.

PRELUDIUM

THE nameless shadowy female rose from out the
    breast of Orc,
Her snaky hair brandishing in the winds of Enith-
    armon ;
And thus her voice arose.

O mother Enitharmon, wilt thou bring forth other
    sons ?
To cause my name to vanish, that my place may not
    be found,
For I am faint with travel,
Like the dark cloud disburden'd in the day of dismal
    thunder.

My roots are brandish'd in the heavens, my fruits in
    earth beneath,
Surge, foam, and labour into life, first born and first
    consum'd !
Consumed and consuming !
Then why shouldst thou, accursed mother, bring me
    into life ?

I wrap my turban of thick clouds around my lab'ring
    head,
And fold the sheety waters as a mantle round my
    limbs,
Yet the red sun and moon,
And all the overflowing stars, rain down prolific pains.

(2)

Unwilling I look up to heaven, unwilling count the
    stars,
Sitting in fathomless abyss of my immortal shrine ;
I sieze their burning power,
And bring forth howling terrors, all devouring fiery
    kings.

Devouring and devoured, roaming on dark and
    desolate mountains,
In forests of eternal death, shrieking in hollow trees.
Ah, mother Enitharmon !
Stamp not with solid form this vig'rous progeny of
    fires.

I bring forth from my teeming bosom myriads of
    flames,
And thou dost stamp them with a signet ; then they
    roam abroad,
And leave me void as death.
Ah ! I am drown'd in shady woe and visionary joy.

And who shall bind the infinite with an eternal bond?
To compass it with swaddling bands ? and who shall
    cherish it
With milk and honey ?
I see it smile, and I roll inward, and my voice is past.

   She ceast and roll'd her shady clouds
   Into the secret place.

A PROPHECY

THE deep of winter came ;
What time the secret child
Descended through the orient gates of the eternal day.
War ceas'd, and all the troops like shadows fled
    to their abodes.

Then Enitharmon saw her sons and daughters rise
    around ;
Like pearly clouds they meet together in the crystal
    house ;
And Los, possessor of the moon, joy'd in the peaceful
    night,
Thus speaking, while his num'rous sons shook their
    bright fiery wings.

Again the night is come,
That strong Urthona takes his rest,
And Urizen, unloos'd from chains,
Glows like a meteor in the distant north.
Stretch forth your hands and strike the elemental
    strings ;
Awake the thunders of the deep.

The shrill winds wake,
Till all the sons of Urizen look out and envy Los,
Sieze all the spirits of life and bind
Their warbling joys to our loud strings ;

VOL. I.
         2 A

Bind all the nourishing sweets of earth
To give us bliss, that we may drink the sparkling wine
    of Los ;
And let us laugh at war,
Despising toil and care,
Because the days and nights of joy in lucky hours
    renew.

Arise, O Orc, from thy deep den,
First born of Enitharmon, rise !
And we will crown thy head with garlands of the
    ruddy vine ;
For now thou art bound,
And I may see thee in the hour of bliss, my eldest
    born.

The horrent Demon rose, surrounded with red stars
    of fire,
Whirling about in furious circles round the immortal
    fiend.

Then Enitharmon down descended into his red light,
And thus her voice rose to her children : the distant
    heavens reply.

                              (5)

Now comes the night of Enitharmon's joy.
Who shall I call ? Who shall I send ?
That Woman, lovely Woman ! may have dominion.
Arise, O Rintrah, thee I call ; and Palamabron thee ;
Go ! tell the human race that Woman's love is Sin ;
That an Eternal life awaits the worms of sixty winters,
In an allegorical abode, where existence hath never
    come.
Forbid all Joy, and from her childhood shall the
    little female
Spread nets in every secret path.

My weary eyelids draw towards the evening, my bliss
    is yet but new.

(6)

Arise, O Rintrah, eldest born, second to none but
    Orc.
O lion Rintrah, raise thy fury from thy forests black ;
Bring Palamabron, horned priest, skipping upon the
    mountains,
And silent Elyaittria, the silver bowed queen.
Rintrah, where hast thou hid thy bride,
Weeps she in desert shades ?
Alas, my Rintrah ! bring the lovely jealous Ocalythron.

Arise, my son ! bring all thy brethren, O thou king of
    fire.
Prince of the Sun, I see thee with thy innumerable
    race,
Thick as the summer stars ;
But each ramping, his golden mane shakes,
And thine eyes rejoice because of strength, O Rintrah,
    furious king.

(7)

Enitharmon slept
Eighteen hundred years.   Man was a dream !
The night of Nature and their harps unstrung.
She slept in middle of her nightly song
Eighteen hundred years, a female dream.

Shadows of men in fleeting bands upon the winds
Divide the heavens of Europe,
Till Albion's Angel, smitten with his own plagues,
    fled with his bands.
The cloud bears hard on Albion's shore,
Fill'd with immortal demons of futurity.
In council gather the smitten Angels of Albion.
The cloud bears hard upon the council house: down
    rushing
On the heads of Albion's Angels.

One hour they lay buried beneath the ruins of that
    hall ;

But as the stars rise from the salt lake, they arise in
pain,
In troubled mists o'erclouded by the terrors of
struggling times.

(8)

In thoughts perturb'd they rose from the bright ruins,
silent, following
The fiery King, who sought his ancient temple,
serpent-form'd,
That stretches out its shady length along the Island
white.
Round him roll'd his clouds of war ; silent the Angel
went
Along the infinite shores of Thames to golden Verulam.
There stand the venerable porches that high-towering
rear
Their oak-surrounded pillars, form'd of massy stones,
uncut
With tool : stones precious : such eternal in the
heavens,
Of colours twelve, few known on earth, give light in
the opake,
Plac'd in the order of the stars, when the five senses
whelm'd
In deluge o'er the earth-born man, then turn'd the
fuxile eyes
Into two stationary orbs, concentrating all things.
The ever-varying spiral ascents to the heavens of
heavens
Were bended downward, and the nostrils' golden
gates shut,
Turn'd outward, barr'd, and petrify'd against the
infinite.

Thought chang'd the infinite to a serpent : that which
pitieth
To a devouring flame ; and man fled from its face and
hid

In forests of night: then all the eternal forests were
    divided
Into earths, rolling in circles of space, that like an
    ocean rush'd,
And overwhelmed all except this finite wall of flesh.
Then was the serpent temple form'd, image of infinite,
Shut up in finite revolutions, and man became an
    Angel,
Heaven a mighty circle turning, God a tyrant
    crown'd.

Now arriv'd the ancient Guardian at the southern
    porch,
That planted thick with trees of blackest leaf, and in
    a vale
Obscure inclos'd the Stone of Night; oblique it stood,
    o'erhung
With purple flowers and berries red, image of that
    sweet south,
Once open to the heavens, and elevated on the
    human neck,
Now overgrown with hair, and cover'd with a stony
    roof;
Downward 'tis sunk beneath th' attractive north, that
    round the feet
A raging whirlpool draws the dizzy enquirer to his
    grave.

(9)

Albion's Angel rose upon the Stone of Night.
He saw Urizen on the Atlantic;
And his brazen Book,
That Kings and Priests had copied on Earth,
Expanded from North to South.

(10)

And the clouds and fires pale roll'd round in the night
    of Enitharmon,
Round Albion's cliffs and London's walls; still Eni-
    tharmon slept;

Rolling volumes of grey mist involve Churches,
　　　Palaces, Towers :
For Urizen unclasp'd his Book, feeding his soul with
　　　pity ;
The youth of England hid in gloom curse the pain'd
　　　heavens, compell'd
Into the deadly night to see the form of Albion's
　　　Angel.
Their parents brought them forth, and aged ignorance
　　　preaches canting,
On a vast rock, perciev'd by those senses that are
　　　clos'd from thought.
Bleak, dark, abrupt it stands, and overshadows
　　　London city ;
They saw his boney feet on the rock, the flesh con-
　　　sum'd in flames ;
They saw the Serpent temple lifted above, shadowing
　　　the Island white ;
They heard the voice of Albion's Angel, howling in
　　　flames of Orc,
Seeking the trump of the last doom.

Above the rest the howl was heard from Westminster
　　　louder and louder,
The Guardian of the secret codes forsook his ancient
　　　mansion,
Driven out by the flames of Orc, his furr'd robes and
　　　false locks
Adhered and grew one with his flesh and nerves, and
　　　veins shot thro' them,
With dismal torment sick, hanging upon the wind, he
　　　fled,
Grovelling along Great George Street, thro' the Park
　　　gate ; all the soldiers
Fled from his sight : he drag'd his torments to the
　　　wilderness.

Thus was the howl thro' Europe !
For Orc rejoic'd to hear the howling shadows,

But Palamabron shot his lightnings, trenching down
    his wide back,
And Rintrah hung with all his legions in the nether
    deep.

Enitharmon laugh'd in her sleep to see (O woman's
    triumph !)
Every house a den, every man bound : the shadows
    are fill'd
With spectres, and the windows wove over with
    curses of iron :
Over the doors, Thou shalt not ; and over the
    chimneys, Fear is written :
With bands of iron round their necks, fasten'd into
    the walls,
The citizens : in leaden gyves the inhabitants of
    suburbs
Walk heavy : soft and bent are the bones of villagers.

Between the clouds of Urizen the flames of Orc roll
    heavy,
Around the limbs of Albion's Guardian his flesh con-
    suming ;
Howlings and hissings, shrieks and groans, and voices
    of despair
Arise around him in the cloudy
Heavens of Albion. Furious,

(11)

The red limb'd Angel, siez'd in horror and torment :
The Trump of the last doom ; but he could not blow
    the iron tube !
Thrice he assay'd presumptuous to awake the dead to
    Judgment.

A mighty Spirit leap'd from the land of Albion,
Nam'd Newton : he siez'd the Trump, and blow'd the
    enormous blast !
Yellow as leaves of Autumn the myriads of Angelic
    hosts

Fell thro' the wintry skies, seeking their graves,
Rattling their hollow bones in howling and lamenta-
    tion.

Then Enitharmon woke, nor knew that she had slept,
And eighteen hundred years were fled
As if they had not been.
She call'd her sons and daughters
To the sports of night
Within her crystal house,
And thus her song proceeds.

Arise, Ethinthus ! tho' the earth-worm call,
Let him call in vain,
Till the night of holy shadows
And human solitude is past !

(12)

Ethinthus, queen of waters, how thou shinest in the
    sky !
My daughter, how do I rejoice ! for thy children
    flock around,
Like the gay fishes on the wave, when the cold moon
    drinks the dew.
Ethinthus ! thou art sweet as comforts to my fainting
    soul,
For now thy waters warble round the feet of Eni-
    tharmon.

Manathu-Varcyon ! I behold thee flaming in my halls,
Light of thy mother's soul ! I see thy lovely eagles
    round.
Thy golden wings are my delight, and thy flames of
    soft delusion.

Where is my luring bird of Eden ?   Leutha, silent
    love !
Leutha, the many colour'd bow delights upon thy
    wings :
Soft soul of flowers, Leutha !
Sweet smiling pestilence ! I see thy blushing light :

Thy daughters, many changing,
Revolve like sweet perfumes ascending, O Leutha,
     silken queen.

Where is the youthful Antamon, prince of the pearly
     dew?
O Antamon, why wilt thou leave thy mother Eni-
     tharmon?
Alone I see thee, crystal form,
Floating upon the bosom'd air,
With lineaments of gratified desire.
My Antamon, the seven churches of Leutha seek thy
     love.

I hear the soft Oothoon in Enitharmon's tents;
Why wilt thou give up woman's secrecy, my melan-
     choly child?
Between two moments bliss is ripe:
O Theotormon, robb'd of joy, I see thy salt tears flow
Down the steps of my crystal house.

Sotha and Thiralatha, secret dwellers of dreamful caves,
Arise and please the horrent fiend with your melodious
     songs,
Still all your thunders, golden hoof'd, and bind your
     horses black.
Orc! smile upon my children!
Smile, son of my afflictions.
Arise, O Orc, and give our mountains joy of thy red
     light.

She ceas'd, for All were forth at sport beneath the
     solemn moon,
Waking the stars of Urizen with their immortal songs,
That nature felt thro' all her pores the enormous
     revelry,
Till morning ope'd the eastern gate,
Then every one fled to his station, and Enitharmon
     wept.

But terrible Orc, when he beheld the morning in the
     east,

(13)

Shot from the heights of Enitharmon,
And in the vineyards of red France appear'd the light
    of his fury.

The sun glow'd fiery red,
The furious terrors flew around !
On golden chariots, raging with red wheels, dropping
    with blood,
The Lions lash their wrathful tails !
The Tigers couch upon the prey and suck the ruddy
    tide,
And Enitharmon groans and cries in anguish and
    dismay.

Then Los arose, his head he rear'd, in snaky thunders
    clad ;
And with a cry that shook all nature to the utmost
    pole,
Call'd all his sons to the strife of blood.

                    FINIS

MEANING OF 'EUROPE'

'*Europe*' *is a term for darkness. Europe and Asia are always the evening and the morning,—North and East.*

After the first page about the Fairy, that Blake omitted from his later copies as quite unsuited to the book, comes the real Preludium in serious symbolic vein. It may be para- phrased. The only service done by the Fairy is to forewarn the reader to expect a symbolic poem, referring to some aspect of marriage. This warning is contained in the very fact that a Fairy is the speaker.

For the 'Shadowy Female' see not only the Preludium to 'America,' but extra page 8, and extra page 17 at the end of 'Milton,'—she is (like 'Vala,' the Shadow 'animated' by Jeru- salem's tears) Nature. We see her here, not under all aspects, but as a thing of the blood. Passion creates the blood and is not created by it. This Female, this visible but vague effusion of unmated desire that rises from the very breast of male energy, standing before his face, prayed Space itself (Enitharmon) to bring into existence no other beings, for she, like each symbolic being, and like each of us mortals, desired her own life to continue. If other visions become moods in man, she, the adolescent preface to mature love, will be superseded. She herself, fainting and travailing, brings forth no permanent mental shape of life, except selfishness, questioning, and the desire of conquest. If such get to have life of their own in space, it is as destroyers of imagination, as mere brute passions, that they must needs live on. A boy's vague emotions are a good preface but a bad volume. Such is the prose equivalent of the Preludium of this book.

The deep of winter, the state of man when most given to the limits of common sense and common egotism, came next. The 'descent' of the 'secret child' through the gates of the day is a counterpart story to that of shadowy female in the Preludium, mere blood-born Desire, rising out of the breast of spiritual passion, for 'above is within,' and both really descend in going outside.

This descent is mortal sunrise, the appearance of that Apollo whom Blake once described, to the alarm of a listener, as 'Satan.' Spiritual war ceased. The struggle that appears to mortals as that of souls striving to enter mortality through the gate of a mortal's realised passion was suspended. It also means more, the struggle of imaginative influences with those that only desire to reason and compare.

The pearly daughters of Space are usually to be seen—so far as most of us know—in the form of clouds in the air. Los, though spirit of Prophecy, yielding to languor, rejoices in the moon (whose light is elsewhere called 'Ahania,' and always shows the dreamy side of passion, as Urizen, the semi-light, shows the practical and tyrannous side of that wakefulness that is more fatal to expanded imaginative life than sleep itself).

So Urthona (Reasoning power of Prophecy) rests, and Urizen, Ruler of Light, becomes in sleep a reflection or echo, a faculty not chained to effort, especially to the effort of suppressing himself—'averting his own despair' ('Vala,' Night VIII., line 136). All of which is due to the getting loose of that nameless thing, the undirected passion of the blood.

Then the Spirits of life are all drawn into the attraction. They are called by name, for there is no space in poetry for the tedium of weary analytical description. Such stuff is only permissible in a note, where it can be read once to avoid bewilderment, and then kept unread for ever, as in times of no

*actual threat against life a once-proved fire-arm is kept for
safety, loaded but not fired.*

*Orc rises in the sun-dream, and his red light is everywhere.
Rintrah and Palamabron, whom Blake at least once associated
plainly and explainingly with Whitfield and Wesley in
'Milton,' page 20, line 55, are called on by the universal
mother to preach against love, and that it is sin in itself, for
the marriage bond is held to permit propagation, but not
to encourage love's delight, at which all churches look askance
('Jerusalem,' page 36, line 45), for churches belong to a God
who does not exist inside man, but outside, 'in an allegoric
abode, where existence has never come.'*

*In a contradictory way this love of dominion is seen to be
the real passion of female or bodily yearning when it once
gets outside of Orc into the cloud. So Rintrah is urged to
bring not only Palamabron, but Ocalythron, jealousy, origin
of the restrictive half of religion.*

*Ocalythron (see 'Milton,' extra page 8, line 19) is the por-
tion of God's jealousy that narrowed the sun into a globe, as
we usually see it, and hid the visionary sun—the sun of the mind.*

*Elynitria did the same to the moon, giving us the natural
sight and taking the imaginative sight away through that
jealousy which narrowed all creation, forbade the tree of life
in Eden, and always 'gains feminine applause.'—See the
verses to 'Nobodaddy.' Elynitria's guard is Palamabron.*

*In the early part of 'Milton' much is to be read about
Palamabron, and a little in 'Jerusalem.'*

*But Rintrah is here called Prince of the Sun. This is
Urizen's title when in his right place. But 'feminine
delusion' has broken loose over the world. In the book of
'Urizen' we are told about the origin of the 'net of religion,'
which is the result of Urizen's feminine mood,—his pity—and
in Night V. and following in 'Vala.'*

*As a result, the net for eighteen hundred years substituted
itself through the different Churches for the real Christianity
about which (like so many other teachers) Blake himself was
certain that he, and he only, rightly knew and delivered, as
the prose prefaces to the four chapters of 'Jerusalem' frankly
show.*

*Enitharmon (space, or the body) slept: these eighteen
centuries were the night of nature: her happiness became like
harps unstrung. Mind (or Man) was a dream—the Sick
Man's Dream, called Theotormon in the 'Vision of the
Daughters of Albion,' line 170, a dream given as a gospel by
Theotormon himself to Jesus when he was the Man of Sorrows,
hearing Oothoon's voice, but not yet entered into the power
that came with his resurrection.*

But war and trouble follow. Imagination will not remain in this tomb of sorrow and literal interpretation, though (to use another phrase of Blake's) 'slain on the stems of generation.'

'*Shadows of men*' *disturb the dream, and* '*divide*' *the* '*heavens of Europe.*' (*A generative symbol, obviously.*)

Albion's Angel (who is seen more distinctly in later books after he has become his Spectre) flies in vain. He and all his like are buried beneath the ruin caused by the demons of futurity that were really at this time (in 1794) agitating Europe.

Albion's leading propensity was rationalistic argument at this period. 'Every man's leading propensity ought to be called his leading virtue, and his good angel,' said Blake in the last of his notes to Lavater's Aphorisms.

Compare for what is to be learned of Demons of the Deep a later passage of 'Vala' than that which touched on the Preludium, Night VII., lines 671 to 794, and also 'Jerusalem,' page 65. It will be seen that these two sets of demons are opposed as blood to judgment.

They, these Angels (Commonsense's reasonings), rise in the form of thoughts, are seen as stars rising after sunset, and therefore as the sons of Albion (see 'Jerusalem') become rationalism, go to Bacon's place of title, Verulam, where 'light in the opake' is to be seen, but where the five bodily senses of man turn to bars against the infinite instead of gates to let it flow into the spirit. Kept out it seems a serpent, Imagination, the atmosphere of Hell, flame; till mind (Man) became conventional (an Angel); Heaven, the origin of the bodily prolific and the mentally restrictive (a mighty circle turning); and God, no longer inside, but outside us, appeared as a crowned tyrant.

At the paragraph 'Now arrived the ancient Guardian at the southern porch,' on page 8, and in what follows, we have what is told as Luvah and Vala leaving the place of seed and flying up into the brain, in 'Jerusalem,' for Luvah when Satanic (love in materialism) is always the 'smiter with death.' Compare the 'Everlasting Gospel' and 'Lafayette,' as well as 'Jerusalem.'

The Angel of Albion, Urizen, seems to have become essentially feminine, 'Milton,' extra page 8. 'The commingling of Albion's and Luvah's spectres was hermaphroditic,' and we know that Luvah's spectre was Satan. Albion's emanation was Jerusalem; his wife was Vala; his spectre (like Vala's) was Satan. Satan thus was ultimately revealed as double-formed, and was in fact Luvah and Vala conjoined, viewed as War and Rahab. From what we read in 'America' about his Angel being fiercely opposed to the West, and so to the soft soul

*of the West, Oothoon, we see how Blake's determination to reveal
the meaning of his visions ripened between this time and the
day when, about seven years later, he wrote 'Jerusalem,' for
War and Rahab are seen joined as the 'dragon-red and
hidden harlot,' and take just the place that in the book
'America' is occupied by Albion's Angel. Albion's Angel
is war, or 'energy enslaved,' or imagination constrained to
argument.   But imagination, or the visionary power that
reveals eternity, is also opposed by love, when love is 'the
infernal grove.'   Luvah-and-Vala become War-and-Rahab
then, or argument-and-law, who after this time vanishes and
is no more heard of in part of the myth that tells of riper
developments, though he may be traced as the 'blind London,
age-bent, led by a child' whom we see in the picture to the
'Song of Experience' called 'London,' and who is referred to
in 'Jerusalem,' page 84, line 11, who ought to have been an
Immortal guardian—he seems to have emanated from Urizen's
book when that was opened in the deadly night with Urizen,
so that, so far as his dragon part was concerned, he really
was both the Dragon Urizen and Tharmas as the Devouring
Tongue, who was, for a while, a dragon and the opposite of
the true Tharmas, whose vegetative portion was America.*

*In a drawing on one page of 'America,' a dragon is seen
hunting through the air the falling figure of an aged man with
a sceptre and book.*

*We must here think twice before we seem to have discovered
contradiction in Blake.   Remembering how 'Luvah was called
Satan because he entered into that state,' and reflecting on the
personages named in the myth as we reflect on real states of the
human soul and not as we consider poetic impersonations like
the dancers at a masked ball, we perceive how one may be called
by the name of another on entering into that other, but not if
unable to do so.*

*To follow the drift of the paragraph on page 8, beginning
with 'Thought changed the infinite to a serpent,' and ending
'God a tyrant crowned,' we must see in it an attempt to sketch
from the symbolic point of view the long history of religious
thought from the old serpent-worship to our own time, getting
it all into a few lines ; and at the same time it will help us to
see into the permanent nature of Blake's own symbolic methods
of thought and speech to compare the often quoted expression,
'The vast form of Nature, like a serpent' ('Jerusalem,' page
29, lines 76 and 80), with the suggestive 'Reasonings, like vast
serpents, infold around my limbs, bruising my minute articu-
lation,'—of which a picture has been noted on page 5 of 'The
Book of Urizen,' though the special symbol and not the wider
interpretation is given in that note (see 'Jerusalem'), page 15,*

line 12; *the passing allusion, page* 42, *line* 76; *the very
mythic, page* 54, *line* 29, *and the valuable hint, page* 55, *line*
13, *which helps the otherwise obscure page* 84, *line* 48.

*Keeping in the mind the naturalistic, serpentine, and
Satanic as all forming phases of one idea, and watching it in
relation to more than one Zoa, we shall come to a comprehension
also of 'Vala,' Night VII., line* 620, *and the earlier lines* 135
to 152, *with the still earlier* 115 *to* 129 *of the same Night, whose
matter is abruptly condensed with fresh ideas added in
'Jerusalem,' page* 30, *line* 30, *where what may be called the
social aspect of the unbrotherliness that follows when the great
human energies are debased into what we call fleshly passion,
which chills the heart, according to the well-admitted rule—
good preface, bad volume.*

The '*Mild*' *Satan will be amply developed in* '*Milton.*'

To return to '*Europe.*' *The southern porch of the North,
of the wintry place, is not the same as the whole region
called South, and Urizen, as Angel of Albion, is not in the
south. It is only a phase of him that is acting. The human
head with hair and skull is used as a symbol. It is the
downward and outward head: the head of the loins and of
nature, not the spiritual upward or inward head. On page
10 we soon hear, as we should expect, of Urizen's pity. Los,
at the beginning of 'Vala,' claimed that* art, *and it is, in the
last line of Chap. V., verse 10 of 'The Book of Urizen,' the
earliest name of Enitharmon. So everything has its good
and its bad side or aspect.*

'*Louis*' *are habitually used as a symbol for argument, and
so is war.*

*Rocks are the 'hard surfaces' of things, the scales of the
serpent, which most of us forget are not reality, but a result
of an intellectual state in ourselves, as much as is a melody
or a colour.*

'*Howling*' *is a symbol of spiritual desire.* '*The flames of
Orc*'—*another symbol for the same thing, heard through
Europe, the North and the Night—cause Urizen in the guise
of a Judge to fly to the wilderness. Rintrah, the lion whose
roarings were Whitefield's eloquence at that time, hung with
his hosts 'of words' in the deep; but Palamabron, who is
'horned,' who seems to have been a bull, and his symbol, the
pen and harrow, wrote on, as people do at night, or 'shot
his lightnings down his back.' He is, by his place in the
quarternary, Rintrah, Palamabron, Theotormon, and Bromion,
a love-force of the second or 'Luvah' rank, for the sequence
Urizen, Luvah, Tharmas, Urthona is a descending sequence
from Sun to Earth, from Zenith to Nadir.*

Enitharmon, urged by the feminine law of jealousy and

desire for dominion, is delighted to see religion turned by the churches from the ideal of forgiveness to the real and moral law, and takes a pleasure in the enchainment and enfeeblement of mind—the male.

Enfeeblement means individuality that appears to be strength to the female, or the emotional. But inspiration knows that in our individual selves we are only a ' worm of sixty winters,' as well as rationalism knows it. Community of minds is Mind and Eternity. These sexes (contraries) are no more.

It seems a function of Albion's Angel, or Guardian, to take care of his ' heavens '—vessels of the strength that derives from blood,—even if his limbs—his mental powers—are burned. He tries in vain while Albion is in this state to awake the moral but deadened faculties of his mind. He cannot. Newton can. Science can arouse a sort of imagination when religion fails to do so. We are in full eighteenth century. The disciplined, conventional, and low-fed mental powers come dropping down like leaves. Such is indeed the result of science on minds whose imagination has been checked until they have only conduct and reason for their two halves of being. And so the century closes. Enitharmon woke (to awake is for the natural heart to love visionary and immortal life and learning) and knew not that she had been merely taught negative virtue or conduct, not aroused to positive virtue or genius, for eighteen hundred years.

Her song—her excitation to the spirits—calls them now to the sports of night.

Ethinthus is one of the set to which Thel and Oothoon belong. We hear that she was buried near that moral tree, the gallows at Tyburn (' Jerusalem,' page 12, line 26); except her name along with Ocalythron, Oothoon, Leutha, Elynitria, Elythiria, Enauld, Manatha, Varcyon, and others not men-tioned here in the long list of the sons and daughters of Los and Enitharmon in Night VIII., line 357 of ' Vala,' we hear no more of her or of several others of these spirits. We can only suppose that their stories were written in Blake's many lost MSS.

Leutha, emanation of Satan's bosom, is heard of in ' Book of Los' and in the early pages of ' Milton,' and the name of Elynitria is in ' Jerusalem,' page 93, line 5 ; and of Ethin-thus, page 12, line 26. Sotha is heard of, and ' Diralada' as Thiralatha, his emanation, or ' joy' is there called. They are spirits of elementary passion ; and as Enitharmon calls for the red light of Orc the sun rises, and she weeps. That is to say, the animating drop soothingly leaves its vessel, and as day dawns, Orc enters into it and Los calls all his powers to

*enter the propagative strife for which all the playfulness of all
hers were but a preparation.*

*This note is but a sketch whose extremely condensed form
must cause it to be obscure to any one but a habitual reader
of Blake, and such a reader will blame its brevity and will
suspect at first that it denies whatever it does not state. It is
not intended as an inclusive account of all the meanings, but
as a suggestive hint where some of them may be sought. It
(along with the Serpent on its title-page) may be summed up in
the line 65 of 'Jerusalem,' page 7—'O holy generation, Image
of regeneration.'*

DESIGNS TO 'EUROPE'

*Frontispiece.—Urizen as the Architect. He kneels in the
sun, stooping and reaching out of it, and measuring the abyss
below with huge compasses. His hair and beard float in the
wind. He is nude. The figure young and strong. Compare
'Vala,' Night VI., line 226, etc.*

*Title-page.—A huge serpent—a form Urizen himself could
take.*

*Preludium.—An assassin, nude, with a dagger, wearing a
pleased grin on his face, sits in a small cave and waits for a
pilgrim with close costume, hat, and pack on his back. This
is 'an idiot questioner, who is always questioning, but never
capable of answering, who sits with a sly grin, silent, plotting
when to question, like a thief in a cave' ('Milton,' page 43,
line 11). At the foot of a page a sort of Devil cherub, a
crumpled face with arms wound over its ears, flying on bats'
wings—Infidelity, a vision of Art that does not believe in
vision. It is also shown flying away near the feet of Blake's
first engraving of himself as 'Glad Day,' dated 1780, and in
'Auguries of Innocence':—*

'The bat that flits at close of eve
Has left the brain that won't believe.'

*A male figure, nude, falls head downwards, with an iron
weight tied to his hands. The mind drawn out into nature
by love (head down, outward; Nature, death; Iron, carnal
love).*

*Page 2. Seemingly elemental spirits of the air. A nude,
flying, bold young man in mid air, catching two others like
himself, and strangling them as they all kick their way*

through space. They have no weight. Another, just escaped, climbs the clouds and gets away. They are the argumentative reasonings that, like the damned, 'contend with one another on the edge of the abyss' (of the Five Senses). This phrase is from the prose account of the 'Vision of the last Judgment.' They are selfhoods, 'little Devils that fight for themselves' in 'woods,' or places of solitude, in the poem 'Los the Terrible,' written at Felpham.

Page 3. Various expressions of love. Two winged figures meet and kiss happily in air. Another floats, looking down sadly at a red planet. A floating, nude virgin, without wings, grasps another, half draped, who writhes away from her. These should be Jerusalem (nude), Vala (partly in robe of natural idea). The red planet may be 'Urizen released from chains,' 'glowing like a meteor in the distant North.'

Page 4. A youthful figure lies on its face on the ground, asleep. Flames issue from its head. A beautiful nude girl hovering over it in clouds raises the cover to look at the flames. Behind, smaller figures of youthful forms lie about in wild repose of love, or rush in wild ecstasy.

The chief sleeping figure is so young, so little seen, so vaguely draped that it can hardly be known whether it is girl or boy. If girl it is Vala, and the nude one above is Jerusalem: the love that dreams and burns the fallen body, and the love that hovers pitying over it in the floating mind.

Page 5. A king, dressed in a suit of chain armour from head to foot, stands at ease, wearing his crown and holding the handle of his sword in his left hand, while its point rests on the ground. Two angels, the same size as himself, drawn like pale, weak, winged virgins in white drapery, stand close behind at each side. This is Og, who is explained in 'Milton,' page 68, lines 33, 35 ; page 20, line 33 ; page 31, line 49 ; page 27, lines 22, 50, 51. The Angels of Pity and Compassion stand behind.

Page 6. A virgin, perhaps ruined, returning to her father, bowing, moving forward, and already kneeling with face down, hiding it against his legs as she flings her arms round him. He, an old man with white beard, stands holding out his arms over his head, level, straight, with hands bent back at the waist, as if warding her off. She seems to have dropped so suddenly on her knees, and so advanced that he has not yet had time to change his position since he was bidding her to keep back. They wear a sort of abstract costume, all over, with sleeves—a similar robe—but both are barefoot. The old man is the jealousy of Jehovah. She is one of the little powers that lead through love to life so long as they do not make common cause with jealousy and seek for dominion,

The story is told as that of Ona, in the 'Song of Experience,' called 'A Little Girl Lost.' Ona is the name of a daughter of Urizen in 'Vala,' Night VII., lines 95 and 101.

Page 7.   Two flying malignant spirits of the air, nude, young, beautiful, without wings; one a youth, one a virgin, blowing blighting breath upon ears of corn.   They must be minute creatures, for the ears of corn are nearly as big as themselves.   The stalks curl up, and black flakes fill the air. This is reproduced in 'Gilchrist.'   The figures have come from Urizen's 'armies of disease.'   They are jealousy (of the Intellect) blighting food (of the Imagination), also jealousy of moral law blighting bodily vegetative happiness—called the cornfield in 'Vala.'

Page 8.   A large serpent up the side of the page, shooting fire at the top.   Orc, among the constellations of Urizen. Compare 'Vala,' Night VIII., line 65.

Page 9.   Two sad girlish angels, draped and winged, lower their sceptres before a wicked-looking fat Pope, rather like Leo XIII., in a tiara, seated on a throne, with a book open before him, and bats' wings behind him.   His face is very red. Of course he is Urizen, the 'primeval priest,' who 'assumed power' and became the 'prester serpent.'   Compare Preludium to 'Book of Urizen,' and 'Vala,' Night VIII., line 600, etc. The only direct verbal allusion to popes in Blake's works is in 'Jerusalem,' page 64, line 15, where Vala, mocking the limits and nature of mortal man, says derisively, 'Go assume Papal dignity, thou spectre!'   The word 'assume' here and in the preludium unites the passages technically in the symbolic story.

Page 10.   'The ambitious spider,' symbolically placed in 'Milton,' page 24, line 15.

Page 11.   The fly in human form.   A naked prisoner newly chained in a dungeon, his mail-clad jailer leaving him.

Page 12.   A caterpillar.

Page 13.   A hero rescuing his wife and daughters from flames.   He is the masculine or intellectual of visionary power rescuing the passive or mere sight from the flames of vegetation.   He is Beauty rescuing flesh from mere passion.   He is the idea referred to poetic power symbolised as Milton, and contained in the line

'her to redeem and himself perish.'

—'Milton,' page 3, line 20.

These designs, like all Blake's, are missionary cartoons preaching his law and gospel, which was—

Seek beauty, even in fleshly passion.
Cultivate vision, even when it is terrible.

Then you will put on the world and put it off, and thus go through the incarnation into brotherhoods through which, by reaching the Universal Mind, you will reach the ascension.

But avoid argument, abstract philosophy, abstract morality, and self-righteousness. These are forces of individualism and naturalism, and lead to death.

THE

BOOK

OF

AHANIA

LAMBETH
Printed by W. Blake
1795

THE
BOOK
OF
AHANIA

LAMBETH
Printed by W. Blake
1795

AHANIA

CHAP. I

1. Fuzon, on a chariot iron-wing'd,
   On spiked flames rose; his hot visage
   Flam'd furious; sparkles his hair and beard,
   Shot down his wide bosom and shoulders.
   On clouds of smoke rages his chariot,
   And his right hand burns red in its cloud,
   Moulding into a vast globe his wrath,
   As the thunder-stone is moulded,
   Son of Urizen's silent burnings.

2. Shall we worship this Demon of smoke,
   Said Fuzon, this abstract non-entity,
   This cloudy God seated on waters,
   Now seen, now obscur'd, King of sorrow?

3. So he spoke in a fiery flame,
   On Urizen frowning indignant,
   The Globe of wrath shaking on high.
   Roaring with fury, he threw
   The howling Globe; burning it flew,
   Length'ning into a hungry beam, swiftly

4. Oppos'd to the exulting flam'd beam,
   The broad Disk of Urizen upheav'd
   Across the Void many a mile.

5. It was forg'd in mills where the winter
   Beats incessant. Ten winters the disk,
   Unremitting, endur'd the cold hammer.

391

6. But the strong arm that sent it remember'd
   The sounding beam. Laughing, it tore through
   That beaten mass, keeping its direction,
   The cold loins of Urizen dividing.

7. Dire shriek'd his invisible Lust.
   Deep groan'd Urizen, stretching his awful hand,
   Ahania (so name his parted soul),
   He siez'd on his mountains of Jealousy.
   He groan'd, anguish'd, and called her Sin,
   Kissing her and weeping over her,
   Then hid her in darkness, in silence,
   Jealous, tho' she was invisible.

8. She fell down, a faint shadow, wand'ring
   In chaos, and circling dark Urizen,
   As the moon, anguish'd, circles the earth,
   Hopeless! abhorr'd! a death-shadow,
   Unseen, unbodied, unknown,
   The mother of Pestilence.

9. But the fiery beam of Fuzon
   Was a pillar of fire to Egypt;
   Five hundred years wand'ring on earth,
   Till Los siez'd it and beat in a mass
   With the body of the sun.

CHAP. II

1. But the forehead of Urizen gathering,
   And his eyes pale with anguish, his lips
   Blue and changing; in tears and bitter
   Contrition he prepared his Bow.

2. Form'd of Ribs, that in his dark solitude,
   When obscur'd in his forests, fell monsters
   Arose. For his dire Contemplations
   Rush'd down like floods from his mountains,
   In torrents of mud settling thick,

With Eggs of unnatural production
Forthwith hatching; some howl'd on his hills,
Some in vales, some aloft flew in air.

3. Of these, an enormous dread Serpent,
Scaled and poisonous, horned,
Approach'd Urizen even to his knees
As he sat in his dark-rooted Oak.

4. With his horns he push'd furious.
Great the conflict and great the jealousy
In cold poisons; but Urizen smote him.

5. First he poison'd the rocks with his blood,
Then polish'd his ribs, and his sinews
Dried: laid them apart till winter.
Then a Bow, black prepar'd: on this Bow
A poison'd rock plac'd in silence.
He utter'd these words to the Bow:

6. O Bow of the clouds of secresy,
O nerve of that lust-form'd monster!
Send this rock swift, invisible thro'
The black clouds, on the bosom of Fuzon.

7. So saying, in torment of his wounds
He bent the enormous ribs slowly;
A circle of darkness, then fixed
The sinew in its rest: then the Rock,
Poisonous source, plac'd with art, lifting difficult
Its weighty bulk: silent the rock lay,

8. While Fuzon, his tygers unloosing,
Thought Urizen slain by his wrath.
I am God, said he, eldest of things.

9. Sudden sings the rock, swift and invisible,
On Fuzon flew, enter'd his bosom.
His beautiful visage, his tresses,
That gave light to the mornings of heaven,
Were smitten with darkness, deform'd,
And outstretch'd on the edge of the forest.

10. But the rock fell upon the Earth,
    Mount Sinai, in Arabia.

CHAP. III

1. The Globe shook, and Urizen, seated
   On black clouds, his sore wound anointed;
   The ointment flow'd down on the void
   Mix'd with blood: here the snake gets her poison.

2. With difficulty and great pain Urizen
   Lifted on high the dead corse:
   On his shoulders he bore it to where
   A Tree hung over the Immensity.

3. For when Urizen shrunk away
   From Eternals, he sat on a rock,
   Barren; a rock which himself,
   From redounding fancies, had petrified.
   Many tears fell on the rock,
   Many sparks of vegetation.
   Soon shot the pained root
   Of Mystery under his heel:
   It grew a thick tree: he wrote
   In silence his book of iron,
   Till the horrid plant bending its boughs,
   Grew to roots when it felt the earth,
   And again sprung to many a tree.

4. Amaz'd started Urizen! when
   He beheld himself compassed round
   And high roofed over with trees;
   He arose, but the stems stood so thick,
   He with difficulty and great pain
   Brought his Books, all but the Book
   Of iron from the dismal shade.

5. The Tree still grows over the Void,
   Enrooting itself all around,
   An endless labyrinth of woe!

6. The corse of his first begotten
    On the accursed Tree of Mystery,
    On the topmost stem of this Tree
    Urizen nail'd Fuzon's corse.

CHAP. IV

1. Forth flew the arrows of pestilence,
    Round the pale living Corse on the Tree.

2. For in Urizen's slumbers of abstraction,
    In the infinite ages of Eternity,
    When his Nerves of Joy melted and flowed,
    A white Lake on the dark blue air,
    In perturb'd pain and dismal torment,
    Now stretching out, now swift conglobing.

3. Effluvia, vapor'd above
    In noxious clouds; these hover'd thick
    Over the disorganiz'd Immortal,
    Till petrific pain scurf'd o'er the Lakes,
    As the bones of man, solid and dark.

4. The clouds of disease hover'd wide
    Around the Immortal in torment,
    Perching around the hurtling bones,
    Disease on disease, shape on shape,
    Winged, screaming in blood and torment.

5. The Eternal Prophet beat on his anvils,
    Enraged in the desolate darkness;
    He forg'd nets of iron around,
    And Los threw them around the bones.

6. The shapes, screaming, flutter'd vain.
    Some combin'd into muscles and glands,
    Some organs for craving and lust;
    Most remain'd on the tormented void:
    Urizen's army of horrors.

7. Round the pale living Corse on the Tree,
   Forty years flew the arrows of pestilence.

8. Wailing and terror and woe
   Ran thro' all his dismal world ;
   Forty years all his sons and daughters
   Felt their skulls harden ; then Asia
   Arose in the pendulous deep.

9. They reptilize upon the Earth.

10. Fuzon groan'd on the Tree.

CHAP. V

1. The lamenting voice of Ahania,
   Weeping upon the void
   And round the Tree of Fuzon.
   Distant in solitary night
   Her voice was heard ; but no form
   Had she ; but her tears from clouds
   Eternal fell round the Tree.

2. And the voice cried : Ah, Urizen ! Love !
   Flower of morning ! I weep on the verge
   Of Non-entity ; how wide the Abyss
   Between Ahania and thee !

3. I lie on the verge of the deep ;
   I see thy dark clouds ascend ;
   I see thy black forests and floods,
   A horrible waste to my eyes !

4. Weeping I walk over rocks,
   Over dens, and thro' valleys of death.
   Why didst thou despise Ahania,
   To cast me from thy bright presence
   Into the World of Loneness ?

5. I cannot touch his hand,
   Nor weep on his knees, nor hear
   His voice and bow, nor see his eyes
   And joy, nor hear his footsteps, and
   My heart leaps at the lovely sound !
   I cannot kiss the place
   Whereon his bright feet have trod.
   But I wander on the rocks
   With hard necessity.

6. Where is my golden palace,
   Where my ivory bed ?
   Where the joy of my morning hour,
   Where the sons of eternity singing ?

7. To awake bright Urizen, my king,
   To arise to the mountain sport,
   To the bliss of eternal valleys ;

8. To awake my king in the morn,
   To embrace Ahania's joy
   On the breath of his open bosom :
   From my soft cloud of dew to fall
   In showers of life on his harvests.

9. When he gave my happy soul
   To the sons of eternal joy,
   When he took the daughter of life
   Into my chambers of love.

10. When I found babes of bliss on my bed,
    And bosoms of mill in my chambers,
    Fill'd with eternal seed ;
    O ! eternal births sung round Ahania,
    In interchange sweet of their joys.

11. Swell'd with ripeness and fat with fatness,
    Bursting on winds my odors,
    My ripe figs and rich pomegranates,
    In infant joy at thy feet,
    O Urizen, sported and sang.

12. Then thou with thy lap full of seed,
    With thy hand full of generous fire,
    Walked forth from the clouds of morning
    On the virgins of springing joy,
    On the human soul to cast
    The seed of eternal science.

13. The sweat poured down thy temples,
    To Ahania returned in evening
    The moisture; awake to birth,
    My mother's-joys, sleeping in bliss.

14. But now alone, over rocks, mountains,
    Cast out from thy lovely bosom:
    Cruel jealousy, selfish fear:
    Self-destroying: how can delight
    Renew in these chains of darkness,
    Where bones of beasts are strown
    On the bleak and snowy mountains,
    Where bones from the birth are buried
    Before they see the light?

FINIS

MEANING OF 'AHANIA'

'Ahania' is often supposed to be the 'Second Book of Urizen,' though not so called by Blake. It is dated the year after 'Europe.'

Fuzon, who opens the poem, is to Urizen what the nameless, shadowy female was to Orc—the product and child of his 'silent burnings.'

He became rebellious at once, being not other than a phase of universal Orc. Urizen's cold will casts him down, but its beam divides his loins—all an obvious symbol. Then the beam turned out to be Ahania—that is, he was always double, as Albion's emotional nature double formed will be seen in 'Jerusalem' as Luvah and Vala,

REFERENCES FOR 'AHANIA'

The following explanatory references to terms found in 'Ahania' are chiefly from 'Jerusalem.' They help when the general idea is remembered, which roughly is this,—that however bad sin may be it does less harm to spiritual life than law, which is actually responsible for that psychic degradation in us that makes us corporeal and opaque, deprives us of prophetic power, clairvoyance, and the state of mind in which all friendship is boundlessly confiding and faithful, and reduces us to such a point that only by going on and breaking forth into actual lawlessness can we expect to unite into one vast soul—Christ's spiritual body—after forgiving one another for the results of this confusion, and entirely casting out the egotism of sin as this has cast out the egotism of righteousness. The terms which the references here are given to illustrate are placed not in alphabetical order, but just as the reader will come upon them when going through the poem.

Chariots—'Execution is the chariot of Genius.' Blake's definition.

Spiked flames—Amorous passion.—'Vala,' Night VIII., line 453.

Cloud of smoke—Abstract philosophy and egotism.—'Jerusalem,' page 5, line 61, combine the passages about Rahab, page 70, line 19, and page 80, line 51. It is also the spectre or reasoning power or shadow ('Jerusalem,' page 6, line 5), and as 'every natural thing has a spiritual cause,' it causes the blood—for the blood is a cloud to clairvoyant vision.—'Vala,' Night IX., line 271. Its connection, the rough tears with Urizen's deceitful religion, is heard of in Night VIII., line 173.

Thunder and flames—Thought and desire.—See verses on preface to first chapter of 'Jerusalem.'

Refusal to worship.—Compare 'Jerusalem, page 29, lines 37 and 57; also 'Vala.'

Shadow and sorrow.—Night III., lines 50 and 70, and the context in both poems.

Globe of Wrath.—Compare its counterpart, the globe of Pity, from blood ('Jerusalem,' page 17, line 51; page 66, line 43; 'Book of Urizen,' Chap. V., etc.). Compare also Los's Globe of Fire, page 31, line 3, and the globe into which the 'Atlantis continent' was caught, page 49, line 20.

Forged in mills.—Compare 'Jerusalem,' page 13, line 56; page 19, line 19; page 38, line 37; page 39, lines 3 and

4 ; *page* 43, *line* 49 ; *page* 60, *lines* 41 *and* 63.   *See also*
'*Vala,*' *Night VIII., line* 224, *etc.*

Loins of *Urizen*—*Cold reasonings desirous of argumentative victory and moral procreation.*—*Compare* '*Jerusalem,*' *page* 18, *line* 44.

Sin.—*The two opposite kinds of emanation seem sin to each
other.   Rahab is sin* ('*Vala,*' *Night IX., line* 158), *so
is Enitharmon* ('*Jerusalem,*' *page* 10, *line* 43).   *Rahab
imputes sin* (*page* 70, *line* 17), *but the idea of sin is an
infection.*—'*Jerusalem,*' *page* 43, *line* 75.

Rock, *snake, tree.*—'*Jerusalem*' *and* '*Vala*' *are full of
passages about these, but the most condensed is that in
'Jerusalem' on page* 92 *containing the line* 25.

Oak.—*Forests are growths of despair.   They are the
entanglements of darkness in the flesh that check and
sadden the spirit ; and entanglements of the moral
laws, only applicable to flesh, that endanger the life of
the spirit and lead to despair and weeping.   See
'Jerusalem,' page* 43, *lines* 6 *to* 11, *and line* 81 ; *page* 44,
line 37 ; *page* 59, *line* 5 ; *page* 66, *line* 55 (*in explanation
of* '*Mystery*') ; *general sorrow, page* 89, *line* 23 ; '*death*'
of Albion in Druid Oaks, page 94, *line* 24 ; *last allusion,
page* 98, *line* 50.

Poison.—*Compare* ' *The Defiled Sanctuary,*' *the last lines of
' Thel,' the first Night of ' Vala,' etc.   In a general
way* '*poison*' *means all the tendency of the beauty of
flesh to take away from the vitality of the spirit*—*it is
the counterpart to the evils of moral restraint that when
applied to vision takes away its spontaneity.*

Bow.—*The bow is not always evil.   It is made of male and
female loves joined.   They are the two ends of the
spring, and their junction is the cord.   They may be
used against, and may be used in favour of, spiritual
liberty.*—'*Jerusalem,*' *page* 50, *line* 22 ; *page* 52, *ballad,
and page* 97, *lines* 6 *to* 17.

Sinai.—*See* '*Jerusalem,*' *page* 16, *line* 68.   *Theosophists
call this the record of the Astral Light.   Magicians use
symbols to read it.*—*See article on Magic in* '*Ideas
of Good and Evil,*' *by W. B. Yeats, published by A. H.
Bullen,* 47 *Great Russell Street.   See also* '*Jerusalem,*'
page 35, *line* 22 ; *page* 68, *line* 6—*a valuable explanation
here of the closing of the western gate.   Page* 96, *line* 9,
which unites the lack of transparency in Nature (*rocks
are the hard surfaces of things*) *with the serpent*—*the
bow, the law, selfhood, reason, etc. ; in fact, all that is
not spiritual brotherhood united in delight and vision.*

Mystery,—*what we call Nature*—*the solid thing that most*

*of us do not dream of piercing with the X rays of the
soul.   Clairvoyants, hypnotists, and prophets, with
some magicians, may say with Blake that it is a mystery
why Nature seems solid.   He added that it is part of
this mystery that it should need to be moral, and that
in introducing any such thing as 'Forgiveness of Sins'
Christ passed 'the limits of possibility.'   Blake, a
natural clairvoyant and magician, preaches 'Forgiveness' as possible by means of imputing sin and
righteousness to 'states' and punishing these or redeem-
ing them.   When sad he ceased to be clairvoyant.
Nature appeared to him as it does to us, and his
'centres were open to pain.'   For 'Mystery,' see all
allusions to Rahab in 'Jerusalem.'   It is 'Rahab' or
'Abstract philosophy,' 'Moral law,' etc.   It is first met
with in the Song of Experience called 'The Human
Abstract.'   See 'Book of Urizen,' and also 'Vala,' Night
VII., line 36.*

*Reptilize.—See 'Jerusalem,' page 49, line 33, etc., and the
long account of the loss of the 'Human' or imaginative
form by Urizen (or scientific intellect) and his going
over to materialism or the 'female death' in 'Vala,'
Night VIII., lines 409 and following.   The rock is
here further explained, and all serpentine attributes of
Nature.*

*Lament of Ahania, Chap. V.—Compare with this the outcry
of Ahania in 'Vala,' Night VIII., lines 485 to 525.*

DESIGNS TO 'AHANIA'

*The frontispiece is a full-page picture representing a white-
haired man of powerful and massive limbs, sitting on his
haunches, with his knees up to nearly his ears, and his head so
bowed forward that no face can be seen.   Between his legs sits
on her heels a female figure so much smaller than he that if they
both rose, she would not come much higher than his elbow.   She
is clasping her hands in pain, and looking up with her head
twisted to one side, for the old man has buried all his clenched
fingers in her hair, and is mercilessly pulling it.   They are
in a dreary landscape outside a rough cliff.   Both nude.
The female figure young and pretty.   They are Urizen and*

Ahania. Urizen is 'groaning, and calling his parted soul Sin.'

On the title-page Ahania is seen as a ray of the moon again, parting the clouds, but the clouds are not seen. She is 'on the margin of nonentity.' At the end is a vague and strange picture; a lot of broken pieces of a giant, smashed like a statue, or hewn asunder like meat, lying on rocks. It belongs to the 'Book of Urizen,' Chap. V., stanza 3.

'Ahania' is not printed from the same sort of plates as the other books, with the exception of the 'Book of Los,' but, like this, is as carefully and neatly engraved throughout as a visiting-card, and the title was given with deliberation.

THE

BOOK

OF

LOS

LAMBETH
Printed by W. Blake
1795

403

THE

BOOK

of

LOS

LAMBETH
Printed by W. Blake
1795

1. Eno, aged Mother,
   Who the chariot of Leutha guides,
   Since the day of thunders in old time,

2. Sitting beneath the eternal oak,
   Trembled and shook the stedfast Earth,
   And thus her speech broke forth.

3. O Times remote !
   When Love and Joy were adoration,
   And none impure were deem'd,
   Not Eyeless Covet,
   Nor Thin-lip'd Envy,
   Nor Bristled Wrath,
   Nor Curled Wantonness.

4. But Covet was poured full,
   Envy fed with fat of lambs,
   Wrath with lion's gore,
   Wantonness lull'd to sleep
   With the virgin's lute,
   Or sated with her love.

5. Till Covet broke his locks and bars,
   And slept with open doors ;
   Envy sung at the rich man's feast ;
   Wrath was follow'd up and down
   By a little ewe lamb ;
   And wantonness on his own true love
   Begot a giant race.

6. Raging furious, the flames of desire
    Ran thro' heaven and earth, living flames,
    Intelligent, organiz'd ; arm'd
    With destruction and plagues.   In the midst
    The Éternal Prophet bound in a chain,
    Compell'd to watch Urizen's shadow,

7. Rag'd with curses and sparkles of fury,
    Round the flames roll, as Los hurls his chains.
    Mounting up from his fury condens'd,
    Rolling round and round, mounting on high,
    Into vacuum, into non-entity,
    Where nothing was ; dash'd wide apart,
    His feet stamp the eternal fierce-raging
    Rivers of wide flame ; they roll round
    And round on all sides, making their way
    Into darkness and shadowy obscurity.

8. Wide apart stood the fires; Los remain'd
    In the void between fire and fire ;
    In trembling horror they beheld him ;
    They stood wide apart, driv'n by his hands
    And his feet, which the nether abyss
    Stamp'd in fury and hot indignation.

9. But no light from the fires ; all was
    Darkness round Los; heat was not, for bound up
    Into fiery spheres from his fury,
    The gigantic flames trembled and hid.

10. Coldness, darkness, obstruction ; a Solid
    Without fluctuation, hard as adamant,
    Black as marble of Égypt, impenetrable,
    Bound in the fierce raging Immortal ;
    And the separated fires froze in
    A vast solid, without fluctuation,
    Bound in his expanding clear senses.

CHAP. II

1. The Immortal stood frozen amidst
   The vast rock of eternity, times
   And times, a night of vast durance,
   Impatient, stifled, stiffen'd, hard'ned.

2. Till impatience no longer could bear
   The hard bondage, rent, rent the vast solid
   With a crash from immense to immense.

3. Crack'd across into numberless fragments,
   The Prophetic wrath struling for vent,
   Hurls apart, stamping furious to dust,
   And crumbling with bursting sobs, heaves
   The black marble on high into fragments.

4. Hurl'd apart on all sides as a falling
   Rock, the innumerable fragments away
   Fell asunder, and horrible vacuum
   Beneath him and on all sides round.

5. Falling, falling, Los fell and fell,
   Sunk precipitant, heavy down, down,
   Times on times, night on night, day on day.
   Truth has bounds, Error none: falling, falling,
   Years on years, and ages on ages;
   Still he fell thro' the void, still a void,
   Found for falling day and night without end,
   For tho' day or night was not, their spaces
   Were measured by his incessant whirls
   In the horrid vacuity bottomless.

6. The Immortal revolving, indignant
   First in wrath, threw his limbs like the babe
   New born into our world; wrath subsided,
   And contemplative thoughts first arose,
   Then aloft his head rear'd in the Abyss,
   And his downward borne fall chang'd oblique,

7. Many ages of groans, till there grew
   Branchy forms, organizing the Human
   Into finite inflexible organs,

8. Till in process from falling he bore
   Sidelong on the purple air, wafting
   The weak breeze in efforts o'erwearied.

9. Incessant the falling Mind labour'd,
   Organizing itself, till the Vacuum
   Became element, pliant to rise,
   Or to fall, or to swim, or to fly,
   With ease searching the dire vacuity.

CHAP. III

1. The Lungs heave incessant, dull, and heavy.
   For as yet were all other parts formless,
   Shiv'ring, clinging around like a cloud,
   Dim and glutinous as the white Polypus,
   Driv'n by waves and englob'd on the tide.

2. And the unformed part crav'd repose ;
   Sleep began, the Lungs heave on the wave,
   Weary, overweigh'd, sinking beneath,
   In a stifling black fluid he woke.

3. He arose on the waters, but soon
   Heavy falling, his organs like roots
   Shooting out from the seed, shot beneath,
   And a vast world of waters around him
   In furious torrents began.

4. Then he sunk, and around his spent Lungs
   Began intricate pipes that drew in
   The spawn of the waters.   Outbranching
   An immense Fibrous Form, stretching out,
   Thro' the bottoms of immensity raging.

5. He rose on the floods ; then he smote
   The wild deep with his terrible wrath,
   Separating the heavy and thin.

6. Down the heavy sunk ; cleaving around
   To the fragments of solid ; up rose
   The thin, flowing round the fierce fires
   That glow'd furious in the expanse.

CHAP. IV

1. Then Light first began ; from the fires,
   Beams, conducted by fluid so pure,
   Flow'd around the Immense.   Los beheld
   Forthwith, writhing upon the dark void,
   The Backbone of Urizen appear
   Hurtling upon the wind,
   Like a serpent, like an iron chain
   Whirling about in the Deep.

2. Upfolding his Fibres together
   To a Form of impregnable strength,
   Los, astonish'd and terrified, built
   Furnaces ; he formed an Anvil,
   A Hammer of adamant, then began
   The binding of Urizen day and night.

3. Circling round the dark Demon with howlings,
   Dismay, and sharp blightings, the Prophet
   Of Eternity beat on his iron links.

4. And first from those infinite fires,
   The light that flow'd down on the winds
   He siez'd ; beating incessant, condensing
   The subtil particles in an Orb.

5. Roaring indignant, the bright sparks
   Endur'd the vast Hammer ; but unwearied
   Los beat on the Anvil, till glorious
   An immense Orb of fire he fram'd.

6. Oft he quench'd it beneath in the Deeps,
   Then survey'd the all bright mass.   Again
   Siezing fires from the terrific Orbs,
   He heated the round Globe, then beat ;
   While roaring his Furnaces endur'd
   The chain'd Orb in their infinite wombs.

7. Nine ages completed their circles,
   When Los heated the glowing mass, casting
   It down into the Deeps : the Deeps fled
   Away in redounding smoke : the Sun
   Stood self-balanc'd.   And Los smiled with joy.
   He, the vast Spine of Urizen, siez'd
   And bound down to the glowing illusion.

8. But no light, for the Deep fled away
   On all sides, and left an unform'd
   Dark vacuity here.   Urizen lay
   In fierce torments on his glowing bed,

9. Till his Brain in a rock, and his Heart
   In a fleshy slough, formed four rivers,
   Obscuring the immense Orb of fire
   Flowing down into night ; till a Form
   Was completed, a Human Illusion,
   In darkness and deep clouds involv'd.

THE END OF THE BOOK OF LOS

MEANING OF THE 'BOOK OF LOS'

*There is a specious facility about this short book which
seems partly to explain itself and partly to have been made
unnecessary as well as explained by the 'Book of Urizen' that
appeared before it, and seemingly ought to have followed it, or
to have been left out as unnecessary because of it.*

*The different stanzas in the order of their numbers may
perhaps be translated nearly as in the Quaritch edition, and
somewhat thus :—*

Chapter I

1. *Since the first day of productive power or creative thoughts,* the thunders of old time, *Eno, the aged mother (Earth), has guided the chariot of Leutha (bodily beauty), for the maternal power rules in the material.*

2. *Beneath the eternal vegetative sorrow—that oak which the mistaken Druids supposed to be imagination—Eno trembled, and, shaking the earth herself, was delivered of children; that is, of speech.*

3. *She called aloud on the times that had ceased to be, when the four quarters of humanity—now known as four evils—were, in right of imaginative freedom, four blameless things. When from the masculine,* joy; *and the feminine,* love; *came the child,* adoration. *The three, as we learn elsewhere, became* Selfhood, Pity, *and* Desire. *But this is their state in our own time.*

She calls to the four regions by their fallen names:—

Envy,		Urizen.
Waste,	Corresponding to the	Luvah.
Wantonness,	four Zoas,	Tharmas.
Covet,		Urthona.

Who, being unopposed, perfectly indulged, and not given 'punishment enough to cause them to commit sins'—to borrow another phrase of Blake's—were harmless.

4. *They were all satiated.* 'Love is too young to know what conscience is,' *according to Shakespeare. The world was then like 'Love.'*

5. *In return, they did good deeds opposite to their own natures. The destruction of obstruction, the amusing of festivity, the protection of helpfulness, and the propagation of beauty and strength.*

6. *At this outcry of the ancient maternity, living flames of the wrath and desire, the heart and loins of imagination that together make creations possible, ran through the generative region of prophecy. The fires were armed with destruction of freedom and plague of the senses that are open to pain. They were thus creative. Creation's first effect is contraction, the next is opacity, the third is pain, the fourth is bliss, the total is an image of regeneration, and the cause is Mercy. This outcry excited the desires of nature and mind, and the prophetic spirit in the midst could do nothing but keep watch on their enemy, the shadow of selfhood.*

7, 8, 9. *The spirit of prophecy had become 'infected.' He fought for a space for himself among the flames, and kept desire from overwhelming him, as though he also had become what he beheld—the spirit of selfhood.*

10. *So matter and reason began where the free spirit once lived in imagination and found it truth.*

Chapter II

1, 2, 3. *As the tomb triumphed over Christ for three days, so for three stanzas the dark water triumphs over the light, materialism over imagination. Eno's error was to call out for a life on earth as in heaven, while still things are as they are. The error of Los was to take sides against this—the ideal. At the third the rock is broken, and the spiritual body is free; Los is impotent in the first stanza, rending in the second, utterly liberated in the third.*

4. *Thus arisen, he suddenly finds his error. He should neither have bound the senses to be only sense, nor have destroyed them for being only sense. He suddenly finds himself in vacuum.*

5. *And so he falls, for truth has bounds, error none. But his fall is fructifying even now, for he whirls as he falls, measuring night and day, and where circles are there the void will presently bear fruit.*

6. *And his fall having done its first work, changes to an oblique motion, and presently his head that had been downwards (for when the bodily man enters into activity of the loins, even though it be to control this activity and find a place for himself between its fires, the spiritual man within him is reversed in all its regions, its head is in the bodily loins, its loins in the bodily head). This moment corresponds in the story of Los to that of the third stanza of the fourth chapter of 'Urizen,' where the eddies of his wrath settle to a lake.*

7. *In the ages of sorrow Los, essentially creative and forced to do something, creates himself; that is, he prepares a system with which to deliver men from systems, as Blake says he does in 'Jerusalem.' For this he had fallen into the region of system—his own loins.*

8. *In the dark, purple air, the region of the heart, he now floated sideways in sorrowful feeling.*

9. *And then the falling but still prophetic Mind organised itself, and became called by mortals Imagination, capable of exploring all the regions of its infinity. The ninth stanza finishes the duties of a ninth gestative month.*

The last three stanzas exactly show the contrast between the book of 'Urizen' and of 'Los.' Both enter the feminine darkness. Both organise themselves. Urizen propagates restrictions and a net from the watery region of tears, from the loins, or pitiful and tearful portion, of the head. Los ends by propagating freedom, the pliant faculty of entering

*into all the vacuity called nature, from the fiery, or mental
and wrathful, region of the head* of (*or spiritual head* in) *the
loins.*

Los being essentially prophetic, Urizen scientific, the reader
must have a Los as well as a Urizen inside him to follow
really the story here told.

Chapter III

1. *The loins are a duplex symbolic region of earth and
water. The earth Los had cast away. The water he must
vivify.* So in this centre, this East, or the void—as East
became when the Zoas, or four forms of life are out of their
homes, as we shall see in 'Jerusalem'—Organisation, or
imagination, begins as a dot that branches, as all selfhoods
begin ('Jerusalem,' page 33, line 20, etc.), and now with lungs
he brings air to the water, or heart to the loins. *Air is the
corresponding symbol to heart, and water to loins: they are
under Luvah and Tharmas.*

2. *Emotion entered the region of sense, and they both
became weary at first, struggling afterwards, for they were
male and female principles.*

3. *Such struggle leads to fruitfulness in eternity, and the
waters became torrents, the lungs became organs.*

4. *Presently, in the region of material sense compared to
which heart is masculine—as head is masculine compared in
its turn with heart—a form is born of heart and loins, collected
from the spawn of the waters as the burning globe of Urizen
from the fires of the air.*

5. *Then, as in 'Urizen' (Chapter V., stanza 4), Los smote
the north from the south region (darkness from light, earth
from fire, or loins from head), so now he separates the 'heavy
from the thin,' west from the east, water from air, loins from
heart.*

6. *The two loins, or female elements, water and earth, clove
together—being the 'heavy'—and sank; that is to say, passed
into the outer or lower of human nature, while the 'thin' or
air, flowing around the fierce fires, coalesced with them, and
going to the upper or inner, really began uniting the scattered
fires into an orb, a selfhood.*

Chapter IV

1. *At this, light or human imagination really first began,
and here we have Blake's immortal hope,—as from the holy
loins arose the holier imagination, so from holy body what we*

call the holy soul. He had the same regard for all loins that Roman Catholics have only for the loins of the Virgin Mary. This selection on their part is due to their rationalistic reading of the myth of the Garden of Eden, with the odd addition given by St. Paul, that the moral taint there acquired was physically inheritable, adding the very proper fancy that at least the mother of Christ should be accounted free of it. We shall see this elaborate account epitomised later into the brief statement that Los is the son of Tharmas (Demon of the Waters). The pure fluid conducted the light from the fires. Air, or the influence of the heart, being added to fire or the passion of the head. Forthwith by this light Los beheld the void's spiritual form. It was a serpent. It was the backbone of Urizen. It was the system of logic or mere coherence without imagination, experience without inspiration, natural tendency without exaltation, the vast 'chain of the mind' that 'locks up' the head, heart, loins of unimaginativeness in the book of 'Urizen' (Chapter VI., stanza 4) into forgetfulness, dumbness, necessity.

2, 3. Los, astonished and terrified at his own experiences, now made furnaces, which we learn in 'Jerusalem,' page 53, line 13, are the stomach, that there might be a counterpart to the pipes that drew in the spawn of the waters. He formed the anvil and hammer of the heart. Just as the loins are a duplex region, so is the heart, a place not only of breathing but of heating, with a fire as well as an air of its own, otherwise the loins would overbalance the region above them, and the outer control the inner. Then began the binding of the cold head—of Urizen. This is the moment of the close of the second and the whole of the third chapter of 'Urizen.' All the rest is a sort of belated introduction to those chapters.

In it we read how, out of Urizen's burning fires that preceded himself, he forged the apparent sun, as mind always forges body, and subject forges symbol. Here also Blake is telling the tale of ancient sun-worship (for Los is Time, and the years turned sun-worship into Monotheism), and he conceives that, when it got off the Sun it did so in the form of a Tyrant. A human delusion, a King Stork instead of King Log. But this seems to have been the origin of the Human Form. There is another reading of this poem equally possible.

4, 5. While outwardly he merely enclosed Urizen's fountain of thought under a roof ('Urizen,' IV., 8), he was really condensing the moods of desire into a selfhood which should eventually bring them forth again as its own, whether under the name of Orc or under any other.

6. Oft the incomplete vitality was quenched in the deeps of its own material. This is a strange alternation of experience and imagination whose ultimate symbol is the ever-buried and ever-rising Christ.

7. And nine ages completed the fruitful circlings of the fires, for the whirling that began in void, went on in torrents of water, after earth was burst, is now in fire, and the four regions are all fructified. Then Los knew that the product he had made was completed. What is called Orc when seen from another portion of the visionary world, and is changed to a rock, and awakens Urizen, is now brought as a glowing rock, or sun, and to it is chained the backbone of Urizen, his system of scientific and moral restrictiveness.

8. On this hot and dark rock Urizen lay—head chained to loins—in torment, as Orc lay in torment on the cold rock—loins chained to head. For the furnaces with their fires had joined the regions that the waters had divided when heavy and thin fell apart, for in this version pity divides, as else-where pity unites, what wrath divides—action and reaction being eternal.

9. And from this orb of fire, a paradise whose four rivers spring from the mount of rocky brain and the marsh of vegetative heart, the completed form, the human illusion, the body form in which we see among clouds, as in glass darkly, the spiritual and real human form, was completed.

DESIGNS TO THE 'BOOK OF LOS'

Frontispiece.—*Ahania as a stony old woman, the very counterpart of Urizen, sitting almost as he did, with her knees up, though she is allowed a low marble seat. Her hair is long, white, and serpentine; her face the essence of dreary despair. Dark cliffs are behind her.*

This picture is more an epilogue to 'Ahania' than a prologue to 'Los.' It was probably designed for that purpose.

The title-page shows a youth sitting doubled up in an aperture in the rocks of a cliff. The stones seem to have grown round him while he sat. Los in Albion's cliffs, or Imagination in difficulties of reason and doubt.

At the head of the first chapter is a slight sketch of an old man (Urizen) sitting in a net, whose further meshes entangle two childish figures, like flies in a spider's web—Los and Enitharmon.

At the end a small drawing—a kneeling figure with hands

up, prophesying in the sky.   Beneath him the earth rolls free in space, and if it stood on a flat cloud beside him, would be a little too large for him to see over if he stood on tiptoe.   Los triumphant.

The book is in the same style as 'Ahania,' and is of the same date, 1795.   They are the only two engraved in exactly this manner, with fine hair-lines.

THE

SONG

OF

LOS

LAMBETH
Printed by W. Blake
1795

AFRICA

I **will** sing you a song of Los, the Eternal Prophet :
He sung it to four harps at the tables of Eternity
    In heart-formed Africa.
Urizen faded ! Ariston shudder'd !
    And thus the Song began.

Adam stood in the garden of Eden,
And Noah on the mountains of Ararat ;
They saw Urizen give his Laws to the Nations
By the hands of the children of Los.

Adam shudder'd ! Noah faded ! black grew the sunny
    African
When Rintrah gave Abstract Philosophy to Brama in
    the East.
(Night spoke to the Cloud)
Lo, these Human form'd spirits in smiling hypocrisy,
    War
Against one another ; so let them War on, slaves to
    the Eternal Elements.
Noah shrunk beneath the waters,
Abram fled in fires from Chaldea ;
Moses beheld upon Mount Sinai forms of dark delusion;

To Trismegistus, Palamabron gave an abstract Law ;
To Pythagoras, Socrates, and Plato.

Times rolled on o'er all the sons of Har; time after time
Orc on Mount Atlas howl'd, chain'd down with the
    Chain of Jealousy ;

Then Oothoon hover'd over Judah and Jerusalem,
And Jesus heard her voice (a man of sorrows), he
    reciev'd
A Gospel from wretched Theotormon.

The human race began to wither, for the healthy
    built
Secluded places, fearing the joys of Love
And the diseased only propagated.
So Antamon call'd up Leutha from her valleys of
    delight,
And to Mahomet a loose Bible gave ;
But in the North, to Odin, Sotha gave a Code of War,
Because of Diralada, thinking to reclaim his joy.

(2)

These were the Churches, Hospitals, Castles, Palaces,
Like nets and gins and traps, to catch the joys of
    Eternity,
        And all the rest a desart ;
Till like a dream Eternity was obliterated and erased.

Since that dread day when Har and Heva fled,
Because their brethren and sisters liv'd in War and
    Lust ;
And as they fled they shrunk
Into two narrow doleful forms ;
Creeping in reptile flesh upon
The bosom of the ground :
And all the vast of Nature shrunk
Before their shrunken eyes.

Thus the terrible race of Los and Enitharmon gave
Laws and Religions to the sons of Har, binding them
    more
And more to Earth ; closing and restraining ;
Till a Philosophy of Five Senses was complete.
Urizen wept and gave it into the hands of Newton
    and Locke.

Clouds roll heavy upon the Alps round Rousseau
    and Voltaire:
And on the mountains of Lebanon round the deceased
    Gods
Of Asia, and on the desarts of Africa round the
    Fallen Angels,
The Guardian Prince of Albion burns in his nightly
    tent.

MEANING OF THE 'SONG OF LOS'

*The 'song' of Los is an influence such as the 'song' of
Enitharmon (its counterpart), which was a 'song of death'
and a song of Vala, and was, in point of fact, the assumption
of the South by the Zoa Luvah, or the flying up of Luvah and
Vala into the brain. Compare 'Vala,' Night I., lines 237 to
266. It is a song of life, whose earliest manifestations were
the giving of laws and religions that should not last, to the
sons of simple men. Los is now Chronos.*

*The instruments of music here used for mental productivity
are harps. Each of the four points has its own inner four,
and in heart-formed Africa, we find four of these creative
instruments.*

*Creation is the intellectual side of that set of three phases of
Ulro—Creation, Redemption, and Judgment,—Head, Heart,
Loins. Here we shall have a story of Loins in Head, and
both in Heart. It begins as Urizen, 'created' his temple out
of the 'void' in the East, Ulro, the 'space' of terror or its
heart. It is a world of (erroneous) generation as well as a
temple ('Jerusalem,' page 58, lines 21 to 51). It had the form
of the human heart, and was sun-worship in old days ('Vala,'
Night VII., line 510). He then faded, though once the 'Prince
of Light,'—for his dark power was to be used. He is the Sun
under the horizon.*

*Ariston, the power of beauty, shuddered, that is, descended
into birth. Changes occur related in compressed world-history
very like those that were told before in anatomical symbols.
Los, by the hands of his four children, ungenerated powers,
during the time when he was too like Urizen, having 'become*

*what he beheld,' causes the world to become more full of rules
of it for individuality and less for brotherhood, which is only
reached by vision when all intellect is perfectly ripe and ready
to be cut off and harvested. We hear the story of the ages that
' rolled over'—stanzas 4 and 5 in ' Book of Urizen,' Chap. V.,
when Los became what he beheld (' Vala,' Night IV., line 285),
before he writhed his neck to Enitharmon, before her shrieks
and the birth of Orc (' Vala,' Night V., line 63) ; before the
building of Golgonooza, or Art, Night V., line 76. In a sense
the date may be while the 'Light was out' (' Vala,' Night VII.,
line 584).*

*The song, the creation, began, and Adam, type of dust,
limit of human contraction, stood in the garden of Eden, the
place of the ' true tongue' who is Antamon, or the ' true west.'*

*Noah, the type of male force, surviving the fine senses of
Man and not destroyed by their flood, stood on the Mount of
Ararat—mount of rescue,—the contrasted symbol opposite to
Sinai—mount of law,—the stone of destruction flung at Fuzon
once by Urizen.*

*Urizen (as from this contrasted region) gave laws to the
Nations, teaching truth to become imperative in its separated
portions, the error of errors, the assuming of will, by what is
not the whole.*

*Just as the writings of the ancients were ' stolen and per-
verted,' so Urizen, who is here what we call intellect, stole the
sons of Los and perverted them from inspirers into restrictors.
Orc was not born yet, therefore it is evident that there must
have been, and were, only the ' ungenerated' sons of Los,
Rintrah, Palamabron, Theotormon, and Bromion, so called
in 'Jerusalem,' page 71, line 51.*

*Adam began to propagate dust, he shuddered with the
throes of procreation.*

*And Noah, the imaginative that never quite dies, faded—
into flesh.*

*Africa, once place of light, became place of darkness. (This
was when thought changed the infinite into a serpent, as told
in ' Europe.') Then under the influence of this darkness
Rintrah gave to Bramah in the East, or region of Luvah, a
love-philosophy abstracted from union with love. Night
spoke to the cloud. The blindness that does not see Eternity
when the tent (the eyelid) is closed (as told of Los in 'Urizen'),
spoke to the cloud, or blood ; an eyeless Reason governed Flesh,
which in its turn grew dark, as the bright sun-drop of inspiration was quenched in the lightless heart.*

*So, just as the four Zoas clouded rage ('Jerusalem,' p. 36,
l. 25 ; p. 41, l. 26 ; p. 58, l. 47 ; p. 74, l. 1 ; and p. 88, l. 55),
so the sons of Los are set against each other when divided,*

and the universal body of Inspiration is split into the mutually opposing separate religions. At this the masculine fell under the feminine dominion (as during the Night of 'Europe'), and thus Noah shrunk beneath the waters. Compare 'Jerusalem,' p. 7, l. 23; p. 15, l. 26; and p. 75, l. 13. The other Noah mentioned in 'Jerusalem,' p, 67, l. 59, is not the builder of the Ark but a daughter of Zelophahad, and one of the sisterhood of heiresses under Mosaic law, symbolising by their number, five, the senses. See Numbers, chap. xxvi. ver. 33.

Abram, the new Noah, in whose loins the Divine was concentrated, fled from Chaldea—from the East—for the place was uninhabitable to him since Rintrah had perversedly given abstract law to Bramah there. (Compare, for Chaldea, 'Jerusalem,' p. 15, l. 28; p. 21, l. 43; p. 36, l. 18; p. 60, l. 20.) And Moses, upon Sinai, beheld in the clouds of that obscured mountain the dark and delusive forms of prohibition. They were delusive because (compare 'Book of Urizen') they were 'laws of prudence' that seemed like 'laws of God.' The true function of Moses is to deliver from Egypt. He should act as Fuzon, but he will not. Moses in Swedenborg denotes the Law. In Blake—see 'Jerusalem,' page 49, line 57, and page 75, line 16. Then Palamabron, the great genius of Rejoicing, who inspired Wesley's hymns afterwards ('Milton,' page 20, line 55)—as Rintrah is of the emotional Pride and Glory and rage of strength, who should one day inspire Whitefield's pulpit thunder—falling in his turn under perversion, and reversing his rightful attributes, gives law, abstracted equally from religion and inspired emotion, to Trismegistus, Pythagoras, Socrates, and Plato, under whose names the Four Quarters of the Philosophic Mind are indicated.

All the sons of Har—all the merely natural men—lived on and propagated as times—creature-divided powers—urged them from generation to generation. All were under law, and rebellious to Har—their natural fatherhood—(compare 'Book of Tiriel'), and Reason's darkness ruled the region of Warmth. Urizen in his Northern darkness was ruler over though hidden under Africa—that is to say, this story belongs to man head downwards.

Times rolled over till Orc was born, or rather began to be born, for till his chains were loose he was hardly in the world. And Orc was howling in chains, the creative force of desire manifesting itself through the flesh. He was chained on Atlas, mount that divides the heavens from the earth. The chain of jealousy bound him there. Note the triad: Sinai, Ararat, Atlas.

At this the sorrows of Jealousy in the person of its victim Oothoon (see *Visions of the Daughters of Albion*) hovers over and rules and influences the inspired and happy Judah and Jerusalem, and the opposite to what should come does come for this reason from them, as from other quarters. They produce a Man of Sorrows, and wretched Theotormon gives to him the gospel of woe.

Three things have become religious—philosophy, law, and jealousy or grief. The head, heart, loins of the mind. For 'Religion' it is necessary at least to remember 'Jerusalem,' page 43, line 35 ; page 44, line 27, and page 45, line 26.

It remained that the loins of the body should be worshipped.

This came when the human race, withered from the healthy generative region of joy (joy is the true holiness to which all this is the opposite), fell into spiritual sterility, and only those mental forces which suffered from the disease of literalness, morality, and materialism propagated. The 'loins' represent argumentativeness.

The only thing to do was to proclaim the gospel of sensuous love as a spiritual code. So Antamon of the morning dew, and Leutha of the rainbow, types of beauty in water, or the region of vegetated growth, gave to Mahomet his 'loose Bible.'

While this was done in the south, Sotha, for the sake of Diralada (written 'Thiralatha' in 'Europe'), gave a code of war to Odin in the north, for war and love are each other's counterparts, and Sotha and Thiralatha are spirits of the eyes—region of marriage.

Then the Architect (who is Urizen) built those ideas and those organs in the four regions that correspond in physical love to the buildings called churches, hospitals, castles, palaces, to catch the joys of eternity as they catch the sorrows of time, and, that being the limit of his power, the rest of men's minds and bodies was desert.

And then, in the heart, in Africa, as in Los and Enitharmon, when the covered tent and curtains were lowered firmly over them ('Book of Urizen,' Chap. V., stanza 11), imagination in the sense of 'Divine Vision' was obliterated as though it did not exist, and thus brotherhood became formularised into conventional states of mind and conventional groups of actions.

But, by the law that 'the eye altering alters all' (compare the 'Mental Traveller,' stanza 16), Har and Hova, once spiritual instincts, having fled from their lawless brethren, because though weak they loved law, became two doleful forms, the mortal masculine, the slave of time and of decay, and its equally pitiable feminine mental counterpart, and all *nature shrunk to the dimensions of the garden where (see 'Book of Tiriel') they were found in a state of imbecile infancy—a return to Vala's garden, where the impressions of Despair and Hope for ever vegetate ('Vala,' Night IX., line 375), and where Tharmas and Enion (the same thing in mythic terms) are innocent children (Night IX., line 507), and Vala herself the sinless soul (Night IX., line 452), that sleeps in the grass and dew (Night IX., line 387), and whose inner soil is in the caverns of the grave, and places of human seed, where impressions of despair and hope enroot for ever (Night III., lines 144, 145), and where contraries are equally true ('Jerusalem,' page 48, line 13).*

Thus the terrible influences of Time and Space gave laws and religions to the sons of instinctive life, closing and restraining them from visionary life, till the Reason-worship of the eighteenth century was complete, and the only conception of God they had left—the 'mistaken demon of Heaven'—Urizen, who became Satan when drawn down into generation (compare 'Milton,' extra page 8, line 1), wept his net-making tears and gave this, the worst mental chain of all, as a system of thought to Newton and Locke.

The weight of the flesh grows heavy on the dry mental and moral code—mountains of Lebanon. It rolls round the 'covering cherub'—here symbolised as Rousseau, Voltaire, resting on the Alps, the Atlas hills of Europe or of the North, and on the deceased gods of Asia—the dry-hearted deserts of Africa, and on the Angels; or those who are before all things obedient, and whose morsel of imaginative existence was sacrificed when they obeyed the trumpet of Newton. (Compare 'Europe.')

But in the fallen Man, or Albion—Urizen—the potency of mind, his guardian Prince, is not quenched though hid by night of experience and the tent of the flesh, but burns darkly with the dark secret fires of Urizen described in the 'Book of Los,' which he, repressing in himself, hated to see others (as in 'America') claim the right to release.

The reader is requested by the editor not to forget that these notes only contain sketches of the meanings they describe. There is much more that should be said were the descriptions to aim at completeness. There are other sets of meanings quite unlike these and not necessarily contradicting them.

(4)

ASIA

THE Kings of Asia heard
The howl rise up from Europe !
And each ran out from his Web,
From his ancient woven Den ;
For the darkness of Asia was startled
At the thick-flaming, thought-creating fires of Orc.

And the Kings of Asia stood
And cried in bitterness of soul.

Shall not the King call for Famine from the heath,
Nor the Priest for Pestilence from the fen ?
To restrain, to dismay, to thin
The inhabitants of mountain and plain,
In the day of full-feeding prosperity
And the night of delicious songs ?

Shall not the Councellor throw his curb
Of Poverty on the laborious,
To fix the price of labour,
To invent allegoric riches ?

And the privy admonishers of men
Call for Fires in the City,
For heaps of smoking ruins,
In the night of prosperity and wantonness ?

To turn man from his path,
To restrain the child from the womb ?

(5)

To cut off the bread from the city,
That the remnant may learn to obey ?

That the pride of the heart may fail ;
That the lust of the eyes may be quench'd ;
That the delicate ear in its infancy
May be dull'd, and the nostrils clos'd up,
To teach mortal worms the path
That leads from the gates of the Grave?

Urizen heard them cry,
And his shudd'ring, waving wings
Went enormous above the red flames,
Drawing clouds of despair thro' the heavens
Of Europe as he went.
And his Books of brass, iron, and gold
Melted over the land as he flew,
Heavy-waving, howling, weeping.

And he stood over Judea,
And stay'd in his ancient place,
And stretch'd his clouds over Jerusalem.

For Adam, a mouldering skeleton,
Lay bleach'd on the garden of Eden ;
And Noah, as white as snow,
On the mountains of Ararat.

Then the thunders of Urizen bellow'd aloud
From his woven darkness above.

Orc, raging in European darkness,
Arose like a pillar of fire above the Alps,
Like a serpent of fiery flame !
   The sullen Earth
    Shrunk !

Forth from the dead dust, rattling bones to bones
Join ; shaking, convuls'd, the shiv'ring clay breathes,
And all flesh naked stands : Fathers and Friends,
Mothers and Infants, Kings and Warriors.

The Grave shrieks with delight, and shakes
Her hollow womb, and clasps the solid stem :
Her bosom swells with wild desire :
And milk and blood and glandous wine,
In rivers rush and shout and dance,
On mountain, dale, and plain.

THE SONG OF LOS IS ENDED

Urizen Wept.

MEANING OF 'ASIA'

*The Kings of Asia are restrainers of the heart of man
wherever we meet them in this life.   They seek obedience before
all things.   We recognise in them the voices of the hypocritic
and dominion-loving daughters of Urizen ('Vala,' Night VII.,
lines 115 to 129), that are explained as being related in the
head in line 130, and in 'Jerusalem,' page 30, where in his
central void or heart, among his oaks (tree of weeping), they
are heard as the voices of 'the oppressors of Albion.'*

*They desire to do some active harm.   They wish not merely
to restrain by nets, but by punishments.   Famine, poverty,
fire, are the engines they would use.   That a little happiness
has become transferred from the State of Eden to that of
generation is unendurable to them.   They call it wantonness.
They would lead mortal worms from the gates of the grave
because these seem to them the gates of feasting and love, and
may by joy, even the lowest joy, lead to regeneration.   They
have nothing else to offer.   But they desire to quench the pride
of the heart, destroy the desire of the eyes to see, especially to
see vision, and to make dull the ear lest it hear an inner
voice.*

'Shall we not do it?' they cried.   Urizen heard the cry.

*It was a howl of Orc in changed form.   It was the desire of
tyranny.   Sad blood, clouds of despair, are all that he brings.
He arose.   His wings (the type of that which covers the mercy
seat, or creative centre) shuddered.*

For the relation between Mercy and Creation, compare

'Jerusalem,' p. 13, l. 45; p. 69, l. 19; p. 73, l. 39, etc. Creation has its evil, or outer side, as now when the wings, and not that within them, propagated, exteriors became fruitful in their own deadly way, for shuddering always has the meaning of parturition.

Urizen's books melted, and their brass, iron, and gold ran down over the regions of heart, loins, and head, as he howled with the passion of sowing his maxims in form of melted metal, and as he wept, that his net of tears (compare 'Book of Urizen,' Chap. VIII., stanzas 7, 8, and 9, and 'Visions of the Daughters of Albion,' p. 5) might still catch souls and form man to his image, even while the melted pages of bodily and mental suffering fell on them drop by drop. Thus he answered to the cry of the kings, and made it productive.

He clouded Jerusalem and Judea—where Oothoon had hovered—darkening what had been his own bright land. It was the land of Christ (symbol of a Rescuer now, who Redeems Man from drowning in sorrow), an Eastern sign, of Adam, symbol of dust, man's limit of materialisation, who rescued man from drowning in dust by help of divine breath, and of Noah, his limit of productivity, who rescued the soul from drowning in instinct, and became the second father of the race. All were gone. The latter two lay visibly dead. Satan, limit of opacity, whose fiery form of Orc rescues man by passion from drowning in reason, flamed above the Northern moralities, Alps. Orc is altogether spiritual here, as when his fires consuming the five gates of the senses, that can no longer be barred against the infinite, at the end of 'America.'

Orc we know to be both Luvah and Satan (according to the 'state' he, though himself a state, may be in). Here we see Satan put off Satan. Each Zoa is Satanic when fighting for himself alone.

The passage about the bones is partly the same as that in which the second, or mature birth of Tharmas, is prepared in 'Vala,' Night III., line 156, but the real context that Blake had in his mind (and probably on his table, for 'Vala' had been in MS. for two years) is in Night IX., around the lines 230 and 242. The resurrection, or delivery into the nakedness of the spirit from reptile dress or prison (line 294), is seen by comparison with these last lines of 'Asia' to be the material joy of the grave, and explanation of the statement that her caverns are the places of human seed. The 'Song of Los' releases, by its prophetic power, the meanings of all symbols in the same way from their dress, and Urizen already begins, weeping, to pervert it all again, for as we shall see from Adam to Luther begins again in eternal circle.

DESIGNS TO THE 'SONG OF LOS'

Title-page.—A bearded old man lying on his back, raised on one elbow and looking up at the sky. He has his hand on a skull. A quiet landscape of hills and lakes behind.

Page 1. Coiled round the sub-title Africa, at the head of the page, a big dark snake, looking downwards.

Page 2. A youth and maid, partly draped, fly together from a sea-coast storm. His arms round her body—one of hers round his head. Her other hand forbids the waves to follow them.

Page 3. A full page. Oberon and Titania, as tiny figures, lying in the hollows of two large lilies that partly interlace their white petals.

Page 4. Below the sub-title Asia, a youth in a cave with a maiden (draped this time), half-lying, backwards, across his knees, looking up at him, and half-kneeling herself at his side. He sits on the ground.

Outside a gloomy figure, nude, sits holding its head. Bromion, Oothoon, and Theotormon again, yet changed. Under any names they are Energy, Opportunity, and Restraint.

Page 5. A man falling head downwards—margin sketch.

THE LAOCOON

THE LAGOON

THE LAOCOON

The Laocoon is referred to in the page on Homer's poetry. Soon after Blake's return from Felpham, he engraved this group for Rees's encyclopædia. He either took a copy of the plate or made another for himself, and printed round it and in every available space the following statements, placing some lines at right angles to others, and some in curves about the limbs of the figures. They partly explain the poem 'Idolatry' to be found above, near the end of the shorter pieces, and are, like the other fragments here given, essential to understanding the odium theologicum with which Blake pursued one form of art while he upheld another.

The order of the sentences is conjectural. There is no ascertained order. The groups are clearly indicated, but we can only guess which were engraved first and which put in later, as space permitted.

Blake's title for the Laocoon statue, engraved under it.

יה‎ and his two sons Satan and Adam, as they were copied from the Cherubim of Solomon's Temple by three Rhodians, and applied to Natural Fact, or History of Ilium.

Added later below this—

Art Degraded, Imagination Denied, War Governed the Nations.

Sentences above the figures, horizontal lines, at the extreme top of the page, crammed in—

Where any view of Money exists, Art cannot be carried on, but War only. Read Matthew, chap. x. 9.

(The reference seems to be to the words 'Provide neither

gold nor silver nor brass in your purses,' and must be read with the statement found further on that Christ and His Apostles were artists. A peculiar use of the word Art recurs in these works. Compare 'Vala,' Night I., lines 307 and 308, and elsewhere.)

He repented that he had made Adam (of the Female, the Adamah), and it grieved him at his heart.

The Angel of the Divine Presence.

מלאך יהוה

(King Jehovah.)

The two serpents in the group are labelled ' Good' and ' Evil.' Good, the one biting the man ; Evil, biting the boy on his right, at left of picture. His name OΦISXƆ *is written over his head. Round his upper hand, that grasps the serpent above, is written—*

The Gods of Priam are the Cherubim of Moses and Solomon, the Hosts of Heaven. Without Unceasing Practice nothing can be done. Practice is Art. If you leave off, you are lost.

Round the upper arm of the bitten boy whom the snake ' Evil' bites is written—

Good and Evil, Riches and Poverty, a Tree of Misery, propagations, generation, and death.

Round the other boy's head is written—

Satan's Wife, the Goddess Nature, is War and Misery, and Heroism a Miser.

In an arch joining this boy's head to the man—

Hebrew Art is called Sin by the Deist Science.

All that we see is Vision from Generated Organs, gone as soon as come, Permanent in the Imagination, considered as Nothing by the Natural Man.

And under the man's left hand—

רירית

which is the name 'Lilith,' considered anciently to be that of Adam's first wife. Blake seems to have considered it that of Satan's, as he writes. Satan's wife, the Goddess Nature, *close to the name, with the definition that she* is War and Misery, *adding the strained inference,* and Heroism a Miser.

On all the blank space to the right of the picture there are more short sayings, whose order can be dimly guessed from the way they fit into each other. Taking those written in largest and boldest hand, edgeways, first, and then those that seem added to fill up gaps and are written more minutely, we read this half of the space as follows:—

Jesus and His Apostles and Disciples were all Artists. Their Works were destroyed by the Seven Angels of the Seven Churches in Asia, Antichrist Science. The Old and New Testaments are the great code of Art. The whole Business of Man Is The Arts and All Things in Common. No secresy in Art. Art is the Tree of Life. God is Jesus. Science is the Tree of Death. The unproductive Man is not a Christian, much less the Destroyer. Christianity is Art and not Money. Money is its curse. What we call Antique Gems are the Gems of Aaron's Breast Plate. Is not every Vice possible to Man described in the Bible openly? All is not sin that Satan calls so,—all the Loves and Graces of Eternity.

The gods of Greece and Egypt were Mathematical Diagrams. See Plato's works.

DIVINE UNION.

Deriding and Denying Immediate Communion with God . . . The spoilers say, Where are his works that he did in the Wilderness? Lo, what are these? Whence came they? These are not the works of Egypt nor Babylon, whose gods are the Powers of this world, Goddess Nature, who first spoil and then destroy Imaginative Art, for their glory is War and Dominion. Empire against Art. See Virgil's *Æneid*, lib. vi. v. 348. For every Pleasure Money is Useless. There are States in which All Visionary Men are accounted Mad Men. Such are Greece and Rome. Such is Empire or Tax.— See Luke ii. 1.

The reference is where Joseph went 'to be taxed with Mary his espoused wife.' So ends the right half of the picture space. Turning to the left we read—

SPIRITUAL WAR.

Israel delivered from Egypt is Art delivered from Nature and Imitation.

A Poet, a Painter, a Musician, an Architect: the Man or Woman who is not one of these is not a Christian. Prayer is the Study of Art. Praise is the Practice of Art. Fasting, etc., all relate to Art. The outward Ceremony is Antichrist. You must leave Fathers and Mothers and Houses and Lands if they stand in the way of Art.

The Eternal Body of Man is The Imagination. That is God himself, the Divine Body. ישוע Jesus. We are His members.

It manifests itself in his Works of Art. (In Eternity All is Vision.) The true Christian Charity, not dependent on Money (the life's blood of Poor Families), that is on Cæsar or Empire, or Natural Religion, Money which is the Great Satan, or Reason, the Root of Good and Evil in the Accusation of Sin.

So end these fragments, unless—as is possible from the style of lettering—they really ended with the uppermost lines at the top of the page, 'Where any view of Money exists, Art cannot be carried on,' etc., down to 'and it grieved him at his heart,' which may have been scratched in afterwards, as a short line under this and above the title, 'The Angel of the Divine Presence,' may indicate a termination. If so, the title was the true beginning.

MILTON

A POEM

IN TWELVE BOOKS

'To Justify the Ways of God to Men'

The Author and Printer W. BLAKE

1804

(The above is Blake's title-page.   The poem was reduced in volume from twelve books to two after the words were engraved.)

MILTON

PREFACE

THE Stolen and Perverted Writings of Homer and
Ovid, of Plato and Cicero, which all Men ought to
contemn, are set up by artifice against the Sublime of
the Bible; but when the New Age is at leisure to
Pronounce, all will be set right, and those Grand
Works of the more ancient and consciously and pro-
fessedly Inspired Men will hold their proper rank; and
the Daughters of Memory shall become the Daughters
of Inspiration.   Shakspeare and Milton were both
curb'd by the general malady and infection from the
silly Greek and Latin slaves of the Sword.   Rouze up,
O Young Men of the New Age !   Set your foreheads
against the ignorant Hirelings.   For we have Hirelings in the Camp, the Court, and the University, who
would, if they could, for ever depress Mental and
prolong Corporeal War.   Painters ! on you I call.
Sculptors ! Architects ! suffer not the fashionable
Fools to depress your powers by the prices they
pretend to give for contemptible works, or the ex-
pensive advertizing boasts that they make of such
works; believe Christ and his Apostles that there is a
Class of Men whose whole delight is in Destroying.
We do not want either Greek or Roman Models if we
are but just and true to our own Imaginations, those
Worlds of Eternity in which we shall live for ever in
Jesus our Lord.

> And did those feet in ancient time
> Walk upon England's mountains green,
> And was the holy Lamb of God
> On England's pleasant pastures seen?

And did the Countenance Divine
Shine forth upon our clouded hills,
And was Jerusalem builded here
Among these dark Satanic Mills?

Bring me my Bow of burning gold,
Bring me my arrows of desire;
Bring me my spear: O clouds, unfold!
Bring me my Chariot of fire!

I will not cease from Mental Fight,
Nor shall my Sword sleep in my hand,
Till we have built Jerusalem
In England's green and pleasant Land.

Would to God that all the Lord's people were
Prophets!—*Numbers* xi. 29.

MILTON

BOOK THE FIRST

DAUGHTERS of Beulah ! Muses who inspire the Poet's
   Song,
Record the journey of immortal Milton thro' your
   Realms
Of terror and mild moony lustre, in soft sexual
   delusions
Of varied beauty, to delight the wanderer and repose
5 His burning thirst and freezing hunger ! Come into
   my hand
By your mild power, descending down the Nerves of
   my right arm
From out the Portals of my Brain, where by your
   ministry
The Eternal Great Humanity Divine planted his
   Paradise,
And in it caus'd the Spectres of the Dead to take
   sweet form
10 In likeness of himself. Tell also of the False Tongue,
   vegetated
Beneath your land of shadows : of its sacrifices and
Its offerings ; even till Jesus, the image of the Invisible God,
Became its prey ; a curse, an offering, and an atone-
   ment
For Death Eternal, in the heavens of Albion, and
   before the Gates
15 Of Jerusalem his Emanation, in the heavens beneath
   Beulah.

Say first, what mov'd Milton, who walk'd about in
        Eternity
One hundred years, pond'ring the intricate mazes of
        Providence?
Unhappy tho' in heav'n, he obey'd, he murmur'd not,
        he was silent,
Viewing his Sixfold Emanation scatter'd thro' the deep
20 In torment, to go into the deep, her to redeem and
        himself perish.
What cause at length mov'd Milton to this unexampled
        deed?
A Bard's prophetic Song! for sitting at eternal tables,
Terrific among the Sons of Albion, in chorus solemn
        and loud
A Bard broke forth! all sat attentive to the awful man.

25 Mark well my words; they are of your eternal
        salvation:

Three Classes are Created by the Hammer of Los, and
        Woven

(4)

From Golgonooza, the spiritual, Four-fold London
        eternal,
In immense labours and sorrows, ever building, ever
        falling
Thro' Albion's four Forests, which overspread all the
        Earth
From London Stone to Blackheath east; to Hounslow
        west;
5 To Finchley north; to Norwood south; and the weights
Of Enitharmon's Loom play lulling cadences on the
        winds of Albion
From Caithness in the north to Lizard point and
        Dover in the south.

Loud sounds the Hammer of Los and loud his Bellows
        is heard

Before London to Hampstead's breadths and High-
    gate's heights, to
10 Stratford and old Bow, and across to the Gardens of
    Kensington,
On Tyburn's Brook ; loud groans Thames beneath the
    iron Forge
Of Rintrah and Palamabron, of Theotorm and
    Bromion, to forge the instruments
Of Harvest, the Plow and Harrow, to pass over the
    Nations.

The Surrey hills glow like the clinkers of the furnace ;
    Lambeth's Vale,
15 Where Jerusalem's foundations began, where they
    were laid in ruins,
Where they were laid in ruins from every Nation, and
    Oak Groves rooted.
Dark gleams before the Furnace-mouth a heap of
    burning ashes.
When shall Jerusalem return and overspread all the
    Nations ?
Return, return to Lambeth's Vale, O building of
    human souls.
20 Thence stony Druid Temples overspread the Island
    white ;
And thence from Jerusalem's ruins, from her wells of
    salvation
And praise, thro' the whole Earth were rear'd, from
    Ireland
To Mexico and Peru west, and east to China and
    Japan, till Babel,
The Spectre of Albion, frown'd over the Nations in
    glory and war.

25 All things begin and end in Albion's ancient Druid
    rocky shore ;
But now the Starry Heavens are fled from the mighty
    limbs of Albion.
Loud sounds the Hammer of Los, loud turn the
    Wheels of Enitharmon.

Her Looms vibrate with soft affections, weaving the
Web of Life.
Out from the ashes of the Dead, Los lifts his iron
Ladles
30 With molten ore; he heaves the iron cliffs in his
rattling chains
From Hyde Park to the Alms-houses of Mile-end and
old Bow.
Here the Three Classes of Mortal Men take their fix'd
destinations,
And hence they overspread the Nations of the whole
Earth, and hence
The Web of Life is woven; and the tender sinews of
life created,
35 And the Three Classes of Men regulated by Los's
Hammer, and woven

(5)

By Enitharmon's Looms, and Spun beneath the
Spindle of Tirzah.
The first, The Elect from before the foundation of the
World ;
The second, The Redeemed ; The Third, The Reprobate,
and form'd
To destruction from the mother's womb : . . . . . . ,
. . . . follow with me my plow.

5 Of the first class was Satan, with incomparable mildness ;
His primitive tyrannical attempts on Los, with most
endearing love.
He soft intreated Los to give to him Palamabron's
station ;
For Palamabron return'd with labour wearied every
evening.
Palamabron oft refus'd ; and as often Satan offer'd
10 His service, till, by repeated offers and repeated
intreaties,
Los gave to him the Harrow of the Almighty ; alas,
blamable.

Palamabron fear'd to be angry lest Satan should accuse him of

Ingratitude, and Los beleive the accusation thro' Satan's extreme

Mildness. Satan labour'd all day; it was a thousand years.

15 In the evening, returning terrified, overlabour'd and astonish'd,

Embrac'd soft with a brother's tears Palamabron, who also wept.

Mark well my words! they are of your eternal salvation.

Next morning Palamabron rose: the horses of the Harrow

Were madden'd with tormenting fury, and the servants of the Harrow,

20 The Gnomes, accus'd Satan with indignation, fury, and fire.

Then Palamabron, reddening like the Moon in an eclipse,

Spoke, saying, You know Satan's mildness and his self-imposition;

Seeming a brother, being a tyrant, even thinking himself a brother

While he is murdering the just. Prophetic I behold

25 His future course thro' darkness and despair to eternal death.

But we must not be tyrants also! he hath assum'd my place

For one whole day, under pretence of pity and love to me.

My horses hath he madden'd, and my fellow servants injur'd.

How should he know the duties of another? O foolish forbearance,

30 Would I had told Los all my heart! but patience, O my friends,

All may be well: silent remain, while I call Los and Satan.

Loud as the wind of Beulah that unroots the rocks
    and hills
Palamabron call'd, and Los and Satan came before
    him ;
And Palamabron shew'd the horses and the servants.
    Satan wept,
35 And mildly cursing Palamabron, him accus'd of crimes
Himself had wrought.   Los trembled.   Satan's blan-
    dishments almost
Perswaded the Prophet of Eternity that Palamabron
Was Satan's enemy, and that the Gnomes, being
    Palamabron's friends,
Were leagued together against Satan thro' ancient
    enmity.
40 What could Los do? how could he judge, when
    Satan's self believ'd
That he had not oppres'd the horses of the Harrow
    nor the servants ?

So Los said : Henceforth, Palamabron, let each his
    own station
Keep ; nor in pity false, nor in officious brotherhood,
    where
None needs be active. Meantime Palamabron's horses
45 Rag'd with thick flames redundant, and the Harrow
    madden'd with fury.
Trembling Palamabron stood ; the strongest of Demons
    trembled,
Curbing his living creatures : many of the strongest
    Gnomes
They bit in their wild fury, who also madden'd like
    wildest beasts.

49 Mark well my words ; they are of your eternal salvation.

(6)

Mean while wept Satan before Los, accusing Palam-
    abron,
Himself exculpating with mildest speech, for himself
    believ'd

That he had not oppress'd nor injur'd the refractory
     servants.

But Satan, returning to his Mills (for Palamabron had
     serv'd
5 The Mills of Satan as the easier task), found all con-
     fusion,
And back return'd to Los, not fill'd with vengeance,
     but with tears,
Himself convinc'd of Palamabron's turpitude. Los
     beheld
The servants of the Mills drunken with wine, and
     dancing wild,
With shouts and Palamabron's songs, rending the
     forests green
10 With echoing confusion, tho' the Sun was risen on
     high.

Then Los took off his left sandal, placing it on his head,
Signal of solemn mourning. When the servants of the
     Mills
Beheld the signal, they in silence stood, tho' drunk
     with wine.
Los wept ! But Rintrah also came, and Enitharmon on
15 His arm lean'd tremblingly, observing all these things.

And Los said : Ye Genii of the Mills, the Sun is on high ;
Your labours call you. Palamabron is also in sad
     dilemma :
His horses are mad, his Harrow confounded, his
     companions enrag'd.
Mine is the fault ! I should have remember'd that pity
     divides the soul,
20 And man unmans. Follow with me my Plow : this
     mournful day
Must be a blank in Nature ; follow with me, and
     to-morrow again
Resume your labours, and this day shall be a mourn-
     ful day.

Wildly they follow'd Los and Rintrah, and the Mills
    were silent.
They mourn'd all day this mournful day of Satan and
    Palamabron;
25 And all the Elect and all the Redeem'd mourn'd one
    toward another
Upon the mountains of Albion, among the cliffs of the
    Dead.

They Plow'd in tears! incessant pour'd Jehovah's
    ruin; and Molech,
Thick fires contending with the rain, thunder'd above,
    rolling
Terrible over their heads; Satan wept over Palamabron;
30 Theotormon and Bromion contended on the side of
    Satan,
Pitying his youth and beauty, trembling at eternal
    death.
Michael contended against Satan in the rolling
    thunder;
Thulloh, the friend of Satan, also reprov'd him;
    faint their reproof.

But Rintrah, who is of the reprobate, of those form'd
    to destruction,
35 In indignation, for Satan's soft dissimulation of
    friendship
Flam'd above all the plowed furrows, angry, red, and
    furious,
Till Michael sat down in the furrow, weary, dissolv'd
    in tears.
Satan, who drave the team, beside him stood, angry
    and red;
He smote Thulloh, and slew him; and he stood
    terrible over Michael,
40 Urging him to arise: he wept: Enitharmon saw his
    tears;
But Los hid Thulloh from her sight, lest she should
    die of grief.

She wept: she trembled: she kissed Satan: she wept
    over Michael:
She form'd a Space for Satan and Michael, and for the
    poor infected;
Trembling she wept over the Space, and clos'd it with
    a tender Moon.

45 Los secret buried Thulloh, weeping disconsolate over
    the moony Space.

But Palamabron called down a Great Solemn Assembly,
That he who will not defend Truth may be compelled to
48 Defend a Lie, that he may be snared and caught and
    taken.

(7)

And all Eden descended into Palamabron's tent,
Among Albion's Druids and Bards: in the caves
    beneath Albion's
Death Couch; in the caverns of death, in the corner
    of the Atlantic.
And in the midst of the Great Assembly Palamabron
    pray'd:
5 O God, protect me from my friends, that they have not
    power over me.
Thou hast giv'n me power to protect myself from my
    bitterest enemies.

Mark well my words, they are of your eternal salvation.

Then rose the Two Witnesses, Rintrah and Palamabron.
And Palamabron appeal'd to all Eden, and reciev'd
10 Judgment: and Lo! it fell on Rintrah and his rage,
Which now flam'd high and furious in Satan against
    Palamabron,
Till it became a proverb in Eden, Satan is among the
    Reprobate.

Los in his wrath curs'd heaven and earth; he rent up
    Nations,

Standing on Albion's rocks among high-rear'd Druid temples

15 Which reach the stars of heaven, and stretch from pole to pole.

He displac'd continents; the oceans fled before his face.

He alter'd the poles of the world, east, west, and north and south;

But he clos'd up Enitharmon from the sight of all these things.

For Satan, flaming with Rintrah's fury hidden beneath his own mildness,

20 Accus'd Palamabron before the Assembly of ingratitude, of malice.

He created Seven deadly Sins, drawing out his infernal scroll

Of Moral laws and cruel punishments upon the clouds of Jehovah,

To pervert the Divine voice in its entrance to the earth,

With thunder of war and trumpets' sound, with armies of disease;

25 Punishments and deaths muster'd and number'd: Saying, I am God alone;

There is no other: let all obey my principles of moral individuality.

I have brought them from the uppermost, innermost recesses

Of my Eternal Mind: transgressors I will rend off for ever,

As now I rend this accursed Family from my covering.

30 Thus Satan rag'd amidst the Assembly, and his bosom grew

Opake against the Divine vision; the paved terraces of

His bosom inwards shone with fires; but the stones becoming opake,

Hid him from sight in an extreme blackness and darkness,

And there a World of deeper Ulro was open'd in the
    midst
35 Of the Assembly.   In Satan's bosom a vast unfathom-
    able Abyss.

Astonishment held the Assembly in an awful silence,
    and tears
Fell down as dews of night, and a loud, solemn,
    universal groan
Was utter'd from the east and from the west and from
    the south
And from the north; and Satan stood opake, im-
    measurable,
40 Covering the east with solid blackness round his
    hidden heart,
With thunders utter'd from his hidden wheels, accus-
    ing loud
The Divine Mercy for protecting Palamabron in his
    tent.

Rintrah rear'd up walls of rock, and pour'd rivers and
    moats
Of fire round the walls: columns of fire guard around
45 Between Satan and Palamabron in the terrible dark-
    ness.

And Satan, not having the Science of Wrath, but only
    of Pity,
Rent them asunder, and wrath was left to wrath, and
    pity to pity.
He sunk down a dreadful Death, unlike the slumbers
    of Beulah.

The Separation was terrible: the Dead was repos'd on
    his Couch,
50 Beneath the Couch of Albion, on the seven mountains
    of Rome,
In the whole place of the Covering Cherub, Rome,
    Babylon, and Tyre;
52 His Spectre, raging furious, descended into its Space.

(9)

He set his face against Jerusalem to destroy the Eon
　　of Albion,
But Los hid Enitharmon from the sight of all these
　　things
Upon the Thames, whose lulling harmony repos'd her
　　soul,
Where Beulah lovely terminates in rocky Albion,
5 Terminating in Hyde Park, on Tyburn's awful brook.

And the Mills of Satan were separated into a moony
　　Space
Among the rocks of Albion's Temples, and Satan's
　　Druid Sons
Offer the Human Victims throughout all the Earth ;
　　and Albion's
Dread Tomb, immortal on his Rock, overshadowed the
　　whole Earth ;
10 Where Satan, making to himself Laws from his own
　　identity,
Compell'd others to serve him in moral gratitude and
　　submission,
Being call'd God, setting himself above all that is
　　called God.
And all the Spectres of the Dead, calling themselves
　　Sons of God,
In his Synagogues worship Satan under the Unutter-
　　able Name.

15 And it was enquir'd : Why in a Great Solemn Assembly
The Innocent should be condemn'd for the Guilty ?
　　Then an Eternal rose,
Saying : If the Guilty should be condemn'd, he must
　　be an Eternal Death,
And one must die for another throughout all Eternity.
Satan is fall'n from his station, and never can be
　　redeem'd,
20 But must be new created continually, moment by
　　moment,

And therefore the Class of Satan shall be call'd the
    Elect, and those
Of Rintrah the Reprobate, and those of Palamabron
    the Redeem'd,
For he is redeem'd from Satan's Law, the wrath fall-
    ing on Rintrah,
And therefore Palamabron dared not to call a solemn
    Assembly
25 Till Satan had assum'd Rintrah's wrath in the day of
    mourning,
In a feminine delusion of false pride, self-deciev'd.

So spake the Eternal, and confirm'd it with a
    thunderous oath.

But when Leutha (a Daughter of Beulah) beheld
    Satan's condemn,
She down descended into the midst of the Great
    Solemn Assembly,
30 Offering herself a Ransom for Satan, taking on her
    his Sin.

Mark well my words, they are of your eternal salva-
    tion.

And Leutha stood glowing with varying colours, im-
    mortal, heart-piercing,
And lovely; and her moth-like elegance shone over
    the Assembly.

At length, standing upon the golden floor of Palam-
    abron,
35 She spake: I am the Author of this Sin; by my
    suggestion
My Parent power Satan has committed this trans-
    gression.
I loved Palamabron, and I sought to approach his Tent,
38 But beautiful Elynittria, with her silver arrows,
    repell'd me,

(10)

For her light is terrible to me.   I fade before her im-
    mortal beauty.
O wherefore doth a Dragon-form forth issue from my
    limbs
To sieze her new-born son? Ah me! the wretched
    Leutha !
This to prevent, entering the doors of Satan's brain
    night after night,
5 Like sweet perfumes, I stupified the masculine per-
    ceptions,
And kept only the feminine awake ; hence rose his soft
Delusory love to Palamabron ; admiration join'd with
    envy ;
Cupidity unconquerable ! my fault, when at noon of
    day
The Horses of Palamabron call'd for rest and pleasant
    death.
10 I sprang out of the breast of Satan, over the Harrow
    beaming,
In all my beauty; that I might unloose the flaming
    steeds
As Elynittria used to do : but too well those living
    creatures
Knew that I was not Elynittria, and they broke the
    traces,
But me the servants of the Harrow saw not; but as a
    bow
15 Of varying colours on the hills, terribly rag'd the
    horses.
Satan, astonish'd, and with power above his own
    control,
Compell'd the Gnomes to curb the horses, and to
    throw banks of sand
Around the fiery flaming Harrow in labyrinthine forms,
And brooks between to intersect the meadows in their
    course.
20 The Harrow cast thick flames ; Jehovah thunder'd
    above ;

Chaos and ancient night fled from beneath the fiery
    Harrow :
The Harrow cast thick flames, and orb'd us round in
    concave fires,
A Hell of our own making : see, its flames still gird
    me round.
Jehovah thunder'd above : Satan, in pride of
    heart,
25 Drove the fierce Harrow among the constellations of
    Jehovah,
Drawing a third part in the fires, as stubble north and
    south,
To devour Albion and Jerusalem, the Emanation of
    Albion ;
Driving the Harrow in Pity's path : 'twas then, with
    our dark fires,
Which now gird round us (O eternal torment !), I
    form'd the Serpent
30 Of precious stones and gold, turn'd poisons on the
    sultry wastes.
The Gnomes in all that day spar'd not ; they curs'd
    Satan bitterly.
To do unkind things in kindness, with power arm'd ;
    to say
The most irritating things in the midst of tears and
    love—
These are the stings of the Serpent ! thus did we by
    them ; till thus
35 They in return retaliated, and the Living Creatures
    madden'd,
The Gnomes labour'd. I, weeping, hid in Satan's
    inmost brain ;
But when the Gnomes refus'd to labour more, with
    blandishments
I came forth from the head of Satan : back the Gnomes
    recoil'd,
And call'd me Sin, and for a sign portentous held me.
    Soon
40 Day sunk, and Palamabron return'd ; trembling I
    hid myself

In Satan's inmost Palace of his nervous, fine-wrought
    brain:
For Elynittria met Satan with all her singing women.
Terrific in their joy, and pouring wine of wildest
    power,
They gave Satan their wine: indignant at the burn-
    ing wrath,
45 Wild with prophetic fury, his former life became like
    a dream,
Cloth'd in the Serpent's folds, in selfish holiness de-
    manding purity;
Being most impure, self-condemn'd to eternal tears,
    he drove
Me from his inmost Brain, and the doors clos'd with
    thunder's sound.
O Divine Vision, who didst create the Female, to
    repose
50 The Sleepers of Beulah: pity the repentant Leutha. My

(11)

Sick Couch bears the dark shades of Eternal Death,
    infolding
The Spectre of Satan: he, furious, refuses to repose in
    sleep.
I humbly bow in all my Sin before the Throne Divine.
Not so the Sick-one. Alas, what shall be done him to
    restore?
5 Who calls the Individual Law Holy, and despises the
    Saviour,
Glorying to involve Albion's Body in fires of eternal
    War?

Now Leutha ceas'd; tears flow'd; but the Divine
Pity supported her.

All is my fault. We are the Spectre of Luvah, the
    murderer
Of Albion. O Vala! O Luvah! O Albion! O lovely
    Jerusalem!

10 The Sin was begun in Eternity, and will not rest to
　　Eternity,
　Till two Eternitys meet together. Ah ! lost ! lost !
　　lost for ever !

　So Leutha spake. But when she saw that Enitharmon
　　had
　Created a New Space to protect Satan from punish-
　　ment,
　She fled to Enitharmon's Tent and hid herself. Loud
　　raging
15 Thunder'd the Assembly, dark and clouded, and they
　　ratify'd
　The kind decision of Enitharmon, and gave a Time to
　　the Space,
　Even Six Thousand years, and sent Lucifer for its
　　Guard :
　But Lucifer refus'd to die, and in pride he forsook his
　　charge ;
　And they elected Molech ; and when Molech was
　　impatient,
20 The Divine hand found the Two Limits, first of
　　Opacity, then of Contraction.
　Opacity was named Satan, Contraction was named
　　Adam.
　Triple Elohim came : Elohim, wearied, fainted : they
　　elected Shaddai.
　Shaddai angry, Pahad descended : Pahad terrified,
　　they sent Jehovah,
　And Jehovah was leprous : loud he call'd, stretching
　　his hand to Eternity ;
25 For then the Body of Death was perfected in hypocritic
　　holiness.
　Around the Lamb, a Female Tabernacle woven in
　　Cathedron's Looms.
　He died as a Reprobate ; he was Punish'd as a
　　Transgressor.
　Glory ! Glory ! Glory to the Holy Lamb of God.
　I touch the heavens as an instrument to glorify the
　　Lord !

30 The Elect shall meet the Redeem'd; on Albion's
    rocks they shall meet,
Astonish'd at the Transgressor, in him beholding the
    Saviour.
And the Elect shall say to the Redeem'd, We behold
    it is of Divine
Mercy alone! of Free Gift and Election that we live.
Our Virtues and Cruel Goodnesses have deserv'd
    Eternal Death.
35 Thus they weep upon the fatal Brook of Albion's River.

But Elynittria met Leutha in the place where she was
    hidden,
And threw aside her arrows, and laid down her
    sounding Bow;
She sooth'd her with soft words, and brought her to
    Palamabron's bed,
In moments new created for delusion, interwoven
    round about.
40 In dreams she bore the shadowy Spectre of Sleep, and
    nam'd him Death.
In dreams she bore Rahab, the mother of Tirzah, and
    her sisters,
In Lambeth's vales, in Cambridge and in Oxford,
    places of Thought,
Intricate labyrinths of Times and Spaces unknown,
    that Leutha lived
In Palamabron's Tent, and Oothoon was her charming
    guard.

45 The Bard ceas'd. All consider'd, and a loud, resound-
    ing murmur
Continu'd round the Halls; and much they question'd
    the immortal,
Loud voic'd Bard; and many condemn'd the high-
    toned Song,
Saying, Pity and Love are too venerable for the im-
    putation
Of Guilt. Others said: If it is true, if the acts have
    been performed,

50 Let the Bard himself witness.   Where hadst thou this
       terrible Song?

   The Bard replied : I am inspired! I know it is Truth!
       for I Sing

                                        (12)

   According to the inspiration of the Poetic Genius,
   Who is the eternal, all-protecting Divine Humanity,
   To whom be Glory and Power and Dominion Evermore.
       Amen.

   Then there was great murmuring in the Heavens of
       Albion
 5 Concerning Generation and the Vegetative power, and
       concerning
   The Lamb, the Saviour.   Albion trembled to Italy,
       Greece, and Egypt,
   To Tartary, and Hindostan and China, and to Great
       America,
   Shaking the roots and fast foundations of the Earth
       in doubtfulness.
   The loud voic'd Bard, terrify'd, took refuge in
       Milton's bosom.

10 Then Milton rose up from the heavens of Albion
       ardorous.
   The whole Assembly wept prophetic, seeing in Milton's
       face
   And in his lineaments divine the shades of Death and
       Ulro ;
   He took off the robe of the promise, and unguarded
       himself from the oath of God.

   And Milton said, I go to Eternal Death !   The Nations
       still
15 Follow after the detestable Gods of Priam, in pomp
   Of warlike selfhood, contradicting and blaspheming.
   When will the Resurrection come, to deliver the
       sleeping body

From corruptibility?   O when, Lord Jesus, wilt thou
    come?
Tarry no longer, for my soul lies at the gates of death.
20 I will arise and look forth for the morning of the grave.
I will go down to the sepulcher to see if morning
    breaks.
I will go down to self-annihilation and eternal death,
Lest the Last Judgment come and find me unannihilate,
And I be siez'd and giv'n into the hands of my own
    Selfhood.
25 The Lamb of God is seen thro' mists and shadows
    hov'ring
Over the sepulchers in clouds of Jehovah and winds
    of Elohim,
A disk of blood, distant, and heav'ns and earths roll
    dark between.
What do I here before the Judgment, without my
    Emanation?
With the daughters of memory, and not with the
    daughters of inspiration?
30 I in my Selfhood am that Satan: I am that Evil One!
He is my Spectre! in my obedience to loose him from
    my Hells,
To claim the Hells, my Furnaces, I go to Eternal
    Death.

And Milton said, I go to Eternal Death.   Eternity
    shudder'd;
For he took the outside course, among the graves of
    the dead,
35 A mournful shade.   Eternity shudder'd at the image
    of eternal death.

Then on the verge of Beulah he beheld his own
    Shadow,
A mournful form, double, hermaphroditic, male and
    female
In one wonderful body, and he enter'd into it
In direful pain, for the dread shadow, twenty-seven-
    fold,

40 Reach'd to the depths of direst Hell, and thence to
    Albion's land,
Which is this earth of vegetation on which now I
    write.

42 The Seven Angels of the Presence wept over Milton's
    Shadow.

(14)

As when a man dreams, he reflects not that his body
    sleeps,
Else he would wake: so seem'd he entering his
    Shadow, but
With him the Spirits of the Seven Angels of the
    Presence
Entering; they gave him still perceptions of his
    Sleeping Body,
5 Which now arose and walk'd with them in Eden, as
    an Eighth
Image, Divine, tho' darken'd; and tho' walking as one
    walks
In sleep; and the Seven comforted and supported him.

Like as a Polypus that vegetates beneath the deep,
They saw his Shadow vegetated underneath the Couch
10 Of death, for when he enter'd into his Shadow, Him-
    self,
His real and immortal Self, was as appear'd to those
Who dwell in immortality, as One sleeping on a couch
Of gold; and those in immortality gave forth their
    Emanations
Like Females of sweet beauty, to guard round him and
    to feed
15 His lips with food of Eden in his cold and dim repose;
But to himself he seem'd a wanderer lost in dreary
    night.

Onwards his Shadow kept its course among the
    Spectres, call'd

Satan, but swift as lightning passing them : startled,
the shades
Of Hell beheld him in a trail of light as of a comet
20 That travels into Chaos : so Milton went guarded
within.

The nature of infinity is this : That every thing has its
Own Vortex ; and when once a traveller thro' Eternity
Has pass'd that Vortex, he percieves it roll backward
behind
His path, into a globe itself infolding, like a sun,
25 Or like a moon, or like a universe of starry majesty,
While he keeps onwards in his wondrous journey on
the earth,
Or like a human form, a friend with whom he liv'd
benevolent,
As the eye of man views both the east and west,
encompassing
Its vortex ; and the north and south, with all their
starry host ;
30 Also the rising sun and setting moon he views, surrounding
His corn-fields and his valleys of five hundred acres
square.
Thus is the earth one infinite plane, and not as
apparent
To the weak traveller, confin'd beneath the moony
shade.
Thus is the heaven a vortex pass'd already, and the
earth
35 A vortex not yet pass'd by the traveller thro' Eternity.

First Milton saw Albion upon the Rock of Ages,
Deadly pale, outstretch'd, and snowy cold, storm
cover'd ;
A Giant form of perfect beauty, outstretch'd on the
rock,
In solemn death, the Sea of Time and Space thunder'd
aloud

40 Against the rock, which was inwrapped with the
    weeds of death.
Hovering over the cold bosom, in its vortex, Milton
    bent down
To the bosom of death. What was underneath soon
    seem'd above ;
A cloudy heaven mingled with stormy seas in loudest
    ruin ;
But as a wintry globe descends precipitant thro'
    Beulah bursting,
45 With thunders loud and terrible, so Milton's shadow
    fell
Precipitant, loud thund'ring, into the Sea of Time and
    Space.

Then first I saw him in the Zenith as a falling star,
Descending perpendicular, swift as the swallow or
    swift ;
And on my left foot falling on the tarsus, enter'd there ;
50 But from my left foot a black cloud redounding, spread
    over Europe.

Then Milton knew that the Three Heavens of Beulah
    were beheld
52 By him on earth in his bright pilgrimage of sixty years.

(15)

*This page contains only a picture of the spiritual form of
Milton struggling with Urizen, and giving him life. Under
the picture is written—*

To Annihilate the Self-hood of Deceit and False
    Forgiveness.

(16)

In the three females whom his wives, and these three
    whom his daughters
Had represented and contain'd, that they might be
    resum'd
By giving up of Selfhood ; and they distant view'd his
    journey

In their eternal spheres, now Human, tho' their
   Bodies remain clos'd
5 In the dark Ulro till the Judgment; also Milton
   knew : they and
Himself was Human, tho' now wandering thro' Death's
   Vale
In conflict with those Female forms, which in blood
   and jealousy
Surrounded him, dividing and uniting without end or
   number.

He saw the Cruelties of Ulro, and he wrote them down
10 In iron tablets ; and his Wives' and Daughters' names
   were these :
Rahab and Tirzah, and Milcah and Malah, and Noah
   and Hoglah.
They sat rang'd round him as the rocks of Horeb round
   the land
Of Canaan ; and they wrote in thunder, smoke, and fire
His dictate; and his body was the Rock Sinai, that body
15 Which was on earth born to corruption ; and the six
   Females
Are Hor and Peor, and Bashan and Abarim, and
   Lebanon and Hermon,
Seven rocky masses terrible in the Desarts of Midian.

But Milton's Human Shadow continu'd journeying
   above
The rocky masses of The Mundane Shell; in the Lands
20 Of Edom and Aram, and Moab and Midian and Amalek.

The Mundane Shell is a vast Concave Earth, an im-
   mense
Harden'd shadow of all things upon our Vegetated
   Earth,
Enlarg'd into dimension and deform'd into indefinite
   space,
In Twenty-seven Heavens and all their Hells, with
   Chaos

25 And Ancient Night and Purgatory. It is a cavernous
    Earth
  Of labyrinthine intricacy, twenty-seven folds of
    opakeness,
  And finishes where the lark mounts: here Milton
    journeyed
  In that region call'd Midian, among the rocks of
    Horeb,
  For travellers from Eternity pass outward to Satan's
    seat,
30 But travellers to Eternity pass inward to Golgonooza.

  Los, the Vehicular terror, beheld him, and divine
    Enitharmon
  Call'd all her daughters, saying, Surely to unloose my
    bond
  Is this Man come ! Satan shall be unloos'd upon
    Albion.

  Los heard in terror Enitharmon's words : in fibrous
    strength
35 His limbs shot forth like roots of trees against the
    forward path
  Of Milton's journey. Urizen beheld the immortal Man,

(17)

  And he also darken'd his brows, freezing dark rocks
    between
  The footsteps, and infixing deep the feet in marble
    beds,
  That Milton labour'd with his journey, and his feet
    bled sore
  Upon the clay now chang'd to marble ; also Urizen rose
5 And met him on the shores of Arnon, and by the
    streams of the brooks.

  Silent they met, and silent strove among the streams
    of Arnon,
  Even to Mahanaim, when with cold hand Urizen
    stoop'd down

And took up water from the river Jordan, pouring on
To Milton's brain the icy fluid from his broad cold palm.
10 But Milton took of the red clay of Succoth, moulding
  it with care
Between his palms, and filling up the furrows of
  many years,
Beginning at the feet of Urizen ; and on the bones
Creating new flesh on the Demon cold, and building
  him,
As with new clay, a Human form in the Valley of
  Beth Peor.

15 Four Universes round the Mundane Egg remain
  Chaotic,
One to the North named Urthona ; One to the South
  named Urizen ;
One to the East named Luvah ; One to the West
  named Tharmas :
They are the Four Zoas that stood around the Throne
  Divine.
But when Luvah assum'd the World of Urizen to the
  South,
20 And Albion was slain upon his mountains and in his
  tent,
All fell towards the Center in dire ruin, sinking down,
And in the South remains a burning fire, in the East
  a void,
In the West a world of raging waters, in the North a
  solid,
Unfathomable, without end. But in the midst of these
25 Is built eternally the Universe of Los and Enitharmon,
Towards which Milton went ; but Urizen oppos'd his
  path.

The Man and Demon strove many periods. Rahab
  beheld
Standing on Carmel : Rahab and Tirzah trembled to
  behold
The enormous strife, one giving life, the other giving
  death

30 To his adversary ; and they sent forth all their sons
     and daughters,
   In all their beauty, to entice Milton across the river.

   The Twofold form Hermaphroditic, and the Double-
     sexed :
   The Female-male and the Male-female, self-dividing,
     stood
   Before him in their beauty, and in cruelties of holiness,
35 Shining in darkness, glorious upon the deeps of
     Entuthon,

   Saying, Come thou to Ephraim ! behold the Kings of
     Canaan !
   The beautiful Amalekites ! behold the fires of youth
   Bound with the Chain of Jealousy by Los and Eni-
     tharmon :
   The banks of Cam, cold learning's streams : London's
     dark frowning towers,
40 Lament upon the winds of Europe in Rephaim's Vale,
   Because Ahania rent apart into a desolate night
   Laments, and Enion wanders like a weeping, in-
     articulate voice,
   And Vala labours for her bread and water among the
     Furnaces.
   Therefore bright Tirzah triumphs, putting on all
     beauty
45 And all perfection, in her cruel sports among the
     Victims.
   Come bring with thee Jerusalem, with songs on the
     Grecian Lyre !
   In Natural Religion, in experiments on Men.
   Let her be Offer'd up to Holiness. Tirzah numbers her :
   She numbers with her fingers every fibre ere it grow.
50 Where is the Lamb of God ? where is the promise of
     his coming ?
   Her shadowy Sisters form the bones, even the bones
     of Horeb
   Around the marrow, and the orbed skull round the
     brain.

His Images are born for War, for Sacrifice to Tirzah,
To Natural Religion; to Tirzah, the Daughter of
  Rahab the Holy.
55 She ties the knot of nervous fibres into a white brain :
She ties the knot of bloody veins into a red hot heart.
Within her bosom Albion lies embalm'd, never to
  awake.
Hand is become a rock : Sinai and Horeb is Hyle and
  Coban :
Scofield is bound in iron armour before Reuben's
  Gate.
60 She ties the knot of milky seed into two lovely Heavens.

(18)

Two, yet but one ; each in the other sweet reflected ;
  these
Are our Three Heavens beneath the shades of Beulah,
  land of rest.
Come then to Ephraim and Manasseh, O beloved-one !
Come to my ivory palaces, O beloved of thy mother !
5 And let us bind thee in the bands of War, and be
  thou King
Of Canaan, and reign in Hazor, where the Twelve
  Tribes meet.

So spoke they as in one voice ! Silent Milton stood
  before
The darken'd Urizen, as the sculptor silent stands before
His forming image : he walks round it patient,
  labouring.
10 Thus Milton stood, forming bright Urizen, while his
  Mortal part
Sat frozen in the rock of Horeb ; and his Redeemed
  portion
Thus form'd the Clay of Urizen ; but within that portion
His real Human walk'd above in power and majesty,
Tho' darken'd, and the Seven Angels of the Presence
  attended him.

15 O how can I with my gross tongue that cleaveth to
    the dust,
  Tell of the Fourfold Man, in starry numbers fitly
    order'd,
  Or how can I with my cold hand of clay? But thou, O
    Lord,
  Do with me as thou wilt! for I am nothing, and vanity,
  If thou chuse to elect a worm, it shall remove the
    mountains,
20 For that portion nam'd the Elect : the Spectrous body
    of Milton
  Redounding from my left foot into Los's Mundane
    space,
  Brooded over his Body in Horeb against the Resur-
    rection,
  Preparing it for the Great Consummation : red the
    Cherub on Sinai
  Glow'd, but in terrors folded round his clouds of blood.

25 Now Albion's sleeping Humanity began to turn upon
    his Couch,
  Feeling the electric flame of Milton's awful precipitate
    descent.
  See'st thou the little winged fly, smaller than a grain
    of sand?
  It has a heart like thee, a brain open to heaven and
    hell,
  With inside wondrous and expansive, its gates are
    not clos'd.
30 I hope thine are not. Hence it clothes itself in rich
    array :
  Hence thou art cloth'd with human beauty, O thou
    mortal man.
  Seek not thy heavenly father then beyond the skies :
  There Chaos dwells and ancient Night and Og and
    Anak old :
  For every human heart has gates of brass and bars of
    adamant,
35 Which few dare unbar because dread Og and Anak
    guard the gates

Terrific ; and each mortal brain is wall'd and moated
    round
Within : and Og and Anak watch here : here is the Seat
Of Satan in its Webs ; for in brain and heart and
    loins,
Gates open behind Satan's Seat to the City of Gol-
    gonooza,
40 Which is spiritual, fourfold London, in the loins of
    Albion.

Thus Milton fell thro' Albion's heart, travelling out-
    side of Humanity,
Beyond the Stars, in Chaos, in Caverns of the Mun-
    dane Shell.

But many of the Eternals rose up from eternal tables
Drunk with the Spirit ; burning round the Couch of
    death they stood,
45 Looking down into Beulah : wrathful, fill'd with rage,
They rend the heavens round the Watchers in a fiery
    circle,
And round the Shadowy Eighth : the Eight close up
    the Couch
Into a tabernacle, and flee with cries down to the
    Deeps,
Where Los opens his three wide gates, surrounded by
    raging fires ;
50 They soon find their own place, and join the Watchers
    of the Ulro.

Los saw them, and a cold, pale horror cover'd o'er his
    limbs ;
Pondering, he knew that Rintrah and Palamabron
    might depart
Even as Reuben and as Gad, gave up himself to tears ;
He sat down on his anvil-stock, and lean'd upon the
    trough,
55 Looking into the black water, mingling it with tears.

At last, when desperation almost tore his heart in twain,

He recollected an old Prophecy in Eden recorded,
And often sung to the loud harp at the immortal feasts,
That Milton of the Land of Albion should up ascend,
60 Forwards from Ulro, from the Vale of Felpham, and
    set free
    Orc from his Chain of Jealousy; he started at the
    thought,

(19)

And down descended into Udan-Adan: it was night:
And Satan sat sleeping upon his Couch in Udan Adan:
His Spectre slept, his Shadow woke: when one sleeps
    th' other wakes.

But Milton entering my Foot, I saw in the nether
5 Regions of the Imagination; also all men on Earth,
And all in Heaven, saw in the nether regions of the
    Imagination,
In Ulro beneath Beulah, the vast breach of Milton's
    descent.
But I knew not that it was Milton, for man cannot
    know
What passes in his members till periods of Space and
    Time
10 Reveal the secrets of Eternity: for more extensive
Than any other earthly things, are Man's earthly
    lineaments.

And all this Vegetable World appear'd on my left
    Foot,
As a bright sandal form'd immortal of precious stones
    and gold.
I stooped down and bound it on to walk forward thro'
    Eternity.

15 There is in Eden a sweet River of milk and liquid
    pearl
    Nam'd Ololon, on whose mild banks dwelt those who
    Milton drove

Down into Ulro, and they wept in long resounding
  song
For seven days of eternity, and the river's living banks,
The mountains wailed, and every plant that grew in
  solemn sighs lamented.

20 When Luvah's bulls each morning drag the sulphur
    Sun out of the Deep,
  Harnessed with starry harness black and shining,
    kept by black slaves
  That work all night at the starry harness. Strong
    and vigorous,
  They drag the unwilling Orb. At this time all the
    Family
  Of Eden heard the lamentation, and Providence
    began;
25 But when the clarions of day sounded, they drown'd
    the lamentations;
  And when night came all was silent in Ololon, and
    all refus'd to lament
  In the still night, fearing lest they should others
    molest.

  Seven mornings Los heard them, as the poor bird
    within the shell
  Hears its impatient varent bird; and Enitharmon heard
    them
30 But saw them not, for the blue Mundane Shell
    inclos'd them in.

  And they lamented that they had in wrath and fury
    and fire
  Driven Milton into the Ulro, for now they knew too
    late
  That it was Milton the Awakener. They had not
    heard the Bard,
  Whose song call'd Milton to the attempt; and Los
    heard these laments.
35 He heard them call in prayer all the Divine Family,
  And he beheld the Cloud of Milton stretching over
    Europe.

But all the Family Divine collected as Four Suns
In the Four Points of heaven—East, West, and North
   and South—
Enlarging and enlarging till their Disks approach'd
   each other;
40 And when they touch'd, closed together Southward in
   One Sun
Over Ololon; and as One Man, who weeps over his
   brother
In a dark tomb, so all the Family Divine wept over
   Ololon,

Saying, Milton goes to Eternal Death: so saying,
   they groan'd in spirit
And were troubled; and again the Divine Family
   groan'd in spirit.

45 And Ololon said, Let us descend also, and let us give
Ourselves to death in Ulro, among the Transgressors.
Is Virtue a Punisher?   O no! how is this wondrous
   thing,
This World beneath, unseen before, this refuge from
   the wars
Of Great Eternity! unnatural refuge! unknown by
   us till now?
50 Or are these the pangs of repentance? let us enter
   into them.

Then the Divine Family said, Six Thousand Years are
   now
Accomplished in this World of Sorrow.   Milton's
   Angel knew
The Universal Dictate, and you also feel this Dictate.
And now you know this World of Sorrow, and feel
   Pity.   Obey
55 The Dictate! Watch over this World, and with your
   brooding wings
Renew it to Eternal Life.   Lo! I am with you alway.
But you cannot renew Milton, he goes to Eternal
   Death.

So spake the Family Divine as One Man, even Jesus,
Uniting in One with Ololon and the appearance of
One Man.
60 Jesus the Saviour appear'd, coming in the Clouds of
Ololon.

(20)

Tho' driven away with the Seven Starry Ones into the
Ulro,
Yet the Divine Vision remains Every-where, For-
ever. Amen.
And Ololon lamented for Milton with a great lamen-
tation.

While Los heard indistinct in fear, what time I bound
my sandals
5 On to walk forward thro' Eternity ; Los descended
to me,
And Los behind me stood, a terrible flaming Sun,
just close
Behind my back : I turned round in terror, and
behold,
Los stood in that fierce-glowing fire ; and he also
stoop'd down
And bound my sandals on in Udan-Adan : trembling
I stood
10 Exceedingly with fear and terror, standing in the Vale
Of Lambeth ; but he kissed me and wished me health,
And I became One Man with him, arising in my
strength :
'Twas too late now to recede, Los had enter'd into
my soul :
His terrors now possess'd me whole ! I arose in fury
and strength.

15 I am that Shadowy Prophet who, Six Thousand
Years ago,
Fell from my station in the Eternal bosom. Six
Thousand Years
Are finish'd. I return ! both Time and Space obey my
will.

I in Six Thousand Years walk up and down, for not
 one Moment
Of Time is lost, nor one Event of Space unpermanent;
20 But all remain : every fabric of Six Thousand Years
Remains permanent, tho' on the Earth, where Satan
Fell and was cut off, all things vanish and are seen
 no more ;
They vanish, not from me and mine ; we guard them
 first and last.
The generations of men run on in the tide of Time,
25 But leave their destin'd lineaments permanent for
 ever and ever.

So spake Los as we went along to his supreme abode.

Rintrah and Palamabron met us at the Gate of
 Golgonooza,
Clouded with discontent, and brooding in their minds
 terrible things.

They said, O Father, most beloved ! O merciful
 Parent !
30 Pitying and permitting evil, tho' strong and mighty
 to destroy.
Whence is this Shadow terrible ? wherefore dost thou
 refuse
To throw him into the Furnaces ? knowest thou not
 that he
Will unchain Orc, and let loose Satan, Og, Sihon,
 and Anak
Upon the Body of Albion ? for this he is come ; behold
 it written
35 Upon his fibrous left Foot black, most dismal to our
 eyes ;
The Shadowy Female shudders thro' heaven in torment
 inexpressible :
And all the Daughters of Los prophetic wail ; yet in
 deceit
They weave a new Religion from new Jealousy of
 Theotormon :

Milton's Religion is the cause; there is no end to
destruction.
40 Seeing the Churches at their Period in terror and
despair,
Rahab created Voltaire: Tirzah created Rousseau:
Asserting the Self-righteousness against the Universal
Saviour;
Mocking the Confessors and Martyrs, claiming Self-
righteousness:
With cruel virtue making War upon the Lambs
Redeemed;
45 To perpetuate War and Glory, to perpetuate the Laws
of Sin.
They perverted Swedenborg's Visions in Beulah and in
Ulro:
To destroy Jerusalem as a Harlot, and her Sons as
Reprobates;
To raise up Mystery, the Virgin Harlot, Mother of
War.
Babylon the Great, the Abomination of Desolation:
50 O Swedenborg, strongest of men, the Samson, shorn
by the Churches;
Shewing the Transgressors in Hell, the proud
Warriors in Heaven:
Heaven as a Punisher, and Hell as One under Punish-
ment;
With Laws from Plato and his Greeks to renew the
Trojan Gods
In Albion, and to deny the value of the Saviour's
blood;
55 But then I rais'd up Whitefield, Palamabron rais'd up
Wesley.
And these are the cries of the Churches before the
two Witnesses,
Faith in God the dear Saviour, who took on the like-
ness of men,
Becoming obedient to death, even the death of the
Cross.
The Witnesses lie dead in the Street of the Great
City.

60 No Faith is in all the Earth : the Book of God is
   trodden under Foot :
   He sent his two Servants, Whitefield and Wesley: were
   they Prophets,
62 Or were they Idiots or Madmen ?   Shew us Miracles !

(22)

Can you have greater Miracles than these ?   Men who
   devote
Their life's whole comfort to inane scorn and injury
   and death?
Awake, thou sleeper on the Rock of Eternity. Albion,
   awake !
The trumpet of Judgment hath twice sounded : all
   Nations are awake,
5 But thou art still heavy and dull.   Awake, Albion,
   awake !
Lo, Orc arises on the Atlantic : Lo, his blood and
   fire
Glow on America's shore.   Albion turns upon his
   Couch,
He listens to the sounds of War, astonished and con-
   founded ;
He weeps into the Atlantic deep, yet still in dismal
   dreams
10 Unwaken'd, and the Covering Cherub advances from
   the East.
How long shall we lay dead in the Street of the great
   City,
How long beneath the Covering Cherub give our
   Emanations?
Milton will utterly consume us and thee, our beloved
   Father ;
He hath enter'd into the Covering Cherub, becoming
   one with
15 Albion's dread Sons. Hand, Hyle, and Coban surround
   him as
A girdle ; Gwendolen and Conwenna as a garment
   woven

Of War and Religion. Let us descend and bring him
  chained
To Bowlahoola. O father, most beloved ! O mild
  Parent !
Cruel in thy mildness, pitying and permitting evil,
20 Tho' strong and mighty to destroy, O Los, our
  beloved Father !

Like the black storm coming out of Chaos, beyond
  the stars,
It issues thro' the dark and intricate caves of the
  Mundane Shell,
Passing the planetary visions and the well adorned
  Firmament.
The Sun rolls into Chaos and the Stars into the
  Desarts,
25 And then the storms become visible, audible, and
  terrible,
Covering the light of day, and rolling down upon the
  mountains,
Deluge all the country round. Such is a vision of Los
When Rintrah and Palamabron spake, and such his
  stormy face
Appear'd, as does the face of heaven when cover'd
  with thick storms,
30 Pitying and loving, tho' in frowns of terrible perturbation.

But Los dispers'd the clouds, even as the strong
  winds of Jehovah.
And Los thus spoke : O noble Sons, be patient yet a
  little ;
I have embraced the falling Death, he is become one
  with me.
O Sons, we live not by wrath, by mercy alone we live.
35 I recollect an old Prophecy in Eden, recorded in gold,
  and oft
Sung to the harp, That Milton, of the land of Albion,
Should up ascend forward from Felpham's Vale and
  break the Chain

Of Jealousy from all its roots ; be patient, therefore,
   O my Sons,
These lovely Females form sweet night and silence
   and secret
40 Obscurities to hide from Satan's Watch-Fiends,
   Human loves
And graces, lest they write them in their Books and
   in the Scroll
Of mortal life, to condemn the accused, who at
   Satan's Bar
Tremble in Spectrous Bodies continually day and
   night,
While on the Earth they live in sorrowful Vegetation.
45 O when shall we tread our Wine-presses in heaven,
   and Reap
Our wheat with shoutings of joy, and leave the Earth
   in peace ?
Remember how Calvin and Luther in fury premature
Sow'd War and stern division between Papists and
   Protestants.
Let it not be so now.   O go not forth in Martyrdoms
   and Wars ;
50 We were plac'd here by the Universal Brotherhood
   and Mercy,
With powers fitted to circumscribe this dark Satanic
   Death,
And that the Seven Eyes of God may have space for
   Redemption.
But how this is as yet we know not, and we cannot
   know
Till Albion is arisen ; then patient wait a little while.
55 Six Thousand Years are passed away, the end
   approaches fast ;
This mighty one is come from Eden, he is of the Elect,
Who died from Earth, and he is return'd before the
   Judgment.   This thing
Was never known that one of the holy dead should
   willing return.
Then patient wait a little while till the Last Vintage
   is over ;

60 Till we have quenched the Sun of Salah in the Lake
　　of Udan Adan.
　　O my dear Sons, leave not your Father as your
　　　brethren left me.
62 Twelve Sons successive fled away in that thousand
　　years of sorrow.

(23)

　Of Palamabron's Harrow, and of Rintrah's wrath and
　　　fury :
　Reuben and Manazzoth, and Gad and Simeon and Levi,
　And Ephraim and Judah were Generated ; because
　They left me, wandering with Tirzah.　Enitharmon
　　　wept
5 One thousand years, and all the Earth was in a wat'ry
　　deluge.
　We call'd him Menassheh because of the Generations
　　of Tirzah,
　Because of Satan : and the Seven Eyes of God con-
　　　tinually
　Guard round them ; but I, the Fourth Zoa, am also set
　The Watchman of Eternity ; the Three are not ; and I
　　am preserved.
10 Still my four mighty ones are left to me in Golgonooza.
　Still Rintrah fierce, and Palamabron mild and piteous,
　Theotormon fill'd with care, Bromion loving science.
　You, O my Sons, shall guard round Los ; O wander
　　not and leave me.
　Rintrah, thou well rememberest when Amalek and
　　Canaan
15 Fled with their sister Moab into that abhorred Void,
　They became Nations in our sight beneath the hands
　　of Tirzah.
　And Palamabron, thou rememberest when Joseph, an
　　infant,
　Stolen from his nurse's cradle wrap'd in needle-work
　Of emblematic texture, was sold to the Amalekite,
20 Who carried him down into Egypt, where Ephraim
　　and Menassheh
　Gathered my Sons together in the Sands of Midian.

And if you also flee away and leave your Father's side,
Following Milton into Ulro, altho' your power is
   great,
Surely you also shall become poor mortal vegetations
25 Beneath the Moon of Ulro. Pity then your Father's
   tears.
When Jesus rais'd Lazarus from the Grave, I stood
   and saw
Lazarus, who is the Vehicular Body of Albion the
   Redeem'd,
Arise into the Covering Cherub, who is the Spectre of
   Albion,
By martyrdoms to suffer : to watch over the Sleeping
   Body.
30 Upon his Rock beneath his Tomb, I saw the Covering
   Cherub
Divine Fourfold into Four Churches when Lazarus
   arose.
Paul, Constantine, Charlemaine, Luther, behold they
   stand before us,
Stretched over Europe and Asia. Come, O Sons,
   come, come away ;
Arise, O Sons, give all your strength against Eternal
   Death,
35 Lest we are vegetated, for Cathedron's Looms weave
   only Death,
A Web of Death, and were it not for Bowlahoolah
   and Allamanda,
No Human Form, but only a Fibrous Vegetation,
A Polypus of soft affections without Thought or
   Vision,
Must tremble in the Heavens and Earths thro' all the
   Ulro space,
40 Throw all the Vegetated Mortals into Bowlahoola.
But as to this Elected Form who is return'd again,
He is the Signal that the Last Vintage now approaches,
Nor Vegetation may go on till all the Earth is reap'd.

So Los spoke. Furious they descended to Bowlahoola
   and Allamanda,

45 Indignant, unconvinced by Los's arguments, and
     thunders rolling,
   They saw that wrath now sway'd, and now pity
     absorb'd him,
   As it was, so it remain'd, and no hope of an end.

   Bowlahoola is nam'd Law by mortals, Tharmas founded
     it,
   Because of Satan, before Luban, in the City of Golgon-
     ooza ;
50 But Golgonooza is nam'd Art and Manufacture by
     mortal men.

   In Bowlahoola Los's Anvils stand and his Furnaces
     rage ;
   Thundering the Hammers beat, and the Bellows blow
     loud ;
   Living, self-moving, mourning, lamenting, and howl-
     ing incessantly,
   Bowlahoola thro' all its porches feels, tho' too fast
     founded,
55 Its pillars and porticoes to tremble at the force
   Of mortal or immortal arm ; and softly lilling flutes,
   Accordant with the horrid labours, make sweet melody.
   The Bellows are the Animal Lungs, the Hammers the
     Animal Heart,
   The Furnaces the Stomach for digestion, terrible their
     fury ;
60 Thousands and thousands labour, thousands play on
     instruments,
   Stringed or fluted, to ameliorate the sorrows of
     slavery ;
   Loud sport the dancers in the dance of death, rejoic-
     ing in carnage ;
   The hard, dentant Hammers are lulled by the flutes'
     lula lula,
   The bellowing Furnaces blare by the long sounding
     clarion,
65 The double drum drowns howls and groans, the shrill
     fife shrieks and cries,

The crooked horn mellows the hoarse, raving serpent, terrible, but harmonious.

Bowlahoola is the Stomach in every individual man.

Los is by mortals nam'd Time, Enitharmon is nam'd Space ;
But they depict him bald and aged who is in eternal youth,
70 All powerful, and his locks flourish like the brows of morning ;
He is the Spirit of Prophecy, the ever apparent Elias ;
Time is the mercy of Eternity ; without Time's swift-ness,
Which is the swiftest of all things, all were eternal torment.
All the Gods of the Kingdoms of Earth labour in Los's Halls.
75 Every one is a fallen Son of the Spirit of Prophecy.
He is the Fourth Zoa, that stood around the Throne Divine.

(24)

But the Wine-press of Los is eastward of Golgonooza, before the Seat
Of Satan. Luvah laid the foundation, and Urizen finish'd it in howling woe.
How red the sons and daughters of Luvah : here they tread the grapes,
Laughing and shouting, drunk with odours, many fall, o'erwearied.
5 Drowned in the wine is many a youth and maiden : those around
Lay them on skins of Tygers and of the Spotted Leopard and the Wild Ass,
Till they revive, or bury them in cool grots, making lamentation.

This Wine-press is call'd War on Earth ; it is the Printing-Press

Of Los; and here he lays his words in order above
    the mortal brain,
10 As cogs are form'd in a wheel to turn the cogs of the
    adverse wheel.

Timbrels and violins sport round the Wine-presses;
    the little Seed,
The sportive Root, the Earth-worm, the gold Beetle,
    the wise Emmet,
Dance round the Wine-presses of Luvah. The
    Centipede is there;
The ground Spider with many eyes, the Mole clothed
    in velvet,
15 The ambitious Spider in his sullen web, the lucky
    golden Spinner,
The Earwig arm'd; the tender Maggot, emblem of
    immortality;
The Flea, Louse, Bug, the Tape-Worm, all the
    Armies of Disease;
Visible or invisible to the slothful, vegetating Man;
The slow Slug; the Grasshopper, that sings and
    laughs and drinks.
20 Winter comes: he folds his slender bones without a
    murmur.

The cruel Scorpion is there, the Gnat, Wasp, Hornet,
    and the Honey Bee;
The Toad and venomous Newt; the Serpent, cloth'd
    in gems and gold:
They throw off their gorgeous raiment; they rejoice
    with loud jubilee
Around the Wine-presses of Luvah, naked and drunk
    with wine.

25 There is the Nettle that stings with soft down, and
    there
The indignant Thistle, whose bitterness is bred in his
    milk,
Who feeds on contempt of his neighbour; there all
    the idle weeds

That creep around the obscure places, shew their
  various limbs,
Naked in all their beauty, dancing round the Wine-
  presses.

30 But in the Wine-presses the Human grapes sing not
  nor dance ;
They howl and writhe in shoals of torment, in fierce
  flames consuming,
In chains of iron and in dungeons circled with ceaseless fires ;
In pits and dens and shades of death, in shapes of
  torment and woe ;
The plates and screws, and wracks and saws, and cords
  and fires and cisterns ;
35 The cruel joys of Luvah's Daughters lacerating with
  knives
And whips their Victims, and the deadly sport of
  Luvah's Sons.

They dance around the dying, and they drink the
  howl and groan,
They catch the shrieks in cups of gold, they hand
  them to one another.
These are the sports of love, and these the sweet
  delights of amorous play :
40 Tears of the grape, the death sweat of the cluster ; the
  last sigh
Of the mild youth, who listens to the lureing songs of
  Luvah.

But Allamanda, call'd on Earth Commerce, is the
  Cultivated land
Around the City of Golgonooza, in the Forests of
  Entuthon :
Here the Sons of Los labour against Death Eternal
  through all
45 The Twenty-seven Heavens of Beulah in Ulro, Seat of
  Satan,

Which is the False Tongue beneath Beulah : it is the
    Sense of Touch.
The Plow goes forth in tempests and lightnings, and
    the Harrow cruel
In blights of the east : the heavy Roller follows in
    howlings of woe.

Urizen's sons here labour also, and here are seen the
    Mills
50 Of Theotormon on the verge of the Lake of Udan-Adan.
These are the starry voids of night, and the depths
    and caverns of earth ;
These Mills are oceans, clouds, and waters ungovern-
    able in their fury.
Here are the stars created and the seeds of all things
    planted,
And here the Sun and Moon recieve their fixed
    destinations.

55 But in Eternity the Four Arts, Poetry, Painting,
    Music,
And Architecture, which is Science, are the Four
    Faces of Man.
Not so in Time and Space : there Three are shut out,
    and only
Science remains thro' mercy ; and by means of Science,
    the Three
Become apparent in Time and Space, in the Three
    Professions.

60 That Man may live upon Earth all the time of his
    awaking,
And from these Three Sciences derives every Occupa-
    tion of Men ;
62 And Science is divided into Bowlahoola and Alla-
    manda.

(25)

Loud shout the Sons of Luvah at the Wine-presses as
    Los descended,
With Rintrah and Palamabron in his fires of resistless
    fury.

The Wine-press on the Rhine groans loud, but all its
    central beams
Act more terrific in the central Cities of the Nations,
5 Where Human Thought is crush'd beneath the iron
    hand of Power.
There Los puts all into the Press, the Opressor and
    the Opressed
Together, ripe for the Harvest and Vintage, and
    ready for the Loom.

They sang at the Vintage. This is the Last Vintage,
    and Seed
Shall no more be sown upon Earth, till all the Vintage
    is over,
10 And all gathered in, till the Plow has passed over the
    Nations,
And the Harrow and heavy thundering Roller upon
    the mountains.

And loud the Souls howl round the Porches of Golgon-
    ooza,
Crying, O God, deliver us to the Heavens or to the
    Earths,
That we may preach righteousness and punish the
    sinner with death ;
15 But Los refused, till all the Vintage of Earth was
    gather'd in.

And Los stood and cried to the Labourers of the
    Vintage in voice of awe.

Fellow Labourers ! The Great Vintage and Harvest is
    now upon Earth ;
The whole extent of the Globe is explored. Every
    scatter'd Atom
Of Human Intellect now is flocking to the sound of
    the Trumpet.
20 All the Wisdom which was hidden in caves and dens
    from ancient

Time, is now sought out from Animal and Vegetable
and Mineral.

The Awakener is come, outstretch'd over Europe;
the Vision of God is fulfilled;

The Ancient Man upon the Rock of Albion awakes.

He listens to the sounds of War, astonish'd and
ashamed:

25 He sees his children mock at Faith and deny Providence.

Therefore you must bind the Sheaves, not by Nations
or Families;

You shall bind them in Three Classes, according to
their Classes;

So shall you bind them, Separating what has been
Mixed.

Since Men began to be Wove into Nations by Rahab
and Tirzah,

30 Since Albion's Death and Satan's Cutting off from our
awful Fields,

When under pretence to benevolence, the Elect
Subdu'd All

From the Foundation of the World. The Elect is one
Class. You

Shall bind them separate. They cannot Believe in
Eternal Life,

Except by Miracle and a New Birth. The other two
Classes,

35 The Reprobate, who never cease to Believe, and the
Redeem'd,

Who live in doubts and fears, perpetually tormented
by the Elect.

These you shall bind in a twin-bundle for the Consummation,

But the Elect must be saved fires of Eternal Death,

To be formed into the Churches of Beulah, that they
destroy not the Earth,

40 For in every Nation and every Family the Three
Classes are born,

And in every Species of Earth, Metal, Tree, Fish,
Bird, and Beast,

We form the Mundane Egg, that Spectres coming by
    fury or amity,
All is the same, and every one remains in his own
    energy.
Go forth, Reapers, with rejoicing, you sowed in tears,
45 But the time of your refreshing cometh, only a little
    moment.
Still abstain from pleasure and rest in the labours of
    eternity,
And you shall reap the whole Earth from Pole to Pole,
    from Sea to Sea,
Begining at Jerusalem's Inner Court. Lambeth,
    ruin'd and given
To the detestable Gods of Priam, to Apollo; and at
    the Asylum
50 Given to Hercules, who labour in Tirzah's Looms for
    bread,
Who set Pleasure against Duty, who create Olympic
    crowns,
To make Learning a burden and the Work of the
    Holy Spirit, Strife,—
The Thor and cruel Odin, who first rear'd the Polar
    Caves.
Lambeth mourns, calling Jerusalem; she weeps and
    looks abroad
55 For the Lord's coming, that Jerusalem may overspread
    all Nations.
Crave not for the mortal and perishing delights, but
    leave them
To the weak, and pity the weak as your infant care.
    Break not
Forth in your wrath, lest you also are vegetated by
    Tirzah.
Wait till the Judgement is past, till the Creation is
    consumed,
60 And then rush forward with me into the glorious
    spiritual
Vegetation; the Supper of the Lamb and his Bride;
    and the
Awaking of Albion, our friend and ancient companion.

So Los spoke: But lightnings of discontent broke on
    all sides round,
And murmurs of thunder rolling heavy, long, and
    loud over the mountains,
65 While Los call'd his Sons around him to the Harvest
    and the Vintage.

Thou seest the Constellations in the deep and won-
    drous Night,
They rise in order and continue their immortal courses
Upon the mountains and in vales, with harp and
    heavenly song,
With flute and clarion, with cups and measures fill'd
    with foaming wine.
70 Glitt'ring the streams reflect the Vision of beatitude,
And the calm Ocean joys beneath, and smooths his
    awful waves.

(26)

These are the Sons of Los, and these the Labourers of
    the Vintage.
Thou seest the gorgeous clothed Flies that dance and
    sport in summer
Upon the sunny brooks and meadows: every one the
    dance
Knows in its intricate mazes of delight, artful to weave,
5 Each one to sound his instruments of music in the
    dance,
To touch each other and recede; to cross and change
    and return.
These are the Children of Los.   Thou seest the Trees
    on mountains;
The wind blows heavy, loud they thunder thro' the
    darksom sky,
Uttering prophecies and speaking instructive words to
    the sons
10 Of men.   These are the Sons of Los, these the
    Visions of Eternity.
But we see only as it were the hem of their garments,

When with our vegetable eyes we view these wondrous
  Visions.

There are Two Gates thro' which all Souls descend:
  One Southward
From Dover Cliff to Lizard Point; the other toward
  the North,
15 Caithness and rocky Durness, Pentland and John
  Groat's House.
The Souls descending to the Body wail on the right
  hand
Of Los, and those deliver'd from the Body on the
  left hand.
For Los against the east his force continually bends
Along the Valleys of Middlesex from Hounslow to
  Blackheath,
20 Lest those Three Heavens of Beulah should the
  Creation destroy,
And lest they should descend before the north and
  south Gates.
Groaning with pity, he among the wailing Souls
  laments.

And these the Labours of the Sons of Los in Allamanda,
And in the City of Golgonooza, and in Luban, and
  around
25 The Lake of Udan-Adan, in the Forests of Entuthon
  Benython,
Where Souls incessant wail, being piteous Passions and
  Desires,
With neither lineament nor form, but like to wat'ry
  clouds,
The Passions and Desires descend upon the hungry
  winds.
For such alone Sleepers remain,—sheer passion and
  appetite.
30 The Sons of Los clothe them and feed and provide
  houses and fields.

And every Generated Body in its inward form
Is a garden of delight and a building of magnificence,
Built by the Sons of Los in Bowlahoola and Alla-
          manda;
And the herbs and flowers and furniture and beds and
          chambers,
35 Continually woven in the Looms of Enitharmon's
          Daughters,
In bright Cathedron's golden Dome, with care and
          love and tears,
For the various Classes of Men are all mark'd out
          determinate
In Bowlahoola: and as the Spectres choose their
          affinities,
So they are born on earth; and every Class is deter-
          minate,—
40 But not by Natural, but by Spiritual power alone,
          because
The Natural power continually seeks and tends to
          Destruction,
Ending in Death, which would of itself be Eternal
          Death,—
And all are class'd by Spiritual, and not by Natural
          power.

And every Natural Effect has a Spiritual Cause, and
          Not
45 A Natural, for a Natural Cause only seems; it is a
          Delusion
Of Ulro, and a ratio of the perishing Vegetable
          Memory.

                                                      (27)

Some Sons of Los surround the Passions with porches
          of iron and silver,
Creating form and beauty around the dark regions of
          sorrow,
Giving to airy nothing a name and a habitation
Delightful, with bounds to the Infinite, putting off the
          Indefinite

5 Into most holy forms of thought (such is the power
  of inspiration),
They labour incessant, with many tears and afflictions,
Creating the beautiful House for the piteous sufferer.

Others, Cabinets richly fabricate of gold and ivory,
For Doubts and fears, unform'd and wretched and
  melancholy;
10 The little weeping Spectre stands on the threshold of
   Death
Eternal; and sometimes two Spectres, like lamps
  quivering,
And often malignant they combat (heart-breaking,
  sorrowful, and piteous).

Antamon takes them into his beautiful flexible hands,
As the Sower takes the seed, or as the Artist his clay
15 Or fine wax, to mould artful a model for golden ornaments.
The soft hands of Antamon draw the indelible line,
Form immortal, with golden pen, such as the Spectre,
  admiring,
Puts on the sweet form; then smiles Antamon bright
  thro' his windows,
The Daughters of beauty look up from their Loom and
  prepare
20 The integument soft for its clothing, with joy and
   delight.

But Theotormon and Sotha stand in the Gate of
  Luban anxious;
Their numbers are seven million and seven thousand
  and seven hundred.
They contend with the weak Spectres; they fabricate
  soothing forms.
The Spectre refuses: he seeks cruelty: they create
  the crested Cock.
25 Terrified, the Spectre screams, and rushes in fear into
   their Net

Of kindness and compassion, and is born a weeping
     terror;
Or they create the Lion and Tyger in compassionate
     thunderings.
Howling the Spectres flee : they take refuge in
     Human lineaments.

The Sons of Ozoth within the Optic Nerve stand fiery,
     glowing;
30 And the number of his Sons is eight millions and eight.
They give delights to the man, unknown artificial
     riches
They give to scorn, and their possessors to trouble
     and sorrow and care,
Shutting the sun and moon, and stars and trees, and
     clouds and waters
And hills, out from the Optic Nerve, and hardening
     it into a bone
35 Opake, and like the black pebble on the enraged
     beach ;
While the poor indigent is like the diamond which,
     tho' cloth'd
In rugged covering in the mine, is open all within,
And in his hallow'd center holds the heavens of bright
     eternity.
Ozoth here builds walls of rocks against the surging
     sea,
40 And timbers crampt with iron cramps bar in the
     joys of life
From fell destruction in the Spectrous cunning or
     rage.   He Creates
The speckled Newt, the Spider and Beetle, the Rat
     and Mouse,
The Badger and Fox : they worship before his feet
     in trembling fear.

But others of the Sons of Los build Moments and
     Minutes and Hours,
45 And Days and Months and Years, and Ages and
     Periods : wondrous buildings.

And every Moment has a Couch of gold for soft repose.
(A Moment equals a pulsation of the artery.)
And between every two Moments stands a Daughter
    of Beulah,
To feed the Sleepers on their Couches with maternal
    care.
50 And every Minute has an azure Tent with silken
    Veils ;
And every Hour has a bright golden Gate carved
    with skill ;
And every Day and Night has Walls of brass and
    Gates of adamant,
Shining like precious stones, and ornamented with
    appropriate signs :
And every Month a silver paved Terrace, builded high ;
55 And every Year, invulnerable Barriers, with high
    Towers ;
And every Age is Moated deep with Bridges of silver
    and gold ;
And every Seven Ages is Incircled with a Flaming
    Fire.
Now Seven Ages is amounting to Two Hundred Years.
Each has its Guard : each Moment, Minute, Hour,
    Day, Month, and Year,
60 All are the work of Fairy hands of the Four Elements.
The Guard are Angels of Providence on duty ever-
    more.
Every Time less than a pulsation of the artery
63 Is equal in its period and value to Six Thousand Years.

(28)

For in this Period the Poet's Work is Done ; and all
    the Great
Events of Time start forth, and are conciev'd in such
    a Period
Within a Moment : a Pulsation of the Artery.

The Sky is an immortal Tent built by the Sons of
    Los,

5 And every Space that a Man views around his dwelling-
　　place,
　Standing on his own roof or in his garden on a mount
　Of twenty-five cubits in height, such space is his
　　Universe ;
　And on its verge the Sun rises and sets, the Clouds
　　bow
　To meet the flat Earth and the Sea in such an order'd
　　Space ;
10 The Starry heavens reach no further, but here bend
　　and set
　On all sides, and the two Poles turn on their valves of
　　gold ;
　And if he move his dwelling-place, his heavens also
　　move,
　Where'er he goes, and all his neighbourhood bewail
　　his loss.
　Such are the Spaces called Earth, and such its
　　dimension.
15 As to that false appearance which appears to the
　　reasoner,
　As of a Globe rolling thro' Voidness, it is a delusion
　　of Ulro ;
　The Microscope knows not of this nor the Telescope ;
　　they alter
　The ratio of the Spectator's Organs, but leave Objects
　　untouch'd,
　For every Space larger than a red Globule of Man's
　　blood
20 Is visionary, and is created by the Hammer of
　　Los ;
　And every Space smaller than a Globule of Man's
　　blood opens
　Into Eternity, of which this vegetable Earth is but a
　　shadow.
　The red Globule is the unwearied Sun by Los
　　created
　To measure Time and Space to mortal Men, every
　　morning.
25 Bowlahoola and Allamanda are placed on each side

Of that Pulsation and that Globule; terrible their
    power.

But Rintrah and Palamabron govern over Day and
    Night
In Allamanda and Entuthon Benython, where Souls
    wail,
Where Orc incessant howls, burning in fires of Eternal
    Youth,
30 Within the vegetated mortal Nerves, for every Man
    born is joined
Within into One mighty Polypus, and this Polypus is
    Orc.

But in the Optic vegetative Nerves Sleep was trans-
    formed
To Death in old time by Satan, the father of Sin and
    Death,
And Satan is the Spectre of Orc, and Orc is the
    generate Luvah.

35 But in the Nerves of the Nostrils, Accident being
    formed
Into Substance and Principle by the cruelties of
    Demonstration,
It became Opake and Indefinite; but the Divine
    Saviour
Formed it into a Solid by Los's Mathematic power.
He named the Opake Satan; he named the Solid
    Adam.

40 And in the Nerves of the Ear (for the Nerves of the
    Tongue are closed),
On Albion's Rock Los stands creating the glorious
    Sun each morning,
And when unwearied in the evening he creates the
    Moon,
Death to delude, who all in terror at their splendor
    leaves

His prey, while Los appoints, and Rintrah and Palamabron guide
45 The Souls clear from the Rock of Death, that Death
himself may wake
In his appointed season when the ends of heaven
meet.

Then Los conducts the Spirits to be Vegetated into
Great Golgonooza, free from the four iron pillars of
Satan's Throne :
Temperance, Prudence, Justice, Fortitude, the four
pillars of tyranny,
50 That Satan's Watch-Fiends touch them not before
they Vegetate.

But Enitharmon and her Daughters take the pleasant
charge,
To give them to their lovely heavens till the Great
Judgment Day.
Such is their lovely charge.   But Rahab and Tirzah
pervert
Their mild influences, therefore the Seven Eyes of
God walk round
55 The Three Heavens of Ulro, where Tirzah and her
Sisters
Weave the black Woof of Death upon Entuthon
Benython.
In the Vale of Surrey, where Horeb terminates in
Rephaim,
The stamping feet of Zelophehad's Daughters are
cover'd with Human gore ;
Upon the tredles of the Loom they sing to the winged
shuttle ;
60 The River rises above his banks to wash the Woof ;
He takes it in his arms, he passes it in strength thro'
his current.
The veil of human miseries is woven over the Ocean
From the Atlantic to the Great South Sea, the
Erythrean.

Such is the World of Los, the labour of six thousand
years.
65 Thus Nature is a Vision of the Science of the Elohim.

END OF THE FIRST BOOK

*Of the three mottoes on this page the first is engraved in
reverse letters by Blake so as to be only legible in a looking-
glass.*

(30)

**How wide the Gulf and Unpassable between
Simplicity and Insipidity!**
Contraries are Positives.
A Negation is not a Contrary.

MILTON

BOOK THE SECOND

THERE is a place where Contrarieties are equally
       True.
This place is called Beulah.   It is a pleasant, lovely
       Shadow
Where no dispute can come, because of those who
       Sleep.
Into this place the Sons and Daughters of Ololon
       descended
5 With solemn mourning into Beulah's moony shades
       and hills,
Weeping for Milton.   Mute wonder held the Daugh-
       ters of Beulah
Enraptured with affection, sweet and mild benevo-
       lence.

Beulah is evermore Created around Eternity, ap-
       pearing
To the Inhabitants of Eden, around them on all sides.
10 But Beulah to its Inhabitants appears within each
       district
As the beloved infant in his mother's bosom round
       encircled
With arms of love and pity and sweet compassion. But
       to
The Sons of Eden the moony habitations of Beulah
Are from Great Eternity a mild and pleasant Rest.

15 And it is thus Created : Lo, the Eternal Great
       Humanity,

To whom be Glory and Dominion Evermore, Amen,
Walks among all his awful Family, seen in every face.
As the breath of the Almighty, such are the words of
    man to man,
In the great wars of Eternity, in fury of Poetic
    Inspiration,
20 To build the Universe stupendous, Mental forms
    Creating.

But the Emanations trembled exceedingly, nor could
    they
Live, because the life of Man was too exceeding
    unbounded.
His joy became terrible to them, they trembled and
    wept,
Crying with one voice : Give us a habitation and a
    place
25 In which we may be hidden under the shadow of
    wings,
For if we who are but for a time, and who pass away
    in winter,
Behold these wonders of Eternity, we shall consume,
But you, O our Fathers and Brothers, remain in
    Eternity.
But grant us a Temporal Habitation ; do you speak
30 To us ; we will obey your words as you obey Jesus
The Eternal, who is blessed for ever and ever. Amen.

So spake the lovely Emanations, and there appeared
    a pleasant
33 Mild Shadow above, beneath, and on all sides round.

(31)

Into this pleasant Shadow all the weak and weary,
Like Women and Children, were taken away as on
    wings
Of dovelike softness, and shadowy habitations pre-
    pared for them.
But every Man return'd and went, still going forward
    thro'

5 The Bosom of the Father in Eternity on Eternity;
Neither did any lack or fall into Error without
A Shadow to repose in all the Days of happy Eternity.

Into this pleasant Shadow Beulah, all Ololon de-
    scended,
And when the Daughters of Beulah heard the
    lamentation,
10 All Beulah wept, for they saw the Lord coming in
    the Clouds,
And the Shadows of Beulah terminate in rocky Albion.

And all Nations wept in affliction, Family by Family:
Germany wept towards France and Italy; England
    wept and trembled
Towards America; India rose up from his golden bed,
15 As one awaken'd in the night; they saw the Lord
    coming
In the Clouds of Ololon with Power and Great Glory.

And all the Living Creatures of the Four Elements
    wail'd
With bitter wailing; these in the aggregate are named
    Satan
And Rahab; they know not of Regeneration, but only
    of Generation.
20 The Fairies, Nymphs, Gnomes and Genii of the Four
    Elements,
Unforgiving and unalterable, these cannot be Regen-
    erated,
But must be Created, for they know only of
    Generation.
These are the Gods of the Kingdoms of the Earth, in
    contrarious
And cruel opposition: Element against Element,
    opposed in War,
25 Not Mental, as the Wars of Eternity but a Corporeal
    Strife
In Los's Halls, continual labouring in the Furnaces of
    Golgonooza.

Orc howls on the Atlantic : Enitharmon trembles, All
    Beulah weeps.

Thou hearest the Nightingale begin the Song of
    Spring ;
The Lark sitting upon his earthy bed, just as the
    morn
30 Appears, listens silent ; then springing from the waving
    Corn-field, loud
He leads the Choir of Day—trill, trill, trill, trill,
Mounting upon the wings of light into the Great
    Expanse,
Re-echoing against the lovely blue and shining
    heavenly Shell,
His little throat labours with inspiration ; every
    feather
35 On throat and breast and wings vibrates with the
    effluence Divine.
All Nature listens silent to him, and the awful Sun
Stands still upon the Mountain looking on this little
    Bird
With eyes of soft humility and wonder, love, and awe.
Then loud from their green covert all the Birds begin
    their Song :
40 The Thrush, the Linnet, and the Goldfinch, Robin,
    and the Wren
Awake the Sun from his sweet reverie upon the
    Mountain.
The Nightingale again assays his song, and thro' the
    day
And thro' the night warbles luxuriant, every Bird of
    Song
Attending his loud harmony with admiration and love.
45 This is a Vision of the lamentation of Beulah over
    Ololon.

Thou percievest the Flowers put forth their precious
    Odours,
And none can tell how from so small a center comes
    such sweet,

Forgetting that within that Center Eternity expands
Its ever during doors, that Og and Anak fiercely guard.
50 First, ere the morning breaks, joy opens in the flowery
        bosoms,
    Joy even to tears, which the Sun rising dries; first
        the Wild Thyme
    And Meadow-sweet, downy and soft, waving among
        the reeds,
    Light springing on the air, lead the sweet Dance; they
        wake
    The Honeysuckle sleeping on the Oak, the flaunting
        beauty
55 Revels along upon the wind ; the White-thorn lovely
        May
    Opens her many lovely eyes; listening, the Rose still
        sleeps.
    None dare to wake her.   Soon she bursts her crimson-
        curtained bed
    And comes forth in the majesty of beauty; every
        Flower—
    The Pink, the Jessamine, the Wallflower, the Carna-
        tion,
60 The Jonquil, the mild Lilly opes her heavens; every
        Tree
    And Flower and Herb soon fill the air with an in-
        numerable Dance,
    Yet all in order sweet and lovely.   Men are sick with
        love.
63 Such is a Vision of the lamentation of Beulah over
        Ololon.

                                                        (32)

    And the Divine Voice was heard in the Songs of
        Beulah, Saying :

    When I first Married you, I gave you all my whole
        soul ;
    I thought that you would love my loves and joy in
        my delights,

Seeking for pleasures in my pleasures, O Daughter of
Babylon.
5 Then thou wast lovely, mild, and gentle ; now thou
art terrible
In jealousy and unlovely in my sight, because thou
hast cruelly
Cut off my loves in fury till I have no love left for
thee.
Thy love depends on him thou lovest, and on his dear
loves
Depend thy pleasures, which thou hast cut off by
jealousy ;
10 Therefore I shew my Jealousy, and set before you
Death.
Behold Milton ! descended to Redeem the Female
Shade
From Death Eternal, such your lot, to be continually
Redeem'd
By death and misery of those you love, and by
Annihilation
When the Sixfold Female percieves that Milton
annihilates
15 Himself : that seeing all his loves by her cut off, he
leaves
Her also, entirely abstracting himself from Female
loves.
She shall relent in fear of death ; she shall begin to
give
Her maidens to her husband, delighting in his
delight ;
And then, and then alone, begins the happy Female
joy,
20 As it is done in Beulah ; and thou, O Virgin Babylon,
Mother of Whoredoms,
Shalt bring Jerusalem in thine arms in the night
watches, and,
No longer turning her a wandering Harlot in the
streets,
Shalt give her into the arms of God your Lord and
Husband.

24 Such are the Songs of Beulah, in the Lamentations
    of Ololon.

(34)

And all the Songs of Beulah sounded comfortable
    notes
To comfort Ololon's lamentation, for they said :
Are you the Fiery Circle that late drove in fury and
    fire
The Eight Immortal Starry-Ones down into Ulro
    dark,
5 Rending the Heavens of Beulah with your thunders
    and lightnings?
And can you thus lament, and can you pity and
    forgive?
Is terror changed to pity, O wonder of Eternity?

And the Four States of Humanity in its Repose
Were shewed them. First of Beulah, a most pleasant
    Sleep,
10 On Couches soft, with mild music, tended by Flowers
    of Beulah ;
Sweet Female forms, winged or floating in the air
    spontaneous.
The Second State is Alla, and the third State Al-Ulro ;
But the Fourth State is dreadful, it is named Or-Ulro.
The First State is in the Head, the Second is in the
    Heart,
15 The Third in the Loins and Seminal Vessels, and the
    Fourth
In the Stomach and Intestines — terrible, deadly,
    unutterable.
And he whose Gates are open'd in those Regions of
    his Body
Can from those Gates view all these wondrous Imagina-
    tions.

But Ololon sought the Or-Ulro and its fiery Gates,
20 And the Couches of the Martyrs ; and many Daughters
    of Beulah

Accompany them down to the Ulro with soft melodious
    tears.
A long journey and dark, thro' Chaos in the track of
    Milton's course,
To where the Contraries of Beulah War beneath
    Negation's Banner.

Then, view'd from Milton's Track, they see the Ulro,
    a vast Polypus
25 Of living fibres down into the Sea of Time and Space
    growing,
A self-devouring, monstrous Human Death, Twenty-
    seven fold ;
Within it sit Five Females, and the nameless Shadowy
    Mother
Spinning it from their bowels with songs of amorous
    delight,
And melting cadences that lure the Sleepers of
    Beulah down
30 The River Storge (which is Arnon) into the Dead
    Sea.
Around this Polypus Los continual builds the Mun-
    dane Shell.

Four Universes round the Universe of Los remain
    Chaotic ;
Four intersecting Globes, and the Egg-form'd World
    of Los
In midst, stretching from Zenith to Nadir in midst of
    Chaos.
35 One of these Ruin'd Universes is to the North named
    Urthona ;
One in the South, this was the glorious World of
    Urizen ;
One to the East of Luvah ; One to the West of
    Tharmas.
But when Luvah assumed the World of Urizen in the
    South,
All fell towards the Center, sinking downward in dire
    Ruin.

40 Here in these Chaoses the Sons of Ololon took their
   abode,
   In Chasms the Mundane Shell which open on all
   sides wound
   Southwards, and by the East within the Breach of
   Milton's descent,
   To watch the time, pitying and gentle, to awaken
   Urizen.
   They stood in a dark land of death, of fiery corroding
   waters,
45 Where lie in evil death the Four Immortals, pale and
   cold,
   And the Eternal Man, even Albion, upon the Rock of
   Ages,
   Seeing Milton's Shadow, some Daughters of Beulah
   trembling
   Return'd, but Ololon remain'd before the Gates of the
   Dead.

   And Ololon looked down into the Heavens of Ulro in
   fear.
50 They said : How are the Wars of Man, which in Great
   Eternity
   Appear around, in the External Spheres of Visionary
   Life,
   Here render'd Deadly within the Life and Interior
   Vision ?
   How are the Beasts and Birds and Fishes and Plants
   and Minerals
   Here fix'd into a frozen bulk, subject to decay and
   death ?
55 Those Visions of Human Life and Shadows of Wisdom
   and Knowledge

(35)

   Are here frozen to unexpansive, deadly, destroying
   terrors,
   And War and Hunting, the Two Fountains of the
   River of Life,

Are become Fountains of bitter Death and of corrod-
ing Hell,
Till Brotherhood is chang'd into a Curse and a
Flattery
5 By Differences between Ideas, that Ideas themselves
(which are
The Divine Members) may be slain in offerings for
sin.
O dreadful Loom of Death. O piteous Female forms,
compelled
To weave the Woof of Death. On Camberwell
Tirzah's Courts,
Malahs on Blackheath, Rahab and Noah, dwell on
Windsor's heights.
10 Where once the Cherubs of Jerusalem spread to
Lambeth's Vale,
Milcah's Pillars shine from Harrow to Hampstead,
where Hoglah
On Highgate's heights magnificent weaves over trem-
bling Thames
To Shooter's Hill, and thence to Blackheath, the dark
Woof. Loud,
Loud roll the Weights and Spindles over the whole
Earth let down,
15 On all sides round to the Four Quarters of the World,
eastward on
Europe to Euphrates and Hindu, to Nile and back in
Clouds
Of Death across the Atlantic to America North and
South.

So spake Ololon, in reminiscence astonish'd, but they
Could not behold Golgonooza without passing the
Polypus,
20 A wondrous journey not passable by Immortal feet,
and none
But the Divine Saviour can pass it without annihila-
tion,
For Golgonooza cannot be seen till, having pass'd the
Polypus,

It is viewed on all sides round by a Four-fold Vision,
Or till you become Mortal and Vegetable in Sexu-
　　ality,
25 Then you behold its mighty Spires and Domes of ivory
　　and gold.

And Ololon examined all the Couches of the Dead,
Even of Los and Enitharmon, and all the Sons of
　　Albion,
And his Four Zoas terrified and on the verge of
　　Death.
In midst of these was Milton's Couch and when they
　　saw Eight
30 Immortal Starry-Ones guarding the Couch in flaming
　　fires,
They thunderous utter'd all a universal groan, falling
　　down
Prostrate before the Starry Eight, asking with tears
　　forgiveness,
Confessing their crime with humiliation and sorrow.

O how the Starry Eight rejoic'd to see Ololon
　　descended !
35 And now that a wide road was open to Eternity
By Ololon's descent thro' Beulah to Los and Eni-
　　tharmon.
For mighty were the multitudes of Ololon, vast the
　　extent
Of their great sway, reaching from Ulro to Eternity,
Surrounding the Mundane Shell outside in its
　　Caverns,
40 And through Beulah, and all, silent, forbore to
　　contend
With Ololon, for they saw the Lord in the Clouds of
　　Ololon.

There is a Moment in each Day that Satan cannot
　　find,
Nor can his Watch Fiends find it, but the Industrious
　　find

This Moment, and it multiply, and when it once is found

45 It renovates every Moment of the Day if rightly placed.

In this Moment Ololon descended to Los and Enitharmon,

Unseen beyond the Mundane Shell Southward in Milton's track.

Just in this Moment, when the morning odours rise abroad,

And first from the Wild Thyme, stands a Fountain in a rock

50 Of crystal, flowing into two Streams, one flows thro' Golgonooza,

And thro' Beulah to Eden, beneath Los's western Wall;

The other flows thro' the Aerial Void, and all the Churches

Meeting again in Golgonooza, beyond Satan's Seat.

The Wild Thyme is Los's Messenger to Eden, a mighty Demon,

55 Terrible, deadly, and poisonous, his presence in Ulro dark;

Therefore he appears only a small Root creeping in grass,

Covering over the Rock of Odours his bright purple mantle,

Beside the Fount above the Lark's Nest in Golgonooza.

Luvah slept here in death, and here is Luvah's empty Tomb,

60 Ololon sat beside this Fountain on the Rock of Odours.

Just at the place to where the Lark mounts is a Crystal Gate:

It is the entrance of the First Heaven, named Luther; for

The Lark is Los's Messenger thro' the Twenty-seven
    Churches,
That the Seven Eyes of God, who walk even to Satan's
    Seat,
65 Thro' all the Twenty-seven Heavens may not slumber
    nor sleep,
But the Lark's Nest is at the Gate of Los, at the
    eastern
67 Gate of wide Golgonooza, and the Lark is Los's Mes-
    senger.

(36)

When on the highest lift of his light pinions he
    arrives
At that bright Gate, another Lark meets him, and back
    to back
They touch their pinions' tip tip, and each descend
To their respective Earths, and there all night consult
    with Angels
5 Of Providence and with the Eyes of God all night in
    slumbers
Inspired ; and at the dawn of day send out another
    Lark
Into another Heaven to carry news upon his wings.
Thus are the Messengers dispatched till they reach
    the Earth again
In the East Gate of Golgonooza, and the Twenty-
    eighth bright
10 Lark met the Female Ololon descending into my
    Garden.
Thus it appears to Mortal eyes and those of the Ulro
    Heavens,
But not thus to Immortals, the Lark is a mighty
    Angel.

For Ololon step'd into the Polypus within the Mun-
    dane Shell,
They could not step into Vegetable Worlds without
    becoming
15 The enemies of Humanity except in a Female Form,

And as One Female. Ololon and all its mighty Hosts
Appear'd, a Virgin of twelve years, nor time nor
   space was
To the perception of the Virgin Ololon, but as the
Flash of lightning, but more quick, the Virgin in my
   Garden
20 Before my Cottage stood, for the Satanic Space is
   delusion.

For when Los join'd with me he took me in his fiery
   whirlwind.
My vegetated portion was hurried from Lambeth's
   shades.
He set me down in Felpham's Vale and prepar'd a
   beautiful
Cottage for me that in three years I might write all
   these Visions,
25 To display Nature's cruel holiness, the deceits of
   Natural Religion.
Walking in my Cottage Garden, sudden I beheld
The Virgin Ololon, and address'd her as a Daughter
   of Beulah.

Virgin of Providence, fear not to enter into my
   Cottage.
What is thy message to thy friend, what am I now
   to do?
30 Is it again to plunge into deeper affliction? behold me
Ready to obey, but pity thou my Shadow of Delight;
32 Enter my Cottage, comfort her, for she is sick with
   fatigue.

(37)

The Virgin answer'd, Knowest thou of Milton, who
   descended,
Driven from Eternity? him I seek, terrified at my
   Act,
In Great Eternity, which thou knowest: I come him
   to seek.

So Ololon utter'd in words distinct the anxious
thought.
5 Mild was the voice, but more distinct than any
earthly
That Milton's Shadow heard, and condensing all his
Fibres
Into a strength impregnable of majesty and beauty
infinite.
I saw he was the Covering Cherub, and within him
Satan
And Rahab, in an outside which is fallacious; within,
10 Beyond the outline of Identity, in the Selfhood
deadly,
And he appear'd the Wicker Man of Scandinavia, in
whom
Jerusalem's children consume in flames among the
Stars.

Descending down into my Garden, a Human Wonder
of God,
Reaching from heaven to earth, a Cloud and Human
Form.
15 I beheld Milton with astonishment, and in him beheld
The Monstrous Churches of Beulah, the Gods of Ulro
dark,
Twelve monstrous dishumanized terrors, Synagogues
of Satan,
A Double Twelve and Thrice Nine : such their
divisions.

And these their Names and their Places within the
Mundane Shell.
20 In Tyre and Sidon I saw Baal and Ashtaroth. In
Moab, Chemash.
In Ammon, Molech : loud his Furnaces rage among
the Wheels
Of Og, and pealing loud the cries of the Victims of
Fire ;
And pale his Priestesses unfolded in Veils of Pesti-
lence, border'd

With War; Woven in Looms of Tyre and Sidon by
    beautiful Ashtaroth,
25 In Palestine, Dagon, Sea Monster, worship'd o'er the
    Sea.
Thammuz in Lebanon and Rimmon in Damascus cur-
    tain'd,
Osiris, Isis, Orus, in Egypt: dark their Taber-
    nacles on Nile,
Floating with solemn songs, and on the Lakes of
    Egypt nightly,
With pomp, even till morning break and Osiris
    appear in the sky.
30 But Belial of Sodom and Gomorrha, obscure Demon
    of Bribes
And secret Assassinations, not worship'd nor ador'd:
    but
With the finger on the lips, and the back turn'd to
    the Light,
And Saturn, Jove, and Rhea of the Isles of the Sea
    remote.
These Twelve Gods are the Twelve Spectre Sons of
    the Druid Albion.

35 And these the Names of the Twenty-seven Heavens
    and their Churches—
Adam, Seth, Enos, Cainan, Mahalaleel, Jared, Enoch:
Methuselah, Lamech—these are Giants mighty, Her-
    maphroditic.
Hoah, Shem, Arphaxad, Cainan the second, Salak,
    Beber,
Peleg, Reu, Serug, Nahor, Terah, these are the
    Female-Males,
40 A Male within a Female, hid as in an Ark and Cur-
    tains.
Abraham, Moses, Solomon, Paul, Constantine, Char-
    lemaine,
Luther, these seven are the Male-Females, the Dragon
    Forms,
Religion hid in War, a Dragon red and hidden
    Harlot.

All these are seen in Milton's Shadow, who is the
 Covering Cherub,
45 The Spectre of Albion in which the Spectre of Luvah
 inhabits,
In the Newtonian Voids between the Substances of
 Creation.

For the Chaotic Voids outside of the Stars are mea-
 sured by
The Stars, which are the boundaries of Kingdoms,
 Provinces,
And Empires of Chaos invisible to the Vegetable Man.
50 The Kingdom of Og is in Orion : Sihon is in
 Ophiucus.
Og has Twenty-seven Districts ; Sihon's Districts
 Twenty-one.
From Star to Star, Mountains and Valleys, terrible
 dimension,
Stretch'd out, compose the Mundane Shell, a mighty
 Incrustation
Of Forty-eight deformed Human Wonders of the
 Almighty,
55 With Caverns whose remotest bottoms meet again
 beyond
The Mundane Shell in Golgonooza, but the Fires of
 Los rage
In the remotest bottoms of the Caves, that none can
 pass
Into Eternity that way, but all descend to Los,
To Bowlahoola and Allamanda and to Entuthon
 Benython.

60 The Heavens are the Cherub : the Twelve Gods are
 Satan.

(39)

Forty-eight starry regions are Cities of the Levites,
And the Heads of the Great Polypus, Four-fold twelve
 enormity,

In mighty and mysterious commingling, enemy with
   enemy,
Woven by Urizen into Sexes from his mantle of years,
5 And Milton collecting all his fibres into impregnable
   strength,
Descended down a Paved work of all kinds of precious
   stones
Out from the eastern sky, descending down into my
   Cottage
Garden, clothed in black, severe and silent he
   descended.

The Spectre of Satan stood upon the roaring sea, and
   beheld
10 Milton within his sleeping Humanity; trembling and
   shudd'ring,
He stood upon the waves a Twenty-seven-fold mighty
   Demon
Gorgeous and beautiful.   Loud roll his thunders
   against Milton.
Loud Satan thunder'd, loud and dark upon mild
   Felpham shore,
Not daring to touch one fibre, he howl'd round upon
   the Sea.

15 I also stood in Satan's bosom, and beheld its desola-
   tions,
A ruin'd Man, a ruin'd building of God, not made
   with hands,
Its plains of burning sand, its mountains of marble
   terrible,
Its pits and declivities flowing with molten ore and
   fountains
Of pitch and nitre; its ruin'd palaces and cities and
   mighty works;
20 Its furnaces of affliction, in which his Angels and
   Emanations
Labour with blacken'd visages among its stupendous
   ruins;

Arches and pyramids and porches, colonades and
   domes,
In which dwells Mystery, Babylon : here is her secret
   place.
From hence she comes forth on the Churches in
   delight.
25 Here is her Cup fill'd with its poisons in these horrid
   vales ;
And here her scarlet Veil woven in pestilence and
   war.
Here is Jerusalem bound in chains, in the Dens of
   Babylon.

In the Eastern porch of Satan's Universe, Milton
   stood and said :

Satan, my Spectre ! I know my power thee to
   annihilate,
30 And be a greater in thy place, and be thy Tabernacle :
A covering for thee to do thy will, till one greater
   comes,
And smites me as I smote thee, and becomes my
   covering.
Such are the Laws of thy false Heav'ns ; but Laws of
   Eternity
Are not such.   Know thou, I come to Self Annihila-
   tion.
35 Such are the Laws of Eternity, that each shall
   mutually
Annihilate himself for others' good, as I for thee.
Thy purpose and the purpose of thy Priests and of thy
   Churches
Is to impress on men the fear of death : to teach
Trembling and fear, terror, constriction, abject selfish-
   ness.
40 Mine is to teach Men to despise death, and to go on
In fearless majesty, annihilating Self, laughing to
   scorn
Thy Laws and terrors, shaking down thy Synagogues
   as webs.

I come to discover before Heav'n and Hell the Self
   righteousness
In all its Hypocritic turpitude, opening to every eye
45 These wonders of Satan's holiness, shewing to the
   Earth
The Idol Virtues of the Natural Heart, and Satan's
   Seat
Explore in all its Selfish Natural Virtue, and put off,
In Self annihilation, all that is not of God alone,
To put off Self and all I have, ever and ever.   Amen.

50 Satan heard ! Coming in a cloud with trumpets and
   flaming fire,
Saying : I am God, the judge of all, the living and the
   dead.
Fall therefore down and worship me ; submit thy
   supreme
Dictate to my eternal Will, and to my dictate bow.
I hold the Balances of Right and Just, and mine the
   Sword.
55 Seven Angels bear my Name, and in those Seven I
   appear.
But I alone am God, and I alone in Heav'n and Earth,
57 Of all that live, dare utter this ; others tremble and
   bow

(40)

Till all Things become One Great Satan in Holiness,
Oppos'd to Mercy, and the Divine Delusion Jesus be
   no more.

Suddenly around Milton on my Path, the Starry Seven
Burn'd terrible. My Path became a solid fire, as
   bright
5 As the clear Sun, and Milton, silent, came down on
   my Path.
And there went forth from the Starry limbs of the
   Seven, Forms
Human, with Trumpets innumerable, sounding articulate,

As the Seven spake ; and they stood in a mighty
    Column of Fire,
Surrounding Felpham's Vale, reaching to the Mundane
    Shell, saying :

10 Awake, Albion, awake ! reclaim thy Reasoning
    Spectre.   Subdue
Him to the Divine Mercy ; cast him down into the
    Lake
Of Los, that ever burneth with fire, ever and ever.
    Amen !
Let the Four Zoas awake from Slumbers of Six
    Thousand Years.
Then loud the Furnaces of Los were heard and seen
    as Seven Heavens,
15 Stretching from south to north over the mountains of
    Albion.

Satan heard : trembling round his Body, he in-
    circled it.
He trembled with exceeding great trembling and
    astonishment,
Howling in his Spectre round his Body, hung'ring to
    devour,
But fearing for the pain, for if he touches a Vital,
20 His torment is unendurable ; therefore he cannot
    devour,
But howls round it as a lion round his prey, continu-
    ally.
Loud Satan thunder'd, loud and dark upon mild
    Felpham's Shore,
Coming in a Cloud with Trumpets and with Fiery
    Flame,
An awful Form eastward from midst of a bright Paved-
    work
25 Of precious stones, by Cherubim surrounded, so
    permitted
(Lest he should fall apart in his Eternal Death) to
    imitate
The Eternal Great Humanity Divine, surrounded by

His Cherubim and Seraphim in ever happy Eternity.
Beneath sat Chaos : Sin on his right hand Death on
    his left.
30 And Ancient Night spread over all the heav'n his
    Mantle of Laws.
He trembled with exceeding great trembling and
    astonishment.

Then Albion rose up in the Night of Beulah on his
    Couch
Of dread repose, seen by the visionary eye : his face is
    toward
The east, toward Jerusalem's Gates. Groaning he
    sat above
35 His rocks. London and Bath and Legions (sic) and
    Edinburgh
Are the four pillars of his Throne : his left foot, near
    London,
Covers the shades of Tyburn : his instep from Windsor
To Primrose Hill, stretching to Highgate and
    Holloway.
London is between his knees, its basements fourfold :
40 His right foot stretches to the sea on Dover cliffs, his
    heel
On Canterbury's ruins : his right hand covers lofty
    Wales,
His left Scotland : his bosom girt with gold involves
York, Edinburgh, Durham, and Carlisle ; and on the
    front
Bath, Oxford, Cambridge, Norwich : his right elbow
45 Leans on the Rocks of Erin's Land, Ireland, ancient
    nation :
His head bends over London : he sees his embodied
    Spectre
Trembling before him with exceeding great trembling
    and fear.
He views Jerusalem and Babylon ; his tears flow
    down.
He moved his right foot to Cornwall, his left to the
    Rocks of Bognor.

50 He strove to rise, to walk into the Deep, but strength
     failing
   Forbad, and down with dreadful groans he sunk upon
     his Couch
   In moony Beulah.   Los, his strong Guard, walks
     round beneath the Moon.

   Urizen faints in terror striving among the Brooks of
     Arnon
   With Milton's Spirit, as the Plowman or Artificer or
     Shepherd,
55 While in the labours of his calling, sends his thought
     abroad
   To labour in the ocean or in the starry heaven.   So
     Milton
   Labour'd in Chasms of the Mundane Shell, tho' here
     before
   My Cottage, midst the Starry Seven, where the Virgin
     Ololon
   Stood trembling in the Porch, loud Satan thunder'd
     on the stormy Sea,
60 Circling Albion's cliffs, in which the Four-fold World
     resides,
   Tho' seen in fallacy outside, a fallacy of Satan's
     Churches.

                                                     (42)

   Before Ololon Milton stood and perciev'd the Eternal
     Form
   Of that mild Vision : wondrous were their acts by me
     unknown,
   Except remotely ; and I heard Ololon say to Milton :

   I see thee strive upon the Brooks of Arnon ; there a
     dread
5 And awful Man I see, o'ercover'd with the mantle of
     years.
   I behold Los and Urizen, I behold Orc and Tharmas ;
   The Four Zoas of Albion and thy Spirit with them
     striving

In Self annihilation, giving thy life to thy enemies.
Are those who contemn Religion, and seek to anni-
     hilate it,
10 Become in their Feminine portions the causes and
     promoters
Of these Religions? How is this thing? this Newtonian
     Phantasy,
This Voltaire and Rousseau; this Hume and Gibbon
     and Bolingbroke;
This Natural Religion, this impossible absurdity?
Is Ololon the cause of this? O where shall I hide my
     face?
15 These tears fall for the little-ones, the Children of
     Jerusalem,
Lest they be annihilated in thy annihilation.

No sooner she had spoke but Rahab, Babylon, appear'd
Eastward upon the Paved work, across Europe and
     Asia,
Glorious as the midday Sun in Satan's bosom glowing;
20 A Female hidden in a Male, Religion hidden in War,
Nam'd Moral Virtues, cruel two-fold Monster, shining
     bright,
A Dragon red and hidden Harlot, which John in
     Patmos saw.

And all beneath the Nations innumerable of Ulro,
Appear'd the Seven Kingdoms of Canaan and Five
     Baalim
25 Of Philistea, into Twelve divided, call'd after the
     Names
Of Israel, as they are in Eden—Mountain, River, and
     Plain,
City and sandy Desart, intermingled beyond mortal
     ken.

But turning toward Ololon in terrible majesty, Milton
Replied: Obey thou the Words of the Inspired Man.
30 All that can be annihilated must be annihilated,

That the Children of Jerusalem may be saved from
slavery.
There is a Negation, and there is a Contrary.
The Negation must be destroy'd to redeem the Contraries.
The Negation is the Spectre, the Reasoning Power in
Man.
35 This is a false Body, an Incrustation over my Immortal
Spirit, a Selfhood, which must be put off and annihilated alway
37 To cleanse the Face of my Spirit by self-examination.

(43)

To bathe in the waters of Life, to wash off the Not
Human,
I come in Self-annihilation and the grandeur of
Inspiration
To cast off Rational Demonstration by Faith in the
Saviour,
To cast off the rotten rags of Memory by Inspiration,
5 To cast off Bacon, Locke, and Newton from Albion's
covering,
To take off his filthy garments and clothe him with
Imagination ;
To cast aside from Poetry all that is not Inspiration,
That it no longer shall dare to mock with the aspersion
of Madness
Cast on the Inspired by the tame high finisher of
paltry Blots,
10 Indefinite or paltry Rhymes, or paltry Harmonies ;
Who creeps into State Government like a caterpillar
to destroy ;
To cast off the idiot Questioner, who is always
questioning
But never capable of answering, who sits with a sly
grin
Silent plotting when to question, like a thief in a
cave ;

15 Who publishes doubt and calls it knowledge ; whose
        Science is Despair,
   Whose pretence to knowledge is Envy; whose whole
        Science is
   To destroy the wisdom of ages, to gratify ravenous
        Envy
   That rages round him like a Wolf day and night
        without rest.
   He smiles with condescension, he talks of Benevolence
        and Virtue,
20 And those who act with Benevolence and Virtue, they
        murder time on time.
   These are the destroyers of Jerusalem, these are the
        murderers
   Of Jesus, who deny the Faith and mock at Eternal
        Life ;
   Who pretend to Poetry that they may destroy
        Imagination,
   By imitation of Nature's Images drawn from Remem-
        brance.
25 These are the Sexual Garments, the Abomination of
        Desolation,
   Hiding the Human Lineaments as with an Ark and
        Curtains,
   Which Jesus rent, and now shall wholly purge away
        with Fire
   Till Generation is swallowd up in Regeneration.

   Then trembled the Virgin Ololon, and reply'd in
        clouds of despair :
30 Is this our Feminine Portion, the Six-fold Miltonic
        Female ?
   Terribly this Portion trembles before thee, O awful
        Man,
   Altho' our Human Power can sustain the severe con-
        tentions
   Of Friendship, our Sexual cannot, but flies into the
        Ulro.
   Hence arose all our terrors in Eternity, and now
        remembrance

35 Returns upon us. Are we Contraries, O Milton, Thou
    and I ?

O Immortal ! how were we led to War, the Wars of
    Death ?

37 Is this the Void outside of Existence, which if enter'd
    into

(44)

Becomes a Womb? and is this the Death Couch of
    Albion ?

Thou goest to Eternal Death, and all must go with
    thee !

So saying, the Virgin divided Six-fold, and with a
    shriek

Dolorous that ran thro' all Creation, a Double Six-
    fold Wonder ;

5 Away from Ololon she divided, and fled into the
    depths

Of Milton's Shadow, as a Dove upon the stormy Sea.

Then as a Moony Ark Ololon descended to Felpham's
    Vale

In clouds of blood, in streams of gore, with dreadful
    thunderings,

Into the Fires of Intellect that rejoic'd in Felpham's
    Vale

10 Around the Starry Eight. With one accord the Starry
    Eight became

One Man, Jesus, the Saviour wonderful ; round his
    limbs

The Clouds of Ololon folded as a Garment dipped in
    blood,

Written within and without in woven letters ; and
    the Writing

Is the Divine Revelation in the Literal expression,

15 A Garment of War. I heard it named the Woof of
    Six Thousand Years.

And I beheld the Twenty-four Cities of Albion

Arise upon their Thrones to Judge the Nations of the
   Earth,
And the Immortal Four, in whom the Twenty-four
   appear Four-fold,
Arose around Albion's body.   Jesus wept, and walked
   forth
20 From Felpham's Vale, clothed in Clouds of blood, to
   enter into
Albion's Bosom, the bosom of death, and the Four
   surrounded him
In the Column of Fire in Felpham's Vale; then to
   their mouths the Four
Applied their Four Trumpets, and then sounded to
   the Four winds.

Terror struck in the Vale.   I stood at that immortal
   sound ;
25 My bones trembled, I fell outstretch'd upon the path
A moment, and my Soul return'd into its mortal state,
To Resurrection and Judgment in the Vegetable
   Body,
And my sweet Shadow of Delight stood trembling by
   my side.

Immediately the Lark mounted with a loud trill from
   Felpham's Vale,
30 And the Wild Thyme from Wimbleton's green and
   unpurpled Hills,
And Los and Enitharmon rose over the Hills of
   Surrey.
Their clouds roll over London with a south wind, soft
   Oothoon
Pants in the Vales of Lambeth, weeping o'er her
   Human Harvest ;
Los listens to the Cry of the Poor Man, his Cloud
35 Over London in volume terrific, low bended in anger.

Rintrah and Palamabron view the Human Harvest
   beneath,
Their Wine-presses and Barns stand open ; the Ovens
   are prepar'd,

The Waggons ready; terrific Lions and Tygers sport
    and play;
39 All Animals upon the Earth are prepar'd in all their
    strength

(45)

To go forth to the Great Harvest and Vintage of the
    Nations.

FINIS

MILTON—EXTRA PAGES

(Not in the complete copy chosen for printing, which is that in the Print-Room of the British Museum. They are numbered by Blake. Only Nos. 3, 5, 8, 17, and 32 have been found.)

(Extra page 3)

BENEATH the Plow of Rintrah and the Harrow of the
    Almighty,
In the hands of Palamabron, where the Starry Mills
    of Satan
Are built beneath the Earth and Waters of the Mun-
    dane Shell,
Here the Three Classes of Men take their Sexual
    texture Woven.
5 The Sexual is Threefold : the Human is Fourfold.

If you account it Wisdom when you are angry to be
    silent and
Not to shew it, I do not account that Wisdom, but
    Folly.
Every Man's Wisdom is peculiar to his own Indi-
    viduality.
O Satan, my youngest born, art thou not Prince of
    the Starry Hosts
10 And of the Wheels of Heaven, to turn the Mills day
    and night ?
Art thou not Newton's Pantocrator weaving the Woof
    of Locke ?
To Mortals thy Mills seem every thing, and the
    Harrow of Shaddai

VOL. I. 2 L

A scheme of Human conduct, invisible and incompre-
hensible.
Get to thy Labours at the Mills, and leave me to my
wrath.

15 Satan was going to reply, but Los roll'd his loud
thunders.

Anger me not ! thou canst not drive the Harrow in
pity's paths,
Thy Work is Eternal Death, with Mills and Ovens
and Cauldrons.
Trouble me no more, thou canst not have Eternal
Life.

So Los spoke. Satan trembling obey'd, weeping along
the way.
20 Mark well my words, they are of your eternal Salvation.

Between South Molton Street and Stratford Place,
Calvary's foot,
Where the Victims were preparing for Sacrifice their
Cherubim.
Around their loins pour'd forth their arrows, and their
bosoms beam
With all colours of precious stones, and their inmost
palaces
25 Resounded with preparation of animals wild and tame
(Mark well my words : Corporeal Friends are Spiritual
Enemies),
Mocking, Druidical, Mathematical
Proportion of Length, Bredth, Highth,
29 Displaying Naked Beauty : with Flute and Harp and
Song.

(Extra page 5)

By Enitharmon's looms when Albion was slain upon
his Mountains,
And in his tent, through envy of the living form,
even of the Divine Vision,

And of the sports of wisdom in the Human Imagination,
Which is the Divine Body of the Lord Jesus blessed
for ever.
5 Mark well my words, they are of your eternal salvation.

Urizen lay in darkness and solitude in chains of the
mind locked up.
Los seized his hammer and tongs; he laboured at
his resolute anvil
Among indefinite Druid rocks, and snows of doubt
and reasoning.

Refusing all definite form the Abstract Horror roofed,
stony hard;
10 And a first age passed over, and a state of dismal woe.

Down sunk with fright a red hot globe, round, burning, deep,
Deep down into the abyss, panting, conglobing,
trembling;
And a second age passed over, and a state of dismal
woe.

Rolling round into two little orbs, and closed in two
little caves,
15 The eyes beheld the Abyss, lest bones of solitude
freeze over all;
And a third age passed over, and a state of dismal
woe.

From beneath his orbs of vision two ears in close
volutions
Shot spiring out in the deep darkness and petrified as
they grew;
And a fourth age passed over, and a state of dismal
woe.

20 Hanging upon the wind two Nostrils bent down into
the deep,

And a fifth age passed over, and a state of dismal
woe.

In ghastly torment sick, a tongue of hunger and
thirst flamed out,
And a sixth age passed over, and a state of dismal
woe.

Enraged and stifled without and within, in terror and
woe he threw his
25 Right arm to the north, his left arm to the south, and
his feet
Stamped the nether abyss in trembling and howling
and dismay.
And a seventh age passed over, and a state of dismal
woe.

Terrified, Los stood in the abyss, and his immortal
limbs
Grew deadly pale. He became what he beheld, for a
red
30 Round globe sunk down from his Bosom into the
Deep. In pangs
He hovered, it trembling and weeping. Trembling it
shook
The nether abyss in tremblings. He wept over it, he
cherished it
In deadly, sickening pain, till separated into a
female pale
As the cloud that brings the snow. All the while
from his Back
35 A blue fluid exuded in sinews, hardening in the
abyss,
Till it separated into a male form howling in jealousy,
Within, labouring; beholding without,—from particulars to generals
Subduing his Spectre. They builded the Looms of
Generation;
They builded great Golgonooza, Times on Times,
ages on ages.

40 First Orc was born, then the Shadowy Female, then
    all Los's family.
   At last Enitharmon brought forth Satan, refusing
    Form.   In vain
   The Miller of Eternity made subservient to the Great
    Harvest,
43 That he may go to his own Place, Prince of the Starry
    Wheels.

(Extra page 8)

Then Los and Enitharmon knew that Satan is Urizen,
Drawn down by Orc and the Shadowy Female into
 Generation.
Oft Enitharmon enter'd weeping into the Space, there
 appearing
An aged Woman raving along the Streets (the Space
 is named
5 Canaan), then she return'd to Los weary, frighted as
 from dreams.
The nature of a Female Space is this : it shrinks the
 Organs
Of Life till they become Finite, and Itself seems
 Infinite.

And Satan vibrated in the immensity of the Space :
 Limited
To those without, but Infinite to those within : it fell
 down and
10 Became Canaan, closing Los from Eternity in Albion's
 Cliffs.
A mighty Fiend against the Divine Humanity mus-
 t'ring to War.
Satan, Ah me ! is gone to his own place, said Los ;
 their God
I will not worship in their Churches, nor King in
 their Theatres.
Elynittria, whence is this Jealousy running along the
 mountains ?
15 British Women were not Jealous when Greek and
 Roman were Jealous.

Every thing in Eternity shines by its own Internal
    light ; but thou
Darkenest every Internal light with the arrows of
    thy quiver,
Bound up in the horns of Jealousy to a deadly fading
    Moon,
And Ocalythron binds the Sun into a Jealous Globe,
20 That every thing is fix'd Opake without Internal
    Light.

So Los lamented over Satan, who, triumphant, divided
    the Nations.

(Extra page 17)

And Tharmas, Demon of the Waters, and Orc, who
    is Luvah
The Shadowy Female, seeing Milton, howl'd in her
    lamentation
Over the Deeps, outstretching her Twenty-seven
    Heavens over Albion.

And thus the Shadowy Female howls in articulate
    howlings :

5 I will lament over Milton in the lamentations of the
    afflicted.
My Garments shall be woven of sighs and heart-
    broken lamentations.
The misery of unhappy Families shall be drawn out
    into its border,
Wrought with the needle, with dire sufferings,
    poverty, pain, and woe,
Along the rocky Island and thence throughout the
    whole Earth,
10 There shall be the sick Father and his starving
    Family : there
The Prisoner in the stone Dungeon and the Slave at
    the Mill.
I will have writings written all over it in Human
    words,

That every Infant that is born upon the Earth shall
 read
And get by rote as a hard task of a life of sixty years.
15 I will have Kings inwoven upon it, and Councellors
 and Mighty Men.
The Famine shall clasp it together with buckles and
 clasps,
And the Pestilence shall be its fringe and the War its
 girdle,
To divide into Rahab and Tirzah, that Milton may
 come to our tents.
For I will put on the Human Form and take the Image
 of God,
20 Even Pity and Humanity, but my Clothing shall be
 Cruelty.
And I will put on Holiness as a breastplate and as a
 helmet,
And all my ornaments shall be of the gold of broken
 hearts,
And the precious stones of anxiety and care, and
 desperation and death,
And repentance for sin and sorrow, and punishment
 and fear,
25 To defend me from thy terrors, O Orc! my only
 beloved.

Orc answer'd: Take not the Human Form, O love-
 liest! Take not
Terror upon thee! Behold how I am, and tremble
 lest thou also
Consume in my Consummation; but thou must take
 a Form
Female and lovely, that cannot consume in Man's
 consummation.
30 Wherefore dost thou Create and Weave this Satan
 for a Covering?
When thou attemptest to put on the Human Form,
 my wrath
Burns to the top of heaven against thee in Jealousy
 and Fear.

Then I rend thee asunder, then I howl over thy clay
and ashes.
When wilt thou put on the Female Form as in times
of old,
35 With a Garment of Pity and Compassion like the
Garment of God ?
His garments are long sufferings for the Children of
Men.
Jerusalem is his Garment, and not thy Covering
Cherub, O lovely
Shadow of my delight, who wanderest seeking for the
prey.

So spoke Orc when Oothoon and Leutha hover'd over
his Couch
40 Of fire in interchange of Beauty and Perfection in the
darkness.

Opening interiorly into Jerusalem and Babylon,
shining glorious
In the Shadowy Female's bosom. Jealous her dark-
ness grew.
Howlings fill'd all the desolate places in accusations of
Sin,
In Female beauty shining in the unform'd void, and
Orc in vain
45 Stretch'd out his hands of fire, and wooed ; they
triumph in his pain.

Thus darken'd the Shadowy Female tenfold, and Orc
tenfold
Glow'd on his rocky Couch against the darkness:
loud thunders
Told of the enormous conflict, Earthquake beneath,
around,
Rent the Immortal Females limb from limb and
joint from joint,
50 And moved the fast foundations of the Earth to wake
the Dead.
Urizen emerged from his Rocky Form and from his
Snows.

(Extra page 32)

And Milton oft sat up on the Couch of Death, and oft
    conversed
In vision and dream beatific with the Seven Angels
    of the Presence.

I have turned my back upon these Heavens builded
    on cruelty ;
My Spectre still wandering thro' them follows my
    Emanation.
5 He hunts her footsteps thro' the snow and the wintry
    hail and rain.
The idiot Reasoner laughs at the Man of Imagination,
And from laughter proceeds to murder by under-
    valuing calumny.

Then Hillel, who is Lucifer, replied over the Couch
    of Death,
And thus the Seven Angels instructed him, and thus
    they converse :—

10 We are not Individuals, but States, Combinations of
    Individuals.
We were Angels of the Divine Presence, and were
    Druids in Annandale,
Compell'd to combine into Form by Satan, the Spectre
    of Albion,
Who made himself a God, and destroyed the Human
    Form Divine.
But the Divine Humanity and Mercy gave us a Human
    Form,
15 Because we were combin'd in Freedom and holy
    Brotherhood,
While those combin'd by Satan's Tyranny first in the
    blood of War
And Sacrifice, and next in Chains of imprisonment,
    are Shapeless Rocks,
Retaining only Satan's Mathematic Holiness, Length,
    Bredth, and Highth,

Calling the Human Imagination, which is the Divine
    Vision and Fruition,
20 In which Man liveth eternally : madness and blas-
    phemy against
Its own Qualities, which are Servants of Humanity,
    not Gods or Lords.
Distinguish, therefore, States from Individuals in
    those States.
States change, but Individual Identities never change
    nor cease.
You cannot go to Eternal Death in that which can
    never Die.
25 Satan and Adam are States Created into Twenty-seven
    Churches,
And thou, O Milton, art a State about to be
    Created,
Called Eternal Annihilation, that none but the Living
    shall
Dare to enter ; and they shall enter triumphant over
    Death,
And Hell, and the Grave : States that are not, but
    ah ! seem to be.

30 Judge, then, of thy Own Self, thy Eternal Linea-
    ments explore.
What is Eternal and what Changeable, and what
    Annihilable?
The Imagination is not a State, it is the Human
    Existence itself.
Affection or Love becomes a State when divided from
    Imagination;
The Memory is a State always, and the Reason is a
    State
35 Created to be Annihilated, and a new Ratio Created.
Whatever can be Created can be Annihilated. Forms
    cannot.
The Oak is cut down by the Axe, the Lamb falls by
    the Knife,
But their Forms Eternal Exist For-ever. Amen,
    Hallelujah.

Thus they converse with the Dead, watching round
    the Couch of Death,
40 For God himself enters Death's Door always with
    those that enter,
And lays down in the Grave with them in Visions of
    Eternity,
Till they awake and see Jesus and the Linen Clothes
    lying
43 That the Females had woven for them, and the Gates
    of their Father's House.

*Against the words 'Human Form Divine' in line 13 above,
Blake has placed a marginal note:*—כירכים *as* multitudes:
Vox Populi.

*The Hebrew word is probably taken by Blake from Job
xxv. 9, 'By reason of the multitude of the oppressions they
make the oppressed to cry.' It there refers to the 'multitude
of oppressions.' Blake would have rendered it 'Druids' or
'Spectre Sons of Albion,' and thus Vox Populi is Vox Diaboli.*

MEANING OF 'MILTON'

*These notes only venture to give a few hints and to indicate
a few places of search where portions of the explanations most
useful to the enjoyment of the writing are to be found.*

*The name 'Milton' is that of the state about to be created
called Self-Annihilation (extra page 32, line 26). It 'annihilates the Self of Deceit and false Forgiveness' (page 15,
beneath illustration), or, in other words, the doctrine of the
atonement, which, being the opposite of 'Forgiveness,' was
Blake's idea of the opposite of the Lamb of God.*

*Milton the poet, who died in 1674, had been dead more
than a century when Blake, executing a life-sized drawing of
his head for a medallion in Hayley's library at Felpham,
began to study for the purpose, and became 'absorbed' by him
as well as by other poets, as he relates in a letter, November
26, 1800.*

*Reading 'Paradise Lost' again he began to feel much of
the influence in it to be poetically akin to his own work ever
since 1774, the centenary of Milton's death, which was, so far
as we can gather, the time when he wrote 'Samson,' his most*

*Miltonic fragment. It is found among the ' Poetical Sketches,'
none of which are later in date than 1775 or 1776. His way
of thinking of the influence of a person as though the acts
caused by that influence were done by the person, would explain
the idea that probably caused him to write here, addressing
the Muses—*

> 'Say first what moved Milton, who walked about in
>   Eternity
>   One hundred years pondering the intricate mazes of
>   Providence,
>   . . . To go into the deep,' . . . etc.

*But this only explains the expression ' One hundred years,'
and shows Blake considering himself as in part acting through
the dictation of Milton, from which he released himself later,
as he relates in last paragraph of the Preface to ' Jerusalem.'
Blake's use of the word ' dictate,' which he makes a noun, can
also be understood from the way in which he employs it as
meaning a mental influence due to action during life, and
surviving the actual period of life, in his letter to Hayley,
dated May 6, 1800, in which he says that he writes by the
' dictate' of his brother Robert, who had been dead thirteen
years. He also held that memory was the personal presence
of the thing or person remembered, as explained in another
letter to Hayley, December 18, 1804.*

*In reading the rest of the book of ' Milton' it is more neces-
sary than even in going through any other works of Blake
to remember that he looked on this world as ' created' only by
the delusion (renewed mercifully morning by morning) of a
hypnotic suggestion whispered in our ears by that Great
Spirit the Poetic Genius, the God whom the Jews worshipped
and have taught us to worship.*

*The ' elements' are eternal—so is the ' void.' There are two
ways of looking at these. The female way believes in them.
The male way disbelieves in them, but believes in the fact that
imagination (part of God's own Substance) may be fed in each
of us by emotions depending on the female delusion of the
reality of nature.*

*The will of Nature (or the Female will) consists in what we
call mathematics. It is the basis of that thing called Morality,
which becomes hateful when it rises to be a delusion : for then,
instead of being inert and dead like this form of Will called
mathematics (which lies without biting, like a sleeping dog
if we do not kick it into activity), it demands to shape our
minds and imaginations, through our bodies, instead of being
satisfied with these. The best it can do to our imaginations is*

to fill them with love through beauty; the worst to occupy them with error, illusion, and self-righteousness.

This creed is implied, both in this poem and in the 'Jerusalem,' in the use, as though they all meant the same thing, of such words as Sin, Morality; Nature, Bacon, Newton, and Locke; The Serpent (from whose jaws we eat the fruit); Rahab and Tirzah (the Biblical account of these names suggests the symbol); the Twenty-seven Heavens and Churches; and the Mundane Shell.

The series includes all ideas of religious restraint of emotion and consequent impoverishment of Imagination, that, taken together, are Adamic and Satanic, and not Deific.

Another result of Blake's philosophy is his use of 'real surface,' which we should usually call 'ideal forms,' in contrast with 'false surface'—which we see every day as 'apparent forms'—and call, because of their apparent solidity, by the name of Body.

He applies this name to apparent cogency of reasoning based on the delusions of Nature, which become alive and grow to the man by the effect they have on his imagination. They should, however, be cast off, and the 'face of his Spirit cleansed' of them. Error has no place in eternal life, whether it be the errors of mind or of will. 'One error unredeemed will destroy a human soul' ('Jerusalem,' p. 46, line 11). The great error of Will, or Morality, corresponds to and springs from the delusion which Nature tricks us into through the senses; although God had only meant these to provide a pleasant shadow in which to rest our minds. It causes the error of condemning the guilty.

Just as poetry seems nonsense to the matter-of-fact mind, so does either redemption or forgiveness seem to the really moral mind. They are the nonsense of Justice.

But besides the Deific Imagination (ultimately inscrutable to us) there is the Human Imagination, His Divine Son, our Saviour. This is not only scrutable and questionable by us, but is so as nothing else can be, being, in fact, our near and only Brother, the Certainty that we may love. He invented 'Forgiveness of Sins.'

But in order that sin may be forgiven, it must be understood. There are two kinds. There is the sin of loving Nature, so as to become One with her, and give her of our lives. This sin, if done as a piece of self-sacrifice, is divine, and is the Redemption itself; for Redemption—as all God's acts—must be performed by us. The typical case and example was, of course, that of Jesus, but every case is a type and an example, and was such from all time.

Under the name 'Milton' another of these infinitely

*numerous Redemptions is told now.   In the narrative it
seems that after being in the Father's bosom a hundred years,
a poetic act, or divine act, or bard's song, released Milton, to
come to a more outward region of the Divine form, or
universe of souls, when he met the influence and spirits of his
three wives and daughters, and through them, and the element
of Rahab and the Covering Cherub in them, suffered painful
contact with what is the Contrary of Imagination—the
Opposite of the Lamb of God—Satan.   The cherub covers the
tree of life, turning it into 'Mystery,' and it is his opacity
which, at its extreme limit, is called Satan, of whom an aspect,
absolutely tyrannous, yet well-meaning, called 'Urizen,'
strives with Milton over the Arnon, a river of love in what we
call the nerves of the human body.   Milton tried to give him
life.   He does so in his poem of 'Paradise Lost,' calling him
God, as noted in Blake's 'Marriage of Heaven and Hell,' for
Urizen is that Dweller on the Future called also Destiny.*

*In doing this Milton's poetry perished, for the dead are
those who are immersed in Moral Law.   His influence, however, re-arising in Blake, is a return.   His selfhood—the
characteristic puritanism of his poetry—perishes while he
thus 'redeems' the feminine portion—the delusions and un-
visionary conceptions of life that had caused that selfhood to
sin, as Eve caused Adam.   The whole idea that sin consisted
in sexual contact is now swept away from the Miltonic influence, and the Biblical creed that an essential part of sin was
that modesty which is based on a Satanic belief in the reality
of Nature is substituted.   An essentially good element in John
Milton is the irresistible tendency of the true poet—not of the
false ones who 'pretend to art to destroy art'—to play the
Redeemer.   This is revealed, and he vanishes from the poem
in line 19, page 44.   Instead of him—*

> *' Jesus wept and walked forth
> From Felpham's vale.'*

*The vision is complete.   A touch of autobiography follows.
Blake, overwhelmed by the trance, falls in a kind of faint in
his own garden-path, and his wife runs trembling out of the
cottage to help him up.*

*Such is this crucifixion—'Mysterious offering of self for
another,' as explained in the closing pages of 'Jerusalem.'*

*But there is much more in the pages of this poem.   It begins
with a reference to Beulah—whose 'daughters,' or minor
influences, are the muses of the poet.   'Beulah' may be
considered as a name for what we should call the beauty
of nature.   The meaning of the word is marriage, and
the symbol is the eye.   Marriage is a Swedenborgian term*

for the influx of spiritual influence into life. He makes all marriage a figure of the act which joined the Holy Spirit and the Virgin Mary, or the same spirit with The Waters, before the creation of the World. Blake, like an artist brought up a Swedenborgian, and going beyond his master, perceiving that this is just what happens when we make beautiful blind nature into visibility by seeing her, reminds us that there is an incarnation when we so much as look at a sunset, and uses a scientific term to say so in the 'Vision of the Daughters of Albion,' page 7, line 1. Here, in the Visions of the Lamentation of Beulah over Ololon, he gives further details of the power of the 'daughters' of Beulah. Ololon (who may be called the sadness of nature without its jealousy) makes a breach from Imagination to Perception, and (like the world's great act by the Man of Sorrows) makes possible the redemption of Rahab, into whom so many of the Satanic qualities unite, whether seen as churches, Milton's wives, the Shadowy Female, or everything else that is emotional, but not inspired. The revelation of Milton, who is now seen to be Jesus after his previous uniting with Los, and that of Los with Blake, recall the well-known allegory of St. Christopher.

The weeping Satan of this poem, like the deceived Urizen, who also weeps, is the sorrow of nature mingled with opacity instead of mingled with inspiration. Urizen (extra page 8, line 1) becomes opaque when drawn down by the Shadowy Female. These are the tears that are the direct opposite of those that woke Lazarus from the dead when they fell on his grave. Satan in whatever form is as opposite to the Lamb of God as Urizen, whose good leads to evil when he goes from his right station, becomes opposite to Orc (or Luvah), whose evil leads to good.

Palamabron is the ideal Tiriel. When Tiriel was regenerated, he became Palamabron, as we are told in 'Vala,' Night VIII., line 488.

Tiriel was a jovial person once, when his beard gathered the smell of ripe figs.

Palamabron is the second, or Asiatic, region of the part of mind that is inspired by Los. Los, or Sol read backwards, who is called 'Time' by mortals, has a way of reading nature backwards, and so refusing to get deception from her, but turning her to poetry. His four sons, long unvegetated and refusing to fly through the gates (of Reuben) into the outer region of mind, are

   Rintrah,   Palamabron,   Theotormon,   and Bromion,
corresponding to the Zoas

   Urizen,   Luvah,   Tharmas,   and Urthona,
in their relative places and characteristics.

Palamabron is old-fashioned, happy London, before the Satanic Urizen has put his (Prester) Serpent's head in Verulam, by aid of experimental Bacon ('Jerusalem,' page 74, line 2). Though London in the 'Songs of Experience' and in 'Jerusalem,' page 84, line 11, descends to Tirielesque qualities, and becomes blind and age-bent, led by a child, younger in the drawing than Hela when she was becoming a maiden, and so could receive the curse of the aged, as part of the same idea. If we looked closely at this 'London,' we should see inside him not only Tiriel and Palamabron, but Urizen, and consequently Rahab, for Mystery is Urizen's tree, and all else, down to Satan, that opposes Vision—the Divine.

Palamabron had a short turn of evil when he tried to serve Satan's mills. This means that Blake tried to produce realistic art. He had been persuaded to attempt it before, and a portion of the Satan and Palamabron story is found in 'Vala,' a book begun in the year 1797. It may have gone on beyond the close of that year. In reading 'Milton,' we must have in hand 'Vala,' Night VIII., line 345—

'I am that shadowy prophet who six thousand years ago
　　Fell from my station.'

This part of the idea in the poem of 'Milton' therefore began long before the name now used for the book was thought of. From line 375 (aided by 'Jerusalem,' page 49, line 68) we begin to gather more about the symbol Satan, and in lines 382 to 480 we have the latter part of the Miltonic story of Palamabron. The former part identifies the 'Satanic' influence with that which Hayley, partly through Mrs. Blake, was trying to exercise on Blake when he finally drove him from Felpham by insisting that he should only do the drudgery of his business. (Compare letter to Butts.)

It is quite impossible to fail to see Hayley and his verses behind Satan and the mills. It is not going further than legitimate conjecture to suspect him of getting Blake to help him with a verse or two before he learned that Blake would endure no such help in return. The line in reverse over the top of the first page of the second part of 'Milton'—'How wide and unpassable the gulf between simplicity and insipidity,' precisely indicating, as it does, the difference between Blake's ballad verse and Hayley's, is conclusive. There is some reason to believe that just at first Mrs. Blake sided with Hayley, talked common sense to Blake, and interfered with his mental happiness. She may even have talked jealousy and interfered with his visits to Hayley's house, where this amiable and profligate gentleman was remembered only a few years ago by a very old gardener as being reported to have kept a Turkish harem of his own. It was said of Mrs. Blake by those who knew her, that she betrayed her peasant origin by an exaggerated suspiciousness of her husband's friends. She may have talked with that old gardener when he was a little boy. Blake would have been furious at his wife's suggestions, and probably hinted in return that if she would be worthy to live in 'Beulah,' and be one of the 'Muses that inspire the poet's song,' she must show herself more really moral by providing him with what Sarah, till a mother, allowed Abraham; and the old William Bond scene may have been acted over again on a reduced scale, for Blake had loved his wife for many years now. William Bond dates about 1783—soon after the publication of the 'Poetical Sketches.' 'Broken Love' seems to have been written about 1803. Page 32 of 'Milton,' and the extra page 32 here printed at the end of the poem, were probably both written, one as a substitute for the other, at this time. Fragments of 'Broken Love' will be found in them. Elynittria, the Emanation of Palamabron, is related by correspondence to Mrs. Blake, in so far as she has qualities in common with Enitharmon ('vegetable mortal wife of Los, his emanation, yet his wife till the sleep of death is passed'), Los becoming one with Blake in this poem, and Blake being in a position closely resembling that of Palamabron. It is evidently meant for a hint to Mrs. Blake when we are told in page 11, lines 31, etc., how Elynittria treated Leutha, who is to her much as Hagar to Sarah. But the fact is that Leutha was not a human being of any sort. She is a name for the tenderheartedness of Hayley's verses (Blake speaks of them as affectionate ballads), which filled him with 'odorous stupefaction,' unlike the arrowy inspirations of Elynittria, as the horses of the harrow—the lines of the poetry—found out.

Leutha is 'made apparent' to Blake seemingly in such beauties of nature as butterflies, rainbows, and flowers. Compare page 9, line 33; page 10, lines 5 and 15; and the book called 'Europe,' page 12. Leutha is the 'luring bird of Eden,' on whose wings 'the many-coloured bow delights.' She is also the 'soft soul of flowers,' and a 'sweet smiling pestilence.' Eden is amorous idea, and so is pestilence, which adorns the wild snake with gems and gold, the accompaniments of excited desire in man or animals, as seen by the visionary. The seven moods of Leutha seek the love of Antamon, who is himself a particular form of beauty, namely, the beauty of gratified desire. Palamabron as a 'horned priest skipping upon the mountains' in this poem is a goat-like and obvious symbol. Blake pays Wesley the compliment of making Palamabron inspire his hymns.

The meaning of this part of 'Milton' is therefore a parable.

Blake makes some of his bard's listeners suggest that the things he tells of under a mask are facts of some kind, page 11, line 49. The bard crushes that gossip by saying that it is all true because inspired. Commentary must here leave the question, only gathering that some sort of incident in which literature, patronage, and jealousy were mixed when referred to in poetry with some impersonations of beauty and desire that were mistaken for persons, occurred and produced those heart-searchings that, under the influence of Blake's absorption in Milton's poetry, led to the composition of the whole book and to the weaving into it of passages from 'Vala,' with explanations, in which Blake's own philosophy is 'justified to men,' under belief that it was one of the 'ways of God.' In the poem of 'Broken Love,' Blake is seen to hint to his wife that they should give up love and root up the infernal grove, living avowedly in future on the joys of imagination only, ending all quarrel in mutual forgiveness.

But the poem of 'Milton' contains expressions that sound as if they meant what they do not; as the word 'Satan' sounds as though it meant the hoofed and horned devil, whom Blake once saw and sketched. Churches or States are not only 'combinations of individuals,' they are combinations of influences (each influence is an individual), and in result produce conditions of perception. The extreme states, Satan and the Lamb, are not properly states at all. One is death, or mind without any spiritual or imaginary light; the other is illumination, or 'existence itself.' We are each alternating between them always. Each intermediate state has powers of clairvoyant, prophetic, and even physical perception that is closed to the state outside it. We can enter into these only by divine grace, being 'of ourselves nothing.'

Stars, Swedenborg says, mean in the Bible, knowledges of faith, goodness, or truth, but wandering stars, evils and falsities. So Milton appeared entering into the 'nether parts of imagination' by his morality, which was only partly Christian and mainly that of the twenty-seven coverings of error, or Heavens of Ulro.

In page 36 is another biographical hint. Blake believes that he left Lambeth (where he wrote the first sketch of the story of Palamabron in 'Vala,' Night VIII.), that he might 'write all these visions' at Felpham. While writing they grew, and he accepted the experiences and the new ideas as all part of his mental growth. This accounts for the portion of Hayley that is to be detected in the 'Milton' story and not in the 'Vala' story of Satan and Palamabron. In the 'Vala' story, 'Satan' seems to have been a figure suggested partly, perhaps originally, by Sir Joshua Reynolds. The rest of the book, especially the peroration, is mainly explanatory. Wherever a word is found both here and in 'Jerusalem,' they explain each other if the leading idea be kept in mind that 'Negation' is pure evil (like murder), and that contradiction (the wars of eternity) is a stage—the sexual stage—on the way towards ultimate brotherhood and good, of which imagination is the essence.

'Nations,' Swedenborg teaches, denote (where this word is used in the Bible), 'in the general sense,' good affections and truth. We are invited now to the 'great harvest and vintage of the Nations.'

These last words of the poem were probably the last that Blake put upon metal, though most of the work was written before most of 'Jerusalem,' and both borrow from 'Vala,' written in 1797, and both are dated on their title-pages, 1804.

The close of 'Jerusalem,' as will be seen, is a cry that all may utter. It is a shout of delight over the discovery in 'Forgiveness' of the breaking down of individualist walls, the annihilation of restriction or contraction (called 'self'), and of the liberty to combine with one another through emotion and imagination till we all become One Grand Man, and each thought and word of ours a human being combining into ourselves, as the selves merge into the only Self. 'Jerusalem is called Liberty among the sons of men.' That is the liberty.

'Milton' goes a step further into the region of art. It has described the phases and changes of the 'self of false forgiveness' under many symbols, and it ends with a cry for those of us who feel that we can make artistic or imaginative use (by mental digestion, leading to mental vigour) of all the contemplation so elaborated.

The 'seed of contemplative thought' has been sown, and it has come up as symbolism, art, and poetry. All our energies may now possess it, nor are we to fear—Blake proudly implies—that one mental faculty will need go empty away.

Every power we possess, if we will only be selfless enough to become saints, artists, and poets, may be nourished into rejoicing and immortality by the soft grapes and firm grain of this harvest and vintage.

DESIGNS TO 'MILTON'

Title-page.—*Milton entering his shadow; a nude figure, full page, walking slowly away from into the back of the picture, which is filled with cloud. The type of head is youthful, the hair long. The motto (' To justify the Ways of God to Men') is beneath the feet, the rest of the title written on the clouds behind the figure.*

Page 3. A heading only. The words 'Milton, Book the First,' are written across the rays or flames shed downwards by a falling star that descends upon a male and female figure that touch only at the feet, in the middle or the foreground, and spread floatingly right and left. The male has corn, the female has grapes mingled with her. They are minute creatures, and would be, judging by the corn and grapes, only a few inches in height. They are the 'human forms' of the harvest and vintage.

Page 4. A half-page drawing. A colossal Druid arch over a hundred feet high, made of three stones only—one at each side and a cross-piece—rears itself among the stars. A traveller on horseback rides under it, not alarmed by a huge stone of a lumpy kind in his way, though it is the size of a balloon. A crescent moon shines in the sky. The design is a counterpart to that on page 70 of 'Jerusalem,' though there are differences. The subject appears to be a traveller passing through Ulro, leaving Druid error and ideas of atonement for sin—Miltonic ideas, in fact.

Page 8. A full page. Three full-length nude figures, one in flames on a pedestal. Of the others, one clasps its hands in pity, and one descends from the pedestal. This one, partly hidden, has the appearance of being female, though the knees and shins are male. It is conjectured in the Quaritch edition to represent Los, Enitharmon, and Orc—the latter in flames. The flames have reference probably to those spoken of on page 10 of the poem. The standing figures have attributes of Los and Enitharmon, and the burning figure of Orc in a secondary sense, but Blake would probably have given the drawing another title.

Page 13. A full page drawing. A nude figure advancing towards us from the rays of a dark sunrise, and dropping as he advances a robe torn in two, and now only trailed in his extended hands. The subject is probably in lines 10 to 14 of the opposite page, where a small drawing, a little figure in a drawing that only displaces a few lines of text, is seen striding away under a tree from a fallen figure. The fallen figure appears feminine, but both are so small and roughly sketched that the subject is doubtful. It may mean the male or symbolic power freeing itself from the feminine or personal.

Page 14. *A very small drawing appears to contain Milton, as an error (or falling star: the symbol seems to be that which Swedenborg attributes to the Biblical writers), entering the nether parts of Blake's imagination—the instep. Some flames and rocks divide this figure from an alarmed female, fully dressed—perhaps Mrs. Blake, who figures later in the poem in personal form as watching with alarm Blake's overwhelming fits of imaginative excitement at this time.*

Page 15. *A full page. The upper half a procession of triumphant musicians—string, brass, and tambourine, youths and maidens dancing slowly through rising sun-rays. One carries 'Urizen's harp' ('Vala,' Night VII., line* 688, *etc.). He is probably Urizen in innocence, as below his feet is Urizen, taught to break law. Probably the others are not in the wild state of servants of the Mill (page* 6, *line* 9), *but they display naked beauty (that of music, not clothed with 'rotten rays of memory,' but made of inspiration only), as this may be displayed with flute and harp and song (extra page* 3). *The figures themselves are draped. Below their feet, just below the surface of the hill on which they stand, Milton (a nude, powerful figure) is seen struggling with Urizen (a melancholy Jehovah) between two tables of the law upon which Hebrew characters are discernible.*

Below, the words 'To annihilate the selfhood of deceit and false forgiveness.' See page 17 *of poem.*

Page 16. *Headpiece—Milton's three wives and three daughters. Tailpiece—Los opposing with fibres the path of Milton. He does so because Milton's morality unlooses the accuser of sins upon man—so at least Enitharmon, his fibrous portion, fears.*

Page 21. *Los seen in Sol behind Blake, who turns round when in the act of fastening ideas of the world to the lower parts of his imagination, as a sandal to a foot.*

Page 24. *A few insects, not in human form, creatures from the winepress of Luvah.*

Page 26. *Two pictures. Large mountains. No figures. The 'two gates' described in line* 11 *and following.*

Page 29. *Full page drawing of Blake, with Milton as a falling star. An enlargement of the drawing on page* 14. *The word 'William' is written large.*

Page 30. *Heading, a few small flying and floating figures, some falling, some rising round the name 'Milton, Book the Second.'*

Page 32. *A diagram. Four circles are drawn through one another so as to touch at a central point. Two are so placed that a line from centre to centre would be level, but a line from centre to centre of the other two would be upright. Each circle is about the size of a five shilling piece. In the midst is placed an egg, about the size of a hen's egg. In the upper part of it is a spot called Adam. In the lower part no spot. The space is called Satan. The top circle is called Urthona, the bottom one Urizen; that on the right Luvah, that on the left Tharmas. They are labelled North—letters also, N., W., S., E. Flames surround them. A line from below on the right is drawn ascending to the spot 'Adam,' and labelled 'Milton's Track.'*

Page 33. A full page drawing, similar to that on page 29. The figure is in reverse, that is, he falls backwards to the right, and not to the left of the picture. His foremost foot is his right, and not his left foot. The name written is Robert, not William, and the star is smaller, and more darkness is in the background. No explanation of this picture has been found in such of Blake's writings as we at present possess.

Page 36. A very rough drawing (not at all correct), labelled 'Blake's cottage at Felpham.' It is childish, and seems to have been done by a little boy of six. Blake (a figure less than an inch in height) walks in the garden, meeting Ololon (the same size), who is stepping down from the sky. Traces of power and dignity are in Ololon and her flying scarf.

Page 38. A full page drawing of a man and woman lying on a rock at the base of a cliff, surrounded by waves. An eagle flies above them, looking down at them. They represented the flesh, powerless without imagination to resist time and space. In the part of the vision of Ahania after line 505 of Night VIII. of 'Vala,' the subject is carried further in verse.

Page 41. A full page drawing of frailty worshipping forgiveness. A nude male figure of Christ, encouraging a draped female figure, who falls on her knees on the banks of a shallow stream, across which he walks. Magdalen and the risen Christ, symbolically understood—

'But I, thy Magdalen, behold thy spiritual risen body.'
                    (*'Jerusalem,' page 62, line* 14.)

'O Melancholy Magdalen, behold the morning (over Malden) breaks.'—(*'Jerusalem,' page* 65, *line* 38; *'Vala,' Night VII., line 679 and following.*)

Page 42. A small sketch of a man underground struggling with monsters of the deep. Man striving with his own intellect under reason's dominion, or Milton as Urizen (into whom he entered by giving him life) in Urthona's den ('Vala,' Night VI.).

Page 43.   A small rough drawing of floating figures holding hands, with arms interlaced above their heads—the human forms of happy words free from 'reason'; and 'memory' bathed in 'waters of life.'

Page 44.   Enitharmon in clouds over the hills of Surrey (line 31 of this page), symbolically; pity weeping on the human harvest, and 'animating by her tears,' as Vala 'built by the reasoning power' was 'animated' by the tears of Jerusalem.

Page 45.   The human harvest growing.

END OF VOL. I.

Printed by T. and A. CONSTABLE, Printers to His Majesty
at the Edinburgh University Press

ERRATA

Vol. I.

Page xvii, 7 lines from top, *for* Crabbe *read* Crabb.
,,   xix, 24 lines from top, *for* Garnel *read* Garnett.
,,   xxiii, 7 lines from top, *for* sun *read* son.
,,   xxxiv, second line, *for* Mr. Grant Richards *read* Chatto & Windus.
,,   96, 15 lines from top, *for* filch *read* fetch.
,,   114, 12 lines from top, *delete* tread.
,,   172, 14 lines from top, *for* Warble *read* Wardle.

Vol. II.

,,   213, 7 lines from foot, *for* Songs *read* Sons.
,,   223, 24 lines from top, *for* lone *read* Love.
,,   228, 5 lines from foot, *for* long heroic line *read* strong heroic verse.
,,   231, fifth line, *for* l. 5 *read* first five lines.
,,   ,, last line but one, *for* 47 *read* 53.
,,   ,, last line, *for* 626 *read* 628.
,,   232, top line, *for* 734 *read* 737.
,,   ,, line 22, *for* long-heroic *read* strong heroic.
,,   234, lines 3, 4, and 7, 8, from top to be deleted (first and third full lines of quotation).
,,   ,, 9 lines from top, *delete* centre (referring to the second full line of quotation).
,,   ,, 17 lines from top, *for* 141 and 142 *read* 145-146.
,,   235, delete references to Night vii.
,,   345, fourth line, *for* plows *read* blows.
,,   347, ninth line from bottom, *for* Shilon *read* Shiloh.
,,   354, fifth line, *for* Forgiven *read* Forgivers.
,,   ,, seventh line from foot, *for* A Voltaire *read* O Voltaire.
,,   ,, 4 lines from foot, *for* Year *read* Tear.
,,   360, 5 lines from top, *for* Ador *read* floor.
,,   365, 10 lines from top, *for* path *read* pain.
,,   406, 22 lines from top, *for* wonders *read* wanders.
,,   415, line 1, *for* in***lement *read* imminglement.
,,   429, 9 lines from foot, *for* on *read* an.
,,   445, 16 lines from top, *for* sendinding *read* sending.
,,   447, 20 lines from top, *for* Ginon *read* Gihon.
,,   464, 13 lines from top, *for* his Bow Fourfold, the Vision, *read* his Bow, Fourfold the Vision, for etc.
,,   465, 5 lines from top, *for* Fourfold, loud *read* Fourfold. Loud.